The Politics of European Integration

A reader

Michael O'Neill

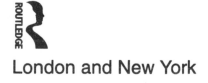

London and New York

First published 1996
by Routledge
11 New Fetter Lane, London EC4P 4EE

Simultaneously published in the USA and Canada
by Routledge
29 West 35th Street, New York, NY 10001

Routledge is an International Thomson Publishing company

© 1996 Michael O'Neill

Typeset in Bembo by Keystroke, Jacaranda Lodge, Wolverhampton
Printed and bound in Great Britain by Mackays of Chatham PLC, Chatham, Kent

British Library Cataloguing in Publication Data
A catalogue record for this book is available from the British Library

Library of Congress Cataloguing in Publication Data
A catalogue record for this book has been requested

ISBN 0–415–11297–4 (hbk)
ISBN 0–415–11298–2 (pbk)

For my parents, James and Gladys O'Neill

'No man is an Island, entire of itself; every man is a piece of the Continent, a part of the main; if a clod be washed away by the sea, Europe is the less. . . .'

(John Donne, *Meditation XVII*)

Contents

Acknowledgements

I have accumulated many debts in preparing this book for publication. I must give particular mention to my colleagues, Barry Harrison, David Cameron and Larry Wilde, for commenting on various parts of the draft manuscript, and to Rhys Dogan for his helpful comments and advice on an early draft. It goes without saying that whatever faults remain are entirely my own responsibility. I have received support throughout the project from Professor Christine Bellamy, the Head of the Politics Section at the Nottingham Trent University. The university authorities have also been generous both with time and financial resources to enable me to complete the endeavour. I owe much to Professor Dennis Austin, who taught all his students to ask the right questions but never to be complacent about the answers.

The library staff in Nottingham, and particularly Moya Leighton and Terry Hanstock, have provided a marvellous and prompt service. I am grateful also to the staff of the libraries at the London School of Economics and the Royal Institute of International Affairs. My debt to Sandra Odell for her patience, good humour and sheer hard work is immeasurable. Without her efforts the manuscript would never have been deciphered. Finally, my wife Wendie has been my constant encouragement and support. It may well be true, as Dr Johnson assured us, that 'a man may write at any time, if he will set himself doggedly to it'. Someone, however, has to provide the conditions most conducive to this essentially selfish task. And in this regard I have been fortunate indeed.

Nottingham, October 1995

Permission given by the following copyright holders and authors is gratefully acknowledged.

Document 1 W. Lipgens, 'The major political consequences of the Second World War', from *A History of European Integration: Vol. One, 1945–1947* (Oxford 1982). © 1982 Oxford University Press.

Document 2 Alan Milward, 'Reconstruction and integration', from *The Reconstruction of Western Europe 1945–51* (London 1984). © 1984 Routledge.

Document 3 W. Lipgens, 'The triumph of the supranational principle in the Resistance', op. cit. © 1982 Oxford University Press.

Document 4 Karl Kaiser, 'L'Europe des savants: European integration and the social services', *Journal of Common Market Studies* Vol. 4: 1964. © 1964 Basil Blackwell Ltd.

Document 5 R.J. Harrison, 'Integration theory: context, scope and method', from *Europe in Question – Theories of Regional Integration* (London, 1974). © 1974 Unwin Hyman.

Document 6 Charles Pentland, *International Theory and European Integration* (London 1973). © 1973 Faber and Faber Ltd.

Document 7 J.B. Priestley, 'Federalism and culture' (1940), cited in R. Mayne, J. Pinder and J.C. Roberts, *Federal Union: The Pioneers* (Basingstoke 1991). © 1991 Macmillan Press Ltd.

Document 8 H.N. Brailsford, 'The federal idea' (1939), cited in R. Mayne, J. Pinder and J.C. Roberts, ibid. © 1991 Macmillan Press Ltd.

Document 9 Lord Lothian, 'The ending of Armageddon' (1939), cited in R. Mayne, J. Pinder and J.C. Roberts, ibid. © 1991 Macmillan Press Ltd.

Document 10 W. Lipgens, 'Motives for European unity: the summing up by the Geneva Conference of Resistance Fighters', op. cit. © 1982 Oxford University Press.

Document 11 J. Monnet, 'A ferment of change', *Journal of Common Market Studies* Vol. 1: 1963. © 1963 Basil Blackwell Ltd.

Document 12 A. Spinelli, *The European Adventure – Tasks for the Enlarged Community* (London 1972). All efforts have been made to trace the copyright owner.

Document 13 M. Burgess, 'The European Community's federal heritage', from *Federalism and European Union* (London 1989). © 1989 Routledge.

Document 14 Samuel Brittan, 'Let fools contest about the forms', *Financial Times* 21 November 1991. © 1991 Samuel Brittan.

Document 15 E. Wistrich, 'A federal democracy', from *After 1992: The United States of Europe* (revised edn, London 1988). © 1988 Routledge.

Document 16 D. Mitrany, 'The prospect of integration: federal or functional', *Journal of Common Market Studies* Vol. 4: 1965. © 1965 Basil Blackwell Ltd.

Document 17 D. Mitrany, 'A working peace system' (1943), reprinted in P. Taylor and A.J.R. Groom (eds), *The Functional Theory of Politics* (Oxford 1975). © 1975 Basil Blackwell Ltd.

Documents 18 and 19 E.B. Haas, *The Uniting of Europe: Political, Social and Economic Forces 1950–1957* (Stanford, Cal., 1968 edn). © 1958, 1968 Stanford University Press.

Document 20 L.N. Lindberg and S.A. Scheingold, 'Alternative models of systems change', from *Europe's Would-Be Polity: Patterns of Change in the*

European Community (Englewood Cliffs, NJ, 1970). All efforts have been made to trace the copyright owner.

Document 21 E.B. Haas, 'The study of regional integration: reflections on the joy and anguish of pretheorizing', in L.N. Lindberg and S.A. Scheingold (eds), *Regional Integration: Theory and Research* (Cambridge, Mass., 1971). The Belknap Press of Harvard University Press, © 1970, 1971 by the President and Fellows of Harvard College.

Document 22 E.B. Haas, 'Turbulent fields and the theory of regional integration', *International Organization* Vol. 30: 1976 (Cambridge, Mass., 1976). © 1976 The MIT Press.

Document 23 S. Hoffmann, 'The European process at Atlantic cross purposes', *Journal of Common Market Studies* Vol. 3: 1964 (Oxford 1964). © 1964 Basil Blackwell Ltd.

Document 24 S. Hoffmann, 'Europe's identity crisis: between the past and America', *Daedelus* Vol. 93: 1964. © 1964 *Daedelus*, Journal of the American Academy of Arts and Sciences.

Document 25 S. Hoffmann, 'Obstinate or obsolete? The fate of the nation–state and the case of western Europe', *Daedelus* Vol. 95: 1966. © 1966 *Daedelus*, Journal of the American Academy of Arts and Sciences.

Documents 26 and 29 M. Forsyth, from *Unions of States: The Theory and Practice of Confederation* (Leicester, 1981). © 1981 Leicester University Press (a division of Pinter Publishers Ltd).

Document 27 J. Pinder, 'Why the single market is a step towards federal union', in J. Lodge (ed.), *The European Community and the Challenge of the Future* (London 1993). © 1993 Pinter Publishers Ltd.

Document 28 W. Wallace, 'Europe as a confederation: the Community and the nation–state', *Journal of Common Market Studies* Vol. 20: 1982 (Oxford 1982). © 1982 Basil Blackwell Ltd.

Document 30 P. Taylor, 'The confederal phase', from 'The politics of the European Communities: the confederal phase', *World Politics* April 1975 (Baltimore, Md., 1975). © 1975 The Johns Hopkins University Press.

Document 31 S. Bulmer, 'Domestic politics and European Community policy making', *Journal of Common Market Studies* Vol. 21: 1983 (Oxford 1983). © 1983 Basil Blackwell Ltd.

Document 32 H. Nau, 'From integration to interdependence: gains, losses and continuing gaps', *International Organizations* Vol. 33: 1979 (Cambridge, Mass., 1979). © 1979 The MIT Press.

Document 33 C. Webb, 'Theoretical perspectives and problems', in H. Wallace, W. Wallace and C. Webb (eds), *Policy-Making in the European Community* (London 1983 edn). © 1983 John Wiley and Sons Ltd.

Document 34 S. Bulmer, 'The European Council's first decade: between interdependence and domestic politics', *Journal of Common Market Studies* Vol. 24: 1985 (Oxford 1985). © 1985 Basil Blackwell Ltd.

Document 35 W. Wallace, 'Less than a federation, more than a regime: the

Community as a political system', in H. Wallace, W. Wallace and C. Webb (eds.), *Policy-Making in the European Community* (London 1983 edn). © 1983 John Wiley and Sons Ltd.

Document 36 F. Scharpf, 'The joint decision trap: lessons from German federalism and European integration', *Public Administration* Vol. 66: 1988 (Oxford 1988). © 1988 Basil Blackwell Ltd.

Document 37 M. Burgess, *Federalism and the European Union* (London 1989). © 1989 Routledge.

Document 38 J. Pinder, 'European Community and nation–state: a case for neo-federalism?', *International Affairs* Vol. 62: 1986 (London 1986). © 1988 The Royal Institute of International Affairs.

Document 39 D. Muttimer, '1992 and the political integration of Europe: neo-functionalism reconsidered', *Journal of European Integration* Vol. 13: 1989 (Saskatoon 1989). © *Journal of European Integration.*

Document 40 R.O. Keohane and S. Hoffman, 'Conclusions: Community politics and institutional change', in W. Wallace (ed.), *The Dynamics of European Integration* (London 1990). © 1990 Pinter Publishers Ltd.

Document 41 A. Moravcsik, 'Negotiating the Single European Act: national interests and conventional statecraft in the European Community', *International Organization* Vol. 45: 1991 (Cambridge, Mass., 1991). © 1991 The MIT Press.

Document 42 A. Moravcsik, 'Preferences and power in the European Community: a liberal intergovernmentalist approach', *Journal of Common Market Studies* Vol. 31: 1993 (Oxford 1993). © 1993 Basil Blackwell Ltd.

Document 43 W. Sandholtz and J. Zysman, '1992: recasting the European bargain', *World Politics* Vol. 42: 1989 (Baltimore, Md., 1989). © 1989 The Johns Hopkins University Press.

Document 44 H. Kastendiek, 'Convergence or a persistent diversity of national interests?', in C. Crouch and D. Marquand (eds), *The Politics of 1992: Beyond the Single European Market* (Oxford 1990). © 1990 Basil Blackwell Ltd.

Document 45 A. Bressand, 'Future for economic integration. Beyond inter-dependence: 1992 as a global challenge', *International Affairs* Vol. 66: 1990 (London 1990). © 1990 The Royal Institute of International Affairs.

Document 46 A. Smith, 'National identities and the idea of European unity', *International Affairs* Vol. 68: 1992 (London 1992). © 1992 The Royal Institute of International Affairs.

Part I

Origins, scope, issues

Chapter 1

The quest for European integration

THE SCOPE OF INTEGRATION

The search for the meaning of European integration operates at two levels. It represents a political ideal to be prescribed or resisted depending on the values of the commentator. At the practical level, European integration consists of particular projects. These are closely related concerns. Both aspects of the debate on European integration have contributed to a long and lively discourse throughout the postwar years. The central issue under review here is the limits or otherwise of nation statehood. The idea of European integration has attracted both support and opposition. Support for the idea of refashioning Europe's political arrangements grew in response to the two 'great' wars of the early twentieth century. Regional integration offered a solvent for the intense national rivalries that had propelled Europe into these two disastrous and costly conflicts within a generation. Opposition to the integration prospectus was focused on the belief in the nation state as the natural limit of humanity's search for a viable political community. From this perspective, regional integration was both un-natural and illusory. It was assumed to be a dangerous experiment which tampered with the natural laws of politics. And one which deflected statesmen from their primary task of encouraging effective government and a stable socio-economic order within defensible frontiers.

The ideological friction between those commentators who recommended a radical shift in the foundations of political community, and those who preferred to maintain the status quo, has been reflected in the academic debate over the future of the European nation state. The literature which has contributed to this fascinating discourse is our principal concern here. The debate on the concept of nation statehood, and the prospects for integrating Europe's existing states into a regional polity, are two sides of the same question. The issues raised here go to the heart of political science's elemental concerns about the nature of political man and the most likely sources of effective governance.

The extracts which comprise Part III of this book provide a flavour of the key issues and principal approaches to these critical questions, across the spectrum of what has been a lively and protracted debate. The constraints on space have limited both the choice and the length of these extracts. We can only highlight here the principal themes of this discourse. The reader is recommended to pursue these issues, by seeking out the original sources of the material cited here.

We need to approach the debate on European integration with a degree of caution. Each of the contributions to the theoretical debate on European integration cited in this introductory chapter or illustrated in the extracts, whatever their theoretical status, conceptual clarity or the accuracy of their empirical insights, are also position papers. None of these theoretical efforts by academic commentators to explain the dynamics of the regional process or to predict its likely outcomes, takes an entirely neutral stance on the momentous issues raised by the prospect of European integration. To that extent, the excerpts reproduced in Part III reflect those implicit values or normative preferences which infuse the social scientific endeavour, as much as they do any other branch of reflective scholarship.

Each contribution, too, resides in its own particular historical context and can better be understood in those terms. The 'great debate' on European integration has been beset by changes in intellectual fashion as the events have unfolded. There is a long established dialectic between politics as scholarship and politics in practice. Aristotle set the precedent for political science in this regard by drawing on the real world as the most reliable source of political insights. Practical politics has continued to confront scholars with those critical questions and perplexing controversies which are the meat of the discipline. The issues raised by the prospect of European integration reflect this long established tradition of a creative interface between the real world of politics and its intellectual evaluation.

The theoretical responses to events on the postwar European political ground reviewed in this study each reflects a distinctive approach to the central question of regional integration. The debate has developed in phases, during which one or other paradigm has tended to dominate the theoretical discourse. The federalist approach, for instance, enjoyed more influence immediately after the end of the 1939–45 war than it has done subsequently, although it has enjoyed a recent revival. The functionalist paradigm has also had a chequered intellectual career and a variable political history. The pure functionalism favoured by the eminent scholar, David Mitrany, although it was not a theory of regional integration as such, did directly influence the European debate. The suggestion that the nation state was a spent force, and that its supposedly 'inalienable' sovereignty could be 'sliced', sector by functional sector, encouraged the endeavours of practitioners such as Jean Monnet, who were seeking ways of bypassing the nation state as the primary unit of political organisation. The Mitranian prospectus also influenced those neofunctionalist theorists whose work did have a regional bias centred on events in Western Europe. The development of a successful regional experiment in practical functionalism in the shape of the Coal and Steel Community established in 1952, and subsequently the Common Market and Euratom launched in 1958, encouraged neofunctionalism's emergence as the dominant explanatory paradigm of the evolving European process during the late 1950s and into the 1960s.

This recurrent pattern of a theoretical scene shift was repeated in the mid 1960s. The hostility of Charles de Gaulle, the ultra nationalistic President of the new French Fifth Republic, to what he regarded as the EC Commission's insidious attempt to extend the scope of supranationalism in the Community's procedures, provoked a backlash in defence of the nation state. The 1965–66 crisis in Community affairs and its resolution in the Luxembourg Accords which confirmed the national veto as the last resort of states determined to protect their interests from unwelcome supranational encroachments, ushered in a new state-centric phase in European integration. These events attracted their own brand of intellectual endorsement. However, this paradigm, too, provided no more than a partial account of the integration dynamic. Events stretched the theoretical credibility of the intergovernmentalist explanation of integration as they had the supranationalist paradigms which preceded it.

Even before the momentous relaunch of the stalled Community project in the shape of the Single European Market in 1985, academic commentators had already begun to modify this prevailing theoretical perspective on regional integration. An altogether new approach was fashioned throughout the 1980s, on the basis of the generic interdependence model of the international process that was beginning to make inroads into the prevailing realist orthodoxy. These recent theoretical developments have assimilated certain broad assumptions about the nature of the international process in general, and the dynamics of international change in particular. Above all, this latest revisionist account of regional integration assumes that regional integration is a multifarious rather than a unidimensional process. And that, as such, its dynamic or momentum is neither teleologically induced or fixed, but is infused instead with mixed motives and variable influences.

At the same time, the increased pace of European integration throughout the late 1980s encouraged the reconsideration of previously discounted explanatory models of the European process. The revisiting of these disputed theories was a tentative rather than a confident endeavour. Both federalism and neofunctionalism were revived, alongside a reformulation of the intergovernmentalist model. All of these revisions took account of the changes in the global order and their impact on the way scholars now perceive the international process. The sudden renaissance of regional integration theory particularly reflected the increased pace of events on the ground with the launch of the Single Market project and all that followed on from that in Community affairs by way of constitutional development and the expansion of the EC's policy competencies. This continuing intellectual ferment emphasises the centrality of the issues raised by European integration, both for political science and for the future shape and direction of the European project per se. It is almost certainly the case that the next decade will see an increase rather than a reduction, in both the academic speculation and ideological debate over Europe's future political shape and direction.

THE CONCEPT OF THE PARADIGM

Opinion in Europe after 1945 was receptive, for the most part, to some degree of closer regional integration. There was, however, far from a consensus over either its organisational shape or the timing of such developments. The debate that has ensued over these critical issues, in both its academic and political expressions, has been, to say the least, lively. It has also followed the conventional pattern of academic political discourse, by giving rise to distinctive schools of thought or 'paradigms'. Paradigms represent those more or less intellectually coherent positions about the state of play in any given theoretical discourse which prevail among the community of scholars at a given juncture and tend to fashion its collective thinking and individual research priorities. As Pentland has maintained, they are not precise formulae or rigid dogmas, but rather maps of related ideas and predicted outcomes. Paradigms claim to reflect the prevailing intellectual consensus about a given phenomenon. As such, they offer a model of 'reality'; or at least what contemporary academic commentators assume to be so.

Used with due caution, a paradigm suggests a line of intellectual inquiry; a useful template which enables the researcher to formulate testable hypotheses about the exigent issues of the moment. Rival paradigms naturally engage in discourse over the nature of their competing 'realities'. As such, they engage one another and compete for critical attention. In the process they invite revision in response to the changes in the world they purport to explain. They are not, then, epistemological fixtures but rather part of the inconstant theoretical universe which characterises the pursuit of useful knowledge. This intellectual flux is even more apparent in the social sciences than it is in the pure sciences. What may stand, then, as an adequate account of the dynamics of European integration at a given historic juncture, will be challenged and discounted as circumstances change and events outdistance it.

The outcome of this ongoing dialectic between events and their theoretical explanation is the 'paradigmic shift' familiar to every discipline of knowledge. European integration theory has experienced a number of such shifts over the postwar years. These have not occurred easily, nor in an indiscriminate or whole-sale fashion. None of the paradigms evolved as accounts of European integration over the duration have entirely disappeared from the academic discourse or ideological debate. The paradigms have been discounted rather than entirely discredited. They continue to coexist alongside the currently dominant accounts of the regional process. The debate on European integration illustrates the flux which is the essence of all political inquiry. The paradigmic shifts here have been as persistent as they have been inconclusive. It would be misleading to suggest that the intellectual search for a definitive explanation of European integration can somehow be neatly captured by such periodic and irrevocable changes in intellectual fashion. Each of the main paradigms discussed here has enjoyed its moment of intellectual supremacy and even of political influence. At the same time, each one of them continues to occupy a place in both the theoretical and political landscape. Knowledge is, in this regard, like any other form of created energy; once in existence, its critical mass tends to be redistributed within its particular environment rather than dissipated entirely.

THE 'IDEA' OF EUROPE

The idea of Europe as a unified political system has enjoyed a long history. The prospect of an 'ever closer' European Union has also provoked considerable opposition. The notion of some form of transnational integration that has sustained this debate is hardly a new one, even if it has moved more surely to the centre of the continent's political agenda since 1945. Proposals for cooperation across Europe's political or cultural boundaries go back almost as far as civilisation itself. The idea of 'Europe' as a coherent historical entity, a cultural concept as well as merely a geographical construct, predates its modern status as an institutional project. This 'idea' of Europe was variously interpreted by theologians, statesmen and scholars, as a geocultural expression commensurate with the boundaries of civilisation itself. The concept of a European core identity has been revived constantly throughout the debate on the continent's future. In the seventeenth century, as Europe's dynastic states found themselves locked into a perennial round of diplomatic crises and military conflicts, the French diplomat Sully, in his 'Grand Design' for Europe, recommended a softening of the continent's rigid division into kingdoms, as a surer route to a durable peace.[1] Similar projects for institutionalising the pursuit of a continental peace were recommended as the antidote to territorial aggrandisement and war throughout the eighteenth century.[2] The Abbé Saint Pierre, Secretary to the French delegation at the signing of the Peace of Utrecht (1713–14), envisaged a permanent league of enlightened European monarchs providing a bulwark against war. Kant, too, in his essay 'On Eternal Peace' (1795), recommended Reason as the counteractant to the atavism of realpolitik. Moreover, Kant put his trust in the legal process rather than in kingship; he recommended the virtues of a federalist republic rather than nation statehood as the best guarantee of the public good.[3]

The turbulent times which had called forth these radical ideas were hardly conducive to their realisation. None of these imaginative projects seemed to amount to anything more than far fetched idealism. The triumph of populism as the fount of modern politics which followed the French revolution of 1789, did little to stem and much to encourage the rising tide of narrow territorial nationalism in European politics. Some luminaries looked askance at the prospect of an intensified competitiveness in European affairs. The French philosopher Saint-Simon, for instance, rejected the statecentric arrangement and anticipated the prescriptions of the European federalist movement by a century or more. Proudhon, too, another Frenchman with an international outlook, advocated a federal solution to what he saw as the artificial and dangerous division of Europe into autarchic and militant nation states.[4]

These visionary schemes nevertheless failed to make inroads into the established, if precarious, balance of power between Europe's leading states. The ideal of separate nationhood and the principle of national self determination captured progressive thought and shaped radical aspirations for a century or more after the fall of the Bastille.[5] The nation state seemed to offer a surer recipe for coping with the urgent tasks of political modernisation and economic development. It appealed in these terms both to established elites and to those emergent publics whose nominal consent to be governed became the new source of political authority and legitimacy.[6] Even in these unpropitious times, however, idealism continued to challenge realpolitik on its own ground, by recommending alternative radical projects for restructuring the international order. The tangled web of imperial rivalries which embroiled the major European powers in a continuous sequence of crises throughout the late nineteenth century, did produce a notional attempt at a continental solution. The Hague Conferences of 1899 and 1907 at least raised the issue of continental organisation as a way of ensuring peace. In the event, the Hague delegates got no further than civilising the conduct of war by codifying its 'rules'.

Even the cataclysm of the Great War (1914–18), fought in the pursuit or defence of national grandeur, failed to dislodge the idea of nationhood as the central organising principle of European politics. Those idealists who continued to canvass an alternative transnational prospectus fared little better than their predecessors. The efforts of Count Coudenhove-Kalergi's Pan European movement to rekindle the federalist principle[7] in the transnational setting came to little, before Europe was swept into a second major conflagration in 1939. Coudenhove's analysis of Europe's contemporary plight was based on an altogether realistic assessment of the impact of recent international change on the continent's political options. He raised the incisive question that has exercised the postwar advocates of European integration ever since: 'Can Europe preserve its peace and its autonomy in the face of growing non European world powers, if she remains politically and economically divided, or is she forced to organise herself as a federation of states to save her existence?'[8]

It seems clear from the developments in Europe between the two world wars, that neither the European political establishment nor its mass publics, were prepared to accept the reasoning behind Coudenhove-Kalergi's appeal for political reorganisation. Although the PEM's manifesto did attract some notable endorsements from progressive statesmen such as Briand and Stresemann, it failed to stem the tide of rampant nationalism that engulfed Europe in 1939. The orgy of violence unleashed with the outbreak of war did, nevertheless, have a cathartic effect. The impact of the second world war did help to educate political opinion away from a fatalistic acceptance of anarchy as the normal condition of international affairs; and even to be more receptive to cooperative solutions to Europe's problems. In this sense, the monstrous self destruction wrought by Europe's states between 1939 and 1945 was, as Lipgens claims, **(Document 1)** undoubtedly a defining moment in modern European history. The issue of regional integration moved from the margins of political debate and became one of its abiding themes. Regardless of political vicissitudes, it has remained at the centre of the European agenda ever since. An abiding sense of moral regeneration tinged with a mixture of shame and realism, touched Europe's political imagination after the armistice. There was renewed urgency devoted to the search for ways of banishing conflict and restoring the pursuit of cooperation to the continent's postwar diplomatic agenda.

This is not to suggest that there was any consensus over the direction of such a common project. By no means was every commentator convinced that Europeans could, or indeed should, devote their energies to building an entirely new continental system to replace the failed system of competing nation states. Many scholarly observers and political practitioners alike schooled in the realist tradition, discounted the prospects of anything more novel or far reaching than various forms of improved but modest intergovernmental cooperation. According to such sceptical opinion, regional integration would amount to nothing more intrusive of the established system of states than the usual bargains and trade offs between sovereign states playing, as they 'must', the usual diplomatic game of maximising their national interests. The most persuasive analysis of the origins of the European Community couched in these terms is Alan Milward's impressive account of the reconstruction of the continent's political economy after 1945 **(Document 2)**. The most that these realists would concede to the notion of change, was to acknowledge that the ancient game of international politics was now being played under quite extraordinary circumstances.[9]

POSTWAR CATHARSIS: THE REINVENTION OF THE 'IDEA OF EUROPE'

Political failure is often the catalyst for radical change at both the national and international levels. Postwar Europe was no exception to this trend. The shortcomings of Europe's nation states in failing to resist dictatorship or invasion did enhance the appeal of the idea of a Pan European antidote to the atavism of nationalism. The European idea took firm root in the political imagination during the war. As Walter Lipgens revealed in his masterly account of the politics of the wartime Resistance[10] **(Document 3)**, the Resistance movement across the continent was active in canvassing the federal prospectus. The prestige of the Resistance helped to raise federalism's profile on the postwar political agenda. The movement's leading political light, Altiero Spinelli, has substantiated this claim. He maintained that

> the platforms of the Resistance movements show an acute awareness of the dangers of nationalist celebrations and national fragmentation in Western Europe. The Resistance itself had a kind of supranational dimension, none of the national resistance movements could have survived without outside support; the nations whose honour they had saved had been liberated rather than victorious.[11]

Other factors reinforced the growing awareness among the postwar governing elites that Europe's nation states now occupied an entirely new geopolitical landscape. The Eastern and Central European sub regions soon fell under Soviet domination. Western Europe was obliged to face this threat to its newly liberated status by accepting Washington's offer to shelter under a Pax Americana. Europe's most perceptive minds also took cognisance of the fact that the new postwar global order placed severe constraints on the continent's economic and political options. This unprecedented situation increased the political support in Western Europe for a degree of closer cooperation at the regional level, without ensuring any consensus over its precise form.[12]

The postwar debate on European 'futures' was essentially a dialectic between two contrasting viewpoints on the integration prospectus. The discourse between the statecentric and supranational paradigms, in both its ideological and academic expressions, has provided the debate on European integration with its enduring axiomatic theme. Both of these influential schools of thought have addressed as their principal concern the future of the nation state and, as its obverse, the prospects or limits of regional integration. A radical shift in direction proved easier to prescribe in speeches, political polemics or manifestos than it was to effect in practice. Nevertheless, the debate on European integration has impacted on and helped to change the course of European politics. The nation state continues to exist as the prevailing organisational unit of governance and the main focus of political obligation in Western Europe. But it does so within a complex network of arrangements, procedures and institutions which increasingly constrain it to pool more facets of what were once wholly national prerogatives. The classical idea of an inviolable national sovereignty reflected in the work of Europe's masters of political thought – Bodin, Hobbes and Hegel for instance – since the sixteenth century has been much eroded in the course of barely a generation. Of course, this process of adaptation and change is by no means straightforward, let alone complete. And it has some considerable way to run yet before the new shape of the political kingdom becomes sharper to even the most discerning eye.

Contemporary theorists have finally at least begun to come to terms with the paradoxes of regional integration. The most recent contributions to the debate have assimilated the mixed or hybrid nature of this unique Community arrangement which spans the threshold between domestic and international politics. The juxtaposition of what the earlier theorists saw as mutually exclusive systems has resulted in the latest and, it has to be said, the most plausible paradigm of the European process to date. Two recent commentators in this vein have captured this syncretic quality of European integration thus;

> the EC (is) a new type of political system. A fundamental aspect of this is the tension which exists between the member states and the emerging transnational authority at the EC level. A peculiar element of the new EC system is that institutional elaboration at the central level lacks the key dimensions which are normally found when studying the formation of a new state. There exists more transnational authority at the central EC decision-making and legislative levels than there does at the corresponding implementation and law enforcement stages. Formulations of legally binding intentions or objectives

may follow procedures for transnational decision-making. However, there is almost no unified EC administrative structure or cohesive force which can reach into member countries.[13]

The debate on the nature and direction of European integration has continued apace. And it has shifted its course in response to events. The clear changes in the regional process which have resulted from the postwar European project have certainly altered the rules of the political game. A new paradigm which draws on elements from its classical forerunners, but reflects the hybrid rather than the singular quality of the contemporary integration process, represents the latest paradigmic shift. This book is less concerned with the historical events of post-war European integration than it is with the way that commentators have perceived, conceptualised and tried to explain them. The theoretical endeavour to uncover the dynamics of the European process has attracted some of the most capable minds at work in contemporary political science. What they have said about this phenomenon has undoubtedly enhanced our understanding of the processes of European integration. The theoretical debate on the regional process in Europe has also enriched our knowledge of the international process at large. For this reason, the intellectual history of European integration is as important and interesting in its own right as any detailed account of what has happened on the ground.

INTEGRATION AND 'MEANING'

Integration is a concept whose meaning depends much more on agreeing a definitional consensus than it does on establishing any abiding or universal properties. The variable nature of regional integration in the political debate, as well as its flexible usage in social scientific discourse, increases the methodological difficulties confronting the theorists of regional integration. The principal problem here is a lack of consensus over the intrinsic properties of the condition under review.[14] As Groom and Heraclides see it, integration is much more a process of becoming than it is a clear outcome or a definitive political end state. Hughes and Schwartz tried to grasp the essentialist nettle, by recommending a systematic approach to the terminology of regional integration. They saw this as a more likely route, both to definitional consensus and to eliciting some sustainable hypotheses about the processes of international change that are amenable to empirical testing.[15]

The imprecision in uncovering a clearcut integration dynamic – the key independent variable that 'makes it happen', and the uncertainty of the momentum or direction of this, as of any other process of political change – has fuelled an energetic academic and political debate over the duration. In these circumstances, subjectivity and political preference are bound to intrude on objective analysis, for 'as a state of affairs certain criteria must be met for integration to have occurred . . . [and these] criteria are usually specified by the observer or the participant, since there is no generally accepted "essentialist" definition of integration.'[16] This variable approach to integration is by no means a surrender to definitional casuistry or mere eclecticism. It represents a necessary philosophical caveat. It offers a way out of the teleological cul de sac, and it avoids the definitional trap of tying down 'integration' to one specific historic outcome or narrowly institutional expression. At the same time, this pursuit of conceptual clarity brings its own problems. To accept integration as a variable condition rather than a fixed entity – a sliding scale involving a minimalist threshold and a maximalist outcome defined as the creation of a new political unity out of the amalgam of distinct and formally separate parts – does suggest a viable theoretical approach, but one that is by no means unproblematical.

The regional integration process in Europe has unfolded at an unsteady and unpredictable pace and in unexpected directions, regardless of the once confident predictions of the classical paradigms to the contrary. The flux in Community affairs makes real difficulties for those whose task is to uncover and explain this process. There are nevertheless some transparent facts concerning the dynamics of integration. Developments so far have certainly carried the European process across the minimalist threshold that demarcates integration from mere inter-governmental cooperation, without realising the ambitious goals outlined at the maximalist or unmitigated supranationalist end of the integration spectrum. This, in itself, does not take us very far towards a satisfactory clarification of the nature of regional integration. And there are other drawbacks in this search for the precise and unequivocal meaning of what is, after all, an immensely complex process of political change. A review of the extensive literature on European integration reveals the extent to which this theoretical endeavour is suffused with the values, prejudices and political prescriptions of those commentators who have been drawn to the study of this fascinating subject.

The subjective element in the academic study of politics is as persistent as it is in every branch of the social sciences. Its pitfalls were signalled in the particular field of integration studies by Puchala's quaint use of the 'elephant parable'. If the sightless, he surmised, were asked to define an elephant, they would almost certainly offer widely divergent and imaginative accounts of the exotic creature, depending on their perception of the part they had touched.[17] The business of constructing theory in the social sciences faces similar difficulties. Not the least of these is the differential meaning attributed to supposedly self evident facts when theorists select, order and build them into what must pass for plausible accounts of 'reality'. The conceptual problems confronting any serious theoretical endeavour are certainly daunting. This should not, however, deter the prospective theorist from trying to make sense of the world. James Rosenau, in a remarkably candid assessment of the limitations on objectivity in a social scientific endeavour in which the observers are also participants in the games of life, felt able to argue nevertheless, for the maintenance of a 'scholarly detachment'. Acknowledging the easy temptation to identify with 'noble' causes and to castigate others as morally unsound, offers a safeguard of sorts. At least it serves to remind against the dangers of subjectivity. As a primary rule of academic engagement it is more than half way to avoiding the ontological trap and ensuring the open mind on which sound scholarship depends. Rosenau's maxim should provide the theoretical yardstick for students of every branch of the human sciences when he maintains that,

> the great problems of war, justice, and poverty are of such overriding import-
> ance that often it seems compelling, if not reasonable, to devote ourselves to
> them as activists and thereby risk exceeding our training and competence as
> we champion worthy solutions. Then, swept along by the intrinsic rightness
> of our actions, we easily mistake the vigor of our advocacy for the rigor of our
> analysis. This is not to argue for isolation in an ivory tower. By scholarly
> detachment I do not mean we should avoid entering the public arena. My
> thought is rather that we remain truly scholarly when we are in that arena.
> How? By adhering to a strict rule-of-thumb which specifies that our conduct
> in the public arena be no different than our conduct in the classroom, the
> library, or the computer center . . . there are good reasons to quell the activist
> temptations and cling to the rule-of-thumb that confines us to the detachment
> of our analytic talents.[18]

The key to good theorising is, by this sensible yardstick, systematic analysis backed by empirical evidence gathered in support of the manageable (that is, research-able) propositions under consideration. Kaiser **(Document 4)** recommends the search for such 'organised knowledge' in just these cautious and measured terms, as 'the first stage in the development of theory'.[19] He also provides a plausible explanation for the curious fact that cogent analytical thinking about European integration evolved originally in the American academy rather than in its European counterpart. Harrison **(Document 5)**, one of the European scholars who rose early to this transatlantic challenge took this conceptual discussion a stage further and related it to the epistemological debate about the 'scientific' quality of social theory per se. Harrison's broad vision helped to connect what many European scholars saw as a rather parochial, even misconceived academic concern, and firmly linked it to the wider issues that had begun to engage and refocus European political sciences in the wake of the 'behavioural revolution'. Integration theory may be precise in its substantive focus; but it has as much to contribute to the generic debate on the philosophy of the social sciences as any other branch of behavioural theory.

Any map of the process of European integration should obviously set out to chart the actual train of events as accurately as possible. Unfortunately the 'facts' of any social situation are never entirely self evident. The 'relevant' data required for fashioning any conceptual model or explanation of events, need to be selected and ordered, and general conclusions drawn from it. To this extent the observer's own predispositions and values are bound to intrude into any theoretical endeav-our. This does not, however, mean that the social scientist should surrender to his value preferences or simply ignore their intrusion into the theoretical task. Any plausible account of events should avoid wholesale subjectivity. The prospect-ive explicator of political events is duty bound, in other words, to be aware of his prejudices and to account for them in his work. The discussion of regional integration would be largely worthless if we were merely engaged in an exchange of ideological prejudices. While we are principally concerned here with academic discourse rather than ideological polemics, the distinction between crude ideologism and social scientific discourse is less clear cut than it ought to be. Nevertheless, this remains a distinctive boundary that every social theorist should strive to maintain. And the extent to which this intellectual frontier is effectively policed should be one of the essential criteria we employ when we weigh the merits of the respective theoretical contributions to the quest for European integration.

THE MEANING OF INTEGRATION

The concept of regional integration would be equally meaningless if it was used in an entirely random fashion. Whatever the substantive differences between the paradigms reviewed here, they all address the same fundamental phenomenon, even if they offer contrasting explanations of its causes and likely outcomes. European integration theory examines the consequences of the increased inter-action of long established nation states within their regional environment. There has been until late an assumption on all sides of the debate that the exchanges and bargains that constitute this process are driven by a singular systemic logic; that a special dynamic is at work here. There is, of course, no agreement about the modus vivendi of this regional process. On the contrary, on one side of the debate are those theorists who detect a supranational momentum, inexorably propelling states into entirely novel transnational arrangements. The realist paradigm on the other side of the argument suggests that regional politics continues to be shaped by the ancient dictates of realpolitik, which invariably limits the scope of these interactions and constrains their institutional or policy outcomes. Even in this minimal or intergovernmental form, regional integration does, nevertheless, imply a special kind of diplomatic transaction with a degree of intensity unique in the long history of interstate relations.

Integration theory covers the entire range of interstate relations implied by these conflicting paradigms. More recently, it has come to embrace some novel attempts to reconcile these conflicting theoretical extremes in the new syncretic or hybrid explanation of the integrative process. The most satisfactory conceptual approach to the meaning of integration is not an exclusive one but the inclusive account recommended by Pentland (Document 6). He prefers to see European integration not as a singular phenomenon or event but as a composite of related actions, joint outcomes and mutual responses to events within a given historical situation. Both the actual process and our understanding of it is further complic-ated by the fact that these reactions to events occur simultaneously, but with variable impact and different outcomes, on three distinct levels: that of the individual citizen, the territorial state and the regional system. Integration is by definition a systemic and multifaceted phenomenon or it is nothing. It does, as Pentland sees it, amount to something substantive at each of these particular levels of social and political experience. The processes of international change invariably alter the balance of relations within the group of states directly involved. This impacts on the domestic politics of each individual state, again with a differential if broadly comparable outcome in each case. Finally, in as much as integration intrudes on national sovereignty and erodes the insular sense of nationhood in which political authority was formerly rooted, it touches the individual at the cognitive level of ideological commitment, value formation and ultimately, political identity itself.

The consequence of this for the development of integration theory suggests a multiplicity of models or paradigms. Accordingly, Pentland offers no grand theory or overarching conceptual scheme for regional integration; 'instead, an attempt is made to determine not only the areas of compatibility but also the points of difference between the major approaches to integration theory'.[20] To do otherwise merely encourages intellectual insularity, in so far as

> groups of scholars tend to equate the progress of the field with the progress of their own particular approach and to ignore scholars whose work begins with different premises and definitions. Integration studies thus proceed along a number of parallel tracks, and passengers rarely transfer from one train to another. In such a situation of mutual incomprehension, productive scholarly debate – let alone cooperation – is hardly possible.[21]

This open minded rather than merely eclectic approach to regional integration remains the most productive way forward in the search for a theory of integration with predictive rather than prescriptive qualities. In other words, the complex and multifarious phenomenon of European integration cannot be captured in any one decisive moment or particular institutional outcome. It is a moveable feast with numerous coexistent meanings rather than a universal or conclusive phenomenon. Integration as a political process covers a spectrum of complex and ambiguous political, social and economic relationships. These involve limited forms of co-operation at one extreme, and also encompass more intensive supranationalist outcomes at the other. The major integration paradigms dwell on one or other of these historic configurations. To this extent, they tend to 'fix' history in the particular aspic of their own subjective preferences. At the same time, even the most cautious and conservative statecentric paradigm has acknowledged flux as a natural condition of international politics. The prospect of change is at least acknowledged in each of these accounts of the integration process. To a greater or lesser degree, each integration paradigm acknowledges that contemporary changes in the scope and scale of international relations have altered the procedures and the pattern of regional politics in Europe. Events have impinged on the autarchic insularity of state actors and refashioned the anarchic order they were deemed to inhabit in the classical realist account. Where these various accounts differ is over the consequences of these changes for the balance of power between state actors and the regional system they now inhabit.

This amalgam of political pressures, economic forces and geopolitical influences has obliged every advanced state to enter what William Wallace has identified as those 'intense patterns of interaction' which occur with increasing regularity in the modern world, generated by its networks of markets, new technologies, intensified communication flows and all manner of cultural, social and educational exchanges. To this extent all of the integration paradigms, irrespective of their profound philosophical differences, do remain in touch with each another. As such, they are part of a common discourse on the nature and prospects for international change. Formal integration, on the other hand, is a clear stage beyond this pervasive pattern of interdependence. In as much as regional integration implies, in the flexible terminology employed by Wallace, those 'deliberative actions by authoritative policy-makers to create and adjust rules to establish common institutions and to work with and through those institutions',[22] it remains, whatever its scope or coherence, beyond the modest range of mere intergovernmental cooperation.

The theoretical debate on European integration concentrates then, on the differential that exists between these competing visions of international change and the impact of this insidious process on Europe's longstanding political arrangements. In the early stages of this discourse a clear antithesis existed between two very different views of this process; those merely cooperative arrangements at the lower end of the projection of possibilities, and the more intensive pattern of transactions associated with formal or maximalist integration of the supranational kind. The classical paradigms were intellectually divided over the future of the nation state, as they were over the prospects, in the face of the unique conditions confronting Europe's nation states after 1945, for rebuilding the continent along supranational (federalist or functionalist) lines. The latest theoretical contributions to this debate have suggested a much less clearcut response to these fundamental questions. But the latter day integration theorists do continue nevertheless to address the same elemental questions. To this extent, the 'meaning of integration' revolves around an on-going debate about the limits or enduring qualities of nation statehood in Europe under contemporary international conditions. This fundamental question at least directs the competing paradigms to a common discourse.

Each of these substantive schools of thought, on the prospects or otherwise for European integration, focuses its theoretical endeavours on the same broad issues; of whether or not there is some intrinsic logic underway in the regional integration process; the implications of these palpable structural changes for Europe's nation states; and the likely political consequences and institutional outcomes of such shifts in the locus of political power. None of these assumptions should be taken at face value or be allowed to pass without serious scrutiny. The maxim in any review of theory making must be its utility as both a plausible and rigorous explanation of events. Two of the leading commentators on the theoretical endeavour to uncover the dynamics of European integration have issued what should be the watchword for those who take up this particular challenge. Pryce and Wessels remind us that, 'from Popper we know that a verification of causal theories in a complex social world is impossible; what we can do, however, is to test theories against the historical record and reject those which manifestly fail to provide a satisfactory explanation of events'. What they suggest in this regard, is

> the modest ambition not of finding and asserting the one and only 'truth' to explain why strategies aimed at achieving a closer union have succeeded or failed, but to clear away some over simplifications, to point towards some probabilities, and to identify a number of factors as likely to be crucial for success.[23]

This prospectus suggests a useful template against which to measure the theoretical contributions reviewed in the chapters that follow.

Part II

The paradigms of European integration

Chapter 2

The supranational paradigm (1)
The federalist approach

TRANSCENDING THE NATION STATE

The costs and consequences of an immensely destructive war cast serious doubts after 1945 on the nation state as the source of effective governance and of a stable socio-economic order. Some contemporary commentators regarded nation states as insular, wasteful and ultimately destructive. A supranationalist school of thought saw the nation state, on the evidence of two world wars, as the least suitable format for reconstructing a devastated continent's infrastructure or for guaranteeing the regional peace. The supranationalists believed that the nation state was obsolescent and must be transcended, even though they disagreed about the most appropriate arrangements for replacing it. The most positive thing these supranationalists could say about the nation state was that it had fulfilled its historic mission. Europe's national states had, over two centuries or more, helped to build viable political communities out of culturally or ethnically diverse components. These states had also resolved some momentous integration and legitimacy crises along the road to political development.

The successes of state building and national integration were indisputable even to those with supranational preferences. But so, too, were nationalism's manifest failings. Critics here believed the time was ripe for Europe to move beyond the limitations and hazards of a regional system consisting of competing nation states, and towards a more positive stage in the continent's political evolution.[1] The postwar mood for change was fuelled in large measure by the assumption that the nation state had outlived its historic usefulness in a century of immensely destructive total war. This positive outlook figured in a characteristically upbeat account of Europe's political development which anticipated a fully fledged transnational polity as the likely end of an arduous adaptive process. The authors of 'Europe's Would-be polity' maintained that

> To the transcenders, re-establishment of the old order would be little more than the prelude to a new round of destruction. Nation states could aggregate terrifying amounts of power, but they could no longer protect their citizens; the hard shells which the territorial states had thrown around themselves were now permeable. Wars were no longer confined to border regions but were

fought centre to centre. Awesome destructive power combined with relatively meagre defensive capabilities led inexorably toward insecurity and war. The weakening of the nation state was thus perceived more as a cause of war than as a result of it.[2]

The supranationalist paradigm was generally sustained by such optimistic assumptions about the likely outcomes of the rapidly changing international system. It included under its broad ambit, federalists and radical constitutionalists, who saw in international law and transnational institutions the only sure safeguard of civility and peace. Federalism also appealed to those who were attracted to an institutionalised social pluralism and cultural diversity as the indispensable bulwarks of tolerance against the structural uniformity and mindless conformity induced by modern, large scale mass society. J.B. Priestley, the English man of letters, spoke for many commentators who shared these fears of an impersonal and indiscriminate social order. Priestley typified the federalist respect for social diversity when he identified what he felt was a clear linkage between the cynical disregard for humanity, forbearance and goodwill, the climate of intolerance and selfishness that thrives in mass societies, and the propensity for unitary states built on such narrow foundations to make war **(Document 7)**. The federalism movement likewise attracted pacifists, and internationalists, with deep ethical roots either in Christianity or Humanism.[3] H.N. Brailsford made no less a claim for federalism than its equation with the salvation of civilisation itself **(Document 8)**. Lord Lothian, the leading light in the influential British federalist movement, combined these concerns and argued for federalism as an antidote to the folly of international anarchy **(Document 9)**. A similar faith in the virtues of international cooperation based on cultural equality was exhibited by the federalist advocates who were active in every European country during and after the end of the war.

The prospect of transcending the extant system of nation states and reallocating their existing sovereignties within international organisations concerned with maximising harmony and minimising conflict, also figured in the recommendations of international theorists in the functionalist tradition. The differences between the various expressions of the supranational paradigm are as important as their similarities. The clearest division here was between the federalist and functionalist traditions. The federalists were convinced of the need to reconstitute Europe's existing political arrangements. Federalism emphasises the priority to be given to making formal changes in political institutions and procedures, as the key to securing social harmony and democracy. As a political doctrine, federalism has until quite recently always been more preoccupied by defining formal outcomes and recommending suitable institutional frameworks for balancing natural social diversity with the requirements for a just governance, than it has been with uncovering the processes or sociological dynamics that lie behind political change.[4] The functionalists, on the other hand, have usually reversed these theoretical and political priorities. Functionalism concentrated on the importance of process as the key to implementing changes in the political order, rather than with prescribing *a priori* its precise form or outcome.[5]

Those federalist theorists who addressed the matter of European integration regarded political change principally as a direct consequence of a radical zeitgeist or shift in the collective political imagination. Whereas, in the functionalist account of international change, the constitutional details of a shift of power and authority away from the nation state were deemed to be much less significant than uncovering those circumstances – both structural and cognitive – under which sectoral integration in specific policy areas might help to build what Mitrany engagingly called 'a working peace system'. Functionalists expected changes in Europe's political arrangements to follow on from increasing cooperation between elites. To this extent, both approaches were modern expressions of the medieval notion of elite complementarity. But there were differences of emphasis and strategy between them. At the risk of oversimplifying important and subtle theoretical differences here, federalism opted for a radical 'bottom up' model of political change. 'Europe' was a grand project that would be built by a cooperative compact between enlightened elites and their peoples. Functionalism, on the other hand, adopted a 'top down' model of international change. 'Europe', rather like 'Christendom' was the outcome of a benevolence bestowed by dedicated elites with a mission to save the masses. Functionalists put their contemporary faith in the wisdom and ambition of administrative elites capable of discerning human welfare needs in response to a technocratic logic rather than a populist one.

FEDERALISM AND EUROPEAN INTEGRATION

Federalism presented a direct challenge to the nation state. As such, it represents the most radical expression of the supranational paradigm. It offers what Preston King defines as an ideological or philosophical outlook,[6] and one which countenances the prospect of a sudden rather than an incremental transformation of existing political arrangements. At the same time, this prescriptive or visionary view implies or indeed overtly recommends a set of institutional procedures, precisely for overcoming the assumed evils or shortcomings of the unitary state. Its leading European advocates, whether active politicians such as Altiero Spinelli or academic theorists such as Henri Brugmans[7] or K.C. Wheare, have canvassed a firm political prospectus that encompassed unprecedented changes in the European political order. Europe's federalists presented a clear alternative to the national atavism and insularity they identified as the principal cause of war, by calling for the dis-aggregation of power away from centralised government in unitary nation states,[8] and its relocation among separate but connected levels of authority within a multinational federal state. The European federalists, concerned to secure and institutionalise a fragile continental peace, drew heavily, both for their inspiration and constitutional format, on the classical federalist doctrine of state building which had been evolving in both theory and practice since the eighteenth century.[9]

European federalism posited a superordinate transnational governance to

regulate the behaviour of the previously fully sovereign state units. This arrangement required a formal compact to be negotiated between these pre-existing
nation states, and implied a contract between their political elites and 'the people'.
These complicated agreements would be struck in a constituent assembly which
expressed the democratic will of Europe's people at large. European federalists,
following on from the classical American model, have concentrated, by and large,
on institutional procedures for ensuring social stability and enshrining an equitable
political balance of power, at the expense of explaining the logics and political
consequences of social change.[10] Politics, in other words, or precise constitutional
formulae and governmental arrangements, are the independent rather than the
dependent variable here. Wheare provided the most lucid account of federalism's
rational appeal when he recommended it as a form of government in which
functions

> are divided in such a way that the relationship between the legislature which
> has authority over the whole territory and those legislatures which have
> authority over parts of the territory is not the relationship of superiors to sub-
> ordinates ... but is the relationship of coordinate powers in the government
> process.[11]

Federalism seemed well placed, both as a political movement and an ideological
prescription, to take advantage after 1945 of the endemic doubts about the virtues
of nation statehood. In the interwar years federalism had attracted some support
from among Europe's liberal intelligentsia.[12] The idea of a transnational European
state organised according to federalist principles had been widely canvassed by
similar elements in the Resistance.[13] Spinelli and Ernesto Rossi used the federal
idea to mobilise the European resistance against Nazi tyranny. The Ventotene
Manifesto[14] composed as a rallying point for this opposition helped to some extent
to popularise what had, under the influence of the prewar English federalist
movement, started out as an elitist doctrine.[15] They argued in this manifesto
that,

> The time has now come to get rid of these old cumbersome burdens (of the
> past) ... Today, in an effort to begin shaping the outlines of the future, those
> who have understood the reasons for the current crisis in European civiliza-
> tion and who have therefore inherited the ideals of a movement dedicated to
> raising the dignity of mankind ... have begun to meet and seek each other
> out ... National independence, freedom, socialism will come alive and will
> exist as beneficial forces only when Federation ... is their basis and not their
> consequence ... To create a European Federation is therefore definitely the
> first task upon which the progressive European movement must concentrate
> all their energy.[16]

Rossi and Spinelli organised a wartime congress of European federalists in
Switzerland in 1944. This congress issued an influential if ambitious declaration
calling for a postwar European federation. It maintained that

all the sacrifice and suffering endured for the same cause have created ties of brotherhood . . . and have given birth to a new consciousness of European solidarity of the free peoples, the maintenance of which will be one of the essential guarantees of peace.[17]

(Document 10)

This progressive momentum was carried over to the Liberation. Another congress of European federalists was held in Paris in 1945. Bosca, in his recent account of the wartime emergence of federalism as a significant political force, concludes that this assembly

> was based on two simple assumptions of fact. First, with the advent of the world market, the process of production, exchange and consumption increasingly unites mankind, particularly in Europe. Secondly, this new world which was shaping itself in an economic and social sphere beyond the nation states, could be politically organised with the method of democratic political participation only if the historical vision of federalism and the mechanism of federal government were added to the prospects and methods of liberalism, democracy and socialism. The only remedy for the evils of national sovereignty was seen by Resistants as a federal union of the peoples, in which every nation was completely self governing in its own internal affairs, yet all people were united into a single federal union for their common affairs.[18]

In spite of its broad idealistic appeal, federalism suffered from some endemic weaknesses that reduced its impact on events. There were deep divisions within the movement between various factions which endorsed different versions of the federalist prospectus. Although these national groups coalesced in 1946 into a transnational federalist movement, the Union of European Federalists (UEF), their abiding differences over strategy and objectives distracted the movement from the task at hand and diverted its energies into damaging internecine squabbles. The prospect of a movement dedicated to universal peace and progressive ideas divided against itself, undoubtedly undermined federalism's credibility too, and with that its political appeal to its prospective constituency.

The moral appeal of federalism and its reputation as a serious force for political change was eventually squandered, and not least because its promise was not matched by its achievements. In the event, the federalist prospectus barely dented the European political establishment. The relative ease with which the discredited nation state system in Europe was restored, requires some explanation. Those of a federalist disposition have tended to attribute this practical shortfall to unfavourable contingencies; for instance to unfortunate political timing, or unexpected circumstances such as the rise of the Cold War, and the natural fear of change brought on by these new uncertainties. While these factors cannot be discounted, European federalism has faced altogether deeper problems. The prospect of replacing even a discredited system of nation states with an untried and fragmented federal political system, held more appeal for academic theorists and idealists on the margins of politics, than it did either for publics exhausted by war, or for mainstream politicians charged with the task of rebuilding the continent and mindful of the fears, prejudices and aspirations of their populations.

The times were out of joint too for this particular expression of political radicalism in quite another sense. The unparalleled energies for change generated by postwar radical movements in Europe, were principally channelled into the redistributive politics favoured by the left. A movement for political change rooted firmly in the nation state was able to muster much wider popular support than federalism could manage, even in its best years. The political elites across the ideological spectrum who occupied the positions of influence after the Liberation, although well disposed to regional cooperation, drew a firm line under what they regarded as a fanciful supranational prospectus. These elites were more concerned to rekindle domestic civic cultures, and rediscover a sense of national purpose in rebuilding their countries' devastated infrastructures. A general indifference to federalism across mainland Europe was reinforced by the hostility of the British political establishment to anything which threatened national sovereignty. Opposition from this quarter proved to be a considerable liability for the federalist cause at a time when Britain was an influential player in postwar European affairs.[19]

Above all, the resilience of the postwar European nation state can best be explained by the sheer weight of political orthodoxy. It is clear, not least from those academic studies broadly sympathetic to the federalist cause, that the movement would have confronted immense obstacles, even under the most favourable circumstances. Political ideas tend to change slowly at the best of times. Even then, they are more likely to change gradually by osmosis rather than by the sort of dramatic sea-change anticipated in contemporary federalist thought. Established elites pursuing conventional agendas continue to wield immense advantages over new movements canvassing more radical ideas. Elites exert a disproportionate influence over political outcomes in any particular historical circumstances. This conservative tendency prevailed in postwar Western European politics too, once the situation there began to regain some semblance of normality. Elites as well as the publics who took their political cues from them, favoured a more conventional approach to resolving the continent's enormous problems.[20] They undoubtedly preferred the predictable to the experimental.

Federalism carried other disadvantages too, that were more of its own making. The ideological differences contained within the movement distracted it from giving due consideration to those very political liabilities that were bound to determine the success or otherwise of its campaign to refocus the European political imagination. In part, the problem was rooted in federalism's preoccupation with constitutional prescriptions.[21] Federalist theory, with its roots in classical liberalism, has tended to assume that rational discourse is all that is required in order to tilt the world on its cognitive axis; and on that basis to refashion its political shape. The federalist movement betrayed its elitist propensities by concentrating its political energies on preaching its gospel of giving priority to constitutional change. Federalists were much less exercised by dealing with the practical requirements of mounting an effective political campaign which took full account of public reticence or establishment hostility to its radical prospectus. In short, many federalists simply wrote or acted as if the mere recommendation by well meaning advocates unburdened by a reactionary political past, of a rational formula for the 'sensible' reorganisation of the continent's political arrangements, was all that was required given the postwar catharsis, to bring it about. They displayed, in the circumstances, a fatal mix of idealism and complacency. They simply took too much for granted; both with regard to federalism's general appeal, and for devising the practical strategies necessary for realising their political ambitions. The evidence for this stringent judgement is there in the failure of the European federalists to mobilise sufficient political support behind their well intentioned cause.

It was by no means the case that all federalists were guilty of political naivety. Jean Monnet stands out as a significant exception here. Monnet's concern with timing and strategy, with cautiously adjusting practical recommendations towards supranational change in order to reflect political realities, was not shared by the federalist movement as a whole. This pragmatism clearly distinguishes his functionalist method from the visionary approach of the federalists. To Monnet's mind, the particular form that integration took was much less important than the requirement to launch the process on a practical footing, and thereby to give it a form that was capable of sustaining transnational cooperation against the opposition from those political elements who felt most threatened by it.[22] Monnet was well aware of those forces which remained favourable to the political status quo and discounted any radical change either as dangerous experimentation or fanciful novelty. In these circumstances, Monnet remained convinced 'that at present there is and can be no Europe other than a Europe of the States except, of course, for myths, fictions and pageants'.[23] The solution as he saw it, was to work with rather than against the political grain. Federalism, to Monnet's shrewd mind, was the culmination of a long and carefully stage managed process, or it was nothing (**Document 11**). It involved modifying conventional expectations about the prospects for international cooperation, rather than confronting them head on as the mainstream European federalists were inclined to do. Instead of waiting as federalists preferred, for a full scale constitutional revolution, Monnet suggested making modest but discernible incursions into national sovereignty. According to this gradualist strategy,

> We believe in starting with limited achievements, establishing de facto solidarity, from which a federation would gradually emerge. I have never believed that one fine day Europe would be created by some grand political mutation . . . (that) the pragmatic method we had adopted would . . . lead to a federation validated by the people's vote; but that federation would be the culmination of an existing economic and political reality, already put to the test . . . it was a bringing together of men and practical realities . . . [24]

This common sense pragmatism, and its implicit compromise with the status quo, was the very antithesis of the constituent method of political change prescribed by Europe's postwar federalist movement. The stark contrast between these positions was highlighted by federalism's failure to capture the political initiative on the back of so much residual goodwill for the resistance movement which had been its principal momentum. Whereas Monnet, in contrast, was remarkably successful in his efforts to establish the foundations of a functional community during the 1950s.[25]

Federalism was further weakened by another outbreak of the political self indulgence that tends to afflict movements driven more by ideology than practicality. The rising ideological differences within the movement as the prospect of real change receded, saw yet more political energy wasted in arcane factional disputes.[26] Instead of the federalists concerting their efforts and concentrating their depleted political resources in a common cause, the movement split asunder over strategy. These internecine differences were less apparent at the start, but had already begun to show by the time the European federalist movement (UEF) embarked on a series of postwar rallies to educate public opinion. The culmination of this publicity campaign, the Montreux Congress of 1947, signalled the divisions already rising within the movement. The 'world federalists' faction saw European integration merely as the precursor of global unity. Whereas the 'integral federalists' faction emphasised Europe's immense cultural diversity and the role of semi autonomous local units as the 'true' foundation of a workable federal polity.[27]

Events served to further widen this schism. The radical or maximalist tendency led by Spinelli[28] remained hostile to any hint of a compromise with their declared goal of constitutional change, legitimised by means of a pan European Constituent Assembly drawing its legitimacy from 'the people'.[29] They argued their case volubly during 1949 in the forum provided by the newly constituted assembly of the Council of Europe. By this time, however, Europe's national political establishments were firmly back in control of domestic affairs, and secure enough to resist these radical demands. Meanwhile, the prospect of an apparently more modest but novel experiment in regional cooperation, in the shape of the Coal and Steel Community, began to attract support from those pragmatic federalists prepared to face facts and follow Monnet's example, by extending the scope of European integration in whatever form seemed most likely to make some positive headway against entrenched intergovernmentalism and national resistance. This fundamental split between the radical and pragmatic federalists was merely consolidated in the tense aftermath of Monnet's failure to extend the ECSC's sectoral approach from matters of technical policy to the 'high' politics of defence and security policy.[30]

The eventual collapse in 1954 of the scheme for political union which followed on from the proposal in the Pleven Plan for a European army, and the return to an altogether more modest route to functional integration, widened the growing rift within the federalist movement. As a direct outcome the UEF formally split in 1956 into two separate organisations. The radicals regrouped into the Mouvement Federaliste Européen (MFE), under Spinelli's aegis, and remained dedicated to nothing less than a fully federalist Europe through the classical constituent route. The discussion of strategy by Spinelli **(Document 12)** is a clear statement of the classical European federalist position: the 'people' remain the only sure guarantors of political progress; governments, even those who feign interest in the European idea, are to be mistrusted; and the EC's supranational institutions are by no means the best or most reliable route to a federal union. The pragmatists of the Action Européen Federaliste (AEF) on the other hand, were prepared to support any positive developments that contributed to further-ing supranational integration, however modest and by whatever means.[31] To this extent, federalism came to be reconciled, in its minimalist expression, with the functionalist paradigm.

Federalism's contribution to the development of European integration turned out, then, to be much less significant than might have been anticipated in 1945. The constraints of national politics, the residual appeal of national interests under-pinned by a revived or continuing sense of national identity, the unpredictable impact of events and the movement's failure in these fluid circumstances to win over key elites or to convert public opinion to its cause, led to deep internal tensions that eventually engulfed the movement in debilitating factional squabbles. Nevertheless, as Michael Burgess has pointed out, federalist principles have continued to impact on both the debate and procedures of European integration **(Document 13)**. At the same time, the longstanding tradition of social and cultural pluralism that is 'the indigenous European federal tradition', has been shaped inevitably, as Burgess sees it, by the continent's own unique historical configurations. The federal idea in Europe has taken on its own peculiar gloss; but it remains, nevertheless, for Burgess, a 'rich' and 'deeply rooted' feature of the political discourse.[32]

On the available evidence this is, to say the least, an optimistic assessment. Subsequent widespread support for the federal idea from within the European Parliament, continued encouragement from the academic community which shadows these events, and even a recent rekindling of admittedly equivocal interest among some national politicians, suggests that the federalist ideal may be severely disadvantaged even if it is far from defunct.[33] An idealist constituency certainly remains convinced of the virtues and indeed the prospects for a federalist route to European integration.[34] Perhaps more significantly for the future shape of European governance, some hard headed realists are gradually coming round to the view that the need to reconcile Community enlargement on the one hand, with the need for efficient decision making, given the sheer scope and complexity of the EU's expansive issue agenda, will require that serious consideration be given to the existing balance of power between the states and the centre, and sooner rather than later. **(Document 14)**. The acceleration in the pace of European integration during the past decade or so has undoubtedly revived the fortunes of the federalist idea. The 'f' word, as it was called by those politicians aware of the acute sensibilities touched by the supranational idea, figured in the deliberations of the IGC's of 1990–1 and at the meetings of the EC's heads of government that prefaced the 1992 signing of the European Treaty of Union at Maastricht. A leading commentator on European affairs was moved to observe, at the time of the Maastricht negotiations on European Union, that:

> Federalism is not dead; it was not even sleeping last night, as negotiations on political union fought towards a conclusion . . . the point will not have been lost on British negotiators. This time, they managed to remove federalism from the treaty. But there will be another summit probably in 1996 . . . When that happens federalism will probably be on the agenda again. It will be there because to most Europeans, federalism is not a pornographic word. If there is one subject over which the last year has demonstrated the cultural and linguistic differences between Britain and the EC, it is this. Europe is federally-minded and will not get any less so.[35]

Again on the current evidence, this is almost certainly an overstatement of the case, but it does contain an important germ of truth. It would be misleading to judge federalism's prospects in contemporary Europe merely from the standpoint of an endemic British hostility to the idea. Practical circumstances as much as ideological prejudices are more likely to determine the EU's future political shape. And in these terms, Wistrich and those who concur with his optimistic prognosis, have a point when they maintain that federalism is probably better placed to impact on European integration than at any time since 1945 **(Document 15)**. The recent enlargement of the EU's membership to 15, and the prospect of over 20 member states by the end of the millennium, suggests that a federalist model may well be the most effective way to balance a cumulative if cautious deepening of the scope of the Community's policy agenda with its inevitable geographical expansion. The genius of federalism has always been the scope it gives to balancing diversity with that degree of political coherence essential for stability; of matching democratic representativeness and social plurality with political order and an efficient but equitable distribution of powers in governance. The EU today is certainly in need of a similar formula as it stands on the threshold of the most daunting challenges – in its economic, political and security affairs – since 1945. Federalism in this latest phase does suggest a practical solution to some of these hugely difficult problems facing the European Union. But by the same token, this latest challenge to the integrity and sovereignty of the EU's member states is certain to invoke the very same concerns and to galvanise a similar resistance to such far reaching change from at least some member states, as federalism raised when it made its early appearance on Europe's postwar political agenda. The most that can be claimed for the federal prospectus in these circumstances, is that it is back on the European agenda, and on somewhat firmer political foundations than it enjoyed in the immediate aftermath of the world war. There is certainly everything to play for but no guarantee that 'history', 'rationality' or any other positivist abstraction, will drive nationhood from the scene without staunch resistance, and submerge it in a fully federal European polity.

Chapter 3

The supranational paradigm (2)
Functionalist models

THE PROSPECT OF INTERNATIONAL CHANGE

Functionalism is a strategy for effecting cooperation and policy coordination between nation states. It is also a theory which claims to explain the logistics at work in the process of international change. The intensification of global exchanges in the technical, communications and commercial spheres had encouraged an organisational response to better coordinate and control these transactions, long before European integration became a realistic prospect. Organisations such as the International Telegraph Union (1865) and the Agreement on Universal Postal Measures (1875) had already helped to regulate interstate relations on a voluntaristic and intergovernmental basis. These developments were, in essence, a managed response to the onset of a global political economy.[1] Claude has described their dynamics as a means of coping with the

> unprecedented international flow of commerce in goods, services, peoples, ideas, germs and social evils; only a short while before the nation state had been too large to serve as the appropriate administrative unit for many of the affairs of man in society; now it had become too small . . . [2]

The functionalist approach to the organisation of international affairs was concerned with identifying those factors which would bring a measure of order and stability to an otherwise anarchic world of untrammelled realpolitik, militarism and intensified economic competitiveness. There was an implicit assumption among the functionalist theorists who addressed these issues that cooperation in merely technical and commercial matters would have positive consequences for political integration. This was more than just a pious aspiration harboured by academic commentators remote from worldly affairs. The effective work of both the League of Nations and the UN in these technical and welfare areas after both world wars was inspired by similar aspirations. Functionalism, in both theory and practice, certainly challenged the conventional realist assumptions that saw the world as a Hobbesian void consisting of competing and narrowly self interested states. They replaced in their model of the international system this image of endemic anarchy with one of a potentially cooperative welfare community united by intrinsic interests, sharing similar aspirations and striving for common goals.[3]

MITRANY'S CRITIQUE OF THE NATION STATE

David Mitrany, among the earliest enthusiasts for a new international order, made the most telling intellectual contribution to the development of a functionalist theory of international society. Writing at a time of gathering international crisis in the 1930s, Mitrany fashioned functionalist theory into an intellectually powerful prescription for global rather than regional integration. Mitrany saw little difference between nation states and regional federations. Both were political entities and, as such, both were equally competitive, divisive and destabilising forces in international society. Mitrany never wavered in his conviction that regional systems were merely nation states writ large. As such, international federations created more problems than they solved. Not least, they increased the difficulties of establishing an equitable and peaceful world order.[4] Mitrany continued to argue the case for a functionalist over a federalist solution to the dilemmas and dangers of international organisation, and for a decentralised global rather than a regional approach to the problems,[5] regardless of the postwar European experience of cooperation **(Document 16)**. Above all, he remained convinced that politics was intrinsically evil; that administration, with its concern for the rational allocation of scarce resources, was the key to human cooperation and to what he called a 'Working Peace System'.[6] This antipathy to politics locates Mitrany's ideas in an intellectual tradition whose roots lie in eighteenth-century rationalism and nineteenth-century utilitarianism.

Mitrany's contribution to the debate on European integration was tangential rather than direct. His ideas were a precursor to the altogether more influential neofunctionalist school. Nevertheless, Mitrany's ideas provided the necessary intellectual touchstone for neofunctionalism. Moreover, his legacy to the subsequent debate on regional integration had both a theoretical and a prescriptive dimension. Mitrany's exposure of the limits of the nation state, and his advocacy of a technocratic approach to solving what he saw as the great issues of the day – the elimination of war and the insurance of global peace – was sustained by moral zeal as well as by intellectual conviction. Mitrany's idealism certainly contributed to the ethical dimension that has informed the pro-integrationist approach to the debate on international society. His theoretical perspective, with its emphasis on the forces for international change generated by modern political economy, also cleared some of the methodological ground and established a defined research agenda for neofunctionalism.

Mitrany developed his critique of the nation state in two important works. In *The Progress of International Government* (1933), published at a time when Europe's states were embarking on another round of regional crisis, he argued that civilised men 'should renounce the pagan worship of political frontiers as the source of our public law and morals'.[7] In the place of nation states he advocated a system of international functional agencies in which 'a continuous transfer of functions and authority should take place from the jurisdiction of the state to that of international organs'.[8] In the decade of exponential political crisis and violence that followed the publication of his book, Mitrany saw nothing to convince him that an international system based on states could guarantee the peace or ensure human welfare. In his classic text, *A Working Peace System*, (1943) Mitrany restated his earlier case for a functional–global approach to installing a peaceful international society. He cited the depredations of the contemporary world to reinforce the moral and practical case for a fundamental reordering of international society **(Document 17)**.

Mitrany believed that the functional solution to the elemental human requirements of peace and social stability was rooted in the fulfilment of joint endeavours and the experience of cooperation required for their fulfilment. As such,

> the functional approach emphasises the common index of need. Very many such needs cut across national boundaries, not a few are universal, and an effective beginning for building up an international community of interest could be made by setting up joint agencies for dealing with these common needs.[9]

Mitrany envisaged investing functionally constituted international organisations with the powers and resources necessary to perform these functions. These would be 'called into being by agreement between several or more Governments, in order to benefit mutually by continuous cooperative action along specific lines, or by the continuous regulation of certain international activities'.[10] This, in turn, implied a fundamental reallocation of authority and jurisdiction away from the existing states and towards these new international organisations. For

> by entrusting an authority with a certain task, carrying with it command over requisite powers and means, a slice of sovereignty is transferred from the old authority to the new; and the accumulation of such partial transfers over time brings about a translation of the true seat of authority.[11]

This seemingly straightforward notion of 'process' raises more problems than it answers. Not least because it is unduly optimistic about both the procedures and the outcomes of the type of international change Mitrany predicts as its likely consequence.

Mitrany's pure functionalist prescription has been criticised on grounds other than its naivety or idealism. Mitrany's work was concerned above all to identify and explain the dynamics of contemporary international relations. To that extent it purported to be a social theory rather than merely an ideology. And it is on these grounds that it is most open to criticism. A persistent problem with Mitrany's model is his faith in narrow technocratic solutions to what are clearly complicated political problems.[12] Mitrany's belief in the prospects for positive changes in human behaviour, based as these are on rational conduct, may well be morally invigorating and appealing on purely humanistic grounds. Whether it offers a plausible account of the nature of international politics is another matter entirely. For idealism, based as it is in Mitrany's case on little more than *a priori* moral preferences, hardly meets the rigorous standards of inquiry required of properly conducted social science. His reduction of the dynamics of an immensely complex international process to the narrowly rational forces of political economy is naive to say the least. More to the point, it confuses ethical prescription with methodological rigour.

Mitrany's many critics have pointed out that he exaggerates the role of rationality in his account of social behaviour.[13] Nor can the vagaries of politics be so easily omitted from any balanced account of the operations of the international process. Politics cannot be so easily discounted from human affairs *ad hominem*, simply because its practitioners may be as corrupt, weak willed or fallible as Mitrany finds them to be. In short, Mitrany's attempt to depoliticise international relations does not stand up to the basic tests we must apply to any theory of international change. It confuses facts with values and ignores much empirical evidence that suggests that the very fabric of international relations is indeed abidingly political. Above all, its ambitious but far from convincing claim to have uncovered the surest route to global peace, raised more questions about the timing and procedures of effecting such a momentous sea-change in human affairs than it answered.[14]

Mitrany's belief in the virtues of decentralisation, technocratic cooperation and international administration as a source of transnational welfare and peace did, however, encourage subsequent theorists in the functionalist tradition. The neofunctionalists adapted Mitrany's basic precepts into an altogether more focused explanation of the dynamics of regional integration in Europe. In the guise of both academic theorists and policy practitioners (of whom Monnet stands out as the supreme example) the functionalist revisionists shared Mitrany's abiding aversion to nationalism, and its 'spirit of domination' as the foundation of a peaceful international order.[15] The neofunctionalist account of international change nevertheless differed from Mitranian functionalism on several counts. It rejected his global focus as wholly unmanageable, both from a methodological perspective and because it was deemed to be unrealistic as a practical way of conducting human affairs.

The neofunctionalists concentrated instead on the prospects and arrangements for manageable integration on a regional scale. Moreover politics played a central role in this revisionist model, without dominating the process of integration. Above all, neofunctionalism claimed to be a scientific methodology rooted in actual behaviour rather than one premised on an ethereal moral philosophy. The basis of this particular claim lay in the approach's intellectual origins. As a distinctive product of American behavioural science, the neofunctionalist methodology was empiricist rather than prescriptive. It was concerned less with the moral exhortation and virtuous indignation that characterises Mitrany's work, and more with charting the actual processes of regional integration. Its claim to a scientific mandate rested on the development of manageable and testable hypotheses, rather than with exhorting a better future, idealising the human condition or with issuing moral injunctions against the iniquities of the nation state.

FUNCTIONALISM IN THE EUROPEAN CONTEXT

Neither federalism, with its expectation of a once and for all constitutional annus mirabilis, nor Mitrany's idealised project for a world peace system, made much headway against the determination of Europe's postwar establishment to restore the status quo ante. These elites were, nevertheless, at least receptive to the need for closer regional cooperation, both as a bulwark against the threat of war and as a means for continental reconstruction. By the late 1940s there were signs that the functional approach, eventually institutionalised as the European Coal and Steel Community by the terms of the Treaty of Paris in 1951, offered a feasible route to regional integration. Monnet's novel proposal for sectoral integration was taken up by the French government, albeit for reasons of state rather than any desire to build a supranational community in Europe. And on that basis European integration was launched as a practical project.

The Schuman Plan that embodied this limited but innovative functional scheme, involved a modest surrender of national sovereignty over important commodities, in exchange for distinct national economic and political advantages. There was, at the same time, a parallel agenda, or long term vision, with more radical implications for the future of regional cooperation in Europe. For Monnet and those 'Europeans' who shared his aspirations, the ECSC suggested a way of integrating Europe by stealth, without directly confronting the interests, offending the national sensibilities or compromising the identity of the existing nation state authorities.[15] In spite of this caution, the ECSC was a novel development and represented a significant change of direction. Schuman, the French Foreign Minister who gave his name to this plan, was prepared to recommend the scheme in precisely these terms. He told the Council of Europe that;

> participating states will be abandoning some degree of sovereignty in favour of a Common Authority and will be accepting a fusion or pooling of powers which are at present being exercised ... by the governments. ... Thus, the participating nations will in advance accept the notion of submission to the Authority. ... The countries associated in these negotiations have indeed set their feet on a new road. They are convinced that ... the moment has come for us to attempt for the first time the experiment of a supranational authority which shall not be simply a combination or conciliation of national powers.[17]

The achievements of the ECSC and its intrusions into the sovereignty of its member states were in the event far less extensive than its founders had anticipated. The ECSC's High Authority proved reluctant to push its putative supranational powers even to the limits permitted by the founding treaty.[18] A subsequent attempt by Monnet in 1950 to repeat his tactical coup and expand the scope of functionalism into the altogether more politically sensitive and contentious realm of defence and foreign policy cooperation, proved to be premature. The six ECSC member states did get as far as signing another treaty in Paris in 1952, by whose terms they would have pooled their defence forces in a common security effort and, in the process, rearmed the West German Republic. An even more ambitious proposal for a form of European political cooperation was subsequently added to this. However, the prospects of further supranational incursions into these elemental national prerogatives led, in the end, to resistance to this proposed extension of functional integration. The European Defence Community (EDC) treaty of 1952 proved to be a treaty too far, or at least too soon. The refusal of the French Parliament in 1954 to ratify the EDC treaty underlined the contemporary limits of regional integration. Even so, the EDC failure slowed the pace of regional integration rather than extinguishing it altogether. The appeal and indeed the practical advantages of a limited degree of regional integration in pursuit of common goals were too apparent to the six participating states even at this early stage to inflict any permanent damage on the functionalist cause.

After a brief hiatus, during which a disappointed Monnet announced his resignation from the ECSC's High Authority,[19] the six again embarked on a more modest functionalist route to integration. The Messina Conference (1955) re-affirmed their common commitment to 'the establishment of a United Europe by the development of common institutions, the progressive fusion of national economies, the creation of a common market and the progressive harmonisation of social policies'.[20] The Belgian foreign minister, Paul Henri Spaak, admirably filled the diplomatic breach left by Monnet's unexpected resignation and saw the proposal through to a satisfactory conclusion. By agreeing to establish a working committee of foreign ministers under Spaak's chairmanship the six kept alive the functionalist idea. And on this occasion Spaak ensured that the participants did not commit the tactical error of trying to push functional integration beyond its current capabilities. Spaak's memorandum on behalf of the three Benelux states proposed an altogether more modest functional integration than that contained in the Pleven Plan. It recommended an atomic energy community and a further extension of economic integration in the shape of a common market.

The six concentrated their integrative efforts on the modest but novel idea of economic integration; in essence, the removal of barriers to commercial coopera-tion and free trade. A clear distinction was drawn here between the primary task of laying the foundations of what Pinder has called 'negative integration'[21] and the altogether more ambitious projects of positive integration which these functionalists assumed would follow on from it.[22] Intensive negotiations followed on the details of these proposals. Spaak chaired what turned out to be a highly successful conference which began its work in Brussels in 1955. The deliberations of its network of committees and sub-committees produced a dual proposal for an integrated approach to atomic energy and for a wider common market, to be enshrined in separate treaties. After a long and predictable period of intergovern-mental bargaining, the two treaties signed in Rome in 1957 relaunched the stalled Community project on the next stage of its functional evolution.[23]

The procedural logic behind this functionalist route to regional integration was assumed by Monnet and those who shared his technocratic faith to move accord-ing to an intrinsic dynamic, which the neofunctionalist theorists subsequently identified as 'spillover'. That is, international change unfolds by incremental degrees and in clear stages. The sectoral cooperation that results from this process of adaptation would instil those political values and habits best suited to eventual political integration. Structural and cognitive change go hand in hand in this account. Monnet had remained convinced of the deeper political and cultural implications of functional cooperation. In his *Memoirs* he claimed to detect an intrinsic momentum at work in the regional process in Europe, that

> little by little the work of the Community will be felt. . . . Then the every day realities will make it possible to form the political union which is the goal of our Community and to establish the United States of Europe. . . . For me there has been only one path; only its length is unknown. The unification of Europe, like all peaceful revolutions, takes time.[24]

The neofunctionalist theorists accepted this basic technocratic premise and set out on the intellectual task of uncovering the precise dynamics at work in this integration process.

THE FUNCTIONALIST PARADIGM REVISED: THE NEOFUNCTIONALIST VARIANT

Neofunctionalism as a deliberative paradigm represented a reaction by a group of American academic theorists to what they regarded as previously inadequate attempts to explain the logic, or to predict the course, of contemporary international change. They were academic social scientists and, as such, were concerned with methodological rigour rather than with the moral prescription that infuses Mitrany's work. This scientific mandate led the principal neofunctionalists to regard integration as a more complex, multivariate and indeed protracted process, than the model of political change prescribed in either the federalist or pure functionalist versions of the supranational paradigm. The neofunctionalists did, however, share some common intellectual ground with these paradigmic precursors. Not least, an abiding sense – at least in their earliest writings – of the obsolescence of the nation state, as well as the dangers to peace and progress inherent in the prevailing realist account of international relations. According to the classical balance of power doctrine that informs this account of global affairs, potentially belligerent states enter into countervailing security arrangements in order to manufacture peace by employing the essentially negative sanctions of deterrence or naked threat.[25] There was, nevertheless, a difference in what we might call theoretical temperament between neofunctionalism and these earlier more idealised versions of supranationalism. Neofunctionalists discounted the nation state as an irrelevance rather than disparaging it as an evil. Functionalism here thus acquired a practical rather than a moral mandate. As they saw it, territorial states had become a redundant force in European politics, on empirical rather than on *a priori* grounds. In short, these traditional polities had been outdistanced by the forces of modern socio-economic change. And in the process, they had become too narrowly focused on pursuing current social or economic requirements. As they were currently constituted, nation states were principally concerned to perpetuate social and ideological divisions along the existing fault lines they themselves had been responsible for creating. They were also too culturally insular and, as such, incapable of meeting the more expansive functional or welfare needs of modern citizens. These needs could only now be met by international cooperation, albeit under more precise conditions than those predicated in the Mitranian prospectus.

The neofunctionalists identified economic transactions and welfare needs as the real source of positive cooperation. Common endeavours here offered the best antidote to the atavistic legacies of nationalism. At the same time, the neofunctionalists were careful not to exclude the creative contribution of politics from their theoretical equation. They were, after all, social scientists concerned to account for things as they are. And they acknowledged that in this less than perfect world, politics and those variable motives that give rise to it – both noble and sordid – remain an ubiquitous aspect of the human condition.

To this extent they were closer to the federalists than to Mitranian functionalism. The neofunctionalists saw regional integration as an intrinsically political process involving, as the federalists had acknowledged, the need to reconcile social diversities and to balance the conflicting interests that exist in all societies, within a community framework. In Haas's famous summary, regional integration was the process of 'how and why states cease to be wholly sovereign, how and why they voluntarily mingle, merge and mix with their neighbours so as to lose the factual attributes of sovereignty while acquiring new techniques for resolving conflict themselves'.[26] Neofunctionalists also acknowledged, and in a way that neither federalism nor pure functionalism had countenanced for reasons specific to the epistemology of each of these theories, the stark fact that political elites determined the outcomes of international integration. In essence, neofunctionalism did its best to correct the normative biases of Mitranian functionalism. In other words to bridge the intellectual chasm that separated Mitrany's *a priori* moralism, embodying as it did an idealistic challenge to the international status quo, from the inductive theory favoured by contemporary political science, concerned to build their models on surer empirical foundations, and thereby to demonstrate the precise behavioural mechanics of the real rather than the speculative process of international change.[27]

In their mission to be social scientists rather than moral philosophers, the neofunctionalists were only partially successful. The neofunctionalist endeavour was rooted, as are all social theories, in certain assumptions about the current human condition. Regardless of their claim to objectivity, to separate empirical observation from particular value preferences, Haas and his colleagues undoubtedly carried their own normative baggage. It is clear from reading Haas's early work that the rising prospect of European integration appealed to him as something more than a mere case study in political science. The nation state seemed to him, and those colleagues who shared his assumptions, on the available postwar evidence, to be slowly but surely becoming redundant as the authoritative source of governance and the focus of unquestioning political loyalties. The steady expansion of the European communities throughout the 1950s was testament to this momentum for regional change.

To recognise an impetus for political change is hardly the same thing as offering a plausible explanation of its causes, or a sound methodological basis for predicting its likely outcomes. The neofunctionalists' claim to have uncovered the intrinsic logic of regional integration was further sustained by their parallel claim to have replaced mere supposition or speculation with methodological rigour. They pursued empirical knowledge about the regional process in the shape of testable hypotheses, rather than the deductive inferences which had figured in the earlier versions of the supranational paradigm. This concern with empiricism, with concrete evidence above mere moral exhortation, and with a methodological rigour that raises the search for hard facts above the prescription of values, at least represents an advance on the deductive reasoning that prefigured previous supranational paradigms.[28] It also provided a way of accommodating the neo-functionalist paradigm to its insistent claim to offer a measurable account of the processes it sets out to explain.

Neofunctionalism's empiricist credentials convinced many commentators that its claim to offer an objective account of the regional process was indeed a more plausible one than that of either federalism or pure functionalism. In the end, this very empiricism undermined the predictive virtue of this paradigm, not least at the hands of its principal advocate. Any social theory that purports to be scientific in this sense of being open to the refutability of its principal hypotheses – that is, to live by facts – is open to obsolescence when those 'facts' can no longer sustain its central propositions. This fate of 'death by detail' proved to be the eventual undoing of neofunctionalism. The alibi of empiricism was both neo-functionalism's strength and its weakness; its best claim to intellectual integrity, but one that made it vulnerable to the litmus test of events.

The 'facts' that dented its certainties about a cumulative process of regional integration became evident almost as soon as the theory surfaced. The strengthening of the grip of the member states on the policy processes of the European Community, the discounting of even the modest supranationalism permitted under the Rome treaties, and the consolidation of a more traditional pattern of intergovernmentalism in regional politics in the aftermath of de Gaulle's confrontation with the European Commission during the Community's 1965–66 crisis, put neofunctionalism on the defensive almost from the start. Thereafter, the paradigm was almost constantly engaged in regular attempts at theoretical revisionism as its advocates struggled to accommodate awkward 'facts' and events that challenged its basic precepts. This revisionism represented a vain attempt to accommodate the theory's fundamental precepts concerning the forces for change at work in the European regional system, with those very facts which challenged the neofunctionalist thesis, and undermined and fundamentally weakened its claim to present a comprehensive account of international change.

When Haas published his seminal work *The Uniting of Europe* in 1958, the prospects seemed altogether more promising for a steady trend towards supranationalism as recounted in his version of the postwar European process. The fate of the European nation state did seem to have been sealed by a modest but inexorable rise in transnational functional cooperation. Although Haas's influential book was principally concerned to account for the development of the ECSC, its publication on the eve of the expansion of the Coal and Steel Community into a full blown common market certainly increased its intellectual appeal. Haas set out to uncover and explain the structural dynamics behind this continuing drive towards European integration. The process, as he saw it, might well in these initial stages be modest, but it was no less dramatic or inconsequential for that. For regional integration implied a virtual revolution in the conduct of politics at both the national and international levels. Haas defined this dramatic challenge to the established and insular political order as 'the process whereby political actors in several distinct nation settings are persuaded to shift their loyalties and expectations towards a new centre, whose institutions possess or demand jurisdiction over the pre-existing nation states'.[29]

Haas did make it clear that the process of change implied by regional integration was of much greater significance than its formal institutional shape or its precise procedural patterns might suggest. The ultimate destination – or 'end state' – of this insidious process of incremental change, held the real clue to the peaceful revolution that was underway in European regional affairs. As Haas saw this process,

> supranationality, not federation, confederation or intergovernmental organisation, seems to be the appropriate regional counterpart to the national state which no longer feels capable of realising welfare aims within its own narrow borders, which has made its peace with the fact of interdependence in an industrial and egalitarian age. It represents the method adopted to secure maximum welfare, including military security, for a post-capitalist state.[30]

Haas was convinced at this stage that this new form of supranational organisation would predominate over the existing nation state format in as much as 'it corresponds to the nature of the New Europe, the Europe of adaptative interest groups, bureaucracies, technocrats and other units with modest but pragmatic interests'.[31]

Unlike the habitués of the federalist paradigm, who were concerned primarily to prescribe a precise constitutional formula to arrest and redirect the negative momentum that had overwhelmed Europe in the shape of economic penury and massively destructive military conflicts, Haas focused his attention on the prospects for positive change, and to determine procedures by which change of this order and magnitude could be effected. The definition he gives to integration is central to this task in as much as it reflects the supposed logic and predicts the direction this process of international change is supposed to be taking. Integration suggests, then, a precise momentum and incorporates those behavioural and cognitive characteristics against which Haas claims we can measure its development and chart its progress.

Haas's apparently objective criteria for measuring integration left much to be desired as an exercise in scientific calculus. As such, his definition of integration is imprecise and, thereby, is difficult to operationalise. It was by no means clear, for instance, whether Haas was inducing a general model of international change retrospectively from recent European history, a model extrapolated from those macro forces deemed to be underway in the institutional structures and interpersonal networks of Europe's expanding and immensely complex political economy, or whether instead he was deducing his particular case study of the ECSC, from a more generalised theoretical notion of international change per se. Although Haas did attempt subsequently to sharpen his theoretical focus,[32] the impression remains from the attempts by many contributors to the neofunctionalist genre to refine the model, of a theory premised on ideologically conditioned assumptions about the way politics *should* work in advanced societies, rather than what was *actually* happening on the ground in Western Europe. There is throughout the abundant neofunctionalist literature published during the 1960s, a persistent doubt that neofunctionalism is more concerned with general outcomes than with the precise dynamics that constitute international political change. This methodological confusion at the heart of neofunctionalism takes several forms: the suspicion that its advocates are less than clear about the precise significance or weighting of their principal dependent variable; whether they are describing the momentum of regional integration on the basis of previous patterns of change; or predicting instead its likely future pattern on the same retrospective basis. This conceptual obtuseness seriously weakened the neofunctionalist claim to offer a comprehensive and plausible explanation of international change. There is every difference between making an intuitive leap or gambling a predictive hunch about the dynamics of the international process, based on the interpretation of the accumulated evidence of a given historical experience, in this case postwar European integration, and neofunctionalism's altogether more theoretically ambitious claim to have identified a universal paradigm of international change.[33]

If the neofunctionalists were less than convincing about the causal sequence and the consequences of the process of change they sought to uncover, they were more certain about its principal agents. And this tells us more about their ideological roots than it does about their scientific candour. The integration process was driven, as they saw it, by similar technocratic imperatives to those identified in the related school of political behaviourism known as modernisation theory. The key actors responsible for directing the regional integration process are much less those national political and administrative elites identified in the federalist paradigm as the source of any new constitutional compact. Although governing elites play their part in accelerating change, they are not in this account the gatekeepers or principal agents of change. They tend to follow the lead of more important actors. These traditional elites – whose predecessors built Europe's nation states – become under contemporary conditions altogether more amenable to transnational cooperation. Neofunctionalism accorded the primary role in facilitating regional cooperation thus, to those more open-minded elites, supranational groups, politicians and lobbies in particular, who have become involved in managing and directing the affairs of an increasingly interdependent and transnational political economy[34] **(Document 18)**. These new elites are ideally placed to perform this function. They operate on the boundaries between national and international policy making.[35] Above all, their experience, interests and career profiles equip them to operate effectively in the immensely complex and expanding interstices between the domestic and regional milieux.

These groups enjoy, in the neofunctionalist account, distinct organisational and resource advantages which predispose them towards an integrative response to mutual problems, and facilitate their efforts to build effective transnational networks. Close collaboration between these elites in the specific policy projects which are part and parcel of the European Community also encourages cognitive change. A mutual sense of confidence and '*engrenage*' – the sense of professional empathy, understanding and trust that facilitates effective joint responses to common problems – follows on from intense cooperation in joint policy making. Moreover, such regular contact became habit forming. Haas predicts permanent changes in political values as a direct consequence of these new patterns of behaviour. The most dramatic outcome of these routinised and persistent elite interactions was, for Haas, the cumulative upgrading of a common regional interest. In Haas's account of this process, '*engrenage*' is a critical factor in facilitating integration; in essence

> the decision making process, in its institutional setting, stimulates interest groups to make themselves heard and political parties to work out common positions; it creates pressure on high national civil servants to get to know and to establish rapport with their opposite numbers.[36]

There is more than a hint here of the ideological certainties that infuse the American pluralist tradition. Contemporary elites, operating increasingly on the transnational plane, are supposedly more likely to be motivated by some intrinsic logic of organisational 'need' and by an administrative or technocratic rationality that points to a higher welfare interest above the narrower perceptions of class, ethnicity or nation. Above all, in the neofunctionalist model the pursuit of suitable policy outcomes inclines governing elites at every level to search for joint rather than singular solutions to what are perceived by them to be common problems.[37] The policy bargains that result from these collective transactions are much less likely in this prognosis to be the narrowly selfish suboptimal trade offs or package deals of conventional intergovernmental diplomacy. They are more likely instead to be those mature cooperative arrangements which increase integration exponentially, by fostering a rising sense among the participants of their shared interests.[38] Brenner, for instance, identified in this unfolding process of functional exchanges an integrative logic by which separate and competitive national interests are gradually assimilated into the general purpose of the commonwealth.[39]

Neofunctionalism also identified the likely social outcomes and political consequences of what it saw as these purported changes in international behaviour.

Under the conditions of contemporary pluralism characteristic of Europe's advanced social systems, cumulative elite bargains eventually transform social expectations and values. Changes in behavioural patterns clearly have a capacity for altering the political culture. In other words, functional spillover leads to cultural spillover, and changes in social behaviour over an unspecified duration are both legitimised and consolidated by normative shifts **(Document 19)**. The causal sequence here is less precise than it should be in what purports to be a rigorous theory of social change. Indeed, different versions of neofunctionalism gave different weightings to the causal linkage between social values and political behaviour. Nevertheless, neofunctionalism did suggest a broad causal sequence underway here. The sociological consequences of the elite transactions which are the core of the neofunctionalist notion of political change were assumed to be both sufficiently cumulative and intrusive to erode over time any exclusive sense of national identity. In short, a cultural osmosis is assumed to be at work in the fabric of these European societies participating in the Community endeavour. And this is a process which will eventually reach beyond those elites who implement it, culminating in the refocusing of popular loyalties away from their traditional attachment to national institutions and the primordial symbols of statehood. The eventual outcome of this process in the neofunctionalist canon is an entirely new European identity.

This is not the place to pursue the important theoretical issue raised here, of the determinitive role of values as the independent variables which cause structural change. Nevertheless, since cultural spillover does figure in the neofunctionalist dynamic, we need briefly to address this issue. Haas and the mainstream neofunctionalists certainly stopped short of crude determinism. The neofunctionalists did not recommend values per se as the independent variables that cause social change to happen. There were, however, indications in the neofunctionalist literature that ideas do have a disproportionate impact on structural outcomes. At best, the relationship between values and behaviour remains as ambiguous as it is in much of the literature in the American pluralist tradition. This is certainly a problem for neofunctionalism's claim to methodological rigour. The imprecise relationship posited between values and behaviour does require much finer tuning than is allowed for by neofunctionalism.[40] The linkage between values and social structure needs to be spelled out rather than implied as it is here. This lack of methodological precision – surprising in a theoretical endeavour that attracted a richly gifted vein of intellectual endeavour – undoubtedly weakened neofunctionalism's claim to have uncovered some of the mainsprings of international political change. In effect, the elaboration of the precise sequences of social change on which the theory's claim to scientific status rests, is implied more than it is adequately explained. Although the neofunctionalists did address the critical issue of process – indeed the pursuit of this dynamic lies at the very core of their theoretical endeavours – the ease with which actual events overwhelmed and invalidated the paradigm's fundamental hypotheses is some indication of the model's weak foundations, and of its oversimplification of what is an infinitely more complex and ambiguous process than the neofunctionalists managed to express in their simplistic employment of the 'spillover' concept.[41]

The theoretical limitations of 'spillover' – neofunctionalism's principal causal dynamic – has quite properly attracted the brunt of criticism levelled against this paradigm. It is important then to understand what neofunctionalists meant by this 'spillover' process. There was a clear assumption in the neofunctionalist account of European integration that the social and political processes, at least as these operated in advanced societies, were universal phenomena rather than culturally discrete or institutionally specific procedures confined to particular nation states. Neofunctionalism's intellectual and ideological roots in the American behaviourist and pluralist traditions predisposed its advocates to think of politics as a ubiquitous process. The neofunctionalists challenged as misplaced the realist assumption that there was an insuperable distinction between politics in the national domain and the international realm. Politics remained for neofunctionalists a universal instinct. It was the only 'legitimate system for the resolution of conflict' and 'for the making of authoritative decisions for the group as a whole at whatever level conflict resolution becomes imperative for order and stability'.[42]

In the neofunctionalist model, contemporary nation states experience difficulties performing these functions effectively. The sheer complexity of policy issues, and the rising interdependence between the national policy processes and the international environment has begun to refashion the political order in ways that enlarge the scope of the decision making function. This has implications for politics at every level. Neofunctionalists defined what they saw as an integrative logic at work, enmeshing elites and publics alike in expansive agreements to resolve joint problems across national boundaries. While these transnational arrangements were initially confined to low level technical issues – as 'negative' integration – and by no means abrogated the traditional policy prerogatives or breached the sovereignty of modern nation states in those areas of 'high' politics by which they have traditionally measured their distinct historical and political identities, the potential here for far reaching change was obvious enough. For a cumulative encroachment on these traditional preserves was implicit in the idea of 'spillover'.

The familiar realist metaphor of the state as an impermeable billiard ball, and the accompanying image of international relations as an exclusive game, played principally between inviolably sovereign nation states occupying an anarchic universe, for whom power politics is the supreme raison d'être, was rejected by neofunctionalists as an archaic description of the modern international process. It was replaced by what neofunctionalists regarded as the more accurate image of international society. One consisting of 'cobwebs' of transnational networks. Accordingly, the politics of those states enmeshed in such functional transactions – culminating in their membership of permanent and institutionalised regional communities – no longer ran in exclusively national channels. Instead, the modern political process was increasingly 'decomposed into sets and layers of diverse interests, some of whom would naturally, by necessity, have links with similar groups in other states'.[43]

This functionalist process was assumed to be more highly developed in the European region than anywhere else. Its structural consequences were equally significant. The pursuit of joint policy goals and common agendas by those administrative, governing and technocratic elites who dominated the European Community was bound to contribute to the restructuring of the regional policy process. Indeed, to Haas and his colleagues the consequences of such critical changes for the conventional statecentric system were quite visible in the recent history of the European project. The impact of the changes wrought by the pressures of modern political economy working in the regional milieu had quite simply changed the shape and direction of Community politics. Sovereignty was being sliced, by degrees and in agreed areas, away from its traditional locale in territorial states and reallocated beyond the boundaries of the nation state and within a rising transnational milieu.[44]

'Spillover' was the term used to capture the impetus and momentum of this radical process. As such, the concept represents the principal dynamic of neofunctionalism's claim to be a plausible theory of international change.[45] In so far as the neofunctionalist model contains an independent variable, it stands or falls by the explanatory power of this 'spillover' concept. The status of neofunctionalism as a rigorous explanation of international change rested on the merits of this concept. Haas was initially confident in his claim to have uncovered a clear dynamic at work behind the processes of European integration.[46] He was sufficiently convinced of this to predict that 'the established nation state is in full retreat in Europe.'[47] Events soon caused Haas and his colleagues to scale down and eventually to recant these predictions. The impact of the Gaullist backlash against the European Commission's modest attempts to curb intergovernmentalism as the driving force of Community politics after 1965 proved to be neofunctionalism's nadir. Things were never quite the same again for the paradigm. The neofunctionalists devoted more time after 1965 to trying to explain the model's limitations than they did to prosecuting the case for a clear functionalist logic at work in European affairs. As the member states reasserted their hold on the Community process, and caution if not a rising pessimism about the project began to prevail over the earlier mood of expectancy, the theoretical initiative moved elsewhere. A new model centred on intergovernmentalism began to dominate the debate on Europe's current condition. In these circumstances, neofunctionalism was discounted.

The demise of neofunctionalism was gradual rather than abrupt and took the form of a slow retreat into revisionism.[48] Lindberg and Scheingold, for instance, began by reformulating 'spillover' in an attempt to account for the variable pace of integration, as they assimilated the uncertainties that surrounded the European project in the aftermath of the 1965 crisis. They abandoned the confident positivism of the 'spillover' concept in the face of the resurgence of national interests as the focus of the Community politics during the Gaullist era (Document 20). These same authors brought together a panel of revisionists in a conference on regional integration held at the University of Wisconsin in 1969. The objective here was to undertake a concerted attempt to review and update neofunctionalism.

Schmitter was particularly candid about the prospects for success here. Summarising the prevailing mood he admitted that

> the first attempt at the statement of a comprehensive, yet parsimonious, model of the political consequences of integration movements by Ernst Haas and myself was, I think it fair to say, a successful failure. It was a failure in the sense that it has proven to be an inadequate and easily misunderstood theory. Variables were sloppily conceptualised; few operational referents were suggested; little attention was paid to specifying relations between variables – to process in other words; and, above all, no sensitivity was shown to the likelihood of different integration outcomes. It was a success in the sense that it proved to be an attractive target.[49]

The admission of failure – however qualified – in the search for a rigorous explanation of the process of regional change, further weakened neofunctionalism's academic credentials. The dilution of the paradigm's principal claim to have uncovered the causal linkages behind political change was bound to damage neofunctionalism's claim to offer the most plausible account of regional integration as a substantive process rather than as an ideology. By permitting in their revised model the possibility of several alternative outcomes to the regional process, Lindberg and Scheingold substituted mere contingency for the clearcut 'scientific' positivism and the certainty of outcome predicted in the earlier versions of neofunctionalism.[50] By embracing the notion of refutability required as a minimum condition of any scientific endeavour, the theory undoubtedly gained in plausibility, but at the cost of losing its claim to have identified the principal causal variables, indeed the very dynamic, of regional integration. This exercise in revisionism cost neofunctionalism its theoretical reputation as the most convincing account of the processes and momentum of regional change in Europe.[51]

Although neofunctionalism was damaged by events its principal advocates failed adequately to explain or predict, it did yield some useful insights into the workings of the regional process. Neofunctionalism's focus on the critical role of key functional elites with roots and interests beyond the nation state, in shaping political outcomes, and its concentration on the crucial linkages between economic or other technical transactions and political change, are undoubtedly important factors in the contemporary political process. To this extent, the neofunctionalists made a useful contribution to breaking the narrow statecentric focus of traditional political science. Indeed, this interdependence theme led to some imaginative developments in the study of regional and international politics. Russett's employment of the idea of transactionalism made an early intellectual connection between neofunctionalist revisionism and the fertile body of ideas that came to represent the new international political economy. Russett identified those 'essential bonds of the social fabric between groups or especially nations . . . such ties as trade, migration, tourism, communication facilities like mail and telephone, and cultural and educational exchange'. This multiplicity of transactions, in Russett's view, had positive consequences for transnational integration. For

these ties serve as channels of communication whereby the needs and perspectives of one group of people are made known to others; they serve to
strengthen the sense of mutual identification within the entire collectivity,
and to promote a readiness to respond sympathetically to the needs of others
within the collectivity. They contribute to mutual predictability of behaviour
and the accurate communication of wishes, without which cooperative efforts
are hazardous.[52]

From the ashes of neofunctionalism there arose then an altogether new perspective
on the connections between domestic and international politics.

Of course, these new behavioural patterns raise as many questions as they
answer about the precise causal linkages involved in these transactions. At the same
time, the early recognition by the neofunctionalists of the importance for political
behaviour of interactions between transaction flows and cognitive patterns, such as
identity formation, launched the debate on the exchanges between domestic and
international politics on a new theoretical trajectory; and one that made a
significant intellectual contribution to the interdependence theory that eventually
replaced neofunctionalism as the leading paradigm of the international process.
The intellectual legacy of neofunctionalism continued to live on in the conviction
of the interdependence theorists about the integrative potential of contemporary
elite transactions. Many of these subsequent theoretical developments in integration theory owe a clear debt to neofunctionalism's intellectual quest to discover the
mainsprings of transnational community building, and their likely consequences
for a form of social solidarity beyond the traditional identity patterns associated
with the nation state. Neofunctionalism undoubtedly helped to uncover some of
the important variables at work in the regional process in Europe. At the same
time, the model's serious limitations encouraged further revisionism. And these
revisions, while confounding the neofunctionalist faith in a clearcut regional
process, have contributed to our understanding of both the regional and international processes. Neofunctionalism shares this accomplishment with every other
variant of integration theory reviewed in this work. While this is an achievement
it is an altogether more modest one than neofunctionalism's initial claim to be *the*
definitive paradigm of regional integration.[53]

The process of theoretical revision was carried furthest by Haas himself. By 1967
he had scaled down neofunctionalism's initial claim to offer clear predictions, to
one of being no more than a useful 'pre theory' of integration.[54] Haas now resorted
to the disclaimer that there was much more empirical work and theoretical refinement to be done before asserting a definitive theoretical breakthrough.[55] In a major
statement of his revisionism, he offered an altogether more conditional account of
neofunctionalism's claims and openly reviewed the model's theoretical difficulties
(Document 21). In a telling passage that exhibited commendable intellectual
honesty even as it pointed to the deep flaws in his model, he confessed that:

The nagging thought persists that we (neofunctionalists) lack clear dependent
variables because we have followed the practice of erecting these terminal

(integrative) states by treating them as ideal types reconstructed from our historical experience at the national level and then of observing the types of behaviour that contribute – or fail to contribute – to the attainment of that condition. These ideal types are not true dependent variables since they cannot yet be observed or measured in nature. The postulated conditions have not yet come about anywhere, at least in the contemporary world. At best we have a putative dependent variable. The EEC in 1962 seemed to be on the point of a breakthrough to a political community de facto . . . instead it settled down into the uneasy equilibrium state. . . . The examples could be multiplied. They suggest that the variety of possible outcomes is considerable, that unions may settle down into a stable system without reaching any of the stages we defined in the earlier phases of our research.[56]

By 1976, Haas was in full retreat even from his earlier conditional revisionism. The aftermath of the first EC enlargement had added three new member states – including Britain – who harboured few illusions about the attractions of a supranational Community. The institutional changes agreed at the 1973 Copenhagen Summit, and implemented at the 1974 European Council held in Paris, had confirmed the Community on an intergovernmentalist trajectory. It was clear that there were deeper reasons for the setback to unalloyed integration after the early triumphs, than merely Gaullist hubris. After all, the General had long retired from the fray and the initial supranational momentum had still failed to reappear. Moreover, the mood of political retrenchment in Europe was deepened by a marked deterioration in global economic conditions. This further eroded any sense, even among the most optimistic commentators, that the EC's governing elites were willing agents of an irrevocable shift from a Community of states to a fully fledged supranational Union. Haas was obliged to pay heed to these circumstances. He was eventually moved, in a valedictory paper published in 1976, to pronounce with intellectual candour the paradigm's obsolescence.[57]

The contrast between Haas's earlier optimism about the momentum and direction of the Community process and this clear retreat in the face of unpalatable facts, was neatly captured in his admission that 'what once appeared to be a distinctive supranational style now looks more like a huge regional bureaucratic appendage to an intergovernmental conference in permanent session'.[58] In another paper, also published in 1976, Haas offered an altogether more balanced review of both the virtues and deficiencies of regional integration theory. He also provided some pointers to the next stage of his personal intellectual journey. In spite of his acknowledgement here of the resilience of the nation state, there was no question of Haas retreating back into intergovernmentalism. Instead, Haas focused his search for effective and collective solutions to international problems on the new interdependence model reviewed in Chapter 5[59] **(Document 22)**.

The conclusions reached by Haas at this stage of his researches reflect his rising awareness of the paradoxical nature of the European process. His diagnosis of these intricate regional arrangements as a 'halfway house', precisely captures the ambivalent quality of regional interdependence that has pervaded Community affairs from the outset. Far from a Europe launched unambiguously on a straight-forward, unilineal trajectory towards the 'ever closer Union' espoused in its found-ing treaty, the Community was caught squarely between two competing 'rationalities'. To that extent, its dilemmas were both real and persistent. And for that matter, have remained so ever since. As Haas chose to see the situation,

> The EC system, as a set of institutions and practices, is a halfway house in more than one sense: the rationalities which animate it are as unfinished and transi-tional as its decision-making procedures. In some areas of collective concern, where the rationality of disjointed incrementalism still dominates, the links among policies are 'functional'. There is a close substantive connection between the policies to be linked. . . . The overall logic of a competitive market establishes the rationale for the functionality of the links. Therefore, the package deals which are made reflect these links, but the scope of the deals is relatively limited. When there is increasing doubt as to relative costs and benefits of transactions associated with joint decisions, it becomes much more difficult to find enough common ground to make such deals. The mode of bargaining which characterises such package dealing tends to be confined to constant-sum games, with an occasional attempt at a variable sum solution. Breaking out of this cycle calls for an upgrading of central institutional capability by enabling Community institutions to devise policies of actively compensating actors who fear that the costs of integration outweigh the benefits. . . .
>
> I have sought to demonstrate that this pattern of action no longer dominates. The competing pattern–fragmented issue linkage depends on 'confined' or 'deliberate' linkages among issues, rather than functional links. The policy areas to be linked are substantively less closely related than the groups of issues involved in the common market. . . . [thus] The chain of causation, as it becomes longer and more complex, gives rise to attempted package deals which involve more uncertainty in the minds of actors. . . . What does this have to do with interdependence? The shift to the rationality of fragmented issue linkage is due to . . . the realisation that these objectives cannot be realised without heavy reliance on, and interaction with, governments who have no intention of joining the regional community. Taken together these [factors] imply increasing interdependence with extra regional forces [and] the growth of inter-dependence is incompatible with the orderly march of regional integration. But it is not incompatible enough to cause a retreat from, or even bring a halt to, the steps already taken.[60]

In providing thus a decent burial for one paradigm of European integration, Haas helped to sustain another model that would offer an altogether more plausible account of the regional process.

THE NEOFUNCTIONALIST LEGACY

No single theory of regional integration can expect to offer a definitive account of the immensely complex international process that is European integration.

Neofunctionalism carried the explanation of this complex and paradoxical process only so far. It undoubtedly took the analysis of the regional process further than either the federalist or pure functionalist paradigms. The virtues of the neofunctional paradigm can be stated clearly. Neofunctionalism at least directed attention to the critical matter of process; that is, with identifying the precise interactions of socio-economic and cultural factors in shaping political change. It held a clear advantage here over its supranational precursors. Unlike federalism, it went beyond the mere prescription of particular institutional outcomes or of simply engaging in a polemic against the 'iniquities' of nation statehood.[61] Its main advantage over pure functionalism was its precise regional rather than global focus, and its emphasis on empiricism, however costly this was to its long term credibility. At the same time, the neofunctionalists laboured hard under their own illusions about the nature, pace and direction of the regional process. In the end, the paradigm was severely dented by its underestimation of the residual power of nation statehood and the national preferences this invariably gives rise to, and that remains at the very heart of the regional process. This is a harsh critique and one that must be balanced, if not mitigated, by broader considerations.

The state of European integration, after the 1965 crisis brought the problems of residual national interests previously subdued by the sheer optimism that accompanied the relaunch of the communities into stark relief, is by no means as clear cut as that painted by neofunctionalism's intergovernmentalist critics. The Community by the early 1970s was already a curious hybrid arrangement; neither the supranational nor the intergovernmental system *in extremis* predicated on either side of the theoretical debate. The balance of the argument had undoubtedly tilted more by this juncture, away from the bold predictions of an incipient supranationalism that had coloured the federalist and functionalist paradigms, than at any time since the intellectual and political ferment of the late 1940s. At this critical moment in its development, the Community was precariously balanced between two competing visions of the new European project. On the one hand it was by no means just another type, albeit a sophisticated one, of intergovernmental organisation; on the other hand, Gaullist retrenchment after 1965 had exposed both the limitations and the facile assumptions of all proponents of the supranational paradigm.

In these circumstances, the prospect from the mid 1960s onwards for far reaching integration was severely discounted by practitioners and academic commentators alike. Not that this fact undermined the idea of European integration as a novel experiment in international politics. The Community did retain a clear sense that its member states were indeed engaged in a unique experiment in transnational cooperation. There were, however, apparent limits to this achievement. The Community seemed to most contemporary observers of its affairs, much less the embodiment of unmitigated regional integration than it was an arena for pursuing and reconciling competing national interests in the shape of what were usually suboptimal policy bargains. An abiding sense of entrenched national preferences continued to confront what had promised to be, in the heady days of the late 1950s and early 1960s, the ineluctable rise of a common regional interest rooted in functional needs. In these circumstances, any sense of a supranational impetus lay dormant – to say the least – although it could not be entirely written off. European cooperation on the ground did produce an impressive catalogue of interstate policy accommodations and diplomatic trade offs that kept these aspirations alive in some quarters at least. Alongside these bargains, the Community did manage to evolve a modest degree of supranational integration, albeit at fairly low levels of policy making. The functionalist – and indeed the federalist – impulse thus remained, as several commentators have acknowledged, however subdued or limited its appeal, as part of the evolving European prospectus.

The relaunching of the integration project in the 1980s, and the renaissance in integration theory that accompanied this process, has seen a rekindling of interest in the neofunctionalist paradigm.[62] The experience of mainstream neofunctionalism in the 1960s has not, however, escaped its subsequent revisionists. Those contemporary commentators who favour the functionalists' explanation of events in the aftermath of the Single Market initiative are more inclined to acknowledge the partial rather than the universal relevance of 'spillover', as an explanation of regional integration. There is, too, among these current neofunctionalist revisionists, a sensible acknowledgement of integration as a paradoxical process with an uncertain outcome. This modesty stands in marked contrast to the positivism that infused the early work of Haas and his colleagues. Indeed, all of the contemporary integration paradigms have apparently learned something from neofunctionalism's earlier tribulations. All of them too, in some degree, as we shall see, now tend to reflect the syncretic or paradoxical quality of regional change. These latest accounts also tend to acknowledge, albeit from different perspectives, the coexistence of a supranational impetus alongside national preferences within the same European process. This attempt to incorporate mixed, indeed competing impulses in the same theoretical account represents a significant shift away from the exclusivism of the classical paradigms. Few seasoned observers of the European scene would take issue with Martin Holland's sober and altogether more balanced judgement of the contemporary integration process in which he maintains that

> the cautious initial integration in specific economic sectors has spilt over into a range of economic activities culminating in the inclusion of Economic and Monetary Union [and] this neofunctionalist effect has also been transmitted into the political arena . . . intergovernmentalism has proved resilient and its announced demise greatly exaggerated. From the failure of EDC, the imposition of the 'Luxembourg Compromise', through to the British problem of the 1980s . . . national sovereignty has been the focus of significant conflict, at times jeopardising the very existence of the Community's unicity.[63]

The pronouncement of neofunctionalism's demise was then, to an extent, premature. At the same time, no serious commentator on contemporary European affairs would seriously argue now in defence of the pristine integrative logic that once sustained the original neofunctionalist model. The resilient sense of nation statehood which continues to reside at the core of the European project and the political prerogatives and interests that sustain it, have provided a persistent reminder of the ambiguities which continue to shadow the regional project. The Community's nation states, and all of those institutional and vested interests who reside within them, continue to provide staunch resistance to those supranational elites with ambitions to effect far reaching transnational integration. And yet, as Holland suggests, these national interests operate in an altogether different universe to that envisaged by the architects of the classical nation state. Modern politics, as we will see in Chapter 5, is characterised instead by a persistent tension between national interests and global impulses.

The very existence of this dialectic at the heart of Community politics challenges, in turn, the presumptions of those supranational theorists who once too readily pronounced the demise of the nation state. Neofunctionalism, along with those other versions of this supranationalist paradigm reviewed above, certainly underestimated the residual impact of ancient loyalties, old political habits, popular expectations and persistent national interests on the momentum and direction of the regional process. This, in its turn, has contributed to the further refinement of integration theory. On the one hand, it has encouraged the emergence of a new approach to the problem of defining the place of statehood in international politics – one which sought to reconcile the impetus for change with the impulse to persistence within a new account of the integration dynamic. We shall review the development of this interdependence model in Chapter 5.

The more immediate outcome of neofunctionalism's demise, however, was the reinstatement of the realist doctrine at the centre of the theoretical debate on European integration. To an extent, this statecentric account of the European regional process had never been entirely overshadowed by neofunctionalism during its theoretical apogee. The realist interpretation of postwar European history had persistently challenged, at every turn, both the theoretical and political assumptions of supranationalism. Drawing on its deep intellectual roots in the academic discipline of international politics, this model had stubbornly resisted the emergent supranational challenge to academic orthodoxy after 1945. And it had more than held its theoretical ground. Those who favoured this conventional outlook saw no reason to bow to what they saw as the whims of academic fashion, by abandoning a rigorous and proven account of the international process that, to their mind, had satisfactorily accounted for the developments of international politics over two millennia. They vigorously resisted the idealistic assumptions that informed the various supranational accounts. As they saw the European process, change might be inevitable but it was a process that was infused with continuity. To this extent, they saw the claims of the supranationalists to have uncovered an entirely new international logic, as exaggerated and entirely misguided. To the realists, the various accounts of international politics couched in supranational terms, amounted to a theoretical heresy that confused fact with fancy. Those theorists who took this particular tack insisted instead on examining the admittedly novel developments in the European project through the familiar lens of realist doctrine. In doing so, they identified at the core of the regional process an unassailable intergovernmentalist logic, one whereby Europe's national states cooperated in *sui generis* arrangements precisely in order to maximise their particular domestic interests.

The statecentric account of the European project replaced neofunctionalism as the dominant paradigm of the regional process for a decade or so after the Gaullist imprimatur was placed on the EC during the mid 1960s. Again, this paradigmic shift was another instance of theoretical art imitating political life on the ground. There seemed every reason to believe that realism had wrested the intellectual initiative back from the supranationalists. After all, neofunctionalism had been weakened by its failure to account for those very events on which its claim was based to have uncovered the impetus to international change. And federalism had never recovered from its own illusions about the prospects for European statehood. The gap between prognosis and practice proved to be the undoing of both major attempts to consolidate a supranational account of the European process. But the intergovernmentalists confronted problems of their own in laying claim to the definitive account of regional change. A familiar theoretical pattern was repeated here; one that mirrored the earlier failure of both federalist and pure functionalist theory to satisfactorily predict outcomes in the real world of European politics. The resurgence of the Community's member states in defence of their respective national interests, and in resistance to the ambitions of the Hallstein Commission, encouraged this latest reappraisal of the regional process. The intergovernmentalist model became, in the circumstances, the latest beneficiary of this paradigmic shift. But as we shall see below, it too was subject to the same sort of strictures as its intellectual precursors, and for that reason, it has by no means had the last word or written the final chapter in the discourse on European integration. As the regional process on the ground shifts in response to unpredictable contingencies and predictable exigencies alike, so too must those concerned with uncovering the dynamics behind such changes adapt their models and refashion their theoretical accounts of what is underway in the quest for European integration.

Chapter 4

The statecentric paradigm

THE RESILIENCE OF THE NATION STATE

The shock registered within European opinion over the costs and consequences of the immensely destructive war of 1939–45 had a profound impact on the general perception of regional politics. At the very least a pervasive sense of uncertainty was evident about conventional political arrangements. A widespread feeling was expressed that there should be some constraints on the unfettered pursuit of national interests. Some political movements went further and canvassed a wholesale replacement of Europe's statecentric system by new regional arrangements. The nation state survived these persistent challenges and, suitably modified, re-emerged as the principal agency of diplomacy and governance, as well as the primary focus of popular allegiance in postwar Western Europe. A half century or so later, the nation state is still with us. Its future is still at the centre of an animated debate among scholars and practitioners. A residual sense of national identity remains the principal obstacle to a pervasive European identity.

The nation state became the focus of a theoretical approach to European integration which identified the 'realities' of nationhood and those distinctive interests associated with the preservation of the nation state, as the principal driving force of the postwar regional process. The notion of a European order consisting of separate but cooperating states, as the best solution to the continent's daunting security and economic problems, has been the antithesis of the supranational paradigm reviewed above. This intergovernmentalist account of the process of European integration prescribed conventional diplomatic transactions and interstate cooperation as the surest route to ensuring continental peace and economic renewal. According to this account, integration was an altogether limited arrangement.[1] There was certainly nothing here to suggest any dilution of the inalienable sovereignty of statehood, let alone its wholesale surrender. Integration amounted in this prognosis to little more than the reaffirmation of a residual sense of national identity and the entrenched national institutions and prerogatives which give this persistent cultural idea its political form.

The postwar European process was seen in this version of events, as it was in Alan Milward's influential account, as a way of saving rather than surrendering the nation state.[2] In Milward's seminal study of the evolution of the Community he interprets history as a continuous process. Historical change is then a dialectic between the powerful and entrenched forces that continue to shape the established political order, along with those radical forces which inevitably rise to challenge the political status quo and call it to account for its stewardship of affairs. The currents of history suggest, to Milward's mind, an altogether more cautious process of political development than that envisaged in the supranational chronicle of events. Historical change is evolutionary rather than teleological. It represents a balance between the preference for the tried and tested, against the pressure to experiment with novel ideas and new arrangements. The outcome of this perpetual dialectic is, in Milward's estimation, a much less dramatic view of international change than the one reviewed above. Accordingly, he set himself the task 'to put this (integration) debate in historical context by showing the development of the European Community for what it really is, one stage in the long evolution of the European state'.[3]

Those international theorists who adopted this cautious, almost Burkian assessment of international change, remained less than convinced of the positive virtues, let alone of the inevitability, of fulsome integration. As they saw it, the European project was driven by an altogether more modest impetus than the radical dynamic at the heart of the supranational thesis. In Milward's analysis 'integration' merely represented the adaptive response of Europe's medium sized and modestly resourced states, as they faced daunting global pressures beyond their immediate control. In these challenging circumstances they were required to cooperate with similarly positioned states, rather than merely to compete, in order to pursue and maximise their interests within the new international order. This, in turn, had significant implications for international relations. At the most, modest forms of regional integration, confined to clearly demarcated areas, were deemed by these 'realists' to be intrusive of sovereignty only in a nominal sense. They provided a means for the survival rather than the obsolescence of the nation state and amounted to a necessary adjustment to the rapidly changing realities of the international political economy.

The leading exponents of this intergovernmental perspective on regional integration remained, by and large, sceptical about the bold and idealistic claims of supranational theorists to have uncovered an entirely novel transnational dynamic at work in the postwar European process. This is not to suggest that all of those commentators who shared this particular outlook held identical views about the role or prospects for the nation state in postwar European politics. There has been as much variation in this paradigm as there is between the supranationalist accounts. At one extreme, the arch Eurosceptics have continued to regard the nation state, in neo-Hegelian terms, as a sacred historic trust, passed down through the generations. The insularity and, *in extremis*, the xenophobia which colours this outlook is entirely opposed on a mixture of moral and practical grounds to even the most limited expressions of regional integration.[4]

Other contributors to the broad intergovernmentalist perspective have been prepared to countenance, on similar grounds, a revision of the role of the nation state in contemporary international arrangements. Even these moderates, nevertheless, confirmed the continuing role of nation states as the principal actors in Europe's new regional arrangements. At this extreme of the generic realist paradigm were thoughtful contributions from commentators such as Ralf Dahrendorf[5] and Helen Wallace[6] who, although committed in principle to the ideal of European integration, refused to be carried away by ideological whimsy. They reflected in their work what they saw as the current limitations and constraints of the regional process. William Wallace captured the sense of ambivalence that pervades these restrained accounts of the statecentric perspective. Wallace identified what he saw as a distinctive and unique Community project, but one nevertheless that by the 1970s was firmly launched on an intergovernmentalist trajectory. Here the facts spoke louder than personal preferences. In Wallace's reasoned estimation, then,

> national governments have been relatively successful at retaining control of the processes of Community policy making in most areas, and at maintaining their position therefore as the most important intermediaries, the confining focus for national lobbying and national debate on Community issues.[7]

What is clear amidst this flux of ideas is that the intergovernmentalist perspective did dominate both the practice and the intellectual discourse on European integration during the decade or so that followed the 1965 crisis. There was more to this intellectual ascendance than the temporary prevalence of a particular idea reflecting a momentary shift in academic fashion. Or for that matter, of a perception of events influenced by the current balance of political power in the Community. The roots of the intergovernmentalist paradigm went much deeper. And this intellectual and political pedigree explains why this view of the European process has been so influential, in academia and Europe's chancellories alike. The intergovernmental approach to regional integration drew its intellectual inspiration and indeed its credibility from an already pervasive realist account of the international process. Realism has shaped the discourse of international politics for as long as politics has been studied. The doctrine had its earliest roots in Thucydides' speculation about the causes of war between the Greek city states.[8] Realists over the duration have seen little to recommend what they regard as misplaced idealism; confusing the actual practice of politics with ideological prescriptions. They share, by and large, Machiavelli's shrewd dictum that 'how we live is so far removed from how we ought to live, that he who abandons what is done for what ought to be done, will rather learn to bring about his own ruin than his preservation'.[9]

According to the realist outlook, the primary concern of international politics, both as an activity and as an academic discipline, is to identify the actual imperatives which continue to govern the interactions of states. The diplomatic detail and political expression of international relations may shift over time, but its axiomatic Hobbesian nature remains constant. International politics is propelled in whatever historical context it occurs by the normal exigencies of interstate rivalry in what is an essentially anarchic universe. The replacement of national or territorial states as the principal actors of the global process, by superordinate agencies or artificial federations following the organisational or moral dictates of some supposedly supranational logic, is deemed here to be unnatural in principle and inconceivable in practice, and as an academic proposition to offer an entirely fanciful account of the European, or for that matter, any other regional process.

Sovereign states pursuing their national interests remain, then, the key international actors; the only legitimate source of authority and the fount of political obligation in the contemporary as they were in medieval and ancient worlds. Any regional subsystem – whether organised as a diplomatic or economic arrangement – that is built on these foundations is assumed by realists to be merely an expression of 'normal' international politics. Regional integration does not imply the unique and irrevocable merger of historically distinct national sovereignties. In truth, it represents an altogether more mundane affair. It is less a question of turning the political world on its head than it is of reconciling, as far and as cooperatively as possible in a world where conflict is costly, those competing agendas that represent continuing national preferences. Of finding, that is, new ways of accommodating distinct sets of national interests in a world where the traditional option of force is no longer as readily available as it once was. The most that can be expected from the experience of regional integration in these circumstances, is enhanced intergovernmental cooperation and the prospective identification of some mutual regional policy interests. The intergovernmentalist paradigm of European integration, both in its theoretical expressions and in political practice, has been shaped by these broadly conservative assumptions.

INTERGOVERNMENTALISM AND EUROPEAN INTEGRATION

The reluctance of Europe's postwar political establishment to allow any major incursions on national sovereignty was evident from their resistance to federalism. Europe's statesmen preferred to limit both the scope and format of such interstate or intergovernmental cooperation as did actually occur. The new regional fora that were originally devised to deal with the twin problems of defence and economic reconstruction – the OEEC, the Council of Europe and the various mutual security treaties negotiated after 1945 – were essentially limited intergovernmental arrangements. The emergence of the Community project in the shape of the ECSC certainly challenged intergovernmentalism's political supremacy during the 1950s, by opening up a new, if modest, supranational route to regional integration. When this project eventually stalled in the mid 1960s, in the face of the Gaullist backlash, the limited intergovernmentalist model of European integration was sufficiently entrenched in the political preferences of statesmen as well as in the academic imagination, to fill the theoretical void left by the demise of the neo-functionalist paradigm.

The Luxembourg Compromise of 1966 which reflected the Community's political retreat from supranationalism enshrined the principle of the national veto.[10] The aftermath of a successful Gaullist resistance to creeping supranationalism confirmed the European project as little more than an attempt to effect a series of national common denominators, manageable compromises or suboptimal bargains between the member states.[11] Indeed, the Luxembourg Accords confirmed the prejudices of a body of mainstream academic opinion about the limits of European integration. This reaction was hardly unexpected, given the abiding tension between these two starkly contrasting approaches to European integration throughout the postwar years.[12] De Gaulle had signalled his determination to pursue a conventional intergovernmentalist approach to the organisation of regional security from the moment he came to power in 1958. The failure of his attempt in the Fouchet proposals of 1962 to impose a confederation organised from Paris on France's five EC partners,[13] merely increased his resolution to resist any further supranational encroachment on national sovereignty, by an ambitious commission headed by Walter Hallstein,[14] than was already enshrined in the Rome treaties.

The Luxembourg Compromise that ended the 1965–6 crisis reflected the prevailing impasse in European integration.[15] None of the member states harboured any great enthusiasm for either a confederal form of regional integration that implied French domination, or for any further supranational incursions into their national sovereignty. At the same time, the balance of power in the Community after 1966 clearly shifted away from supranationalism and moved markedly in favour of intergovernmentalism.[16] On the intellectual plane, the intergovernmentalist literature that discussed the Community's political crisis and reviewed its consequences, set the tone of the integration debate for a decade or more. In its most theoretically coherent and sensible expressions this revised intergovernmental paradigm made a positive contribution to the European debate, not least because its proponents accepted, by and large, the need for some form of regional cooperation.

The impetus for a modest degree of regional intergovernmental integration was confirmed by events. Changes in the scale and complexity of global political economy had increased the sense of vulnerability among Western Europe's governments. The deep anger in Europe's political capitals, induced by Washington's unilateral decision in 1971 to abandon their responsibilities under the Bretton Woods Accord to manage the international monetary system, and the rise of superpower bilateralism or détente, likewise encouraged both the EC states and those candidate states negotiating entry into the club, to search actively for closer forms of political cooperation, outside the reach of supranational arrangements. A similar peremptory response by the Americans to the world energy crisis, following on from the OPEC cartel's hike in the oil price, likewise reinforced Europe's rising sense of a common regional interest. At the same time, those of an intergovernmentalist disposition, both statesmen and those academics reflecting on these events, prescribed limits to the scope and purpose of such initiatives.

A model of regional integration that closely conformed to this limited prospectus for transnational cooperation found its institutional expression in the institutional changes that accompanied the EC's first enlargement negotiated in the early 1970s. On the one hand, the Community had embarked on a new phase of integration, and one that involved something more than numerical enlargement. They established, for instance, new institutional machinery and policy making procedures outside the 'first' Europe of the founding treaties, with its cautious mix of supranational and intergovernmental arrangements. At the same time, this new organisational impetus largely confirmed the intergovernmentalism of the late 1960s and refashioned it in a distinctive confederal mould. The Council of Ministers in particular consolidated its hold on Community affairs by developing its presidency functions and by extending the involvement of COREPER – the members' permanent diplomatic corps in Brussels – in shaping the strategic direction and influencing the detail of the EC policy process.

After 1974 the EC's member states consolidated this distinctly confederal approach to managing their affairs. The Community harnessed whatever political momentum it could muster in a geographically expanding Community, from the newly instituted tri (later bi) -annual summit meetings of the European Council. This new Council was part of a clear intergovernmental strategy to keep the Commission's supranational ambitions under the control of the national governments. The Council consisted of heads of government and their foreign ministers. Although the Commission president was eventually admitted to these proceedings it was clear, at least at this stage, that he was regarded by his political peers among the leaders of the member states, as a less than equal partner and much more as an amalgam of administrative supplicant and mere observer. In short, these new confederal arrangements were unambiguously intergovernmental. They were primarily concerned with facilitating consultation and maximising agreement between governments. And, whenever feasible, with effecting policy convergence among the member states, most especially in the foreign policy field. These institutional innovations certainly extended the scope of regional integration, but without deepening the process in line with supranationalist expectations. At the same time, they confirmed the ascendancy of the member states over the Commission as the principal determinants of the Community's political direction. And with that, established the pre-eminence of intergovernmentalism over supranationalism as the prevailing ethos of the European regional process.

THE FATE OF THE EUROPEAN NATION STATE; THE HOFFMANN THESIS

The most intellectually sophisticated and persuasive account of European integration as an intergovernmental process appeared in the published work of the American academic, Stanley Hoffmann. Hoffmann recognised that throughout the postwar era both the logic of internal circumstances and external constraints had induced Europe's states to revise their approach to regional issues. The traditional or exclusive model of sovereignty had become 'obsolete'. Under the prevailing conditions regional integration was certainly a fact, but for all that it remained a modest interstate arrangement,[17] for these changes had hardly altered the essentials of the 'great game' of international politics. Nor were they driven by the inexorable integrative logic anticipated in the supranational paradigm. Hoffmann remained entirely unconvinced of the claims by supranational theorists in general, and the neofunctionalists in particular, to have uncovered a unique functional momentum which threatened to erode national sovereignty, and thereby to replace the nation state as the focal point of international politics. In Hoffmann's account of the limits of European integration, the nation state, modified but omnipotent, remained the principal actor in the regional process.

According to Hoffmann's thesis, the nation state persists, changed but unbowed in its role as the main agent for the conduct of international politics. It likewise remains as the critical building block of the contemporary international system. And it does so for several good reasons. In the first place, Hoffmann shared those fundamental realist precepts about the logistics of the international system.[18] Accordingly, states continue to 'collide' in what remains an essentially anarchic universe. The nation state is more in this paradigm than the historically conditioned contrivance performing temporally specific tasks – such as political development and socio-economic modernisation – that it is deemed to be by functionalists or international federalists. In essence, states retain their elemental and ubiquitous qualities. They represent natural and timeless, rather than merely conditional human needs; in essence, they are communities of belonging and identity as much as they are organisations for coercion or governance. They embody the human need – both functional and spiritual – to belong somewhere; the need to locate a communal, ethnic or linguistic identity within distinct political bounds. As such, they are a more culturally rooted, organic and clearly conservative force, than is envisaged by the political engineers or textbook constitutionalists of either the federalist or functionalist paradigms. As Hoffmann saw the condition of contemporary European politics,

> the past lives on . . . as a series of problems, tensions, atavisms – old institutions, modes of authority . . . models of rationality that no longer fit the advanced industrial societies of Western Europe. . . . The future too, of course, is viewed in national terms because of those same idiosyncrasies that have kept the Western European nations from building a common state; they are partly deep residues of the past, partly distinctive features of their present political and social systems. Old blinders or worries, present crises, and opportunities loom large in such visions.[19]

There is more than an element here of the Burkian belief in tradition as the cement that reinforces the reality of statehood. Especially so where Burke places his faith in custom over political engineering as the one sure basis of political community on the grounds that we are afraid to put men to live and trade each on his own private stock of reason; because we suspect that this stock in each man is small, and that the individuals would do better to avail themselves of the general bank and capital of nations and of ages.[20]

Hoffmann's firm intellectual roots in the realist doctrine suggested to him that any account of the development of postwar European regional politics that confuses, as the neofunctionalists' apparently did, merely low level cooperation pursued for limited purposes, and the more intrusive transactions impinging on national sovereignty in those critical areas of 'high' politics, simply misconstrues the real dynamics that underpin the international process. Hoffmann remained convinced of the impermeable nature of the boundaries between modest integration and the abandonment of sovereignty. He was moved to reject neofunctionalism out of hand.[21] He believed it to be tendentious, even driven by ideology, and as such to be intellectually misconceived and its premises to be unsubstantiated by the abundant evidence from the practice of postwar European statecraft.[22] Contrary to its own empiricist assertions, neofunctionalism had substituted wishful thinking for the sound reasoning grounded in firm historical evidence that can be the only sure basis for rigorous political science. This model amounted, in what still stands as one of the most damning indictments of the neofunctional paradigm, to be little more than the latest expression of a long tradition of technocratic determinism with its roots in philosophical positivism. For Hoffmann, neofunctionalism missed entirely those enduring political dynamics of competing national interests that had shaped the continent's destiny for half a millennium or more. European political history was thus replete with perpetual differences that to Hoffmann's mind must always limit the extent of cooperation, and colour its purposes, even between otherwise close regional allies.[23]

Hoffmann dismissed the notion of 'spillover' as nothing more than an unproven deduction and a misleading metaphysic – one which follows on more from the ideological preconceptions of those theorists and practitioners who had claimed to identify it at work in the regional process. In short, Hoffmann discounted neofunctionalism as no more than a chimera, 'an act of faith' **(Document 23)**. These reflections on supranationalism go to the heart of Hoffmann's case for realism. 'Spillover' and all that is implied by this for the processes and outcomes of international politics, threatens to replace a common sense realism by a metaphysical concept that clouds the truth of politics as a perpetual conflict over interests. Hoffmann is clear about the implications for knowledge about the way people actually live their lives in society, of allowing the neofunctional case to go uncontested. Hoffmann regarded neofunctionalism to be misconceived but also dangerous; it substituted a myth for an imperfect but tested game plan. He took comfort, at the same time, from his belief that the facts had driven out the myths. As Hoffmann puts it,

For it (neofunctionalism) to be true, it would be necessary to envisage that very death of politics, that very replacement of government of men by the administration of things . . . (and) we are not at that stage. . . . The only states which can behave as if the external political function has withered away are those that leave the whole burden of their protection to others.[24]

Neofunctionalism, in particular, and supranationalism per se, were thus discounted by Hoffmann as utterly misguided, a gross distortion of the facts of political life in both the national and international domains. Its account of the regional process missed the abiding sense of cultural and political differences, and the enduring impact of particularistic historical identities. It ignored too the unique place each European state occupies in the geopolitical universe. The implications of this distorted picture of the real world are that the sort of far reaching integration proposed by supranationalists simply,

> cannot work when each government, however much lip service it pays to the idea of a common good, actually wants to follow a road of its own, and when the roads the governments propose to travel are so far apart that the statesmen are not willing to trust their travel plans to an agency that may push them into detours they do not want to take towards destinations they do not want to reach.[25]

Any suggestion that a Europe composed of distinct nationalities, rooted in pervasive cultural identities and riven by entrenched linguistic divisions could, as the supranationalists had suggested, somehow overcome such massive obstacles to unity, and follow the American route to political union, was to Hoffmann's mind, entirely fanciful.[26] Europe, unlike the America of the eighteenth century as it forged its common political destiny, had a diverse past. One that presents too many obstacles, at least for the foreseeable future, to the cosy idea of an effective 'common' political identity with a system of governance to match. The memories of past conflicts and the residual mistrust generated by them, to say nothing of the pervasive social differences and the continuing divergent interests, have weighted Europe down with legacies that will not be easily overcome. And certainly not by surrendering to facile myths about submission to the dictates of benevolent technocratic elites; or for that matter the equally misguided elitist prescriptions implied by a federal compact for Europe. Although here Hoffmann was prepared to concede in principle a federal Europe as at least the 'best chance of being an effective entity' that did not go beyond the nation state but offered instead the prospect of becoming a larger nation state. Federalism, then, 'would be a tribute to the durability of the nation state'. At the same time

> its failure so far is due to the irrelevance of the model. Not only is there no general will of a European people because there is of now no European people, but the institutions that could gradually (and theoretically) shape the separate nations into one people are not the most likely to do so.[27]

Europe's political future thus remains in the same autarchic hands that have fashioned its national divisions over the centuries.

In other words, Europe cannot be what some of its nations have been: a people that creates its state; nor can it be what some of the oldest states are and many of the new ones aspire to be: a people created by the state. It has to wait until the separate states decide that their peoples are close enough to justify the setting up of a European state whose task will be the welding of the many into the one.[28]

And for Hoffmann, the political will to bring about such a transformation neither exists now, nor is likely to exist for the foreseeable future.

The European past contrives, then, to continue to shape the continent's present arrangements. The problem here, for launching any significant degree of European integration beyond a modest intergovernmental cooperation was, to Hoffmann's mind;

> not just the absence of a precedent, it is also the avalanche of rocks that have battered and buried . . . Europe as a whole; they have bloodied each European state in a different way. A common fate has created a unity of concern in this little 'cape of Asia' but there is no unity of reaction. For each nation fate has been slightly different, and the common fate is not perceived alike.[29]

Of course, the present train of events, while similar in essentials to what had gone before, was also different in important details. Hoffmann was sufficiently perceptive and attuned to the rhythms of postwar European politics to accept that history never repeats itself in every precise detail, regardless of those broad imperatives that permanently operate to fashion the minutiae of events. He did acknowledge, for instance, the remarkable and unique achievement that was the postwar Community project. At the same time, the experience of post-war European cooperation itself – and not least the Cold War 'luxury' that had allowed the Europeans to shelter under the Pax Americana after 1945 – had sharpened these differences of perception about Europe's 'best interests' as much as it had reconciled them. Postwar cooperation in Europe had pointed up new differences of geopolitical interest as much as it had ameliorated many of the lesser ones **(Document 24)**.

To that extent, 'each nation . . . finds itself placed in an orbit of its own from which it is quite difficult to move away; for the attraction of the regional forces' is offset by the pull of all the other forces to which every nation state is subjected.[30] The endemic anarchy in which international politics continues to be conducted will always countervail, then, any supposedly straightforward tendency to effect a 'natural' regional harmony as prefigured in the idealist model of inter-national relations. In so far as regional integration is possible in these awkward circumstances, it must always be for Hoffmann a contrived and limited arrange-ment between 'real' states. Not, in other words, an exercise in myth making. The realist doctrine lies at the heart of this sceptical account of the European project. The dynamics of the international system, at whatever level, are for Hoffmann certainly more predisposed towards the preservation and pre-eminence of the nation state than to its submersion in a new international *gemeinschaft*. For international politics is, by its very nature,

> profoundly conservative of the diversity of nation states . . . The nation state prevails in peace, they remain unsuperseded because a fragile peace keeps the Kantian doctor away, they are unreplaced because their very involvement in the world, their very inability to insulate themselves from one another, preserves their separateness. The 'new Europe' dreamed up by the Europeans could not be established by force. Left to the wills and calculations of its members, the new formula has not jelled because they could not agree its role in the world.[31]

In essence the nation state remains for Hoffmann the obstinate rather than the obsolete player in the great game of international politics **(Document 25)**:

> Thus, the nation state survives by the formidable autonomy of politics, as manifested in the resilience of political systems, the interaction between separate states and a single international system, the role of leaders who believe both in the primacy of 'high politics' over the kind of managerial politics susceptible to functionalism, and in the primacy of the nation, struggling in the world today over any other form, whose painful establishment might require one's lasting withdrawal from the pressing and exalting daily contest.[32]

When Hoffmann was invited to re-examine his view and reflect on the place of the Western European nation state some 16 years after these words were written, he reaffirmed his original verdict, albeit with an acknowledgement that things were no longer quite what they had been in the heyday of realism. Even so, he was confident enough of the nation state's resilience to pronounce that 'the nation-state co-exists with (the) European enterprise', rather than being subsumed within it. Regardless of the changes that had enveloped it, and indeed because of them, Europe's nation states had accommodated well to the Community game. Hoffmann agrees with those other realists who continue to argue the case that regional integration has come to the rescue of the European nation state, and has enabled it to adapt to the new exigencies of global political economy rather than burying it in altogether new political arrangements.

> Indeed, the relations between the Community and its members are not a zero sum game; the Community helps preserve the nation-state far more than it forces them to wither away. . . . The most striking reality is not the frequent and well-noted impotence of the so-called sovereign state. It is its survival, despite the turmoil.[33]

CRITIQUE

Hoffmann's trenchant analysis of the modest prospects for European integration has invariably attracted its own critique. Commentators more convinced of the prospects for deeper regional integration and more ideologically favourable to the supranational idea, have challenged as fanciful his assumption that an inviolable boundary exists between national states and the wider environment in which they operate. The evidence of increasing global interdependence has certainly raised serious doubts about the ability of modern states to operate as primarily independent international actors. Commentators who have taken this line of thought have challenged Hoffmann's rather dogmatic conviction that, while transnational cooperation and the sharing of functions might well occur in those 'low' policy or functional issue areas which did not challenge to any great extent fundamental national interests, the scope for such integration in the more sensitive areas of 'high' politics remained slight.

The case for holding out for such a rigid demarcation between those areas of low political significance available for integration and core national interests, was questioned on the basis of accumulated evidence from students of contemporary political economy. The recent surge in European integration that accompanied the completion of the Single Market has certainly drawn attention to the artificial nature of these policy boundaries. Recent policy developments in Europe and for that matter in other regional arrangements, has encouraged a greater degree of complementarity between these policy areas than Hoffmann had countenanced in his early writings. Hoffmann's latest writings duly acknowledge this fact. But in the process of revision he has softened rather than abandoned altogether his realist perspective. And with good reason.

It is certainly reasonable to conclude, on the basis of recent research into the contemporary political economy, that modern territorial states do inhabit an altogether more interdependent universe than that predicated in the narrowly focused account of international politics which figured in Hoffmann's classic defence of the European nation state. Every advanced nation state finds itself increasingly drawn into immensely complex global networks, regional regimes and all manner of transnational arrangements. These experiences, in turn, shape every participating states' international orientations and erode, even if they do not entirely supersede, the autarchic sense of sovereign autonomy that once prevailed as the crucible of national identity and shaped the pursuit of exclusive national interests. There are structural and behavioural reasons why this should be so. The problems that confront all states big and small now have an extra-territorial dimension. They all face what are increasingly regional issues or global problems requiring common solutions. Moreover, the governing and other key elites whose task it is to address these issues also inhabit what are increasingly common experiences, and share similar lifestyles and aspirations. We are hardly yet dwellers in the global village of Mitrany's fertile imagination. But we are, at the same time, some way removed from the narrowly exclusive atavism of Bismarckian realpolitik.

The cumulative experience of such rising interdependence raises doubts about Hoffmann's narrow concept of international relations. And, by extension, about his insistence on claiming that a clear distinction persists between those aspects of national policy amenable to integration, and those which are precluded from such joint approaches and common strategies. To say this is by no means to endorse the supranationalist perspective on the prospects for further integration. However, this issue does highlight a critical question that lies at the very centre of the theoretical discourse on regional integration. The debate over the momentum behind integration touches on the process variables that propel or retard regional integration. Hoffmann's distinction between types of issues susceptible or anti-thetical to transnational cooperation, raises serious questions about how and why such changes occur. It confronts the critical issue of dynamics; the identification of those forces which are at work in and underlie the process of international change; the extent to which the process is 'moved' by some inexorable momentum, or whether change is merely a contingent outcome of policy interactions, which may have any number of possible political consequences. On balance, it is reasonable to say at this stage that neither the supranational nor the intergovernmentalist paradigms discussed so far, have addressed this critical issue as plausibly as the revi-sionist paradigm to be discussed in Chapter 5. Both the classical paradigms insist on an exclusive view of the process of international change. The interdependence of advanced societies suggests that their relationships are shaped in fact both by what they share in common and what they continue to perceive as their competing national interests.

The evolution of the European Community has illustrated this continuing flux between distinctiveness and commonality that is the principal defining characteristic of contemporary international politics. It reflects the fluidity of what were once regarded as the impermeable boundaries between states and their wider international environments. Indeed, the European project offers the best example in contemporary international politics of the engagement of individual states with their regional and wider international hinterlands. The EC's institutional patterns and procedural arrangements have thus become the focal point of an energetic debate about the nature of international politics per se. The Community has witnessed the expansion of common agendas, with a tendency to intrude into policy areas once staunchly defended by statesmen and realist theorists alike, as the sole and legitimate preserve of national governments.[34] The recent history of the European project has likewise witnessed similar tensions between supranationalism and intergovernmentalism. It has become a crucible of conflicting forces; the centripetal pressures to defend national interests on the one hand, confronted by the centrifugal 'pull' of transnational tendencies to cooperate in order to survive.

The requirement of modern governments to respond to the structural demands imposed on them by modern economic management leads them to pool sover-eignty and share in common policy competences across an expansive range of issue areas. This in turn, has challenged head on the resistance of Europe's statesmen to any form of international cooperation that significantly dilutes national sover-eignty. The evidence seems to suggest that regional integration is in fact propelled by a combination of forces drawn from these two competing impulses which impinge on every contemporary national state. Hoffmann's original claim that regional integration is nothing more intrusive of traditional national prerogatives than a series of modest accommodations to these global pressures in non critical policy areas is, on the available evidence at least, a highly questionable one. Hoffmann was of course a realistic realist! He was persuaded by the evidence of a rising interdependence in Community affairs to revise rather than to abandon his earlier view that nation states remain essentially resistant to intrusive global pressures in critical areas of policy. This subsequent review is discussed in the conclusion to this work. While it does meet some of the critical objections raised here, it remains for all that, an essentially intergovernmental and statecentric account of the European process.

The latest phase in the Community's development has certainly revealed some of the obvious shortcomings of the realist account of regional integration. The realist model of international politics provides useful insights as well as narrow prejudices. The case for an intergovernmentalist model of integration is neither proved nor invalidated by contemporary events. Instead, current developments suggest that an altogether more complex process is underway than is reflected in either of the classical paradigms. We might just as easily conclude from these events that the exponential pressures of global change in general, and the particular modalities of regional integration, continue to find the nation state caught in two minds. Hoffmann was surely right to point out the shortcomings of the supranational version of events in Europe, the tendentious claim that some inexorable logic is at work here, unravelling the fabric of the national body politic and eroding the sense of community and identity which sustains these processes. As Hoffmann rightly concludes, the very suggestion is at the least premature and quite possibly far fetched. It is a conclusion based on a distortion of the evidence and a gross oversimplification of the contours of international politics.

At the same time, the very complexities of the new international order, and not least the constraints these have placed on effective independent action by individual states, does raise similar doubts concerning Hoffmann's assertion that as far as the essential qualities of sovereignty go, little has really changed. In common with other realists, he sets as much store by a persistent sovereignty as the supranationalists place their faith in innovation. National sovereignty retains, more or less, a uniform quality. Certainly, states have to pursue their interests in a rapidly changing world order. But they continue to do so by steering by ancient lights. Sovereignty and the sense of statehood it represents in the minds of actors and publics alike, remains capable of resisting those insistent transnational pressures which seek to undo the world of states and replace them with a novel international order. And while sovereignty is fraying at the edges, as economic and social interdependence make the world a much smaller place, it remains most resilient in Hoffmann's view in those critical areas of 'high politics' which have always encapsulated the very essence of distinctive nationhood.

The development of the European project over the past decade or so seems to sustain a more paradoxical view of the state of regional integration. Governments may well continue to harbour the illusion that they are responding to the exigencies of international politics in accordance with the dictates of their own sovereign prerogatives. Statesmen too may well intend to be resolute in their pursuit of what they see as their fundamental national interests. And they certainly make domestic political capital out of their diplomatic forays abroad. But merely to lay claim to a clear sense of national purpose is not quite the same thing as corroborating the realist thesis in full. The intention to act in the national interest clearly prefigures much that happens in the international arena, in Europe as anywhere else. However, this intent in no way covers or explains the range of motives or actions available to modern statesmen. Nor, of course, does it guarantee their success. No state today, however resourceful its statesmen are, is an island. Few statesmen, however purposive or powerful, have effective control over outcomes. This implies much less a failure of will, or any deficiency in the arts of statecraft, than a reflection of the real constraints on independence and, indeed, sovereignty itself. The limits on sovereign independence are, then, an important factor in the contemporary international equation. The reasons for this lie in the structural shifts that have occurred in global political economy.

The interpenetration of modern states by global forces beyond their control, and the need to make adjustments to these prevailing forces is a fact – perhaps the most palpable and important fact – of modern political life. It is a situation that demands compromises, precludes autarchy and imposes severe constraints on state sovereignty. These facts raise serious doubts about the rather outmoded notion of statehood employed in the realist paradigm. Hoffmann, too, regardless of the reservoir of common sense that represents his opus, tends to narrow his vision and, to that extent, he misconstrues the *sui generis* quality of the contemporary international system. To this extent too, he misses much of the novelty of the European project. It is by no means the case, as Hoffmann claimed – even on a cautious assessment of the tenor of European international relations over the past generation – that 'each (European) nation remains encased in its present self, giving an occasional backward glance at the recent past for remorse or consolation and a worried glance at the near future'.[35] This was a selective view of affairs, even for the time – the late 1970s – when this was written. There was certainly some hard evidence to support Hoffmann's contention that the momentum of regional integration had stalled. But much depends on the reasons given for this hiatus. Hoffmann, in realist fashion, doubted the very enterprise itself. He was persuaded by events to seriously question the Community project; as if 'only a uniting Europe that could look at the whole of its fragmented past would be able to will a future (and) how can it emerge, if its members have neither the drive nor the necessary incentives to transcend themselves into Europe?'[36] Hoffmann's assessment of the situation in the late 1970s was, to say the least, selective. He took recent events largely out of context. For instance, he chose to minimise the significance of the current recession on the will to build a positive Europe. Macroeconomic factors have the potential for both a positive and negative impact on regional integration. At the time Hoffmann wrote his 1979 paper, economic privations had encouraged an autarchic and insular response. Within a few years those same statesmen and politicians drew entirely opposite conclusions about the benefits of further integration. It was ever thus in the unsteady quest for European integration.

These developments must of course be weighed carefully. To concede the impact of global developments on national aspirations, to allow for their dramatic effect on notions of sovereignty, and to concede their consequences for contemporary international relations, is by no means to confirm the relevance of the supranationalist over the intergovernmentalist account of the European regional process. These events did take their toll of the status quo, but not in ways that corroborated one of these classical paradigms at the expense of the other. Modern global interdependence in fact took its toll of both accounts of the regional process. As far as the intergovernmentalist paradigm was concerned, it did raise serious doubts about the explanatory virtues of a school of thought that had dominated both the intellectual discourse and the practice of European statecraft for over three centuries. To that extent, the conventional rationale of European and international politics came under serious review. The notion of a 'picket fence' raised around the legitimate prerogatives of statehood against allcomers was severely dented by the recent shift in global affairs. Sensible realists such as Hoffmann took some account of these changes, but their revisionism at this stage only went so far.

States certainly do retain their place at the centre of the regional process. Nothing that has happened in the field of European integration since the 1960s challenges that singular fact. At the same time, states are by no means the only, or for that matter, the most influential actors in the regional process. Nor are they any longer the cohesive actors of classical realist theory, standing for a clear sense of national purpose as represented in international transactions undertaken by an authoritative governmental elite. On the evidence of the contemporary regional process in Europe, modern states are much less cogent and altogether more ambivalent players. Even when they engage in their most conventional, and we might say here traditional role in the diplomatic process, as defenders or prosecutors of the security interests – protecting the national boundaries of the 'homeland'. The straightforward billiard ball metaphor favoured by realists which supposedly captures this pristine quality of sovereignty, looks much less convincing when we measure it against those multiple horizontal networks which connect the various levels of intrastate activity to an increasingly interdependent transnational society.

Modern territorial states are far from being the obsolescent, outdated agencies of the supranational paradigm. But, neither are they those cohesive actors speaking with a single national voice, and engaged in the pursuit of a concerted national interest, that colour the realist account of international politics. To this extent, the realist paradigm fails to reflect contemporary circumstances. As we will see in the review of the increasingly influential interdependence paradigm below, the narrow insularity of the statecentric concept of integration hardly fits the facts of the regional process in Europe as it is presently organised. There are altogether more suitable models available that capture the flux and the mixed motives at the heart of the region's affairs. In these circumstances, the conceptualisation of regional politics as a multiple series of interlocking networks offers an altogether more plausible picture of European statehood than the classical realist account, under the prevailing conditions of European political economy.

The shortcomings of this conventional intergovernmentalist account of European integration became apparent during the 1970s. The academic response to political developments on the ground which increasingly called into question the explanatory value of the classical realist account of regional integration, was broadly two fold. One response to the limits of the classic intergovernmentalist thesis was to adapt it, in order to better explain the paradoxical and some might even say confused, responses of the Community's member states to their changing international environment. Paul Taylor's development of the confederalist model discussed below represents the most cogent attempt at theoretical revisionism here.

A more radical response to the limits of the intergovernmentalist account of events in Europe encouraged some theorists to suggest an entirely new paradigm altogether. The new paradigm which emerged from these intellectual endeavours was bound to offer a much less cohesive theoretical model than either of the classical paradigms it confronted. It was, after all, based on the fundamental premise that regional integration was an intrinsically ambiguous rather than a singular process. As such, it sought to synthesise a range of previously conflicting assumptions about the dynamics behind international change. In the process it drew on schools of thought about international politics that were by no means easily reconciled. What the various exponents of this diffuse school of integration theory do share in common, however, and what distinguishes theoretical contributions here from the modest revisionism which the same events forced on the intergovernmentalist or supranationalism paradigms, was the acknowledgement of ambivalence as the key to understanding the momentum behind European integration.

The assumption here was that the integration process was driven neither by a singular dynamic, whether a statecentric or supranational one. Nor was it propelled in any clear direction, or for that matter towards any certain outcome. Instead, these syncretic theorists, as we will identify them, defined integration as a hybrid process; one in which the immensely complex interactions of both national and transnational actors determines the shape, pace and outcomes of the European project. The dualism of the regional process, the necessary balance between specific domestic interests and an emergent regional outlook in which nascent common interests play their part, was the principal concern of the new theoretical modelling that began to accrue from the late 1970s. This significant paradigmic shift did not of course emerge overnight. Paradigmic shifts are as tentative as they get underway as they are inevitable. This latest shift in intellectual perceptions began with an attempt to adapt the intergovernmental model to the new exigencies of the 1970s. It was prefigured in the confederalist refinement of the intergovernmentalist model that became currency in the debate during the decade of the 1970s.

THE MEANING OF CONFEDERALISM

A confederation is the antithesis of a federation. Federations are states in their own right. They amount to a contract between governors and governed and are recommended ethically and practically as the best way of ensuring the liberties of citizens, by dispersing power as widely among the constituent parts of the state as possible. A confederation on the other hand is a concert of sovereign states principally arranged for their members' mutual advantage. In this community of states the participants choose to interact with one another in predictable patterns, according to agreed procedures and with varying degrees of shared endeavour. Regardless of their political cohesion, commonality of purpose and the policy convergence that may result from this, the members of confederations do acknowledge one another's rights as sovereign states. Not least the primary right to sovereignty itself. Even at their most advanced stages of development, confederations amount to little more than a pooling of non critical elements of their members' de jure sovereignty. They are practical arrangements convened to better facilitate the usual diplomatic intercourse and transactions of international politics. They are interstate rather than intrastate arrangements. The rules which apply to confederations are essentially those of international rather than domestic politics. Members perceive themselves to be engaged in the conventional game of diplomacy; albeit with the objective of lessening their differences, or in pursuit of mutually beneficial policy outcomes. In either case, a special degree of cooperation is deemed desirable or suitable for achieving these goals.

Confederalism is, then, a special form of the intergovernmental arrangement discussed above. Conventional intergovernmental procedures cover the entire spectrum of interstate relations. They encompass everything from security and crisis management to the closest expressions of diplomatic collaboration. Confederalism, as Murray Forsyth argues in his analysis of the phenomenon[37] **(Document 26)**, does go a clear stage further down the intergovernmental route to international cooperation. As an international strategy, confederalism concentrates on maximising positive collaboration between states which share a strong sense of common purpose, rather than dwelling on the negative pursuit of policy suboptimality or the narrow transactional trade offs associated with more mundane and conventional forms of intergovernmental cooperation. Confederations are, in these terms, a special type of intergovernmental arrangement; one that aims to formulate practical procedures for cooperation and to facilitate by institutional devices beyond ordinary diplomatic intercourse, the smooth conduct of interstate relations. The attempt here to move beyond nominal intergovernmentalism and to fashion it into formal codes and procedures that minimise the risks of conflict, encourages crisis management. And indeed it reinforces a mood of harmony and a propensity to collaboration between the participating states, and certainly mirrors to a degree the fundamental federalist concern with peace and with ensuring the political conditions conducive to a stable social order. Confederalism may, in certain historical circumstances, be no more than a recipe for a civilised international society. At its most productive, it may even be a way station on the road to a fully federal polity. This is certainly the positive conclusion that some commentators on European integration have drawn from the Community's recent confederalist phase[38] **(Document 27)**. But this is by no means the inevitable outcome of a confederal arrangement at the international level. By and large, the adoption of a confederalist framework in the debate on European integration, as much as in the Community's political arrangements, has been an attempt to refine an intergovernmental paradigm. As a model of the Community process, confederalism was an attempt to adapt the prevailing intergovernmentalist or statecentric paradigm that was apparently losing touch with political realities, to those very changes of circumstance and procedure that had overtaken the Community during the course of the 1970s **(Document 28)**.

EUROPEAN CONFEDERALISM IN PRACTICE

This shift of emphasis had practical as well as intellectual consequences. The procedural and institutional changes that represented the EC's confederalist phase were far from incidental or haphazard occurrences. They were an attempt by the Community's members to accommodate intergovernmentalism to the new international demands of globalism. These changes consolidated the Community's role in international affairs and confirmed its members' perception and that of its international partners, that it had finally arrived as a force to be reckoned with in world politics. The development of the Council Presidency, the new system of foreign policy coordination (European Political Cooperation) and the formalisation of regular European Councils, agreed at the Paris Summit of 1974,[39] all contributed to the general impression that the Community did indeed occupy a uniquely important international status. The steady expansion of functions and constitutional competencies and the increased scope of the Community's policy agenda reinforced the sense of a Community on the move. The metaphor of a journey was frequently cited by commentators at this time. As, of course, it has been subsequently. What was less certain was the direction or the likely outcome of these changes.[40]

The contemporary debate began to reflect this *sui generis* quality as one suspended somewhere between intergovernmentalism and supranationalism. William Wallace, for instance, saw a 'Community (that) remained stuck between the recognition of the need for more effective common action and the inability – or unwillingness – of its constituent states to concert their actions or to concede authority'.[41] Forsyth, too, pointed to the EC's unique intermediate status as among its most significant characteristics **(Document 29)**. A new level of international or rather transnational relations had evolved. Forsyth was convinced that

> the Community represents the replacement of external economic relations between members by economic relations similar to those that obtain within a single state. The economy of each state has not ceased to exist, but it has been replaced by a new economy – that of the Community as a whole.[42]

The new procedures which were superimposed on the Community's residual legacy from the founding treaties, were widely acknowledged as a novel institutional arrangement,[43] one that was unprecedented in the modern history of international society. A consensus began to form that these transitional arrangements had moved the Community into a new category of international organisation altogether. Taylor made these institutional changes, and the political attitudes they signified, the focus of a confederalist account of the EC project.[44] This model was particularly influential during the 1970s and into the early 1980s. While this new theoretical account, with its emphasis on change in response to external as well as internal stimuli, was certainly an improvement on the narrowly conceived intergovernmentalist model, it did suffer from its own limitations. Fashioned in the intergovernmentalist mould, it tended to focus on institutions rather than on processes; on structures rather than functions. As such, its value as an account of what was really underway in the European project was partial. In retrospect, it reveals less about either the Community's political status or the dynamics that were changing the regional process than we might expect from a model that had perceptively identified an incipient tension in Community affairs between national interests and emergent common aspirations. Of course, these limitations are more easily seen with benefit of hindsight. Nevertheless, Taylor's confederalist thesis did provide some useful insights into the new complexities of the European process.

In the event, political exigencies – the search for manageable solutions rather than idealised prescriptions – dictated, as we might reasonably expect, the shape and momentum of the European regional project during this latest critical juncture in its development. The supranational ambition, whether in the federalist form that was favoured by key elements in the European Parliament, or in the administrative, technocratic or functionalist expression preferred by the Commission, was quite easily obstructed by the tenacious pursuit of national preferences within the Council of Ministers. And it was this intergovernmental machinery that continued to hold the whip hand in the management of Community affairs. The Council retained, after all, the legislative prerogative awarded to it by the Treaty of Rome. The inter-institutional frictions that persisted throughout this troubled decade were largely resolved in the Council's favour. The supranationally motivated institutions took, however reluctantly, a back seat. Events confirmed in Taylor's mind that the Community's development was contained within demonstrably intergovernmentalist bounds. The Community, far from being orchestrated from a supranational centre was directed, in so far as anything akin to a common purpose emerged from the clamour of interests in the policy process, by shifting constellations of competing national interests negotiated within variable coalitions made up from its principal states. These were entirely ephemeral arrangements that moved with the shifts in the Community's agenda.

There was sufficient evidence from the flux in Community affairs to support the idea that the Community had indeed entered a confederal phase. Taylor's account of the Community in the 1970s certainly offers some useful insights into the new level of intergovernmental arrangements. Moreover, Taylor's confederalism provided a far from doctrinaire account of the regional process. Taylor, whose original theoretical inquiries into integration had favoured a functionalist perspective,[45] was intellectually disposed to the notion of tension as the principal force for change in the Community. His account of EC politics in the 1970s breaks away from the narrow focus of intergovernmentalism, and allows for a degree of positive integration as well as acknowledging those negative frictions which encouraged the sort of impasse and Euroschlerosis that have periodically overtaken the European project.[46] In Taylor's hands, the confederalist model pointed to an altogether new level of regional integration; one which was statecentric, if not exclusively so. And when centred as it increasingly was on cooperative arrangements, was entirely appropriate to the particular requirements of the member states who cut these bargains, in response to a rapidly changing international environment (Document 30).

The confederalist version of the statecentric paradigm was plausible in another sense too. It took account of the wider international environment. Not an environment perceived merely as the void or vacuum that figures in classical realist accounts; but rather as the source of cooperative stimulus and of positive challenges requiring calculated responses and imaginative solutions. Taylor's confederal model accounted for the international constraints which have increasingly impinged on this Community of medium sized and not particularly well resourced states – at least when compared with those available to the economic and military superpowers. If there is a 'dynamic' in Taylor's model it is essentially a utilitarian and reactive one. Confederalism – less than a halfway house between the old notion of international governance and a radical transnational one – amounts to a rational regrouping of nation states in order quite simply to survive the ravages of global change. These institutional adaptations are no more than the practical ways that small regional states of medium status and modest diplomatic resources might mobilise, the better to cope with the exigent pressures of the changing international environment. According to Taylor's account of the EC's confederalist phase, the institutional innovations of the 1970s were primarily an attempt by otherwise vulnerable regional states to coordinate their efforts in the international political and economic fields, in order to facilitate cooperation and maximise their common interests, in so far as this was possible between independent states. The principal object of this exercise was for the participants to expand their individual national interests through collective action; and, in the process, to maximise their global leverage.

Political strategies are always a balance of probabilities. Taylor was always realistic about the Community's prospects for a successful accommodation with those powerful global forces that encompassed it. On balance, the confederal strategy can be viewed as a considerable achievement, with many positive policy outcomes. But for Taylor these accomplishments did not imply that structural change, even the successful adaptation to global exigencies, implied anything more than a case of likeminded states taking their international bearings and responding accordingly. As far as Taylor and those other commentators who shared this perspective were concerned, the integration process in Europe was by no means driven by the sort of inexorable integration momentum identified in both versions of the supranational paradigm. These common initiatives were purposive, expansive even; but they fell a long way short of surrendering state sovereignty over critical policy areas. On the contrary, for Taylor this limited strategy was followed precisely in order to pursue abiding national interests. Above all, it was a way of ensuring the prosperity, security and the stable political order which are the preconditions for the survival of any territorial state. The bottom line here remained the inviolability of national sovereignty. In spite of a noticeable expansion of consultations on the ways of resolving common problems, even as far in the EC's case as the penetration of national legal systems by the overarching jurisdicial framework of Community law, the critical boundaries between the domestic and Community competencies remained intact. It takes, of course, a particularly conservative view of EC law to sustain this view, but Taylor was sure of his ground. So while,

> in the drawing up of the detailed, day to day decisions [the states] agreed to be bound, they could equally disagree to be bound – they could take back what they had given and, the argument ran, this did not amount to a breach of sovereignty. The procedures were novel, the Community legal system was indeed unique, and might be justifiably called supranational, but it was still an expression of the states' adjustment to new conditions . . . the supranational elements helped states to survive rather than placed them in new integrated structures.[47]

The essence of confederalist integration was in these modest terms, a kind of international 'clubmanship' among states who found themselves facing common problems and opportunities vis-à-vis the wider global environment, yet whose distinctive and abiding national interests precluded any deeper form of integration. Taylor identified this balance of opportunities as a novel, but for all that an inherently limited, form of integration. It amounted to a situation in which,

> Each (EC) state perceived the benefits of membership in the club for its own interests, but also in the existing institutional context was reminded of the costs of moving towards greater 'supranationalism' in the procedure for coordinating foreign policy. The state of each member in diversity was increased by the very procedures that were intended to assist with coordination. It was indeed ironic that in accepting the form of Communities De Gaulle had sought – a political union – member states were also reinforced in any propensity they had to act like him. The problems that had emerged in international cooperation were therefore made more difficult rather than reduced by the experience of foreign policy coordination. In reinforcing the governments' propensity to stress their immediate separate interests within the common system, the problems of tackling 'positive' integration were increased: governments became less willing to make the kind of mutual commitment necessary in those politically more sensitive areas.[48]

Confederation in practice was of course a more complex set of arrangements than those suggested by classical intergovernmentalism. The member states were part of something bigger than the sum of its constituent parts, however tenuous their sense of commitment or limited their obligations to this project. And to this extent, Taylor did acknowledge that regular participation in these arrangements might eventually induce changes in the behaviour of these states. Or at least in the principal agents of these states, which amounted to much the same thing. He was already aware of an incipient ambivalence in this new European confederation. But when the chips are really down, states do revert to type and follow their primordial instincts for survival. In Taylor's estimation, national states continue as the central actors in the integration process, whatever their increasing disposition to resolve their policy differences in ways that enhanced their sense of mutual advantage, and by procedural means that contained real potential for consolidating an abiding sense of their common interests. The outcomes of such joint endeavours were of course by no means as clear cut as they are in classical realist accounts of diplomatic bargaining. The impact on the Community in general, and on attitudes to integration per se, of this culture of policy bargaining was for Taylor both positive and negative. On the one side, it exposed the still raw nerves of national interests. It revealed too, the deep and abiding differences of national interest across the expanded range of policies addressed by the member states. The deepening of integration associated with the confederal phase by no means ensured the suspension of normal political instincts.

At the same time these close encounters occasionally encouraged some notable instances where a discernible regional interest emerged to tone down or overcome narrow atavism. Taylor's account is far from blind to the steady erosion of the formal prerogatives and the cultural insularity taken for granted in mainstream realism. The classical nation state is exposed to altogether new influences within these confederal arrangements. Taylor acknowledged the impact of the rising interdependence which was impelling the EC's member states to coordinate more closely their responses to the persistent problems of the contemporary international political economy and global security arrangements. These structural pressures, too, enhanced the centrifugal pull of regional integration; although this has more to say about the structural impact of these changes than it does about the process variables that underlie them. Whatever the precise causes, the consequences are not in doubt. For this change in the circumstances of regional politics has,

> contributed to the weakening of the Gemeinschaft of the nation state, has helped to undermine the hierarchy of values and attitudes, and has reduced the authority of governments. Membership (of the EC) has also exacerbated the problems of control over national economies and has disposed governments to seek allies with other organisations in an attempt to regain control. . . .[49]

This interpretation of events implies change, of sorts, yet remains in its essentials within the intergovernmental tradition. Change here owes more to states – albeit coming to terms with and even accommodating transnational and global pressures – than it does to supranational forces. There was no suggestion in the developments of the 1970s, as Taylor saw them, that the EC's discernible impetus to closer integration was in any sense propelled by any deeper supranational impulse. Regional states pursuing national interests – albeit in ever close proximity and with a rising sense of common purpose vis-à-vis the wider world – remain the critical actors and continue to be the raison d'être of the regional process. To that extent the confederal experience suggested that there was,

> no tendency for governments to be eliminated as actors from the European Gesellschaft. In fact, their right to remain as actors has, if anything, been reinforced by developments in the Community over recent years. The absence of a Gemeinschaft at the European level means that there is no means of establishing the priority of any one set of interests.[50]

FROM CONFEDERALISM TO INTERDEPENDENCE

The confederal model refined an intergovernmentalist account of integration that appeared to be increasingly outdated as the Community responded to the particular challenges it faced during the 1970s. It managed for the most part to avoid the rigidities and didacticism of classical realism. Taylor's work in particular captured something of the ambivalence of the European project, that had become its most palpable characteristic after the Community and its member states were drawn more closely into the orbit of global interdependence. De Gaulle's political passing – he resigned in 1969 after a defeat in two of his many referenda – was a symptom of this new direction. The French president had long supported the idea of European political union – as long as it was a 'small', non Anglo-Saxon Europe under firm French control. The new confederalism was an altogether less exclusive affair. And although de Gaulle's immediate political heirs, Pompidou and Giscard d'Estaing, had been the main protagonists of the institutional changes that gave it political form, the new European Confederation reflected the interests of all its members. Confederalism was a deliberate institutional response to a raft of problems confronting the Community in a rapidly changing international environment. Doubts replaced certainties and pessimism replaced optimism at the heart of the European project. Ambivalence describes the prevailing mood well enough; an uncertainty of attitudes and mixed expectations about the prospects available to Europe's states in a new world order.

At the theoretical level, the confederalist refinement of a clearly misplaced intergovernmental thesis did help to restore some conceptual subtlety to the cruder versions of the statecentric model of integration. To this extent the confederalist account provided a useful theoretical bridge between two mutually exclusive accounts of the regional integration process represented in the classical paradigms. Confederalism contributed to this paradigmic shift precisely because it saw regional integration in Europe as a two way process. On the one hand, the confederalists acknowledged the resilience of the nation state and its continuing role in the international and regional processes.[51] At the same time, confederalism represented change; the rising sense of joint endeavours and mutual interests, the search for common regional strategies and shared policy making competences necessary to save the European nation state from those impending global forces which threatened its survival.[52]

Those commentators who took their intellectual cue from the confederalist revision of the conventional statecentric paradigm duly acknowledged the hybrid quality of the regional integration process. Although Taylor's analysis was by no means the only one to highlight the interaction and complementarity of the domestic interests and regional impulses in the Community, his account was the most cogent exposition of this particular perspective. But it was a revision of a pre-existing paradigm rather than an entirely fresh account of integration. It looked backwards for inspiration rather than forwards. To this extent the limitations of the model were at least as significant as its virtues. It was, after all, premised on broadly intergovernmentalist assumptions, even though it did address some of the limitations of that conventional paradigm. Taylor's work did, nevertheless, help to encourage another paradigm shift in the intellectual quest for the meaning of European integration: it opened a new line of debate about the paradoxes at the heart of regional politics. This sense of political flux was reflected even more clearly in the theoretical revisionism already underway in the mainstream discipline of international relations.

The emergence during the latter years of the 1970s of a theoretical literature which posited an entirely new integration dynamic marks the real turning point in this discourse. The development of theories that maintained a symbiosis or interdependence between domestic preferences and global forces provided an entirely new account of European integration.[53] The theorists who developed this interdependence model based their account of international change on a different momentum from that which drove the confederalist model. The regional momentum here was instilled by a creative tension generated by the coexistence in the same Community processes of both intergovernmental and supranational impulses. This was bound to be an unpredictable, potentially volatile mix, even in the best of circumstances, and one which permitted any number of possible regional outcomes, depending on the actual balance of political forces in play on any particular policy issue. The interdependence theorists broke with both of the earlier paradigms that had dominated the discourse since 1945. The writing that contributed to this new account of the regional process thus represents a full paradigm shift in the proper sense of that term.

There was more substance to this new integration paradigm than merely the fusing of two opposing interpretations of the role of nation states in the international process. The new revisionism presents a uniquely syncretic view of the regional process. The syncretic paradigm was a far from cogent account of international change. The established notion of integration as a singular process – one which involved either the withering or the consolidation of the nation state – was replaced instead by a variable model. The new model premised its assumptions about the dynamics behind regional change on ambivalence rather than certainty about outcomes.

The revival of academic interest in both the theory and processes of European integration after 1984, as the Community emerged from one of its familiar cycles of institutional torpor and policy ennui, by launching itself into the most extensive round of positive integration on the back of the Single European Market programme, contributed much to this paradigm shift. The pattern here was a familiar one in the history of intellectual discourse, of a creative dialectic between practical politics and political theory. This was by no means the first occasion in the EC's history when the thrust of events had challenged the capacity of the prevailing theoretical paradigms to explain them adequately.[54] The sudden, indeed unexpected, end to the impasse surrounding British budgetary payments at the Fontainebleau European Council of 1984, had removed the most serious obstacle in the way of a new round of integration. This solution to an issue that had dogged Community affairs for a decade, and done much in the process to reinforce a mind set that elevated the idea of *juste retour* as the raison d'être of EC membership, opened up Community politics to a new agenda which appealed to the supranationalists in the Commission and the Parliament, as well as to the member governments. The installation of a new and energetic Commission, the rehabilitation of the Franco-German entente as the central driving force of integration,[55] and the widespread perception among the member states and the Commission alike of the unpalatable consequences for European competitiveness of the latest world recession, all helped to reinforce this new momentum for change.[56] And this sea-change brought a ready acknowledgement from the academic community that something new was afoot; a shift that the traditional models of integration had failed to explain adequately – or had missed altogether.[57]

This remarkable turn of events, from a pervasive mood of Europessimism to the relaunching of a positive integration initiative of unprecedented reach and potential, was itself the outcome of a trade off between national and supranational interests at the Milan summit of 1985. The academic community has warmed to this revisionist task. The past decade or so has seen a remarkable revival of interest in, and some remarkably creative thinking about, the meaning of European integration. During this time there has been a positive renaissance in integration theory. The European Community has been subjected to more detailed and sophisticated academic scrutiny than at any time since integration became a matter of serious theoretical interest during the 1950s. A plethora of case studies, many of which had their empirical origins in the policy outcomes and procedures of the '1992 project', have refocused the efforts of the academic community on the task of explaining the dynamics of the regional process. The cumulative impact of this rich vein of scholarship has undoubtedly been to refine and deepen our understanding of this intellectually challenging and immensely complex process. This theoretical renaissance has taken the current debate about European integration further than any previous paradigmic shift. At the same time, the classical paradigms have survived, albeit changed by the experience of academic dialogue. The current debate reflects a rich theoretical confection; a confluence of the established but modified paradigms and an entirely new revisionism. There is clearly still much to play for in the intellectual quest for European integration.

The new paradigm has undoubtedly had the better of the recent argument. It became clear during this round of febrile academic debate that the latest push for integration, this present standoff between the member states and those actors who steer the Community's supranational institutions, simply could not be explained exclusively in realist or supranational terms. Both the statecentric and supranational paradigms have focused theoretical attention on the durability of the nation state. Each of these models interpreted the European project as a contest between an established and a new way of organising international politics, even if they drew entirely opposite conclusions about the consequences of this engagement. The statecentric account continued to see regionalism as another arena for the traditional game of international politics. Revisionists in this school of thought modified what they saw as the traditional rules of this engagement between states to reflect new global factors. They recognised the presence in this global system of ambitious supranational interests, each with their own explicit agendas. But these interests lacked the power or the leverage to refashion the system in their own image.

By the same token, the supranationalist paradigm identified what its theorists saw as an inexorable process for change driven by pervasive structural forces, in the shape of technocratic, functional and, ultimately, a political impulse to reshape international institutions the better to cope with these same global pressures. Neither paradigm managed, however, satisfactorily to encompass the complexities of the regional integration process. Both were partially focused and ideologically skewed. Each paradigm suggested a far too simplistic and exclusive image of the logistics of contemporary regionalism. To that extent, both paradigms gave an equally misleading account of the European process.[58]

The new syncretic paradigm confronted rather than ignored these paradoxes at the heart of regional integration. Its principal theoretical virtue lies precisely in a sensible attempt to accommodate the conflicting impulses, competing interests and mixed motives which continue to inhabit the European project. This essentially hybrid quality, which focuses primarily on ambivalence rather than certainty, reflects far more accurately than the exclusive accounts of the regional process in the classical paradigms, that cautious balance between still competing domestic agendas, and those altogether broader definitions of shared regional interests which are becoming part of the currency of European politics. This amalgam of theoretical perspectives mirrors, more closely than either of the classical paradigms whose exclusivism it challenged, the mood of paradox that has come to pervade Europe's regional affairs. To this extent, the new paradigm represents merely the latest and almost certainly not the final phase in the evolving discourse on European integration.

Chapter 5

The syncretic paradigm
The ambiguities of European integration

INTEGRATION AS A HYBRID PROCESS: COMPETING PARADIGMS AND MIXED METAPHORS

European integration has been a far less clearcut process with more uncertain outcomes than those predicted by the classical paradigms. The paradigmic shifts reviewed in this book reveal the futility of any claim to have uncovered *the* elemental nature of the process. The search here for a version of the philosopher's stone remains a vain one. Integration theory is concerned with the elusive quality of change. The world of politics refuses to stand still. Those who track it are faced by cycles of events not with certainties. The relatively brief history of this debate proves the point. Theory-making on this issue has been a constantly shifting dialectic between events as they have unfolded on the ground, and the efforts of scholars to track and accurately explain them. This is as it should be. Social science is a constant endeavour to square the 'facts' of any phenomenon with those concepts or hypotheses which seem best to accommodate them; but only for as long as they 'fit'. Theoretical revision in any field is, after all, a cumulative process that reflects and builds on previous endeavours. The sort of paradigmic shifts reviewed here represent, then, the normal business of social scientists; the continual refinement of our understanding of the dynamics of the phenomenon under consideration. To that extent, the periodic shift of ideas about European integration reviewed in this book by no means represents a failure of intellectual effort. On the contrary, it is the usual outcome of any properly conducted theoretical discourse. These paradigms and the intellectual tension generated by them, have helped to map more accurately the actual developments in European integration, and to clarify our understanding of what the process means.

The latest of these paradigmic shifts does, however, take us closer to an understanding of what is at stake here than its predecessors did, for it represents a clear break with the previous discourse on integration. Instead of the certainties of both process and outcome that tend to characterise the classical paradigms, it prefers the language of ambiguity and replaces certitude with paradox. Above all, this latest theoretical appraisal of European integration chooses to see the EU as a hybrid composed of international and domestic variables; a process driven by mixed motives, in several directions and at variable speeds. European integration is, then, a contingent process which depends on the issue agendas, leadership skills and the configurations of both the supranational and domestic agencies involved in its policy making. It should come as no surprise here that the fluid metaphors of variable geometry or multi-speed change have been employed to challenge the old certitudes of the established paradigms.[1] The new syncretic model which has emerged to confront these orthodoxies offers an altogether less predictable account of the regional process. This flight from prescription is to be welcomed. Integration was always an infinitely more complex process than the one described in these classical accounts. At the same time, the new modelling of European integration does share certain broad assumptions with these precursors. Its particular appeal is its hybrid quality. The 'syncretists' – a term which covers a wide variety of contributions to the debate – incorporate assumptions about the nature of the European project drawn from both sides of the classic debate. They incorporate into a coherent account of the European process, ideas about the dynamics of regional and international politics which a previous generation of scholars and practitioners alike had assumed were irreconcilable.

There was more to this merging of two supposedly conflicting accounts of the integration process than theoretical eclecticism for its own sake. The weight of empirical evidence from the plethora of detailed research into Community affairs which followed on from the relaunching of the project in 1984–5, did tend to suggest that the European integration process was indeed an equivocal one: that it was open to several different impulses simultaneously. Contributors to this new generic approach shared one fundamental premise in common: that no single factor or impulse could adequately explain, nor any one theoretical model capture, the complex dynamics of the regional process in Europe.[2] For all their variety, the 'syncretists' do share as their fundamental premise the idea that the processes of international change are neither straightforward nor teleologically driven, and that they amount instead to a mixture of impulses, a competition between interests who hold very different perceptions about the objectives and possibilities for international cooperation.

The syncretic approach to European integration has tried to marry together these apparently conflicting impulses within a new paradigm. The preference of national actors for defending or advancing their narrow interpretation of interests is juxtaposed with the recognition of the impetus towards transnational cooperation in order to facilitate these bargains between neighbouring and 'allied' states under the conditions of contemporary globalism. There is, at the same time, some acknowledgement here that what appears to be 'mere' intergovernmental cooperation in pursuit of national preferences and domestic agendas, may well encourage, over time, new habits: the pursuit of mutual objectives and joint endeavours. Domestic and supranational interests are thus accommodated within a more or less coherent theoretical account of international change. The syncretists define integration as a process driven neither by a statecentric logic, where statesmen are motivated solely by the constraints imposed by their domestic environments, nor by those teleological assumptions implied in the versions of the supranational paradigm. This hybrid account of integration brings together participants at every level, regardless of their disparate expectations and competing policy agendas, in what is broadly conceived of as a joint but not – or at least not yet – a common endeavour. The EC operates in this sense as a functioning but limited rather than an organic community; a *gesellschaft* rather than a *gemeinschaft*, but one, nevertheless, in which integration is a fact and an increasingly pervasive and significant fact at that.

THE ROOTS OF REGIONAL INTERDEPENDENCE

In order to grasp the novelty of this new theoretical model and its contribution to the discourse on European integration, we must put it into historical context. By the late 1970s, after a generation or more of largely inadequate or inappropriate theoretical accounts of the regional process, and with events changing much faster than the existing paradigms could explain them, the debate on European integration had become confused, to say the least. At the same time, the mixed impulses at work in the regional process were increasingly evident to those who surveyed developments on the ground. The paradoxical quality of European integration was aptly captured in Fritz Scharpf's summary of these events, as a process characterised by 'frustration without disintegration and resilience without progress'.[3]

It was clear, even before the relaunch of the Community project with the Single Market proposal of 1985, that European integration was by no means the modest intergovernmental enterprise reflected in the dominant statecentric paradigm. The regional process has never been driven solely by the domestic priorities of its member states, even though they have all utilised the Community's policy procedures to pursue their respective national interests. Although the statecentric paradigm did reflect the national preferences that continue to motivate the member states, exclusive domestic agendas were by no means their only concern. At the same time, the evolving Community process was far from being the sort of inexorable push towards a Pan European polity predicted by the supranationalist account of events. Although the experience of European integration had encouraged both federalists and functionalists in their view that the nation state was obsolescent, the facts told a very different story.

The syncretic paradigm avoided such theoretical exclusivism. It acknowledged instead the contribution of both domestic and regional interests to the Community process, by incorporating both elements into the operating logic of the regional process. This exercise in theoretical revisionism received a significant boost from the revival of the integration project in 1985 after the torpor of a decade or more of Eurosclerosis. The decision taken at the Milan European Council in 1985, to embark on the completion of the Single Market, led, by degrees, to fundamental changes in both the EC's institutional arrangements and in its policy agendas. These events, in turn, encouraged academic commentators to subject the prevailing theoretical accounts of the regional process to a searching examination. The largely unexpected resuscitation of the European project and its cumulative deepening and enlargement, influenced the direction of the theoretical debate throughout the following decade. The abundant theoretical literature published from 1984 onwards illustrates more than a rekindling of academic interest in the European process. The revival of academic interest sparked an energetic search for a paradigm that was capable of reflecting the new complexities of regional integration.

To claim the emergence of an entirely new paradigm here tells only part of the story. There was no simplistic consensus among these revisionists about either the critical dynamics at the heart of the process of regional change, or over the likely outcome of European integration. Some of this 'revisionist' literature retained a sense of theoretical caution; it merely revisited, albeit with a more discerning eye for the complexities of what is underway, the theoretical terrain colonised by the classical paradigms. Other commentators, however, did go further. They focused instead on explaining the integration process in entirely novel terms. They rejected as unfounded the narrow premises of the statecentric account of regional politics, just as they questioned on similar empirical grounds the idea that an 'inexorable' momentum lay behind the clearly discernible supra-national impulse within the fabric of the Community. The syncretists focused instead on those very tensions generated by the interaction of these conflicting impulses. Seen from this perspective, European integration was far from being the straightforward, one dimensional process identified in either of the classical paradigms. On the contrary, a properly balanced account of the contemporary European process – its real achievements as well as its shortcomings – suggested the need for an entirely new theoretical perspective altogether.

The syncretists have contributed much to this revisionism, but they have done so in a way that draws insights from those very paradigms they set out to challenge. European integration has been not so much reinvented as revisited. The statecentric paradigm, with its acknowledgement of the centripetal pull of domestic factors on international politics, and of national interests and inter-governmental diplomacy as significant variables in the shaping of international outcomes, continues to contribute to the new paradigm, but in ways that tone down its autarchic view of politics. The 'state' remains as a key, even the deter-minative actor in the 'new' international politics. However, in this account 'states' are defined in less than cogent or exclusive terms. They are not the impermeable 'black boxes' or hard shelled billiard balls of the realist metaphors. Instead, the boundaries of modern states are porous and their linkages with the wider environment remain fluid. To this extent, these revisionists are behaviouralists rather than structuralists. And, as such, they are intellectually closer to the socio-logical roots of functionalism than they are to the jurisdicial roots of federalist thought; process here takes precedence over institutions and informal exchanges and political relationships offer more revealing insights into the way we live now than the sort of formalism and institutionalism that prevails in both the classical realist and federalist doctrines. As the syncretists see it, regional integration is more process than form and as such its boundaries are not as easily policed as the realists imagine. The fluidity of national boundaries – the ease with which, for instance, national law is superseded by EC law – in the new Europe is a powerful case in point. The patterning of regionalism is, then, open to influences in both directions. Domestic politics touches and shapes the regional processes and the global dimension spills back too and imposes its own powerful influences and special constraints in reverse, as it were, on home turf.

States here consist of bundles or aggregates of competing interests. These networks, in turn, possess a capacity provided by the fruits of technology, to flow across national frontiers more than used to be the case. And, in the process, to compete with or accommodate similar domestic networks from elsewhere. What we are talking about here is interdependence. The boundaries between the domestic or national, and the regional or international milieux, are replaced in this model by altogether more fluid transactional flows within and between the different levels and agencies of the Community. This *engrenage* draws on the neofunctionalist idea of elite bargains, without the technocratic determinism that persuaded Haas and his colleagues to exaggerate their case. These exchanges foster in their turn all manner of bargaining relationships, without suggesting a clear momentum to encourage or resist integration. Indeed, the experience fosters both respect and empathy alongside more atavistic impulses, as the recent history of the Community confirms. Cooperation at close quarters in no way ensures the abiding common interest that underpins both versions of the supranational paradigm. On the contrary, it is as likely to have mixed consequences depending on the issue and the particular configuration of forces lined up behind it.

In some circumstances, these contingencies have encouraged the convergence of national preferences in pursuit of a more or less common position, whereas on other issues, such networking merely foments conflicts between entrenched national interests. Alliances and hostilities thus are the meat of Community politics. They are complementary not exclusive phenomena; part of the natural order of things in modern regional organisations. They occur, for instance, in the EC over every type of issue – in inter-institutional conflicts or even as alliances, such as those between the Parliament and the Commission, or even between the Council and the Commission, brokered by the two presidencies or by COREPER. Or they may take the form of competing coalitions between different groups of member states within the Council machinery. Either way, this conceptualisation of the regional process as both a source of transnational cooperation and intergovernmental discord is far removed from the uncompromising realist notion of statehood as

> a political organisation that has the capacity, within a territory . . . to make laws and effectively sanction their upkeep; exert a monopoly over the disposal of the means of violence; control basic policies relating to internal political or administrative forms of government; and dispose of the fruits of a national economy that are the basis of its revenue.[4]

It casts doubt just as surely on the simplistic neofunctionalist or federalist assumptions about the forces behind regional change.

According to this syncretic paradigm, states do play under contemporary conditions, an altogether less exclusive role in the international process. The power of even the most favourably positioned and best resourced of states, to effect suitable policy outcomes or direct events to their national advantage, is reduced to the extent that the sheer scale and reach of the global process has depleted their scope for independent action.[5] As a consequence, the effectiveness, and with that the legitimacy, of modern states has been diminished vis-à-vis their domestic clienteles. National identity in its broadest, most inclusive sense, is thus short circuited by macroeconomic and other such global forces beyond the immediate control of national elites.[6] The authority of national governments is likewise undermined by the impact on popular perceptions of increasingly well organised transnational influences, which possess the resources, as well as the technological capacity to participate in the new globalism to their best advantage.

In other words, states are now inadequately equipped to play the Hobbesian role defined for them by the realists. They are by no means obsolete; but neither are they the determinitive and exclusive actors who once dominated the traditional narratives of international politics. They are less able under contemporary conditions to articulate, let alone to pursue successfully, these exclusive national preferences. Instead, 'the state' in its domestic arena is viewed through the syncretic lens as a composite of political, economic and sociological interests, which shape its politics, determine its international capacities and in no sense confirm the romantic idea of an historically determined, sociologically permanent and culturally fixed identity. Domestic interests shaped by modern pluralism, compete for influence within the state's formal procedures and informal networks. At the same time, external forces intrude on these manifold transactions via the multiple transmission belts that connect the domestic and international environments in a bewilderingly complex network of interest bargaining and exchange. In these circumstances, the traditional notion of a single national interest is somewhat fanciful.

This condition of interdependence has undoubtedly modified the patterns of international politics at every level. The experience of transnational flows both enhances the sensitivities of societies to one another and increases their mutual vulnerability.[7] The implications of this state of affairs for regional integration are significant. As Keohane and Nye see it,

> such efforts if pursued by more than one government make government policies sensitive to one another, since one government may deliberately or inadvertently thwart the others purposes, governments must design their policies with the policies of others in mind. The result of this may well be attempts at coordination which will increase bureaucratic contacts among government subunits, and which may, particularly in a multilateral context, create opportunities for international organisations to play significant roles.[8]

None of these changes, important though they are for the impact and intrusion of global influences into domestic politics, suggests the demise of the nation state, let alone any suggestion that supranationalism in whatever form is an imminent or even likely outcome of such cumulative interdependence. States are not replaced then as the central actors of international politics. But their place in the scheme of things is revised. For states do, however, stand alongside, and are supplemented in their activities as articulators and aggregators of the multiple interests that reflect the aspirations of modern civil societies, by other international agencies, institutions and policy networks.[9] Keohane coined the epithet 'complex interdependence' to characterise these multiple transnational transactions. To this extent, 'complex interdependence' has a pervasive quality and operates at every level of the global system, not least in regional communities such as the EU.

The impact of interdependence on the theoretical debate on European integration was evident from the literature. The material published from the late 1970s onwards clearly reveals an awareness of the shortcomings of the existing integration paradigms. A number of commentators on European affairs had already highlighted the endemic ambiguity of the Community policy process. Helen Wallace, for instance, identified the significance of the interface between domestic and regional concerns at the centre of the regional project.[10] She revealed this dualistic quality at a time when the academic debate continued to engage in the familiar 'dialogue of the deaf' across a paradigmic 'no man's land' that separated the mutually exclusive statecentric and supranational narratives. Two complementary studies by Simon Bulmer[11] and Stephen George[12] further developed this notion of the Community as a hybrid that combined domestic and supranational impulses within the same policy process. These particular revisionist accounts questioned the insularity of the crude intergovernmentalist account of European integration. They also took issue with the equally questionable assumption that supranationalism provided the EC with its principal momentum. Bulmer **(Document 31)** regarded the 'mixed intellectual parentage' of his domestic politics approach as its best claim to authenticity.

The revisionist bandwagon began to roll. Writers in this vein clearly outnumbered either unreconstructed realists or closet federalists. Contingency replaced certainty as the defining characteristic of much of this literature. Its advocates acknowledged that the Community was not evolving towards a particular outcome, nor was it moving according to the lights of a certain logic. In short, the EC was neither the incipient federation nor the welfare *gemeinschaft* of the supranationalists' imaginings. Nor was it, at the other theoretical extreme, an intergovernmental arena, a confederation of exclusive and competing national interests favoured by contributors to the realist schools of thought. Rather, the Community was defined as an arena where multiple preferences, mixed motives and competing visions remained in play. The typical policy outcomes of this regional regime were those suboptimal bargains concocted by actors – domestic and transnational – motivated by a variety of interests and competing expectations. 'States' here are composite rather than cogent actors. Although they are represented 'abroad' by statesmen and women who possess the authority to speak for 'the nation', conflicts between government officials, interest group spokespeople and assorted political movements, make it difficult to identify a clear cut national interest. And these disparate corporate interests are also significant political actors in their own right. Given their considerable resources, they are often formidable ones too. At the same time, the patterning of influence as between the domestic and regional policy environments of modern states is a far from one way traffic. The very institutional and procedural channels which carry those multiple demands and factor them within the national policy environments, also provide opportunities for breaching national boundaries. To this extent, the domestic policy system remains open to external influence. Politics is, then, a two level game; a metaphor that well reflects the persistent ambiguities of the contemporary regional process, and, not least, the blurring between the domestic and international milieux.

THE LOGIC OF INTERDEPENDENCE

By the late 1970s the regional project in Western Europe was increasingly perceived by a new generation of academic commentators to be a hybrid rather than a singular process. They could hardly fail to identify the close connection between national policy debates, global events, and the consequences of both outcomes for the regional process itself. These developments confirmed the limitations of the prevailing realist paradigm. They challenged the idea of the Community as a system of impermeable and insular nation states, as they did too the notion of the wider international process as one of endemic anarchy without any intrinsic sense of common purpose. The interdependence or globalisation thesis drew entirely opposite conclusions about the logistics of international politics. Anarchy is replaced, or at least tempered here, by an awareness of issues of transnational concern. Moreover, this degree of commonality of purpose is deemed to encourage cooperation between states of similar political disposition and mutual outlook. Regional organizations or regimes provide the arenas for the trade offs between national preferences that are necessary for the joint pursuit of sustainable policy bargains, to alleviate or redress their common problems. Such cooperative outcomes are by no means random occurrences. They are most likely to occur in this thesis between states who share similar political values, and face similar problems in the global environment. The convergence of, as much as the conflict between, national interests is one outcome of modern international regimes. These conditions are particularly encouraged by the experience of the sort of common decisional procedures which typify the EC's elaborate institutional arrangements. Indeed, the EC is the epitome of institutionalised interdependence; it stands as the most sophisticated, developed and intensive form of interstate cooperation anywhere in the world.

The urgent search by regional partners for practical and broadly acceptable solutions to these common problems, as modern states confront altogether new and demanding challenges – and in ways that preserve their national identity, without foreclosing on the prospect of cooperative regime bargains – captures the abiding paradox of international interdependence. This dilemma is well illustrated in Community affairs. The challenges which have confronted the EC as a whole in recent years, particularly the shortfall in effective competitiveness in global markets, and the demands of the new security situation imposed on the region by the collapse of communism and other shifts in global forces, were bound to take their toll of rooted, cosy shibboleths. These dramatic shifts in Europe's fortunes demand imaginative responses to unprecedented problems. The pressures facing the EU's states on all sides had tended to drive them closer together in their urgent search for solutions to these serious challenges.

This was a rational rather than merely a reactive response. Europe's political elites recognised that there was, if not strength in numbers per se, at least the prospect of exerting some additional leverage over global outcomes by making such regional accommodations. What we see in Europe's affairs is the rising sense of a common agenda, if not yet the acceptance on all sides, of a common fate. There was, of course, another side entirely to this novel experience. The experience of regular and increasingly institutionalised regional cooperation sharpens as much as it dulls these states' abiding sense of their own distinctive national interests. What is 'common' about the experience of regional integration is a recognition, grudging in some instances, of a shared dilemma. Finding agreements to these problems at a level of cooperation that upgrades the regional interests above a merely suboptimal trade off between national preferences, is another prospect entirely. The other side of closer regional cooperation is, then, a reinforcement of a sense of nationhood.

These facts of life were assimilated into the debate on regional integration. One line of theoretical inquiry here focused on regional integration as something less than the *sui generis* process that had figured in the federalist and neo functionalist paradigms.[13] In other words, the search for a discrete integration logic applicable only to Europe was futile. According to the interdependence thesis, European states were merely responding, and in predictable ways, to the new global arrangements that impinged on states elsewhere. Transnational cooperation – the Community acquis and its policy consequences – was seen here to be a typical, indeed in rational terms an unavoidable, response by medium sized states to their fast changing global predicament. This interdependence approach to regional integration owed much to parallel developments in international relations theory.[14] Two of the pre-eminent exponents of the syncretic account of regional integration saw the process in precisely these structural terms. It was a way of accommodating the particularities of European regional politics to those global forces for change that states everywhere were now forced to address. These new constraints demanded new policy solutions and political strategies to match.[15] From the intellectual perspective, they also demanded new theoretical models to better explain these processes. According to Keohane and Nye, regional integration theory should not then be defined 'as a separate and arcane set of notions applicable only to Europe and perhaps a few other areas, but as a highly important part of the literature on world politics'.[16] William Wallace, too, shared this view. He observed that,

> The European Communities may thus be seen, from one perspective, as part of the general response of the governments of industrialized countries to the problem of an interdependent international economy, as part of an overall trend towards the management of interdependence, together with the other industrialized organizations which bring together different and overlapping groups of countries from the industrialized world.[17]

Henry Nau **(Document 32)**, writing at a time when the interdependence model was making inroads into the integration debate, resisted this theoretical eclecticism. Nau certainly endorsed the continuing value of the special insights into the process of international change yielded by the revisionist endeavour. At the same time, he cautioned against submerging the search for a generic brand of integration theory within a broader category of ideas that missed or misinterpreted the unique quality of the regional process. His appeal for caution is understandable enough. But it was hard to resist the potency of the interdependence model as converts climbed aboard from all sides of the intellectual spectrum. This inter-dependence frame of reference continued to attract considerable, and sometimes indiscriminate, support among students of European integration. By and large, these commentators tend to see integration not so much as an inevitable outcome of international change – for the resilience of nationhood and the centripetal pull of national identity continues to build powerful barriers of resistance to integration, even in its most promising locales – but as a rational strategic response. These doubts were not confined to statesmen either. As Carole Webb **(Document 33)** has perceptively observed, 'interdependence seems to be the answer for scholars and politicians who wish, for different reasons, to keep their options open on the evolution of the EC'.[18]

The European regional project was regarded then by the syncretists who shared the interdependence outlook, as a critical response to a generic global process. Seen in these terms, the experience of European integration reflected the abiding doubts and dilemmas about futures, rather than the glib certainties that infuse realist and supranationalist theory. Above all, interdependence, in theory and practice, was a direct response by both statesmen and those transnational interests alike that play a critical role in determining outcomes at the Community level, to the increasingly difficult challenges confronting every modern nation state.[19] To this extent, the interdependence perspective opened up a new line of inquiry in the study of European integration. The tendency of earlier paradigms to identify the momentum of international change by an unequivocal dynamic, with a certain outcome – the preservation or the obsolescence of the European nation state – gave way to accounts that made a positive virtue out of the paradoxical nature of the European regional process.

REGIONAL INTEGRATION AND THE TWO LEVEL GAME

Many of the commentators on European affairs who adopted a version of the syncretic model shared this seamless view of the political process. Modern politics blurred, even if it did not entirely obscure, the traditional distinction between the domestic and international levels of the 'game' of nations. This state of affairs implied an increasing congruence or interpenetration between the domestic and external parts of the political processes. The close interaction between two levels of what both classical paradigms assumed to be more or less exclusive political realms, reinforced the salience of the new interdependence paradigm of regional integration. In short, opposite and indeed competing political impulses are brought together here within a single model of politics. And one that emphasises the importance of process over formal structures. This dualist model was not of course the preserve of any one theorist. It was developed piecemeal in the work of several contributors to the broader debate on the political science of international change.

Putnam made a particularly influential contribution here. His employment of a gaming metaphor for the international process challenged the conventional realist assumption that domestic politics was, by and large, insulated from international politics and vice versa. Putnam evaluated the political process in a way that was particularly suitable as model for European integration. The implications of his account of politics as a contingent process involving strategic calculus is refreshing, even if we have to make some allowance for the rather narrow utilitarian and overly rationalist precepts on which most gaming theory is based. Politics is, after all, a strategic business. Even ideologues engage in quite mundane calculations. It was Oliver Cromwell after all, who advised his troops to trust in God but also to keep their powder dry! We are perhaps closer to the truth about international behaviour with such straightforward, parsimonious but above all testable models of political behaviour, than we are with the grand designs of the macro theories and metanarratives discussed above.

Putnam and those other commentators who have taken their pedagogic cue from the middle range, remind us of some fundamental and common sense truths about the political process. In the search for understanding and explanation the straightforward is often more appropriate than the arcane or over elaborate. And why complicate matters unnecessarily? Yet theorists often pursue 'truth' through obfuscation, as if there is a hidden mystique in the world that speaks of higher insight. And they tend to do so by building elaborate concepts on flimsy evidence. Regional integration theory has suffered as much from this temptation as any other branch of the social sciences. International change in Europe – or anywhere else for that matter – is not driven by some deep metaphysic or hidden force. The higher the theoretical edifices raised on these assumptions, the more fragile these structures have been found in the face of remorseless changes in circumstances that have proved them wrong. This rubric applies as much to the study of

European integration as to anything else. None of the classical paradigms have survived as plausible accounts of what is actually underway in the European project.

The underlying truth behind the process of change that is European integration is altogether more straightforward, though no less easy to conceptualise for that. All politics is based on the normal human instinct to survive and prosper. This basic reflex takes many different forms, depending on 'local' exigencies, temporal contingencies, available resources, leadership skills and so forth. The 'game' that decides these outcomes – and it is a 'game' only in the serious sense that all human relationships involve strategic calculations – is a multifarious one; it brings into play a variety of motives – from greed to idealism – and creates in the process immensely complicated patterns of behaviour. Whether the dynamics of the game, let alone its outcomes, are predictable is disputable. But social science starts – *has* to start – from the assumption that a kind of intellectual order can be imposed on apparent disorder. Otherwise we must abandon our intellectual game as a futile exercise, and accept that a kind of chaos reigns – an unacceptable defeatism for any half rational individual.

Putnam, and those theorists who followed his lead, accept the intellectual challenge to uncover the non specific dynamics that provide politics with its momentum. We can certainly argue about whether these middle range theorists have done proper justice to the political process. What is clear, however, is that the sort of non metaphysical, even mundane, hypotheses formulated by the syncretists do abide by the first, the essential rule, of the social sciences: not to build theories whose intellectual ambitions outreach their capacity to suggest hypotheses that are testable by the minimal rules of evidence, and by this means, to show how the game of politics actually works, rather than how it 'should' work in a 'perfect' world. We do not inhabit a 'perfect' world. Politics is much less the outcome of mysterious forces than it is of the sort of contingencies Putnam identifies in his gaming metaphor. Putnam's model meets some of these critical requirements. It is straightforward without being by any means simplistic. It adapts a familiar and plausible metaphor to the exigencies of contemporary politics.

This image of politics as seamless – a constant feedback between the domestic and the international 'loops' of the game – challenges head on the pervasive realist assumptions about statehood. At the same time it questions the idea, implicit in federalism and functionalism alike, that international, or at least non national, factors are the primary influences on political outcomes. As Putnam sees it, inter-dependence is closer to the mark; for we 'need to move beyond the mere observation that domestic factors influence international affairs and vice versa, and beyond simple catalogs (sic) of instances of such influences, to seek theories that integrate both spheres, accounting for the areas of entanglement between them'.[20]

Putnam responded to this intellectual challenge by defining the contemporary political process as two distinct but interacting environments. These correspond to the domestic province of national politics; and beyond that, the interactions between nation states in the international sphere in pursuit of their interests. This is a model of politics that encompasses the better insights of the statecentric and supranationalist models. Politics is thus a two level game. The first level or 'loop' of the game is played out at the domestic level. A variety of interest groups and clienteles compete to persuade the governing authorities to defend or prosecute their particular interests. There is nothing radical in this view. You will find similar if dated accounts in Aristotle's *Politics* or Burke's *Reflections* or in any number of the classical texts of politics. But Putnam takes his analysis a clear stage further. This domestic arena is connected – and more than tenuously – to the international realm. For under the pressures imposed on states by the conditions of contemporary global interdependence, domestic requirements necessarily carry the actors who manage the affairs of modern states beyond the confines of the state. Of course, politicians have always 'doubled' as statesmen. The difference today is that political leaders need to engage in their international role in order to carry out their domestic functions. To this extent the boundaries between the domestic and international domain are no longer as inviolable as they used to be. The imperative to satisfy domestic needs and fulfil national agendas simultaneously frequently makes Europe's politicians into statesmen and engages them – on a more or less constant basis in the interstices of the EU's various councils and its COREPER arrangements – in an altogether new level of diplomatic action that Edberg identifies as the fourth, or international, loop of decision making.

The fourth level of government is especially appropriate as a concept for defining the contemporary processes of regional integration. European integration involves an almost permanent pursuit of elaborate bargains and requires the reconciling of competing domestic preferences within what is certainly the most sophisticated regional regime anywhere in the world. As a consequence, an entirely new dimension of governance has evolved – one that deals at a high level of transnational institutionalisation with precisely those problems 'normally associated with domestic politics'. This new level of governance in Putnam's account is:

> A complex network of political–administrative relations across national boundaries, accompanied by a correspondingly complex agenda, and without clearcut hierarchial arrangements [and] implies that we should expect lines of conflict and cooperation to be found across as well as along national boundaries. And, in the process of bargaining and consultation, international organisations, or parts of them, are assumed to play a crucial role, regulating and relating the streams of participants, problems, solutions and choice. ... Altogether, this organisational contact seems decisive for understanding most public policy today. And from this perspective, the distinction between domestic and foreign politics becomes blurred.[21]

This is a relatively straightforward but for all that, an up to date, imaginative and above all, a unique version of the timeless Aristotelian observation about the ubiquitousness of politics. These policy loops under contemporary conditions remain permanently connected. And to the extent that they are, the principal theoretical claim of the realist thesis stands discounted. Putnam took his cue here from Gourevitch who had earlier maintained that 'international relations and domestic politics are therefore so interrelated that they should be analyzed simultaneously, as wholes'.[22] The implications of this hypothesis for European integration is obvious enough. Under the conditions of advanced interdependence, all states are confronted by similar problems and face comparable constraints in their search for answers to them. Solutions to pressing national problems are much less likely to be found 'at home' in the shape of unilateral domestic policy decisions. Rather, these answers are increasingly part of a broader policy environment, one that includes transnational, although by no means exclusively supranational, accommodations. By these connections, rather than by the big intuitive leaps of the grand theories, we come close to a model of the regional process that encompasses elements from both classical paradigms.

The patterns of joint decision making that follow on from this fundamental premise more plausibly fit the facts than either of the orthodox accounts on their own. It is an account of an aspect of the contemporary international process sustained more by common sense, the evidence of what we actually know about international politics, than what we might prefer to be the case on a priori moral grounds. A case of facts over values, is over ought. An account borne out by careful observations rather than one sustained by flights of fancy or vain attempts to contort moral prescriptions to fit the world as it really is. For statesmen do stand at the interstices of both the domestic and global systems and there are countless examples in the most recent politics of the EU to corroborate the view. Why else would John Major or Jacques Chirac for that matter, be so concerned to avoid being seen to make unacceptable 'concessions' at European summits to ideas that reflect other states's interests, and thereby alienate domestic political support?

The process, of course, can be reversed and frequently is. After all, what we might call the 'fourth level mentality' has clearly begun to impinge on the EU's diplomatic networks. EU summits are no longer Gaullist ramps, even for politicians – Mrs Thatcher clearly springs to mind here – who might wish they could act as if the world outside their native shores mattered little and affected them even less. Those halcyon days of splendid isolation have long gone and the interdependence model takes account of and explains some of the political implications of this important fact of life. Statesmen do inhabit two overlapping universes. And to this extent they are the classic gatekeepers of both systems. They are the ferrymen who ply their increasingly awkward trade between two convergent territories. They represent on the one hand, an aggregation of multiple and conflicting domestic interests 'abroad'. As such, they seek to reconcile, as far as possible, and to accommodate the political demands of several domestic constituencies in a coherent bargaining position within those international fora where the management of the international political economy is increasingly located. At the same time, the persistence of an alert and mobilised domestic opinion, and the sheer political costs of alienating it, deter national statesmen from settling, as the supranationalists would prefer to see it, for those collective solutions based on functional need that supposedly reflect an upgraded trans-national interest.

There is, of course, more to the process of transnational bargaining than accommodating a constellation of interests, whether based on mere utility or on an altogether narrower calculus of national interest. Nevertheless, the electoral costs of ignoring or betraying 'local' interests abroad have to be balanced by the equal dangers of diminishing national prestige vis-à-vis allies and partners in those international networks that decide, more and more, the fate of nations. Another consideration in this delicate calculus has to be the negative costs to 'national interests', of resisting a degree of compromise and pursuing domestic preferences 'come what may', rather than engage in suboptimal bargains that deliver a reasonable trade off between the interests of all concerned. This symbiosis of the domestic and foreign policy processes has steadily encroached on the conduct of modern politics, and to this extent it does confront statesmen with a kind of double indemnity. On one side, they need to remind their regime partners of their domestic constraints as a mitigation of resistance to unacceptable compromises. John Major has become as adept at this as any current EU head of government. At the same time, statesmen are required to justify their behaviour in the international domain to a restive and often censorious domestic audience. Again, 'international realities' are often used as an alibi for those compromises entered into 'abroad', alongside a claim that these concessions favour the national self interest. The prime minister's behaviour in the House of Commons after every Euro Summit again illustrates this strategy at work.

The two loops of the 'great game' of politics remain, then, irrevocably connected. Putnam identified in this seamless quality of modern governance, a deep dilemma facing statesmen who seek to maximise their utilities in both parts of the game; for

> across the international table sit [his] foreign counterparts; and at his elbow sit diplomats and other international advisers. ... Around the domestic table behind them sit party and parliamentary figures, spokesperson's for domestic agencies, representatives of key interest groups, and the leaders' own political advisers.[23]

We are not yet, even in this arrangement, inhabitants of the supranational universe of the federalist or neofunctionalist imaginings. But we have travelled some considerable way from the autarchic states and anarchic milieu of Hobbes, Bodin and their latter day disciples. Indeed, Wessels has identified, in this complex interactive framework, an entirely new type of European state, one whose processes, public expectations and goals encourage a sense of integration; a sharing of experiences and even of aspirations between states who also inhabit a common predicament. Again this seamless quality of politics speaks of a level of regional interdependence undreamt of and, to an extent, uncalled for even a generation previously. The key to this new state of affairs lies for Wessels in the structural changes that accompany the new global order. Thus,

As interdependence rises, whether the result of market forces or government policy, the propensity to move to Community activity increases, as common or coordinated actions become more effective. . . . The institutional evolution of the EC is thus connected with the post World War II history of West European states, which is characterized by a combination of participatory mass democracy, capitalistic market economy, and the development of a welfare and service state. . . . In the history of the nation state, we have entered a new phase of a 'cooperative state'. . . . This new European state is not a reborn revision of those European nation-states that died in the two world wars but a qualitatively new entity with some major new attributes.

Wessels identifies the characteristics of this new cooperative polity as 'persistent interdependence'. This condition has both structural and functional consequences for the shape and direction of modern politics. Cooperation leads, if not to common identity, then at least to a degree of empathy as unthinkable among the 'little capes' of prewar Europe as it was in other regions of the world. This gradual sharing of aspirations is a discernible feature of the politics of contemporary Europe. Who would really question today the massive progress made since the mid 1970s towards defining common European goals? The same progress is evident at the institutional level. The Maastricht treaty was certainly less than the Euro enthusiasts expected, but more than the Eurosceptics hoped to see enacted. Domestic and international politics are linked then, by a deepening functional endeavour. And by the unprecedented encroachment of those joint decision making procedures by which the European regime tries to resolve the dilemmas its members share in common. One particular dilemma – the principal concern of the European Community from the outset – prevails over all other concerns. Economic integration continues to occupy the box seat in this cumulative drive for cooperation. Economics is the key to all those other civic aspirations that have always stood between the fragile bloom of democracy and those atavistic and destructive forces that threaten it. As Wessels assesses this situation,

> The dilemma of West European governments is that successful economic performance is a major prerequisite for the stability of these welfare and service states. Governments in power see their electoral fate as being directly linked with the state of their economy and a sufficient performance of state services. To achieve this goal, West European economies have to be open to an international and European division of labour. With economic interpenetration, however, interdependencies increase and the (at least de facto) autonomy of national systems decreases.[24]

This uncomfortable fact is as true as ever it was. And in a political milieu where public expectations seem to increase exponentially, at the same time as material resources and political control of the levers of global forces make satisfying these demands less likely, the fate of the Community as well as the stability of its individual states continues to hang by this critical thread. It is no accident that economics rather than pure politics, and functionalism rather than federalism, have provided the principal cement of the European project. The solution to this critical dilemma, and the key to survival in both games, given that each game remains highly visible to ever critical and electorally volatile audiences under modern social and technological conditions, is to construct a workable compromise. That is, neither to submerge statehood in the sort of fanciful universe of welfare organisations dreamt up by Mitrany, nor to turn away from the practicable arrangements – the halfway house between anarchy and federation recommended by Monnet. The acknowledgement of this state of interdependence allows those who steer the affairs of contemporary societies to find a satisfactory accommodation between the concurrent and heavy demands placed on policy making elites from both levels of the game. To this extent, the present arrangements of European integration do represent a suitable compromise – an unavoidable compromise – between two equally unpalatable and increasingly unrealisable extremes. The world – or the Europe – prescribed in either the classical supranationalist or realist paradigms is no longer on offer. Interdependence, and all that this entails for a two level game is, however, realisable. It is where we are now. In fact, there is no other international strategy available to modern states, especially those of modest resources such as the EU members and prospective members, that maximises their options quite as effectively.

The rationale of this particular two level game, if the players are to avoid incurring serious costs at either of its 'tables', is to strike a balance, to negotiate a trade off, between the competing interests all states confront in the actual game of politics. This is of course much easier to prescribe than it is to carry off. The rational choice imagery of the deductive metaphors rather glibly employed in academic game theory bears little resemblance to the hard choices and the flux of 'real politics'. All sorts of contingent factors – luck, happenstance, the fortuitous as well as the avoidable – play their part in determining actual outcomes here. To this extent, political outcomes are determined much more by the roulette wheel of Hoffmann's colourful metaphor,[25] than they are by the automatist metaphysics predicated in the positivist theories of the political process. Moreover, strategic skill also plays its part in this equation. The history of Europe has taught us never to discount the impact of political leadership in determining events, whether in a positive or negative direction. Some statesmen play their respective hands with consummate skill; others with much less diplomatic aplomb or minimal political cunning. Carole Webb has linked the problems of devising effective strategy inherent in modern interdependence, in a way that questions the overly utilitarian notion of statehood preferred by the realists. It is not a difficult feat of the imagination to call to mind her altogether credible image of contemporary European statesmen as those 'far from . . . efficient and effective gatekeepers' who uneasily straddle the fluid threshold between their domestic milieu and the world beyond; nor to concur with her claim that 'national governments more closely resemble the juggler who must apply himself simultaneously to the tasks of keeping several balls in the air and not losing his balance on the rotating platform'.[26]

These are altogether more plausible images of the constraints imposed and options available to Europe's statesmen than anything on offer from the classical paradigms reviewed earlier in this essay.

Developments in the EC by the 1980s certainly seemed to fit this new model of the regional process, as one of multiple and interconnected levels of decision making suffused with ambivalence and short on certainties.[27] And the EC was far better placed in terms of its institutional and political resources to resolve these awkward dilemmas than any of the world's other nascent regional regimes. As Bulmer (**Document 34**) argued in his own cautious application of the gaming metaphor to the EC's new institutional dynamics, institutionalised interdependence offered a more apposite account of the emergent Community process than it did of any comparable regional organisation. The accelerated pace and the expansive scope of the EU's joint decision making and pooling of sovereignty – even before the quantum leap of the 1992 project – was represented by a growing and sophisticated body of Community law.[28] This was far from the whole picture however. Integration was by no means the one-way street implied by the supranationalist prospectus. The enhanced quality of unicity was more than matched by the continuation of hard bargaining within and between the Community's institutions, to protect or advance the domestic preferences of the member states.[29] This dualism between national interests and common endeavours was rooted, after the Milan Summit of 1985, in the Single Market project. Project 1992 was not about a federal Europe – at least not for the majority of the participants. It was primarily about the survival of Europe's nation states by ensuring their continuing capacity to compete in a highly competitive world economy. Survival demanded, of course, mutual adjustments, common strategies and even a degree of pooled sovereignty. And even the most sceptical member states bought into the project on these limited terms. The supranationalists, as has been their pragmatic wont since Monnet first conceived his idea of the long game – the patient wait for the 'historic breakthrough' he always believed would arrive – bought into it too, as a sort of speculative investment in political futures. We shall one day see which of these gambles pays off; or whether, as is more likely, both options continue to coexist at the heart of the enterprise. For the time being, this medium or interdependent position seems best suited to fit the facts of European integration as they currently stand. The eventual outcome of the policy developments and institutional changes which followed on from this deepening of the Community project may well be uncertain. Above all, the project does resonate with an abiding sense of competing impulses and mixed motives. Only a fool or a prophet would challenge the present currency of integration as all things to all men. And this balance of opposites is hardly novel. It has provided the mainspring of the European project ever since Monnet first sold his Community idea to more cynical minds, of a merging of the capacity to make war as the surest way of shackling any future German ambitions for European hegemony.

It has become clear from the increasingly sophisticated accounts of the European policy process that appeared throughout the 1980s, that the state of integration theory has finally assimilated these paradoxes that were inherent in the European project from the outset. The style and conduct of Community business continues to suggest a policy process which is neither entirely intergovernmental nor wholly supranational, but is instead a hybrid system that draws its momentum from political impulses identified in both of the preceding paradigms. The significant shifts in decision making procedures represented by the Single European Act and the Treaty of Union negotiated at Maastricht in December 1991 have merely consolidated rather than resolved these paradoxes of European integration.

REGIONAL INTEGRATION AS 'INTERNATIONAL REGIMES'

The emergence of increasingly intricate and formalised interactions between the EC's member states as a way of resolving these dilemmas, encouraged one branch of the theoretical endeavour on regional integration to refine the generic interdependence model into a more focused theory of Europe as an international 'regime'. Keohane and Nye have defined regimes as essentially those 'networks of rules, norms, and procedures that regularise (international) behaviour and control its effects'.[30] International regimes occupy that increasingly important 'second level' of decision making between the domestic and international systems.[31] It seemed natural to some commentators to define the Community process in these terms. The discussion of the EC as a 'regime' has certainly provided some useful insights into the complexities and ambiguities of the integration process. At the same time, the regime concept is less than precise. It is a pretheoretical device and hardly amounts to a theory in its own right. The regime concept is one of those useful analogies which abound in political science, capable of yielding insights but too generalised, notional and descriptive to furnish those deeper insights into the global process which merit the status of a fully fledged theory of international behaviour. As it stands in the literature, the regime concept achieves little on its own account.[32] The concept's usefulness depends on it being operationalised and adapted to fit altogether more rigorous theoretical constructions of the process of regional integration.[33]

Some regime theorists have nevertheless made a useful start here. They have identified in the multiple transaction flows of the international political economy, a kind of cooperative logic at work, which encourages, even if it does not ensure, a mutuality of outlook capable of nurturing empathy and the potential for further transnational integration. As Diehl saw this exponential process, the proximity and complexity of modern issue agendas eventually encourages those regimes with more developed institutional procedures to address the important question of governance, rather than merely confining themselves to contingent matters of policy substance. This inferred incremental 'logic' is familiar to students of the classical European integration paradigms. And, on the available empirical evidence, it cannot easily be discounted. The urgent requirements under contemporary conditions of interdependence, for effective decision making, and the need for consistent rule enforcement to ensure equity and compliance in the world's most advanced intergovernmental arrangements, has deepened and widened the scope of functional integration. More even than that, it has encouraged an important degree of political integration. The EU does tend to lead as Diehl suggests, by degrees, to those 'sets of explicit or implicit principles, norms, rules and decision making procedures around which actors' expectations converge in a given area of international relations, and which may help to coordinate their behaviour'.[34] This process is clearly visible in the politics of European integration, and it has become more apparent therein since the early 1980s.

The regime concept offers, nevertheless, a far from sufficient account of the logic of regional integration. It has attracted as much criticism for its vagueness as it has praise for its perceptive insights into the functional currency of the international process.[35] 'Regimes' is a useful middle range concept, an aid to hypotheses formation and data collection. It is not a substitute for a fully articulated theory.[36] The regime concept has nevertheless been useful in developing our understanding of the dynamics and exposing some of the myths of contemporary international change. Above all, it suggests useful avenues for empirical research, as well as a procedural matrix for collecting empirical evidence about the intricate patterns of international transactions and bargaining relationships that are the essence of the European regional process.[37] Haas himself saw the regime concept as an aid to theorising rather than a substitute for it. He concluded from an exhaustive discussion of the regime concept, that 'the best service to be expected from an ideal-typical discussion of regimes is to make people pause and think'.[38] The regime concept has, then, assisted with the refinement of the interdependence paradigm. The idea of regimes as bridges between old fashioned ideas of national sovereignty and the new transnational milieu created by the exigencies of modern political economy, has helped international theorists to find a middle way between the extreme perspectives reflected in the clash of the old paradigms. The regime concept accommodates the continuing existence of nation states to the multiple patterning of regional and global transactions which now characterises international relations and is taking modern states and their peoples into unchartered waters.[39]

The impact of this idea of multiple transactions beyond the traditional scope of states, has raised some perhaps predictable responses from the adherents of the conventional paradigms. Supranationalists are content to bide their time. In the idea of regimes they see evidence, however tentative or equivocal, of those radical shifts in perception and behaviour that promise to bring about, sooner or later, a very different world order. Realists – or neorealists in their contemporary guise as revisionists – have had rather more difficulty accommodating the idea of interdependence into their theoretical perspective. Not that their acknowledgement of changing patterns of international behaviour amounts to the wholesale abandonment of the statecentric view of the international process. We shall see in the discussion in Chapter 6 that neorealism remains remarkably chipper about the future of their singular account of international politics. Nevertheless, the increasing evidence of regime patterning in contemporary international relations, as the embodiment of rising interdependence at both the regional and global levels, has done as much as any full blown deductive theory out of the supranational stable, to qualify the intellectual ascendance of the realist paradigm.[40]

The regime concept embodies in identifiable structures, the process 'logic' behind contemporary interdependence. At the very least it offers some useful insights into the rationale and the ways and means of transnational cooperation. Regimes provide the institutional location for the international brokering of the two level game discussed above. Applied with caution, and as an aid to theoretical endeavour rather than as a substitute for it, the regime concept does suggest a useful conceptual framework for charting and making sense of the multiplicity of transactional flows between these domestic and international environments. For it is these bargains that increasingly shape the destinies of states and determine the tenor of international politics. The impact of the latest GATT round on the participating states (governments and people) and on international relations per se, illustrates precisely the significance of regime exchange in the current scheme of things.

Some commentators have taken on board the concept's obvious limitations and have begun to offer refinements designed to improve its utility to students of the regional process. Haggard and Simons for instance, warn against glib usage and the tendency of some commentators to treat all regimes as if they operated on an equal footing. Indiscriminate use and generalisation are pitfalls for any concept. Refinement is the key to proper usage and clarification can only come from judicious and above all from comparative application. Too many writers use the regime concept as a kind of conceptual shorthand for the empirical type of regime in which they happen to have invested research time. Clearly some examples of regime interaction exhibit more integrative potential than others. The rigid employment of the regime concept by structuralists focusing only on visible or formal procedures, has tended to encourage the misplaced assumption that all regimes are much the same, as to their degree of empathy, their potential for mutual problem solving and so on. This is certainly not the case. A comparison between the EU and any number of less cohesive or purposive regional regimes – from the Arab League to the OAU – illustrates this point. Haggard and Simmons are right to recommend discernment in employing the concept. Context here is everything. As these revisionists observe, when identifying the potential of any given regime to either instil common habits and empathy, or encourage their very opposite, 'much depends on past history, knowledge and purpose'.[41] In short, some regimes are much better placed to facilitate and sustain patterns of integration than others. The critical determinants here lie in the precise history, and the structural and cultural underpinnings of the regime in question, and in order to determine which regimes are likely to fit this particular bill requires much detailed empirical work.

Regimes, then, merely imply that what exists at face value as a general inclination to cope with the rigours of an interdependent world, may also exhibit potential for going further and for changing an intergovernmental arrangement into something altogether more inclusive. This prospect cannot be taken for granted. It has to be tested against events, in order to elicit the potential for, or constraints on, closer integration. Haggard and Simmons are careful to demarcate levels of regime interaction: that all regimes provide almost by definition, the limited means for 'regularising expectations' and facilitating more effective problem solving than normal diplomatic intercourse.[42] And by the same token, 'most regimes . . . are likely to have at least some minimal administrative apparatus for the purpose of dispute settlements [and] the collection and sharing of information'. Some regimes, however – and the EU does seem to fit this mould better than almost any other regional or global arrangement – are altogether more complex, coherent and exclusive arrangements. They go beyond the minimalist threshold and engage in what Haggard and Simmons call 'complex coordination tasks', which 'require more elaborate, and potentially autonomous organisational structures'. In essence, the constant experience of collaboration, bargaining and transacting within regimes instils what starts out as an intergovernmental and routine diplomatic enterprise with a degree of empathy, and may, in particularly close encounters, install the institutional means for facilitating and patterning these exchanges in altogether more predictable ways. Something of this order of enmeshment – functional, cognitive and institutional – seems to be underway in the EU.

The regime concept encapsulates, then, a dual potential whose precise outcomes cannot be taken for granted. They depend on circumstances and events. On the one hand, the politics of every international regime exhibits the normal impulse of all those states who join them to advance their own national interests. 'Normal' that is, measured against their behaviour and their public's expectations for the foreseeable future. At the same time, there are palpable signs that changes are afoot in the conduct and even in the aspirations for politics at both levels of the game. Without in any sense exaggerating the trend or drawing unwarranted conclusions from it, we must acknowledge from the evidence of contemporary world politics – and certainly from Community practice since 1984 or so – a new cooperative quality in international affairs. This tendency encourages states to engage in transnational bargaining, and collaboration at various and often interconnected levels. Nor did this condition simply happen by chance. It is a considered behavioural response to structural shifts in the global process. Regime formation is, in these terms, a predictable reaction to those patterns of complex interdependence which characterise contemporary international relations.

The regime concept made its appearance in the literature on European integration during the period of theoretical revisionism which overtook the fixed and doctrinaire notions of the classical paradigms during the late 1970s. Its application to the European process is patently obvious to anyone outside the ideological laager of unreconstructed realism. Puchala, for instance, used the regime concept to reflect what he took to be the rising ambiguities of the European integration process under the contemporary conditions of intense global change. He defined the Community in these terms as a 'concordance system' which 'does in fact 'go beyond the nation state' both organisationally and operationally; [although] it none the less does not go very far beyond'.[43] The image here was of the Community as a regime propelled by a unique momentum, yet also one constrained by the differential and competing expectations of its member states. As such, it was somehow suspended *in partibus*, between the classical paradigms – the conflicting statecentric and supranational impulses – on both sides of the debate. This challenge was by no means the cause of academic defeatism in either camp. The most negative outcome here was merely to encourage the advocates of the classical paradigms to fight a rearguard in defence of their respective dependent variable – whether of sovereignty or supranationalism. A more positive response was to embrace interdependence itself as the dependent variable, and to take up the intellectual challenge of searching for more cogent theoretical accounts of a process that had yet to be explained, and in which the impulse to protect domestic or local interests had to be properly accommodated to the steady impetus towards joint endeavours at the transnational or Community level.

THE EUROPEAN COMMUNITY AS A REGIME

The interdependence thesis and the regime concept it gave rise to made a distinctive contribution to this revisionist activity. Interdependence theorists are disposed to regard international relations as a process driven by conflicting impulses. The facts of socio-economic convergence encouraged by policy harmonisation, and a geopolitical proximity that underlines, however inchoate, a sense of a shared fate, do tend to impel those elites who manage the affairs of regional states to adopt a regime strategy. This is driven more by pragmatic considerations than it is by ideological preferences. The primary objective here is not integration for its own sake, as the supranationalists tend to define the push for change, but for making those practical arrangements that maximise the potential for cooperation and minimise those persistent conflicts of interest which distract states from the search for mutual accommodations between their national preferences. This strategy involves procedural arrangements as well as a tendency to negotiate policy outcomes which foster and reinforce this sense of common interests. This strategy too, tends to be pragmatically rather than idealistically driven. Certainly, no international enterprise on this scale can survive without some measure of empathy outside the strictly utilitarian calculus of policy bargaining. At the same time, the regime participants, aware of historical legacies that remind them and their electorates of less civil times, and constrained by this cultural residue of nationalism and by the popular expectations it fosters – played out as these are at the domestic level – continue to operate as discrete states whose distinctive national interests assume priority in any transactions at the second or international level of the political game. The EU certainly fits this model of a regime caught between the past and the present needs of its members.

The EU is for all that, undoubtedly a highly developed regime, one whose sophisticated institutional structures and activities are capable of generating a considerable degree of empathy among its membership. In these circumstances, history is a mixed blessing. Europe's states cannot ignore their different pasts, those cultural legacies that have made them what they are today. These 'folk memories' undoubtedly stand in the way of the generic European identity necessary as the cognitive cement of a fully federal Union. But history in Europe is a shared experience too, as well as a spur to narrow atavism. The EU has worked as a regime precisely because its members share more positive attributes than bad memories. They are all committed without exception to the values of liberal democracy and the virtues of the free market economy. Likewise, they share a strong and growing sense of common rather than identical purpose, vis-à-vis their own region and the wider world. These generic principles are important; they provide the cultural give for much of what has occurred in the Community since the last great European war. But even positive cultural perceptions can only carry cordiality and good intentions so far. The EU states have volatile populations who now expect more from governance and from life itself than millennia of their ancestors ever did. Alongside the shared experiences – not least the self inflicted horrors that stemmed from their own xenophobia – the Community harbours within its political arrangements the sort of deep-rooted ambivalence that afflicts even the most entrenched and purposeful international regimes. The EU's principal actors – its member states – continue to inhabit, alongside their shared experiences, different political universes. The steady momentum towards closer integration recently witnessed, as a safer anchorage in the maelstrom of a rapidly changing and still unpredictable world order, is countered by equivalent forces in the other direction. Not least the equally insistent pull on the political imagination of its principal statesmen, of pressures which originate not only in the member states' domestic environments, but also from the variable impact on each member state of those events which unfold remorselessly in the regional and global environments.

Not every EU state, for instance, is affected by currency instabilities, ecological threats, immigration flows or perceptions of security crises to the same extent. It has become a commonplace assumption that the EU regime works precisely because its members share identical problems or shoulder the same burdens as a result of international change. In a key passage in a recent working paper contributed by Carlos Westendorp, the Spanish chairman of the EU Reflection Group charged with preparing the agenda for the 1996 IGC, he notes that

> the Group has come to the conclusion that the coming reform must give priority to the real problems, ie those which preoccupy Europeans most. A majority of personal representatives include employment, internal security and environmental degradation among the problems to be tackled as a matter of immediate urgency.

Westendorp expands on this idea of integration and recommends that the EU must 'take all the necessary steps to become a world force in international relations, so that it can promote its values, defend its interests, and help shape a new world order'.[44]

These are, on the one hand, commendable principles. But they reflect, too, a glibness that typifies much diplomatic and even some academic 'Eurospeak'. How, we might reasonably enquire, are these noble aspirations to be realised in a Community where the present continues to be shaped by the past, and where any of the generalised values every member state would subscribe to in principle reflects their own distinctive domestic agendas? This fact certainly does not preclude cooperation, or even an eventual consensus on some at least of the critical issues that will face the Union into the next century – not least, the construction of full monetary Union and a genuinely common regional Defence Identity. But identifying the sheer scale of the problem and the size of the hurdles to be surmounted if such positive integration is to occur is no substitute for politics. Enduring conflicts of interest alongside a putative common endeavour are always likely to make bargaining in the Community regime a protracted and frequently a suboptimal business. For these continuing and occasionally deep differences do tend to pull the EU's policy makers in various directions over different issues. The political permutations here are not infinite, but the ensuing coalitions of interest conjured by this multiplicity of interests do shift with circumstances, and in ways that, as recent events post-Maastricht have indicated, can easily throw the Union off track, even if the members are too well aware of what is at stake to wish to see the project derailed altogether. This, in turn, ensures that a political dissensus deeper than the unity envisaged in the federalist idea of Europe, or in the administrative consensus dreamt of by the neofunctionalist technocrats, continues to prevail at the heart of the EU's affairs. To this extent, the EU regime is a magnetic field with two poles in which both centrifugal and centripetal forces operate simultaneously.

This persistent ambivalence over both the pace and direction of the European project has conditioned the type of integration that has ensued, rather than prevented it altogether. The Community regime from the outset has been a more cohesive and focused entity than it has been merely an intergovernmental arena. The momentum for deepening this project, encouraged by the onset of the Single European Market proposal, has extended both the structural and operational aspects of this unique regime. Even the erstwhile realist Stanley Hoffmann felt obliged to acknowledge the significance and scope of this unusually sophisticated international regime, well before the momentous changes that followed on from the 1985 White Paper and the Single European Act caused him to review his original account of the EC project. As early as 1982, and even as the Community was still gripped by its latest protracted bout of Eurosclerosis, Hoffmann was constrained to tone down his earlier scepticism about the prospects for political integration among the EC states, and to acknowledge freely their unique potential for policy cooperation. The influence of the interdependence model in general and the regime concept in particular on his academic judgement, was evident from his particular description of the Community as 'a set of norms of behaviour and of rules and policies, covering a broad range of issues [and] dealing with procedures and with substance and facilitating agreements among members'.[45]

Hoffmann was well aware, of course, that this unusual compound of cooperation and compromise still fell a long way short of supranationalism. The Community continued to combine, then, the conventional impulses of states, alongside the rising momentum for closer cooperation imposed by contemporary circumstances. To that extent, the Community regime was the apotheosis of structural developments in the very fabric of the modern international system. Hoffmann spoke for a legion of revisionist commentators who were beginning to break ranks with the unreconstructed realist doctrine, but without going over to the supranationalists, when he observed that:

> The best way of analysing the EEC is not in the traditional terms of integration theory; which assumes that the members are engaged in the formation of a new, supranational political entity superseding the old nations – an outcome that was originally possible but has become increasingly more unlikely – and that there is a zero sum game between the nation state on the one hand, the EEC on the other – a very false notion. It is to look at the EEC as an international regime . . . From the viewpoint of the participants, such a regime provides both restraints and opportunities, it limits the state's freedom of unilateral action . . . and it imposes financial loads . . . but it gets others to share one's burdens . . . or to accept restraints in one's favour . . . (for instance) . . . it provides the participants with external support, hence the crucial importance of coalition building, issue by issue, year by year.[46]

Given the rapidly changing conditions of the global political economy, the regime concept appeared to capture precisely the duality of purpose which characterises the current policy imperatives of the EU's member states. Their urgent search for solutions to particular national interests, as well as the need to define mutual interests and common purposes as a response to current geopolitical conditions is, after all, what drove them together as a regional regime in the first place. And it is certainly what keeps them together. Not every member state gets what it wants from every regime bargain that ensues, but the EU does have the capacity for fulfilling its members' interests on many things, at least some of the time. Enough certainly to make the exit option unthinkable for all of its members. Since the Community was launched, its membership has risen steadily and is likely to do so again in the near future. A queue of candidate states waits patiently in line to embrace the commitments implied by accession to full membership. Only Greenland has left the Community and then under unique circumstances. This may not be the cumulative drive for a United States of Europe prefigured by the supranationlists; but it is a remarkable testament to the efficacy and pulling power of the world's most elaborate international regime. The essential purpose of this project, as Hoffmann defines it, has not been to replace the nation state as the building block of international society but, rather, to consolidate it; to better equip it to face these current global exigencies. For as Hoffmann saw this process, the impulse to regional integration was merely a contemporary response by the states concerned to address both familiar and altogether new dilemmas. Thus,

> Analyzing the EEC as an international regime allows one also to see better what, to integrationists, is a paradox or a contradiction: such regimes, in exchange for curtailing the state's capacity for unilateral action, serve to preserve the nation state as the basic unit in world affairs – and actually help governments perform their domestic tasks. Although the traditional model of sovereignty is clearly obsolete, the nation state today survives even though many apparently sovereign decisions are seriously constrained or made ineffective by the decisions of others as well as by economic trends uncontrolled by anyone. International regimes help the nation state survive, by providing a modicum of predictability and a variety of rewards. . . . Far from leading to a supranational European nation state (the EEC regime) has put pressure on the members to modernise their economies. . . . The EEC has also served as a playing field for 'inter-issue bargaining', allowing for complex deals in which concessions in one realm were offset by gains in another. In all these ways, and despite its internal flaws, the EEC regime has strengthened the member states' capacity to act at home and abroad.[47]

Other commentators drew somewhat less cautious conclusions from these same events. The outcome, either way, was a clear shift of theoretical emphasis away from paradigms predicated on the narrow realist account of the processes of international changes. This, in turn, underlined a trend in the theoretical literature that identified a more syncretic or mixed dynamic as the principal momentum at work in the regional process.

Developments within the EC throughout the 1980s certainly confirmed the impression that this theoretical ferment was sustaining the development of an altogether more accurate account of the integration process. The sense of paradigmic shift was palpable here with the emergence of a model that better explained this juxtaposition of significant structural changes with persistent national interests, far more plausibly than any of the existing paradigms. The adaptation of the regime concept – as an extension of the confederalist thesis discussed in Chapter 4, and as a bridge to even bolder versions of the new revisionism – helped to facilitate the steady shift in theoretical momentum that was underway from the late 1970s. The contemporary discussion by William Wallace (**Document 35**) illustrates how much those clear-sighted commentators in touch with actual events, rather than seduced by appealing illusions, were coming round to the view that the Community was the far from straightforward or indeed static arrangement captured in the prescriptive aspic of the classical paradigms. In similar revisionist fashion other commentators contributed to the refinement of this somewhat basic regime concept, in order to accommodate better the EC's novel procedural arrangements and the special characteristics of its institutional procedures, which distinguish it from other, less well structured, cohesive or integrated regimes. The rapidity with which the Single Market project unfolded, and particularly the important institutional changes and political decisions which accompanied the project throughout the 1980s, reinforced this sense of uniqueness in Community affairs. The 1992 project gave a fillip and injected new intellectual energy into the search for appropriate models that better explained the process underway in the new Europe.

COOPERATIVE FEDERALISM

Regime theory is a branch of generic international relations theory. It identifies the broad characteristics of transnationalism across all manner of policy bargains, and at several political levels simultaneously. By and large, its exponents have been concerned to uncover the logistics of the global process rather than to explain its specific policy styles. Some commentators have taken this analysis further and focused attention on the coexistence of different policy styles as the principal defining characteristic of regional regimes. 'Cooperative federalism' is one concept that has emerged from this endeavour. Pentland gave a passing mention to co-operative federalism in his early and stimulating account of European integration. He briefly discussed the concept in the context of national federal arrangements such as the one operating in Canada, where linguistic differences and a continuing ethnic tension between the Quebecois and Anglo-Canadians called for novel political solutions to reflect diversity within an overarching common purpose. Pentland might have been nearer to the heart of the perennial problem of European integration than he imagined at the time. He saw the solution to this problem of balancing distinctive interests and managing cultural or linguistic diversity alongside a real commonality of purpose, not in outright federalism or in unitary government, but rather by engineering a political hybrid that responded to unique local needs and sensibilities. Thus,

> it might therefore be more useful to recognise that a variety of [political] relationships can exist simultaneously between the units of a federal state. There can be direct confrontation between some states and the central government over jurisdiction or taxation; there can be uncoordinated, duplicated activities by several governments; there can be cooperation.[48]

The essence of this 'cooperative federalist' model remains unchanged, in spite of subsequent refinements by theorists who have more recently revisited the idea. It remains a mixed system; a cohabitation within the rules, institutions and policy framework of a single regime, of entirely different policy styles and decision making philosophies. This state of affairs – of multiple aspirations, both competing and cooperative – was and remains the way of things in the EU. Pentland of course was not to know this. He undertook his researches before the Community had fully got into its stride as a confederal regime. Even so, his remarkably per-ceptive account of EC affairs up to the early 1970s, when intergovernmentalism was in the theoretical ascendance, has more than a hint of what was to come, on both the political plane and in the academic discourse on these events. Pentland reached a tentative conclusion even then; that while the international system does, in part, evolve 'according to its own dynamics' and that these 'dynamics' impinge on and influence the behaviour of the states, 'much of the integrative process cannot be explained except at the level of the nation-state as actor'. At the same time, an altogether unique process is underway here. For 'this treatment of the state as a major actor in integration diverges considerably from the classic realist picture'. What Pentland sees, in place of the oversimplistic federalist or realist prescriptions is 'the notion of the 'penetrated state' and the suggestion of a distinctive 'community policy' issue area which blends characteristics of the foreign and domestic issue areas'.[49] Other writers subsequently, did pay closer heed to what in Pentland is little more than a tantalising footnote, but one that pointed the way forward.

Cooperative federalism has clear implications for integration theory under present circumstances. It implies that integration is a process with its own intrinsic logic; that it is by no means an interim stage or halfway house between the minimal expressions of integration and its maximalist or fully fledged outcome, as suggested by the supranational paradigm's assumption of a cumulative momentum building towards a certain federal or functionalist end state. Neither does it suggest that integration amounts to intergovernmentalism and little else, as the new realists tend to suggest. 'Cooperative federalism' avoids these narrowly exclusive definitions. It defines the regional process as primarily one of the coexistence, as Pentland's commentary reflected on it, within a hybrid policy system of common procedures and institutions, of two entirely distinct policy styles. The concept reflects very closely those abiding tensions that continue to inhabit the contemporary European project. It also expresses the mixed policy dynamics underway in a regional process where is continuing animus over the direction of international change, rather than any certainty over its eventual outcome. Above all, this concept captures the intrinsic ambiguities of the two level political game under conditions of interdependence, which is the essence of the contemporary European regime.[50]

The mix of policy styles that characterises the EU system, and the particular and very real dilemmas faced by its member states from the frequent interaction in its councils and inter-institutional exchanges of the domestic and regime 'loops', are among the unique features of the Community's procedural arrangements. The unprecedented range and intensity of the EU's policy transactions, as between the functional and transnational interests which operate at every level of the process, and the governments and their official agencies caught squarely in the two level game, has encouraged the coexistence of two entirely different styles of Community decision making. To this extent, the EU is clearly a regime which faces in two directions at once. There is, on the one hand, a suboptimal approach to decisions that is quite consistent with the intergovernmentalist or confederalist notion of the European regime discussed in Chapter 4. This involves the splitting of national differences on the basis of negotiated and often cumbersome package deals. The resultant common denominators are much less than the rational policy outcomes anticipated in the supranational paradigm. There is no sense here of the cement of any putative common interest holding the Community together or guiding its policy makers towards a broadly acceptable consensus. How could there be in an arrangement predicated in no small measure on more efficient ways of defending or prosecuting domestic interests? Suboptimality in this sense is an entirely unpredictable matter. It involves the apportionment of costs and benefits as equitably as possible between the member states, but above all in line with the current balance of political power, and in order to keep the Community show on the road, rather than in the vain pursuit of a commonly acceptable and fully integrative agenda.

If this was the whole story, the EU would be little more than a sophisticated intergovernmental organisation. In fact, this suboptimal mode of decision making is only part of the overall picture. Interdependence masks national interests but as we have seen it also modulates and, on occasions, tames them. The suboptimal instinct which is one outcome of the need to balance out or reconcile both sides of the political game, coexists with a complementary approach to policy making in the EU regime that reflects an entirely opposite impetus. The emergence of a genuine, if by no means ascendant supranational element – itself the direct outcome of interdependence – has seen the consolidation in the EC's institutional arrangements of a cooperative decisional approach to settling policy differences. This policy style is practised tentatively, is far from extensive in its use, and causes member states quite genuine anxieties, especially the prospect of extending its practice to the more sensitive domain of high politics – particularly to foreign, security and fiscal policy. This policy style is characterised by the technique of qualified majority voting in the Council of Ministers. Thus is the Community's identity crisis – the schizophrenia of two ways of doing business – incorporated into the very fabric of its body politic. The situation is complicated precisely because both of these policy styles cohabit within the Community's political fabric. There is undoubtedly a persistent tension here between two entirely different policy styles, coexisting within the same organisational skin, yet representing two competing philosophies of integration.[51]

This tension, rather than any inexorable drive towards federalism, or the persistence of statehood, provides the momentum at the heart of the project. For Europe's states are indeed caught in two minds about the meaning of integration. The suboptimal policy style is essentially intergovernmentalist, both in orientation and in practice, whereas the joint policy style corresponds closely with the supra-nationalist ethos. The emphasis here is on identifying mutual problems, defining a common perspective, and with prosecuting the best, the most rational use of the Community's own budgetary and other resources, whether these are apportioned horizontally across national frontiers, or vertically between specific functional sectors or issue areas. This cooperative federalist approach characterises the sort of multiple issue linkages which figure in the maximalist or supranational prospectus. Together this combination of policy styles as cooperative federalism, demarcates this most sophisticated of international regimes from less cogent attempts to square the circle of national independence with an ever more interdependent global superstructure.

The notion of cooperative federalism captures the very essence in the EU of this coexistence of competing policy impulses and alternative decision making styles. To this extent, it reflects the underlying paradox of contemporary inter-dependence. On the one hand, is the fact that modern states may well retain their special status as the primary actors of the international process, while at the same time, these states also remain permeable to those multiple transnational influences which threaten to expose their lack of clout, independent resources or diplomatic initiative; unless they embrace regime solutions that also, in other ways, compromise their sovereignty. The key to identifying and explaining the dynamics of European regional integration lies precisely in gauging the momentum, direction and reach of these global political and economic changes on national prerogatives. Or indeed, the obverse of this: the consequences of closer integration for the other level of the games, for refashioning the way politics is conducted within the national state itself.

The concept of cooperative federalism is, then, another useful addition to the theoretical armoury of those concerned to uncover the critical dynamics of modern European politics. It helps to pinpoint the creative tension that underlies modern regionalism, and to do so with a greater precision than is available from the generalised regime or gaming concepts reviewed above. Indeed, cooperative federalism was developed by those who picked up on Pentland's useful hint, specifically as an aid to explaining the unique dilemmas underway in European integration. Bulmer and Wessels, for instance, utilised this concept to explain the critical distinction between the pooling of sovereignty which characterises the Community's decisional process, and the fusion of sovereignty associated with full or complete statehood. The distinction here between confederal or regime arrangements and full blown federalism remains an appropriate one. Scharpf particularly has focused on the significance of these important demarcations of de jure authority and de facto competences, in order to illustrate the uniquely hybrid quality of the EU's political and policy processes.[52]

The cooperative federalism model was adapted from the consideration of the consequences for governance of the shared competences of the Swiss and West German models of federalism. Unlike the American experience of federalism, these European variants seemed to offer a more promising analysis of the prospects for transnational federalism in a multicultural, multilingual and multi-ethnic European context.[53] Unlike much previous thinking on international federalism, the model was not prescriptive. It was concerned above all with uncovering the necessary and sufficient conditions for effective transnational cooperation. In par-ticular, the model offered some penetrating insights, both into the complexities of the Community's decision making system, and into the abiding ambivalence of the regional integration process. American federalism had been constructed around the classical doctrine of a separation of powers, with clearly demarcated state and federal jurisdictions. These European variants of federalism, however, consisted of overlapping jurisdictions, or what Scharpf calls '*Politikverflechtung*'. According to this arrangement, neither the centre nor the constituent parts of this type of federal system are empowered to act on their own, or without full cognisance of the 'other' level of government. In these joint arrangements, policy outcomes are determined by the interactions of these two interdependent jurisdictions. The policy decisions that result from these exchanges are not only mixed, in as much as they must reconcile conflicting expectations about goals, they are also predisposed to decision traps and policy pathologies. In other words, shared competencies lead to stand offs, impasse and 'decision traps'; or, at best, to suboptimal decisions that split differences between entrenched national positions, rather than rationally solving the problems they purport to address **(Document 36)**.

Scharpf adapted this model to account for the special procedures and problems of the EU's mixed decisional system. The founding treaties had installed a decision making system which combined supranational and intergovernmental elements; an uneasy coexistence that has by no means been resolved by subsequent constitutional changes. On the contrary, later reforms, and most especially those changes implemented by the Single Act and the Maastricht Treaty, have only consolidated this unique and uneasy blend, rather than resolving it in one direction or another. The reference in the European Treaty of Union to three distinct pillars under a single institutional 'roof' captures precisely this composite quality.[54] The persistent debate since the less than overwhelming ratification of the new treaty, about the balance of powers, the prospect of revisions in 1996–7 and the form these might take, provides further evidence of the continuing unease about the meaning of the EU's version of '*Politikverflechtung*'. The member states remain willing to consider joint policy approaches, and to accept a degree of pooled sovereignty, at least in those policy areas which do not compromise their fundamental national interests or intrude unduly on their sovereignty. Most of them do so because they have no realistic alternative in today's world. These same states do, however, continue to resist encroachments on their national prerogatives in those critical policy areas by which they measure their independent statehood; for instance, in the areas of monetary, fiscal, foreign or security policy. Others, certainly, accept these limits on their pursuit of national preferences because they genuinely do see this as a testament of their 'Europeanness'; and a few accept them because pooling sovereignty, however limited the initial impact, is seen as a real step towards a fully fledged European Federation.

The Community continues to combine, then, within its policy framework, both cooperative and suboptimal procedures. The coexistence of conflict and consensus, flux and equilibrium, within this unique policy system provides the key to understanding the variable, hybrid and indeterminate quality of the European integration project. Scharpf's particular model of the state of European integration, measured by its policy making arrangements, is both plausible and realistic.

It works because it avoids the narrow determinism of the classical paradigms and acknowledges the hybrid nature of the European process. Its claim to explanatory credibility is precisely that it balances those supranational/maximalist and inter-governmental/minimalist aspects of integration which continue to inhabit the European project, and provide it with its principal momentum.

The Single Market project is the most recent example of the endemic conflict between these different aspirations for European integration. At one level, the 1992 programme was an attempt to effect extensive vertical and horizontal linkages across an impressive range of economic and related policy sectors.[55] This led, in turn, to important political changes and rekindled speculation, even in the most sober circles, about the prospects for a federal state in Europe.[56] Without in any way wishing to diminish the significance of these achievements, this latest stage of European integration must be put in its proper perspective. The 1992 project was driven, primarily, by the imperatives of global interdependence discussed above. This was not the annus mirabilis, the democratic compact between Europe's governments and governed of the federalist prospectus; nor for that matter, the steady technocratic erosion of governmental legitimacy propounded by the neofunctionalists. Neither could it be seen merely as a clever piece of interstate diplomacy writ large: '1992 and all that' was something more than the further refinement of an intergovernmental confederation; and something less than a federalist revival. Again, the European project was relaunched as a practical exercise in utilitarianism, as it had been in 1950 and 1955 and, for that matter, during the early 1970s. Closer integration was projected as a way of dealing with European welfare needs, defined in their broadest terms. As on these previous occasions too, the project seemed modest in outline, but had more far reaching implications once it was embarked upon. It began in response to a general concern that the Common Market's potential for erecting a liberal free trade regime had failed, for various reasons, to materialise.[57] This concern was shared by intergovernmentalists and supranationalists alike, both among the member states and in the EC's institutions. While they all agreed on the need to pursue this specific goal, the sudden and largely unexpected relaunch of the integrative project, after a long period of torpor, sparked off all sorts of sub plots and alternative agendas. The SEM, as with the ECSC and the Common Market that preceded it, soon became an arena for testing competing integration prospectuses.

The Single Market project as it unfolded in the mid 1980s lacked any clear certainty of purpose about its ultimate destination. The 1992 programme seemed to confirm, to all sides of the debate about the idea of Europe, their own particular aspirations for the future outcome of integration. Neither the supra-nationalists nor the intergovernmentalists enjoyed a monopoly of influence over the process, or for that matter of wisdom about the current state of, or prospects for, regional integration. The intergovernmentalist theorists on one side of the debate were reassured that the renewed vigour with which the removal of trade barriers was being pursued, could be reconciled easily with their preference for the survival of the European nation state. The supranationalists, on the other hand, remained just as convinced that the economic rationale behind this latest bout of integration would eventually reach its critical mass and 'spillover' into altogether deeper forms of political integration.

In fact, as this project unfolded, it again revealed the persistent ambiguities of the integration process. Indeed, the Single Market project was sustained by these very ambiguities. The coexistence of a suboptimal decisional style alongside an expanded but still modest degree of joint policy making, and of national interests balanced against an upgraded regional interest, and all within the same sophisticated confederal regime, gave the 1992 programme its distinctive momentum. This coexistence of competing notions of integration and conflictual decision making styles, perpetuated the longstanding animus between very different expectations of integration at the centre of the European project. The consequences of this were reflected in the catalogue of failures, delays, compromises and indeed, in the successes of the Community's policy process. The consequences of the decision traps that threatened to overload or stall the 1992 programme, not least, memories of long cycles of Euroschlerosis that cost the Community dear in the pursuit of global competitiveness throughout the 1960s and 1970s were, after all, the best incentive to participants to strike the bargains and make the sort of deals that enabled the Community to move forward and quickly, compared to previous experiences, in both types of policy province.

In short, '1992' meant different things to the various actors who participated in its elaborate policy programme. Moreover, the working consensus that ensued was only effective because those states who took part in it eschewed any attempt to go beyond the usual diplomatic practice of bargaining on the basis of sustainable deals and common denominators. Those participants with supranationalist inclinations – especially the Commission – undoubtedly harboured altogether more far reaching aspirations, but Delors was a master tactician who was well versed in the political arts. The Delors Commission was blessed with a fair economic wind before recession set in. Nor was it yet blown off course by what Delors himself called 'the acceleration of history', that led to the implosion of communism symbolised by the memorable November night in 1989 when the Berlin wall was breached. These subsequent events have raised even more searching questions for the EU to address and the outcome of its deliberations on Monetary Union and on a new security architecture to enable Europe to police its own heartland as the Pax Americana falls into abeyance, will offer the strongest tests yet of these competing visions of European integration.

These momentous matters were not the immediate concern of the 1992 project. The Community took it upon itself to address its competitiveness; a limited prospectus, certainly, but one with wider implications than were immediately apparent to those – not least Mrs Thatcher – who signed up to the Commission's project. The key to success in liberalising the European marketplace and stimulating economic growth as a response to global pressures, lay in a hitherto low key legal precedent – the 1979 Cassis de Dijon ruling of the European Court. This ruling maintained, unremarkably at the time, that national regulations per se were insufficient grounds for prohibiting imports from another member state. The long term implications of this judgement were more far reaching. By ensconcing mutual recognition of product standards as the basis of free trade, this ruling offered the Community's bargain brokers a neat way of avoiding the usual delays of common policy making, where costs to national interests were seen as a consequence of commercial concessions.[58] Deregulation thereby replaced the altogether more politically delicate method of harmonising existing national regulations, as the solution to the delays and impasse that had previously overshadowed attempts at removing the obstacles to genuine economic integration.[59]

The EC's member states set out, on the basis of this judicious compromise, to legislate an extensive programme of some 300 separate policy enactments. As this elaborate process gradually unfolded, it became clear that the Commission's preferred route of a cooperative or joint decisional approach, shared with varying degrees of enthusiasm by the European Parliament and at least some of the member states, seemed to promise, more by default than intent, a new era of supranationalism. An unprecedented degree of issue linkage in the four broad policy areas at the centre of this enterprise; the prospect for 'spillover' from functional sectors of 'low' or minimal political significance, into matters of 'high' politics per se; a revival of the prospect of federalism itself in the small print of the institutional changes enshrined in the SEA; the proposals of various IGCs on constitutional and policy reform, culminating in the terms of the Treaty of European Union itself, all suggested a much increased momentum towards political integration. By the late 1980s there was a distinct impression that the Community had indeed entered altogether new political territory. And that, as such, it had strayed across the rubicon of political integration, and was embarked on an entirely new phase in its development towards 'ever closer Union'.

This perception became much less convincing as the optimism of the mid 1980s gave way to the altogether more sober reflections of the early 1990s. The integration process does seem, at its present juncture, to be as delicately poised between its minimalist and maximalist extremes as ever it was. The coexistence of two divergent policy making strategies within the European Union's political system continues to support the idea of regional integration as a two level game, played by dissimilar rules, in front of different audiences and in pursuit of conflicting goals. A recent account of the current state of play by a group of leading commentators dwells on the uncertainty that still hangs over the outcomes here. The integration debate remains as open and is as dogged by differential aspirations as ever it was. In short, there remains

a fundamental argument about the eventual nature of the post-1992 Community which is unlikely to be resolved by the current (i.e. 1990–91) IGCs. It will probably not be until 1996 at the earliest, and possibly not until the close of the end of the century before we have a clear idea of how the states of Europe intend to organise their cooperation and manage their interdependence as they enter the next millennium.[60]

In the circumstances this seems an entirely reasonable conclusion.

COOPERATIVE FEDERALISM AND EUROPEAN INTEGRATION

Scharpf's discussion of these competing yet coexisting policy models residing at the core of the Community system, offers a useful template against which to chart its actual operations. The particular appeal of this model is its ready acknowledgement of the abiding paradoxes of the European project. The concept of cooperative federalism is relevant precisely because it avoids the narrow exclusivism of the two classical paradigms. Moreover, it can be accommodated to those other equally useful concepts discussed above, which also reflect the hybrid quality of the contemporary European process, whether the cumulative logic of structural interdependence, which connects national and regional events to global circumstances, or the equally instructive concept of the international regime. The political dynamics of each of these partial but informative glimpses into the mechanics of the contemporary international process does reveal something of the continuing interaction between domestic and transnational politics in the shape of a two level game. Scharpf is surely right to question the insularity of the classical paradigms of regional integration in these terms. Neither the statecentric nor the supranational approaches have adequately explained the unique format or the direction of the European process over the duration.

The realist model simply cannot account for the recent shifts towards greater mutuality of interests and the rising sense of common purpose which has infused Community diplomacy since the 1970s. By the same token, the supranationalists fail to account for the residual resistance at the domestic level, to those policy developments and institutional changes which appear to challenge the central role of nation states in the Community process. The cooperative federalism model is useful, then, precisely because it questions the narrowness of focus and the resultant theoretical distortions, of both these classical perspectives on integration. Its focus instead on the hybrid quality of Community decision making has been borne out by events on the ground. In the syncretic account of the regional process, integration is neither as tentative or as conditional as the intergovernmentalists suggest. Nor is it driven by some inexorable momentum towards the unicity predicted by the confident advocates of the supranationalist paradigm.

A close examination of the EC's procedures, and the way these operate across the Community's policy agenda, reinforces the aptness of a model of integration that incorporates conflicting expectations and suggests a momentum driven by the competing impulses that have inhabited the European project from the start. The residual tensions between the Commission and the European Parliament on one side of the institutional equation, and the Council of Ministers and European Council machinery on the other, are bound to mitigate against any easy going or fully 'cooperative' relationship,[61] let alone to facilitate any extensive sharing of policy making prerogatives or the straightforward settling of those joint tasks necessitated by global interdependence.

Although the Community's institutional arrangements have improved considerably since the signing in 1988 by the respective presidents of the three political organs of an Inter-Institutional Agreement to facilitate budgetary cooperation, tension and dissensus rather than unanimity of purpose continues to shadow the European regional process. Misgivings rather than clearsighted consensus about the meaning of the European project remain the norm, even where the member states are increasingly obliged, by the sheer impact on their domestic affairs and national outlook of the wider political environment they all inhabit, to acknowledge the mutual advantages in striking joint policy deals wherever possible.[62] The extension of parliamentary prerogatives in the form of the cooperation and co-decision procedures is a mixed blessing in this regard.[63] Wolfgang Wessels acknowledged this enduring tension between supranational and intergovernmental tendencies at the heart of the EC's policy system when he observed that:

> This EC pattern of administrative and political interactions reflected a trend by which members 'pool' their sovereignties and mix them with competencies of the EC into a system to which the notion of 'cooperative federalism' can be applied. Competences are not shifted from the nation to the EC level without any compensation ... but a different pattern can be observed. The more intensive are the forms, and the stronger are the impacts of the common policy making, the more extensive and intensive are the organisational devices for access and the influence which national officials and politicians preserve for themselves.[64]

In these unpredictable circumstances, contentions within and between the principal institutions may easily exacerbate confusion and even lead to conflict, over both the pace and direction of integration. Events throughout the duration of the European project certainty bear out this prognosis. Policy pathologies and decision traps are, as Scharpf suggests, the most likely consequences of the continuing animus between the statecentric and supranational impulses within the Community's body politic. An activist Commission under Delors' aegis harboured an ambition for maximalist integration, and its steady pursuit of this goal gave rise to a palpable tension between the centre and at least some of the member states or their domestic clienteles.[65] The Commission's potential for exerting excessive influence on the policy processes, over and above its formal role as a proposer of legislative initiatives and a conciliator or broker between the various sectoral interests who have a vested interest in the policy outcomes, as well as the principal mediator between the Council and the Parliament is, of course, not a foregone conclusion. The powers reserved to the Commission are conditional rather than absolute. Their exercise and consequences depend on the particular play of contingencies and situational factors, and not least the strength of the personalities involved.

In other words, there are no foregone conclusions here; no guaranteed or inevitable outcomes. The precise balance between the EC's complex political forces, at any stage of what is an intricate and frequently byzantine legislative process, is contingent. It is conditioned by the prevailing domestic political climate of its leading member states, and a host of other contextual factors, all of which determine the Community's political shape and policy orientation at any given juncture. To this extent, the state of integration is far from being a static process, or one whose momentum points in any certain direction. At best, these contending forces which determine outcomes in the EU reflect a conditional equilibrium. Events speak for themselves here. The Community's development has been fraught with cycles of Euroschlerosis, followed by even briefer periods of substantial achievement. When these cooperative intervals are overwhelmed by the incipient anxieties, doubts and conflicts that visit every transnational community faced with the task of addressing the consequences of global inter-dependence – and sooner rather than later given what is at stake – the characteristic struggle over the pace and direction of integration returns to centre stage. This incipient flux between two antithetical notions of European integration provides the EU's policy process with its principal motive force.[66] Scharpf, and those other writers who have utilised the notion of cooperative federalism as a conceptual lens through which to focus on the Community's elaborate policy process, are surely closer to the mark than those who argue for a more singular position when they pinpoint ambivalence rather than certainty of purpose or direction as the critical dynamic of European integration.

The precise equation between successful policy outcomes – whether as sub-optimal bargains or more ambitious cooperative solutions – and policy pathologies, is also unpredictable and depends on a complex mix of events, personalities, and those other contingent factors that shape political arrangements within any international regime or organisation. These determinants can, however, be stated in broad outline. They form a matrix that consists of the ongoing policy dialectic between the EU's cooperative and suboptimal arrangements, the continuing tension between the Community's supranational and intergovernmental properties, and the maximalist and minimalist aspirations for integration harboured by the principal institutional and political actors. Policy outcomes are not 'given' or determined by ideological prescriptions. They are altogether more mundane but no less complicated for that. They depend on the interplay of these forces of change and conservation. The state of integration, and how far it approximates to the minimalist or advances towards the maximalist options, depends on constantly shifting coalitions of political forces at work within and between the member states and the EU's institutional centre. These abiding tensions are exhibited constantly in the Community's inter-institutional arrangements. There has been at various times some slippage backwards, or a forward momentum, but no conclusive out-come in favour of one side or the other of this discourse. The Community remains, in essence, what it has been from the time when supranationalism engaged intergovernmentalism in the Council of Europe and in other regional fora at the end of the war. Understanding the essentially hybrid nature of the Community's decisional system is, then, the key to unlocking its precise dynamics. The concept of cooperative federalism helps to put that syncretic quality into an appropriate theoretical perspective.

CHANGING CIRCUMSTANCES AND REGIONAL INTEGRATION

The syncretic model offers the latest and most plausible account so far available of the complex dynamics of European integration. It does so precisely because it occupies a medium position between extremes: on one side, the unreflective idealism of those who have detected the incipient prospect of supranational integration in almost every concrete development of the Community project, however apparently modest; and on the other, the excessive caution, amounting in some cases to myopia, of those confirmed sceptics who continue to view the Community's operations from an unerring intergovernmental perspective. Of course, when applauding the virtues of any new paradigm, we must be careful to avoid the dogmas and narrow prescriptions that turned the two classical paradigms into ideology rather than heuristic theories. The same operational rules must be applied to our assessment of the syncretic model as to any preceding account. Social scientists work in accordance with strict rules of intellectual engagement. They must keep their minds open to the constant interaction of hypotheses about how the world might work and those empirical 'facts' which record what actually happens. Social scientists must expect disappointments when cherished assumptions fall foul of unexpected eventualities. They must constantly refine and refute carefully crafted predictive models of the world. And they must accept, too, the prospect that unexpected outcomes are always on the cards and likely to challenge and overturn their best efforts at theoretical preconception, however promising these might seem to be at any given moment. Events retain the capacity to be wholly unpredictable. Scharpf's measured account of the regional integration process meets this criterion too. He allows for the prospect of momentous and far reaching change in the patterning of international arrangements to impinge on and refashion the shape and direction of the European project. He remains alert to the prospect that war, diplomatic crisis or some other cathartic event may well tip the delicate balance that currently exists between intergovernmentalism and supranationalism, and tip it either way. There is much to commend this approach to political knowledge; not least, that it avoids the rigid determinism that has blighted other theoretical excursions into the intellectual quest for European integration.

We might draw some tentative conclusions on the basis of these judicious comments about the exigent quality that suffuses all international change. From the current perspective, the balance of probabilities seems to indicate the likely continuation, at least for the foreseeable future, of an unsteady oscillation between an optimistic and pessimistic outlook surrounding the European project. The prognosis for integration seems likely, then, to follow the mixed impulses rooted in Community affairs from the outset. The persistence and the continuing inter-action of two competing notions of integration within the Community project, will undoubtedly continue to throw up variable policy responses and unpredictable political outcomes. We are hardly in uncharted territory here, nor are we at the end of the quest for European integration; the Community has passed this way before, and more than once. Even so, the terrain remains as difficult, the signposts just as misleading and the way through the integration maze, as uncertain as ever it was. In these circumstances, the underlying dynamic remains driven, as it always has been, by the persistent tension between two clear but unreconcilable options. In these circumstances, the likely outcomes of this stand off are a combination of undoubted successes and frustrations. One one side positive achievements that confirm the Community's place as a remarkable and indeed unique political arrangement, and on the other, those now familiar derogations, crises and impasses that constantly visit the project with turbulence rather than outright chaos. The EU's flaccid response to the Bosnian imbroglio is merely the latest and almost certainly not the last episode when expectation and necessity lamentably failed to come within touching distance of effective policy solutions. In the circumstances, the intellectual quest to explain this immensely complex and variable process remains as challenging as ever. At the very least, those who embark on the search for answers here must confront the hybrid quality of the integration project. Ambivalence of purpose, ambiguity of procedures and uncertainty of outcome continue to provide the debate on the idea of Europe with its theoretical focal point. If integration theory loses sight of these parameters, it cannot begin to match the daunting intellectual task it has set itself.

Those who set out to explain the meaning of European integration would do well to assimilate and learn from the failures of the earlier, more confident para-digms. Caution must replace certainty as the first principle of theory making. Juliet Lodge, in her recent impressive overview of the complex modalities of the regional process, sensibly offered the student of integration a list of pertinent questions rather than simplistic prescriptions, as a template for gauging the state of the European Union. She wondered aloud about the meaning of integration, about

> What is the likely shape of European integration in the 1990s? Has a new phase started? Is it merely a composite of preceding stages? Is it self contained? Is European integration unpredictable, random and self limiting? Or can it be inferred that the EC in seeking to establish itself as a European Union is making a transition from a Gesellschaft to the Gemeinschaft? In that process, has the role of the state and the nature of governance in the modern age been irrevocably altered?[67]

Lodge has thus set an agenda students of the European integration process would do well to follow.

These are surely the critical questions confronting anyone who seeks to understand the current state of European integration. The surest route through this theoretical maze is not the one that resorts to narrow teleological certainties or settles for self verifying or tautological accounts of political change. Such complacency merely confuses the task of explanation with facile prophesies. What is required instead is an altogether more rigorous and balanced account of the regional process than that contained in the classical paradigms which for four decades or more dominated the theoretical discourse on European integration. A new revisionism prospectus must instead open up the regional process to a thorough and fully comprehensive review of all the paradoxical forces at work within it. The syncretic model reviewed above, in as much as it draws on a tradition of international thought which emphasises the universal processes underway in international change, rather than dwelling on what are assumed to be *sui generis* regional impulses, is better equipped than either of the classical integration paradigms, to undertake the daunting theoretical challenge outlined in Lodge's indicative research prospectus.

This interactive approach to European integration theory began to make its mark as part of the theoretical renaissance of the 1980s. Since then, it has made an important contribution to improving our understanding of the regional process in Western Europe. Yet, as we have seen, paradigm shifts are rarely if ever entirely conclusive. Intellectual coexistence is a more usual outcome of theoretical discourse than a clean break, even with paradigms heavily discounted by the force of events.[68] The syncretic model recommended here has continued, then, to share the theoretical stage with those classical paradigms which preceded it in the theoretical lists. As the European project unfolded with renewed vigour over the course of the 1980s, scholars from every theoretical tradition refocused their efforts to explain the 'essence' of integration. In the process, all of these classical paradigms have been revisited, revised and, to a degree, reinstated in the debate. The reprise of theories once thought to be misplaced or even obsolescent, suggests a neat intellectual symmetry. To this extent, the intellectual quest to explain the dynamics of European integration has come full circle. We have, however, learned much in the process. The poet's maxim, that we return from whence we came and know the place for the first time for what it really is, holds good too for this intellectual journey.

Chapter 6

Theoretical *déjà vu?*

THE DEBATES REVISITED

It is clear from the foregoing discussion that no single theory has proved capable of explaining adequately the critical dynamics of the processes of international change that are the key to regional integration. The recent emergence of altogether more conditional accounts of these immensely complex processes is evidence of the acknowledgement of this fact by contemporary contributors to this debate.[1] Theoretical revisionism has gained considerable impetus during recent years, as the Community was transformed into a Union and new challenges were confronted, with the potential for both confirming and challenging the members' sense of common purpose. At the same time, the momentum for integration provided by the 1992 project also revived interest in the pre-existing paradigms. Federalism and neofunctionalism have both been revisited by those theorists who continue to define a supranational dynamic as the driving force of the European regional process.

On the other side of the debate, the abiding scepticism of the pervasive realist tradition continues to colour those theoretical accounts of the European process which remain rooted in the statecentric paradigm. To this extent, we are still confronted with old theoretical wine, even if it has been decanted into somewhat newer bottles and marketed under different labels. The resilience of the old paradigms, in part, denotes academic vested interests, rather than the continuing relevance of these ideas and concepts per se. It is also a reflection of a more excusable persistence; the fact that, however much the political landscape seems to change, the very same questions continue to occupy the contemporary students of EC affairs that exercised their predecessors. This is hardly surprising. The future of the European nation state or the prospects for supranational integration are the two sides of a theoretical coin that has been the principal currency, in one form or another, of European political theory since the Enlightenment.[2] And more than that, political science continues to address those very fundamentals of agency, community, legitimacy and power – in whatever institutional format or historical context – that have been the principal concern of political science since Aristotle first turned his forensic mind to these perennial issues. In this sense, we are as much his students as we are his heirs.

FEDERALISM REVIVED

Federalism, both as a political ideal and as a theoretical account of European integration, had lain dormant since its defeat at the hands of Europe's political establishments in the early 1950s. Dormant but by no means dead. And as Burgess[3] reveals, federalist ambitions continued to be nurtured within the Commission, among the Strasbourg parliamentarians, and even nominally among some of the Community's national elites **(Document 37)**. The relatively sudden re-emergence in the European Parliament in 1980 of a campaign for political union under Spinelli's auspices,[4] revived interest in the federalist idea at both the political and academic levels. The pressing problems of the third enlargement – Greece acceded to membership in 1981, followed by Spain and Portugal in 1986 – and the increased scope of the Community's joint policy endeavours, gave added impetus to the federalist prospectus.

Both the challenge and likely pitfalls of accommodating twelve member states and rising, with their respective cultural diversities and socio-economic disparities, within a coherent and effective policy making framework, has increased the appeal of the federalist formula. Federalism makes a constitutional virtue out of social diversity. Its political rationale rests on the accommodation of a separation of powers and the sharing of sovereignty within an effective, democratic and progressive polity.[5] The federalist genius for balancing social diversity and reconciling dispersed jurisdiction with effective governance has done much to restore federalism to the centre of the integration debate, with the prospects of an altogether new stage of deepening and enlargement; and even in these present circumstances, to recommend federalism beyond its usual constituency, as a practical solution to what might otherwise be the daunting problems of ensuring effective decision making and equitable resource allocation in such a geographically amorphous and large scale union of states.[6]

This in itself does not obviate the immense difficulties that have accompanied the federalist account of integration outlined in Chapter 2. For one thing, federalist thinkers who have addressed the issues of the shape and destiny of the European Community, find it hard to agree on a clear definition. There is as much vagueness and allusion in the debate on federalism as there is conceptual clarity or political precision.[7] This mirrors the persistent political divisions within the European federalist movement referred to in the above account.[8] The revival of a federalist prospectus as the EU's most appropriate constitutional formula in the frenetic debate which emerged in the aftermath of the Single European Act did, however, give this particular paradigm greater credence than federalism has enjoyed at any time since its brief postwar ascendency. Contemporary federalist theorists have taken their cue from events and responded readily to the challenge. They choose to see, in the ferment of ideas and the positive endeavours to build Europe in the aftermath of the 1992 initiative, a new and positive start, however tentative, down the road to a fully fledged union.

Although neither the Single European Act (1985), nor the European Treaty of

Union (1992) were overtly federalist, the tone of both of these constitutional land marks did at least imply that the Community had arrived at an important crossroads in its uncertain political development. There was a sense, on all sides, that a critical juncture had been reached. Federalists felt encouraged by events. There was a discernible sense throughout the late 1980s of history in the making; that the major political shift towards European Union that seemed imminent, might well require – and sooner rather than later – a more overtly federalist component in its procedures and institutional arrangement than had previously been permitted by those more cautious member states who had retained their hold on the direction of the Community's affairs. There is a danger here, however, of confusing two entirely distinct phenomena. The unquestionable decline in the sovereign autonomy of Europe's nation states neither guarantees the inexorable rise of federalism nor ensures the obsolescence of territorial polities. In their enthusiasm to find proof positive of an ineluctable federal logic at work in the European process, its supporters often confuse and conflate these parallel but by no means identical phenomena.

The claims of the current federalist case are based on the very same precepts that exercised their postwar predecessors. The contemporary federalist prospectus exhibits a familiar mixture of motives; the concern with ensuring the regional peace, with protecting civil society against undue concentrations of centralised power, with guaranteeing citizen redress against the overbearing state and pluralism over cultural hegemony. And, above all, the abiding belief in the limitations of the nation state as a means for providing the minimum governmental and social requirements for ensuring a civilised domestic and international order. The Italian political scientist, Lucio Levi, has summarised the essence of the contemporary federalist case in terms that would have been readily acknowledged by its postwar predecessors. Levi saw the constraints of modern globalism as propelling Europe's nation states towards federalism; that

> the internationalisation of the productive process and the formation of the world system of states has contributed to the growing awareness that the nation state is no longer a sufficient basis for guaranteeing either economic development or political independence in the contemporary world. In particular, reflection on the process of European unification has encouraged considerable maturation as regards the deeper aspects of federalist theory. The search for European unity represents the most consistent attempt to overcome the political formula of the nation state, which has led to extreme consequences as regards compressing mankind into closed, uniform, hostile and belligerent communities, a principle which is radically incompatible with the deepest requirements of the contemporary world.[9]

The linkages proposed here are too vague and generalised to pass for an adequate explanation of the forces for international change. This is a common problem with many expositions of federalism. They continue to be more prescriptive than analytical. Moral injunctions masquerade as apparently self evident 'facts'. The heart continues to rule the head here. Burgess, in his recent account of this process certainly cannot be accused of vacuity. He makes an intelligent effort at showing how federalism has become ensconced in the actual European process. But in the end, even he resorts to a familiar piece of federalist legerdemain; he tends to identify an integral federal dynamic at work in Europe leading to what he calls 'an evolving organic whole'.[10] This is more ideology than it is good social science. It exhorts and recommends, but does not substantiate or otherwise prove the case for an incipient federalism in Europe's body politic. Burgess identifies the institutional loci of the Community as those frameworks in which federalism might easily take root and exert influence. But this assumption too, amounts in effect to little more than wishful thinking. Burgess perceives federalism as a process of value change; a cultural shift as much as a constitutional compact. The process variable as it is conceived here is cognitive rather than structural; thus, 'by regular contact and political intercourse federalist influences can be spread widely and often imperceptibly across a network of Community actors so that policy and decision making environments become more receptive to alternative options and strategies'.[11]

While value shifts are undoubtedly a significant aspect of all forms of political change, this particular causal sequence raises more questions than it answers. The role of values as causal factors is problematical and exaggerated, to say the least. At most, they are intermediate variables rather than independent ones. Values reflect deeper structural changes more than they cause them. If federalism is indeed firmly back on Europe's political agenda as Burgess suggests, we need to know more about the 'trigger' factors which have given what were previously peripheral values a new political salience. Contemporary federalist thought still tends to confuse prescription with inductive analysis. Burgess's assertion that the empirical studies of concrete decision making on which we must surely rely for an informed insight into the actual dynamics of the regional integration process, are little more than 'a coward's way out of a theoretical dilemma',[12] pinpoints precisely the severe limitations of this sort of methodology.

Ernest Wistrich is even less circumspect than Burgess about the positive prospects for European federalism. As Wistrich sees it, federalism is not only desirable but inevitable: it will come about because it must![13] This may well be an inspiring thought, but it is hardly rigorous social science. What is clear from these accounts of the federal idea is the important distinction to be drawn between an approach which examines empirically the role of ideas and ideology in shaping the direction of international change, and a reflective approach which settles for mere subjectivity. Keohane recommends an approach to ideas which balances the contribution of values to our understanding of international politics, with a rigorous endeavour to test their impact and cultural salience far more precisely than any merely prescriptive approach manages to do.[14] The balance here between hypothesis and verification is crucial to the theoretical endeavour, and much that passes for federalist theory fails to meet this exacting methodological requirement.

This critique of course by no means discounts the contribution of the current federalist thinking per se to the integration debate. Some writers in this vein offer an altogether more balanced and plausible assessment of the federal prospectus. John Pinder, for instance, shows an acute awareness of the need to address the question of change as process rather than merely as a vague cultural shift driven by ideological preference or political prescription **(Document 38)**. A federal union, as Pinder sees it, must evolve in stages rather than as the annus mirabilis or sudden political transformation projected in the classical federalist thesis. In other words, a federal union in Europe will only ensue if the conditions for it are in place. No amount of wishful thinking or moralising will bring about such a massive political transformation unless the structural and anthropological conditions are fully in place. A federal union or for that matter any other political regime, will be to Pinder's mind nothing more mystical than the working through of a process of political and cultural change; the gradual and frequently unintended outcome of incremental policy linkages and network building, and the cumulative sense of commonality of interests which will flow from such developments.[15] While this graduated or 'neofederal' process is by no means guaranteed to end in a fully fledged federal polity,[16] the success of the Single Market project did encourage Pinder to believe that a federal state would be a more realisable outcome at some stage in Europe's future than it was ever likely to be after 1945.[17] Nathan, too, offers a more conditional assessment of the federal prospect in Europe as the outcome of a similarly complex and conditional process of political change.[18]

Although the re-emergence of the federalist goal has been apparent in both the ideological and theoretical debate on European integration, we need to put this revival into perspective. Some of federalism's staunchest advocates continue, as their predecessors did, to confuse hyperbole with hypothesis. They still tend to substitute idealistic prescriptions for sober analysis. Regardless of the far reaching changes that have recently occurred in the EU's affairs, its constitutional arrangements and the political mood of its elites and public opinion alike, continue to fall some way short of a federalist zeitgeist. The period of public disquiet and political disaffection that accompanied the ratification of the Union Treaty underlined, as clearly as any resurgence of optimism about a radical sea-change in the continent's political affairs, the doubts and unease that continue to surround the European project. This persistent ambivalence about how the idea of Europe might be translated into concrete political and institutional arrangements, suggests that the populist foundation on which the federalist prospectus depends for its fulfilment, is still some considerable way off.

These are all important reservations and need to be properly addressed if the federal idea is to make its mark in the current integration debate. If federalism does have a future in the EU's arrangements, it will be facilitated by practical needs rather than by appeals to idealism. The present debate on subsidiarity and the hard thinking that is presently going into the political preamble to the forthcoming IGC, offers some indication of the need to balance enlargement and the increasing scope and immense complexity of the Community's policy process with more efficient decision making. Common sense dictates that changes will have to be made in the Community's procedures to this extent, and the federal principle rather than a fully fledged federal system per se – with all of the likely objections to formal loss of sovereignty conjured by such a monumental political shift – suggests a practical way forward here. Ivo Duchacek's work on the sociology of federalism pointed to the feasibility of accommodating cohesive political communities with a strong sense of their own political identities, within a viable and larger scale system of governance.[19] Daniel Elazar has pointed to a critical demarcation here between process and system, when he observed that:

> using the federal principle does not necessarily mean establishing a federal system in the conventional sense of a modern federal state. The essence of federalism is not to be found in a particular set of institutions but in the institutionalization of particular relationships among the participants in political life. Consequently, federalism is a phenomenon that provides many options for the organization of political authority and power; as long as the proper relations are created, a wide variety of political structures can be developed that are consistent with federal principles.[20]

Common sense also suggests that this practical rather than prescriptive approach to the question is more likely to contribute to federalism's reinstatement on the EU's political agenda in the short and medium term, than any more ambitious prospectus that promises a full blown Pan European state legitimised by a meaningful and primary sense of a European 'national' identity.

NEOFUNCTIONALISM REVISITED

The Single Market project was also claimed by latter day neofunctionalists, as evidence of the re-emergence of spillover as the modus vivendi of European integration. Aware of the difficulties that befell the original neofunctionalists, revisionists here have settled for an altogether more modest version of this paradigm. Muttimer **(Document 39)** for instance, offers a conditional definition of spillover as a 'process variable'. The teleological implications of the classical neofunctionalist paradigm are expunged.[21] The original sense of a certain destination for a Community, propelled by some inexorable if hidden force, is replaced in the latest versions by a more qualified behavioural account of political change, in which key actors, possessed of disproportionate power over policy outcomes and driven by calculations of advantage, transact their bargains more or less rationally and according to perceptions of self interest and the contingencies that shape them. At the same time, the cumulative effect of such transactions on the tenor of Community politics does lead, as Muttimer interprets the process, beyond those merely suboptimal bargains or at best, complementary and convergent national preferences, which dominate the intergovernmentalist paradigm.

The journey, then, may be unpredictable, even tortuous in the short term. But it leads, nevertheless, to some sort of destination that reflects the deeper instincts of supranational pedagogy. Muttimer remains convinced that significant changes in both the structures and culture of European regional politics are underway. He concludes that

> in the 1950s Ernst Haas promised that international integration would lead beyond the nation state, but subsequently argued that the lessons of the 1970s were that the nation state was not yet ready to be surpassed. It is at least possible that 1992 will act the midwife to the birth of the world's first truly trans-national political organisation.[22]

Moreover, these revisionists do not treat the current stage of positive regional integration as a theoretical abstraction. They follow neofunctionalism's methodological insistence on manageable hypotheses and empirically testable causal linkages. This makes for an altogether more measured account of integration. The contemporary neofunctionalists attribute such changes to the interaction of discernible political processes, operating on both the national and regional levels, rather than to 'hidden hands' or metaphysical forces. In his account of these processes, Tranholm-Mikkelsen hedges his methodological bets but still backs his predictive hunch that 'something' is happening out there in the 'here and now'. So, the 'automaticity of spillover' is not abandoned but qualified by other parallel (occasionally disintegrative) processes that delay or deflect the development of integration. At best, neofunctionalism

> Provides us with a framework for informed guesses about the future pace and direction of integration on the basis of assessments of the relative strength of the two forces. At present, for example, such a guess would be likely to involve a continuation of the dynamism leading up to 1992 and beyond.[23]

This subdued optimism for European futures was conceived before the impact of those events that tipped the scales the other way. The pressures raised by the fall of communism, the sharpened ethnicity of Europe's new politics, the post-Maastricht jitters and the brake on monetary union caused by a long recession, all reopened the more than incidental questions about timetables, and whether indeed any kind of 'journey' was in train.

Other writers who shared the neofunctionalist hunch also hedged their bets. Muttimer identified similar structural processes at work, although these processes for him were far from being consistent or mutually reinforcing, and were by no means aspects of some grand if hidden design. They suggested instead to Muttimer an equation of interests similar to Tranholm-Mikkelsen's notion of a 'dialectic' of opposing forces, and with similarly important consequences for regional integration. Cumulative functional linkages, even where these are transacted for motives other than integration for its own sake, tend to deepen the scope of supranational integration. The new neofunctionalists cast their ideas on receptive waters. The 1992 project seemed to have taken up the technocratic drive for integration where Haas's optimism had left off. And yet even these revisionists could see the flaws and certainly knew the risks of engaging in unqualified model building of this notoriously fluid project. And they were, of course, right to be nervous of resurrecting a model that was clearly out of its time. Tranholm-Mikkelsen, although persuaded of the continuing relevance of neofunctionalism for explaining the regional process, is a good enough social scientist to recognise the continuing flaws in this paradigm. The European process is too complicated to lend itself to narrow systemic modelling. Its interactive qualities and competing forces must be accounted for, then, in behavioural terms. For,

> Although we can discern pressures, constraints, tendencies and trends, European integration, like politics in general, ultimately depends on intentional acts by individual human beings. Integration cannot, therefore, be reduced to anonymous processes whose inexorable 'laws' it is for academics to discern.[24]

Notwithstanding the modest theoretical claims made by the current neo-neofunctionalists, the revised model continues to carry some of the same methodological drawbacks as the discounted classical version. Regardless of the caveats already outlined, 'spillover' remains the imprecise and misleading concept it always was. And a largely meaningless one, except as a truism or as a highly selective description of events. Tranholm-Mikkelsen was obliged to recognise the theoretical limitations that prompted Haas to declare his own efforts redundant. Tranholm-Mikkelsen likewise concluded from his attempt to resurrect neofunctionalism, that, 'it helps us to describe and explain but it does not allow us to predict'.[25] 'Spillover', then, is rather like a mirage; it is there if you want it to be. To this extent, it continues to anticipate the future rather than concentrating on the present. It justifies *a priori* assumptions about the development of the European project rather than providing a useful template against which to plot and explain the development and actual processes of international change.

The 'spillover' concept, with its emphasis on cumulative linkages, appealed especially to those commentators who thought they detected in the development of the Single Market Project, the same functional logic, the predicted political consequences of technical and economic policy, and the determinitive role of transnational elites upgrading the common European interest, identified by Haas and his colleagues. However, a more objective appraisal of these events raises some awkward facts which confront the notional logic of 'spillover'. The difficulties confronted by the Community during the 1990s have further dented the neofunctionalist case. There are now as there were in its original form, clear limits to the 'spillover' dynamic. For all their candour, these recent and more modest revisions have not entirely resolved these theoretical flaws. A close look at recent developments suggests an altogether more complex process unfolding in the EU, and one that depends for its momentum on a mixture of variables. Far from providing evidence of a clear momentum based on forward linkages, any accurate account of regional integration must draw attention to the abiding tension between supranationalism and intergovernmentalism. It is surely the interaction of these distinct but interdependent sets of political impulses which provides the European Union with its central dynamic? William Wallace has accounted for the renewed momentum of integration in precisely such terms. As he sees the process, national interests compete and coexist with a rising sense of regional identity. At the same time, these are, in Kirchner's view, complementary rather than mutually exclusive impulses. To this extent, Europe's

> governments tread a treacherous path between increasing transnational cooperation (needed to fulfil important service functions for their citizens) and maintaining sufficient national control over EC decision making. However, this national control is not individual control of single governments but the control of national governments collectively.[26]

At the most, 'spillover' remains unsatisfactory because it is a crude metaphor for the momentum which is implied by the idea of regional integration as a sequential and cumulative process. But we can never assume that political or economic developments are always positive and exponential. The same mixture of ambiguous impulses and conflicting interests that has dictated the unsteady and unpredictable course of European integration to date, might just as easily unravel in less favourable circumstances. Integration and disintegration are, therefore, two sides of the same theoretical coin. There are no certain outcomes from the processes of political change, whether at the level of the state or in international politics. There are only prospects and possibilities whose precise configurations depend on the complex variables identified most plausibly above by the syncretic theorists. As such, the 'spillover' concept is suggestive more than it is precisely analytical or empirically accurate. The neofunctional model does identify some of the principal supranational agencies at work in the processes of international change. What it fails to offer, however, is any plausible account of how such actors manipulate or direct the regional process. Nor does its notion of cultural 'spillover' adequately account for the endemic conflicts, frictions and genuine dilemmas which constantly visit the participants in the regional process.[27] To this extent, neofunctionalism remains as theoretically incomplete and as methodologically deficient as ever it was.

INTERGOVERNMENTALISM RECONSTITUTED

It should be clear from the foregoing discussion of the attempts to revive earlier versions of the supranational paradigm, and accommodate them to contemporary circumstances, that old paradigms do not travel easily in an unfamiliar political landscape. This caveat also applies to those attempts to adapt the inter-governmentalist paradigm to present events. The realist paradigm had to a degree accommodated the notion of interdependence, whilst accepting that the new globalism merely increased the challenges facing contemporary nation states and altered the context in which they must operate. By the 1980s it was apparent, even to those commentators who remained well disposed to a statecentric approach, that its crude application to the current international situation was at best distortive and at worst entirely misconceived. This tendency to engage in modest but insistent revisionism was as apparent within the realist genre of integration theory as it was among the doyens of its rival paradigms.

Theorists who continue to see European integration through an intergovernmentalist lens have tended to adopt a neorealist perspective.[28] Neorealists assume that states are self regarding actors with differential resources, coexisting within a system characterised by 'anarchy'. At the same time, neorealists discern a potential for order as much as unmitigated chaos in the contemporary arrangements of the international process.[29] Axelrod and Keohane refer for instance to the positive payoffs that await those 'governments (who) are, prepared to grope their way toward a better coordinated future . . . in a world where states have often been dissatisfied with international anarchy . . . so that despite the reality of anarchy, beneficial forms of international cooperation can be promoted'.[30] States in pursuit of their respective interests interact in all manner of regimes, international organisations and institutions. These structures concentrate on agreed solutions between states in ways that were simply not conceivable even a generation ago. Accordingly, modern states do not inhabit the disorderly, atavistic international universe of the classical realist models. Or at least the emergent pattern of regimes of which regional organisations are a significant example, provides channels or networks for negotiating mutual non zero sum accommodations, even between the most adversarial states.

There is even scope here for altogether more cooperative arrangements. States whose socio-economic systems are convergent, who share the same fundamental political values and inhabit the same geopolitical environment may go beyond mere peaceful coexistence or the usual diplomatic bargains of the international system, and enjoy altogether more positive forms of integration. Paul Taylor has identified this process as a form of consociationalism. Consociationalism represents the inherent paradox of states' elites cooperating in pursuit of their separate interest agendas. Integration is construed here as another and immensely intricate version of the two level game.[31] These cooperative ventures are hardly driven by the supranational momentum identified by the federalist or functionalist paradigms. Instead, the participants orientate themselves to one another, as a response to their respective and sometimes mutual national dilemmas, as much as in pursuit of any putative common interest.[32] The sort of 'integration' that ensues in this neorealist construction, is not the outcome of some inexorable supranational momentum towards an upgraded common interest. It is an altogether more mundane matter. International bargains, wherever they are transacted, provide the most likely means for maximising national interests in a rapidly changing international milieu; and one that demands altogether new and cooperative responses from its component states.[33]

The theorists who have approached the recent study of European integration from this neorealist perspective remain far from convinced by the supranationalists' implicit claim that the phenomenon can only be explained by developing a *sui generis* brand of integration theory; a novel theory to explain an exotic process. If, as the contemporary realists continue to believe, the European project is nothing more than a useful strategy for maximising national interests, and preserving the nation state in response to the new conditions of global interdependence, it also follows that its most appropriate explanation requires only a refinement of the conventional realist paradigm. This is broadly how the neorealists have approached the study of European integration. Some of the leading neorealists have identified in contemporary events, genuine prospects for limited regional integration. Waltz[34] and Grieco[35] have both maintained that conventional expressions of interstate rivalry might, under certain circumstances, be replaced by more cooperative relationships, albeit principally pursued for national advantage. The endemic competition between states over what they continue to define as their primordial national interests are not, however, likely to be effaced by their institutionalisation in regional communities; they will, nevertheless, be transformed and perhaps even tamed by this salutary experience.

This essentially utilitarian account of integration was further developed in the neoliberal institutional variant of this type of realist doctrine.[36] The neoliberals build both conflict and cooperation into their model of the international process. They dwell on the creative tension between those mixed impulses we have identified as the driving force of regional integration. While they accept neorealism's emphasis on anarchy, state interest, and power, they also acknowledge the positive consequences of international regimes and the experience of regular 'second level' contact, formal and informal, in their procedures and institutions, as a way of ameliorating some of the worst aspects of unmitigated anarchy which used to be the normal condition and ultimately the most destructive outcome of international 'society'. Cornett and Caporasa have weighed the neoliberal contribution to integration theory thus:

> In particular, scholars in this tradition explore how international institutions mitigate the most divisive and stressful effects of anarchy. Without questioning the anarchic character of international relations, they seek to understand and explain how the spread of information, norms, and rules may change states' options and influence the order, if not the ordering principle, of international relations.[37]

There have been many adaptations and refinements of this broad neorealist model. Keohane, for instance, whose contribution to the interdependence thesis had never entirely discounted states as the principal actors in the international process, interpreted regional integration in terms similar to the neoliberals, as a form of 'preference convergence'. States may well continue to hold their traditional place as the central players in the regional process. At the same time, unmitigated conflict or competitiveness, under the conditions of complex interdependence, is likely to be as costly as it is rewarding, even to the most resourceful or formally powerful states. The structural constraints implied by the conditions of interdependence suggest that real and mutual advantages accrue to states from the establishment of those norms, procedures and networks which increasingly govern the conduct and decide the outcomes of interstate transactions.[38] These arrangements are far removed from either the constitutional provisions or the underlying ideological motives of a fully fledged federal or any other variant of the supranational system. They are less concerned with the unrealisable project of supranationalists to prescribe the conditions for universal peace or welfare cooperation in a truly international society. Instead they amount to a far more limited recommendation of a condition that Rosenau called 'governance without government'.[39] The essential concern here is with the survival of the nation state – the only repository of civilised society as the neorealists know it – but in ways that take account of the endemic tendency to international disorder in humanity's conduct of its affairs. The guiding light of this line of thought might well have been inspired by Addison's warning that 'from hence, let fierce contending nations know, what dire effects from civil discord flow'.

Keohane and Hoffmann **(Document 40)** have applied this modified realist framework to the analysis of the latest stage of European integration. They maintain that in present circumstances, this project requires a fresh theoretical approach. The politics of contemporary European integration can only be understood in the context of the changing global political economy. Integration in some degree is an undeniable fact of European political life. But this, in itself, does not imply a supranational momentum; rather, the complex policy procedures and networks of the Community project suggest only that an unprecedented pooling of sovereignty has occurred, in order to maximise the benefits of intergovernmental cooperation to the EC's various and competing national interests. The patterning of convergent but by no means identical interests in this particular account, conjures images of technocratic complementarity similar to those found in the neofunctionalist paradigm,[40] except that here there is no sense of a *deux ex machina* or inexorable teleological force at work. Instead, Keohane and Hoffmann identify integration merely as a structural imperative rather than an unstoppable and deterministic force. As such, the process and its particular outcomes represent the cumulative outcome – the 'spin off' rather than the 'spillover' – of the usual bargains negotiated between state actors.

Integration, even in these terms, is little more than the outcome of a rational strategy employed by states operating within those institutional networks developed precisely to meet their needs and to minimise their vulnerability, given the heightened costs of failure and the dangers inherent in the new global anarchy. Hoffmann had already argued in an early assessment of the Single Market project, that 'the (EC's) national governments and bureaucracies remain the chief players'. And that 'while the earlier supranationalists often saw the states as the enemy, today's activists see them as indispensable partners, whose sovereignty is to be pooled rather than removed, and to whom enforcement of Community decisions is entrusted'.[41] According then to this neorealist–neoliberal variant of the old statecentric paradigm, European integration is 'an elaborate set of networks, closely linked in some ways, and particularly decomposed in others, whose results depended on the political style in the ascendance at the moment'.[42]

Networks, as employed here, are by no means cohesive systems of procedures based on common norms, let alone a full blown federal polity vested in agreed constitutional procedures and amounting to an authoritative patterning of powers and responsibilities. They are instead limited arrangements entered into freely for mutual convenience; devices for salvaging a degree of order and policy coherence from an unpredictable political universe; an organised alternative to the ever present prospect of chaos that surrounds international politics. Participants within these networks are deemed to enjoy a propensity for cooperation, but in pursuit of potentially mutual interests, rather than an unrealisable universal interest. In the process, the traditional business of statecraft is changed; new styles of bargaining emerge and a propensity for sharing the heavy costs and responsibilities of their new international roles. But this is not the same thing at all as the aspiration to concoct a single, overarching regional interest. Networks provide another of those useful middle range concepts that yield insights into the actual mechanics of international politics, and one that expresses those adaptive mechanisms in the real world of transnational, two level politics which accommodate political actors at every level – from states and supranational agencies, down to interest groups and even those active citizens who participate in them – to the vagaries of international change.

There has been some remarkably perceptive work on European integration cast in this particular theoretical mould. Moravcsik is a good case in point. Moravcsik further refined the statecentric model in similar if rather more uncompromising terms. In his forays into the theoretical lists, he disclaimed as whimsical if not far fetched, those optimistic or open ended interpretations placed on the import of the Single European Act by adherents of the supranational school of thought. As he saw it, this latest stage of the European 'story' in no way represented the great leap forward heralded by the latter day federalists or new functionalists **(Document 41)**. Moravcsik remained convinced that 'the historical record does not confirm the importance of international and transnational factors'. He affirms instead 'that the primary source of integration lies in the interests of the states themselves'.[43] In a more recent article Moravcsik again purports to explain the latest phase in the EU's development as 'a successful intergovernmental regime designed to manage economic interdependence through negotiated policy coordination'[44] **(Document 42)**. Integration is, seen in these limited terms, merely the latest response of regional states to the increasing constraints on independent action downloaded by the new international environment. Moravcsik draws instead on conventional international theory in general and on realism in particular, for his explanation of recent developments in the European Community. Accordingly, any plausible account of integration would

> rest on the assumption that state behaviour reflects the rational actions of governments constrained at home by domestic social pressures and abroad by their strategic environment. An understanding of the preferences and power of its member states is a logical starting point for analysis.[45]

In essence, then, the driving force behind regional integration remains, for Moravcsik, what it always had been, according to the classical lights of the inter-governmentalist perspective. Change at the regional level – and he does not dispute that the European venture was transformed by events after 1984 – continues to mirror the perceptions held by governing elites of their domestic political and economic priorities. And these are shaped, as ever, by domestic calculations – not least electoral ones – rather than by supranational aspirations. In these terms any regional strategy is little more than a rational assessment of those international strategies most likely to reduce national opportunity costs and better ensure their maximisation.[46] There remains, then, in the conduct of all statecraft, that elusive but persistent quality that once caused Joseph Conrad to observe that 'there was a completeness in it, something solid like a principle, and masterful like an instinct . . . of that hidden something, that gift of good or evil . . . that shapes the fate of nations'.

The attempt here to adapt the inadequacies of the old realist paradigm to the circumstances of the new interdependence has much to recommend it. At the same time there are as many limitations to this revised account of realism as there are merits. The assumption of national preference convergence that lies behind this model suggests, at best, another useful metaphor, rather than satisfying all the necessary conditions of a well honed theory of international change. Even in these modest terms, it still falls some way short of suggesting an entirely satisfactory explanation of even the remarkable degree of interest convergence that has undoubtedly been generated by the Single Market project over a relatively short time span. This model does not move far beyond the essentially realist assumption that it was the EU's leading states who were the principal moving force behind the recent moves to deepen regional integration. In this the new realists are only partially correct. Intergovernmental bargains in defence of perceived national interests[47] have been a key element in Europe's recent endeavours to respond to the global challenge, but they are by no means the whole story. The role of the Commission as an initiator of the project, and the prominent place of transnational business interests in the 1992 process cannot be so easily discounted.[48] And these two agencies have canvassed their own distinctive agendas, agendas that complement but by no means replicate those of the member states. It is clear, from the work of the principal contributors to the neorealist account of the European project, that any revisionist account of the classical realist paradigm which emphasises national interests as the sole priority of the EU to the exclusion of the supranational dimension, continues to offer an unbalanced account of the regional process.

Revisionist versions of all the classical paradigms have tried to account for the recent developments of the regional process. As we have seen, in spite of commendable attempts to refine and adapt these old models, they remain too narrowly focused and are no better equipped to capture the subtleties and paradoxes of this process than they were when they first visited the European integration debate. For that reason, the syncretic models, premised on the notion of integration as a mixed and ambiguous process, have continued to more than hold their own during this latest stage of the debate.

THE SYNCRETIC MODEL REFINED

By the 1990s European integration theory had assimilated the complexities of what was an unsteady rather than a confident movement towards an 'ever closer union'. That term itself was more conditional than clear cut. It was used by commentators on every side of the debate to reflect their preferences or prejudices rather than as an accurate account of what was meant by integration per se. The old paradigms, for all of their resistance, were patently inadequate, and even in their revised forms missed the ambiguities and subtleties of the contemporary regional integration process. Many close observers of the vagaries of the European process had become convinced that the search for a universal paradigm of what was undoubtedly an immensely complex and paradoxical process, was a fruitless endeavour. The academic community, as we saw in Chapter 5, responded well to this revisionist mood. The ambitious metanarratives of the classical paradigms were replaced instead by less exclusive and altogether more modest middle range theories based on ideas about the international process generated by the new global interdependence. These models have largely abjured grandiose attempts at inductive macro theorising. They offer instead manageable and testable hypotheses which focus attention on the actual logistics of integration, not as systemic or functional imperatives that carry mankind in their wake almost regardless of will, nor as moral crusades that would refashion the world and its ways in the image of a code of ethics made, as Raymond Aron once observed, by intellectuals and those who follow their cues. Instead, they are processes conducted between a range of actors who exhibit an infinitely complex mix of motives, and those competing interests which form the constellation that is the European Union's policy process, and a process, above all, subject to careful and measured scrutiny, where scholars interpret rather than impose their own ideological preferences on events.

The recent academic accord about the limits and limitations of integration theory by no means implies an academic consensus, let alone an ideological one, on the meaning and direction of the European project. The debate here remains as febrile as ever it was. Even so, its terms of engagement are now much less stark, as a sense of the sheer heterogeneity of the European project has settled over the academic mind. Even those who continue to ply singular theoretical notions, preface them with cautious caveats. All of this suggests an altogether more open minded debate than was once the case on this subject, and one that has a real prospect of the sort of intellectual cohabitation that is likely to get us closer to the truth of things. This entirely sensible notion of the regional process as a hybrid process – a mixture of domestic and transnational imperatives, in all sorts of combinations – represents the syncretic model's most significant contribution to our understanding of the regional process.

The concept of the EU as a 'network' captures something of the fluidity and variability of the contemporary regional process. Networks in this usage are no more than a descriptive device for arranging data and charting complex and shifting transactional patterns. Several contemporary commentators have identified network patterns running through the EU's policy system. These networks reflect the recondite nature of modern international society. They represent the plethora of both formal and informal linkages that connect subnational groups, governmental agencies and transnational interests. The European process is in this sense but one dimension of what Rosenau has called 'an era of cascading interdependence'.[49] The literature is full of imaginative modelling cast in the syncretic mould. Brewin for instance argued the case for a revised version of the confederal concept to take account of the new globalism, as the most suitable theoretical means for reflecting the Community's unique international position; one that is 'equal in status to states but lacks unity of government'.[50] This is by no means a new idea. Even at a time when the confederal model of integration was in the ascendance, Carole Webb concluded, on the basis of an exhaustive empirical study of the Community's policy framework, that the European project was a kaleidoscope of networks of collaboration which brought together state actors, functionalist lobbies and the transnational interests that had already begun to change the shape and direction of international politics.[51]

Other writers have adopted and subsequently refined the network model as a means of charting a clearer route through the complexities of the European maze. Helen Wallace, too, saw such networks as a direct consequence of multinational organisation. In her account, 'this development is in part a direct consequence of involvement in the Community process'.[52] John Peterson, in a recent study of the Community's Research and Development policy,[53] has suggested that the accommodations and policy bargains that result from such multilateral networking lead to the establishment of layers of stable policy communities. The language is variable but the underlying meaning of these analyses is clear enough: European integration is essentially a project driven by complicated and by no means convergent forces.

Sandholtz and Zysman **(Document 43)** in their account of the 1992 project, have analysed the Single Market project in similar terms. They define the remaking of the Community as a syncretic accommodation of competing interests. The Single Market process illustrates the underlying dynamic of integration as an amalgam or interdependence of those different interests and ideologies that have always infused the European project. To that extent, the equation remains the same, even if the weight or influence of the component elements has shifted over the duration, and in response to novel circumstances. '1992' is, then, a new arrangement or series of bargains, concocted in the Community's policy networks between governmental elites and transnational actors. These are seen, primarily, as a response to the manifest threats to both domestic and regional interests from a much enhanced Japanese and American competitiveness, once this danger was assimilated at every level of the Community.[54] The specifics of regional integration – what is actually happening in the EU's policy networks at every level – in this

latest phase amount to both structural and behavioural responses to the rising interdependence that accompanies the development of modern political economy. As
Helen Wallace has interpreted the unfolding logic of this process, these networks
in which the European game is played are both indispensable to, and a direct
outcome of, the new levels of policy interdependence represented by the
Community's expansive patterns of interaction. To this extent,

> Functioning coalition patterns are observable within the system based on a mix
> of complementary (rarely identical) interests and tactical alignments. . . . Those
> coalitions are a necessary part of a negotiating process with so many players with
> such wide ranging and often contrary interests. . . . The European negotiating
> process has acquired an inbuilt dynamic observable in the EC. . . . It does not
> follow that there is an irreversible accumulation of agreements in prospect, but
> it does appear that West Europeans have acquired the negotiating capabilities
> to pursue, if they so choose, an incremental path. . . . Collective interests are
> perceptibly pursued. This should not be taken to imply that a starry-eyed supra-
> nationalism inhabits the portals of state power in Western Europe. However,
> both governments and the economic groups affected by the current policy
> repertoire make the careful calculation that a negotiating process that delivers
> results is more valuable than the frustration of stalled debate.[55]

This stands as a succinct account of what syncretism is all about. We can expand
on this brief definition of the current state of play but not improve on it. To go
beyond this modest but intelligent synopsis would be to allow back into the
theoretical quest, paradigmic ideas that have had their day and failed, when they
did hold the stage, to capture the essence of what was really underway in Europe's
postwar affairs. The EU's multilateral networks are, however, more than just
a vehicle for particular, temporal pressures. They do reveal something of the
momentum and the mechanics at work in the regional process. They are also
more than innocent bystanders, pawns in a game controlled from elsewhere. On
the contrary, what goes on in these networks does affect both perceptions and
outcomes. These networks serve then, an experimental purpose; they allow us to
'test' hypotheses about the precise operation of the European 'game'. For they
provide channels or outlets which facilitate that perennial debate over the pace,
policies and direction of European integration which has dominated both the
academic and political landscape for almost half a century. And if at the level of
real politics, its particular policy outcomes are less – or more – than either its
supranational or intergovernmental protagonists might prefer, both camps can
find a sufficient pay off in these networked bargains to induce them to stay in the
game.

In other words, Europe's extant networks are where the intellectual as well as
the practical contest for the political soul of Europe is fought out. What occurs
there shapes how we perceive the current state of play, and sharpens or dulls
our expectations for future developments accordingly. An interim and sensible
assessment on the current evidence would seem to corroborate the ambivalence

exhibited by the syncretists, rather than the supranationalist optimism or neorealist pessimism. The policy bargains that have resulted from this latest phase of integration are not so much unpredictable as inconclusive. Clearly *something* is unfolding in the European project. The EU today is more than the sum of its national parts. But the result of this momentum is by no means the certain, maximalist outcome confidently predicted by the supranational paradigm. The ultimate direction and shape of the European project remain indeterminate, in a way that the certitudes implied in the classical paradigms simply failed to countenance. Contingency plays its part here, as do leadership qualities and the steering skills of elites charged with the task of building the project, negotiating its institutions and procedures, and determining its policy priorities. Nor can we discount the steady fluctuations in either domestic circumstances or the flux of global events.[56] The very different emphases given to this network model and the conclusions that follow on from it in the essays by Kastendiek[57] **(Document 44)** and Bressand,[58] **(Document 45)** indicate its value as a lens for analysing what remains a multifarious and variable process. It is not the case that European integration defies all attempts to pin it down; but rather that it is a process too complex and fluid to be confined to the narrowly didactic categories of the mainstream paradigms.

While Kastendiek interprets the 1992 project as a 'networked bargain' in which national interests are temporarily rather than conclusively reconciled, Bressand prefers to see this process as a synergy of national, regional and global trends. Not that either of these particular approaches to the European policy process ignores the range of inputs – from individual statesmen to powerful macro forces – from what are, under the conditions of contemporary political economy, the interactive and interlocking networks which comprise the international system. The facts as opposed to the fantasies of European integration speak for themselves here. These writers underline what is the elemental truth of the matter; the multifarious nature of the regional process as it has unfolded over the past decade. Undoubtedly, accounts of the integration process cast in this syncretic mould are better able than either of the two classical paradigms to paint a more plausible picture of the processes that contribute to and shape the process of political change that is European integration – not least because this new revisionism combines assumptions about the dynamics of international change and brings together in the same intellectual framework behavioural and cognitive variables that the classical paradigms wrongly took to be inconsistent and mutually exclusive.

POSTSCRIPT: SYNCRETISM – NOT THE END OF THE QUEST, BUT WHERE WE ARE NOW

The notion of the European Union as a hybrid system is the only one that adequately fits the political facts. Of course, recommending any new paradigm requires the obvious caveat. Students of European integration should avoid the narrow prescriptions that translated the classical integration paradigms into polemics and ideology rather than into heuristic political theory. And we must be aware of the contingent quality of politics, which limits the relevance of even the most candid theoretical endeavours. Politics is a fluid rather than a mechanical process. To explain its exigencies requires imagination and intuition, but not where these qualities degenerate into whimsy or prejudice. Every political phenomenon must be periodically, and objectively, reviewed. With a suitable degree of humility we might reasonably expect more informed judgements and clearer insights into the actual dynamics of this immensely complicated regional process. The notion of a syncretic form of integration works precisely because it avoids the trap of narrow determinism or preconceived ideas that distorted some of the contributions to the earlier integration paradigms. Social scientists should be concerned only with explaining the world as it is, rather than justifying their own *a priori* preferences. This tendency to subjectivity has coloured the accounts of the classical paradigms on both sides of the argument.

This tentative conclusion about the shape and prospects for European integration has been easier to sustain as the optimism of the late 1980s has given way to altogether more sober reflections during the 1990s. European integration remains as conditional as ever it was, and just as delicately poised between its minimalist and maximalist extremes. The coexistence within the European Union of two different policy making styles, alongside competing institutional arrangements and policy agendas, reaffirms the syncretic quality of the enterprise. The European Union remains unquestionably a unique regime; but one in which a two level game is underway, played by different sets of rules, in pursuit of competing goals and conflicting aspirations, and for the benefit of different audiences.[59] The incomprehension registered among Europe's statesmen and bureaucrats by the public disquiet that followed Maastricht, served to underline that there is more than one version of what the European project is about. The balance of probabilities suggests, for the foreseeable future, an unsteady fluctuation between hope and caution among those political actors – national and supranational – charged with building the European project. This equivalence between optimism and pessimism is also likely to be reflected in the work of those academic commentators who have set themselves the task of assessing the project and its consequences for the nature of politics.

And so the process of explaining the meaning of European integration continues. It remains in essence what it has always been; events shadowed by commentators whose task it is to order and account for them. The 1996 IGC will cause both participants and commentators to take up these ideological cudgels once again and to try and clarify the significance of the European project. But almost certainly they will do so with as little success as previous attempts to square the circle of European integration. Unless, that is, they accept the fact that the process remains rooted in ambivalence rather than impelled by certainty. The evidence of the early manoeuvrings over the present IGC suggests that the same deep divisions between the institutional and national contributors, maximalists and minimalists are still very much in play in the European project. The task of the political scientist is to gauge this continuing animus and to explain it. The syncretic model seems better placed to provide the framework and suggest the hypotheses that will test the current state of European integration, than those didactic models it has so successfully challenged.

CONCLUSIONS

European integration theory has in one sense come full circle. Academics are currently debating as vigorously as ever, the same fundamental issues identified by the initial contributors to the classical paradigms. Nevertheless, something has changed in the tone if not the focus of this discourse. There is now much less exclusivism or theoretical insularity surrounding the debate. And far more uncertainty, about both the processes and outcomes of European integration.[60] Contemporary contributors to the debate on European integration are also more aware of the intricacies and unpredictable outcomes of international change. Pedersen distilled this theoretical turbulence in his observation that,

> Europe is changing complexion almost overnight. Though as political scientists our natural inclination is to look for precedents and theoretical constraints, most analysts would probably agree that what is happening has a strong flavour of uniqueness about it. We are all reaching for intellectual lifeboats to take us safely through the rough sea of systemic change. No one really knows what new European patterns of cooperation will emerge once the smoke has cleared.[61]

The positivism which infused the earlier paradigms of international society has been replaced by an altogether more conditional appraisal.[62] This theoretical flux has found its way into the discussion of the European subplot. Again, this is a case of a dialectic between events and theoretical accounting. There has been much talk of late, in both political and academic circles, of the Community's apparently irrepressible diversity being translated into a multi-speed or variable geometric approach to integration.[63] At most, the recent stalling of the EMU project and the resistance of some member states to embrace deeper political integration seems to endorse what two practitioners identified over a decade ago, as an unavoidably 'graduated' route to integration.[64] The increased pace of the changes in the Community's affairs during the 1980s by no means suggests that some inexorable momentum towards regional integration has, after all, finally broken free of the narrow, 'artificial' and historic constraints imposed on 'human welfare' by out-dated nationhoods. Indeed, one way forward out of the impasse that periodically grips the European project whenever the critical issue of sovereignty is raised by those charged with managing the Community's affairs, may well be to institutionalise diversity within the Community's procedural framework. The recent vogue for subsidiarity seems to offer a useful bridge here between the conflicting impulses of commonality of purpose and the continuing scope for 'local' initiative.[65] The maximalists predictably resist this as a concession to anti-Europeanism. It is instead, a concession to realism – a recognition that the project may fall apart altogether unless it acknowledges the different aspirations covered by the quest for 'European integration'.

The requirement for a proper reconciliation of these persistent differences and for continuing accommodations of deep laid interests will become ever more urgent as the Union enlarges its geographical extent and increases its population.[66] The nascent Committee of the Regions undoubtedly has a role to play in putting institutional flesh on the conceptual bones of subsidiarity.[67] Without possessing any effective powers beyond its nominal advisory role, and in the absence of a more fundamental reshaping of the Community's political and policy making procedures, it is unlikely that such cosmetic changes will be enough to avert a serious crisis of political authority. The prospects for fundamental changes in the Community's governance that will be debated as a matter of priority in the forth-coming IGC are pregnant both with opportunities and dangers. Nation states remain under severe challenge from powerful global forces above, and from all manner of citizen discontent, regional movements and political factionalism below.[68] The pattern of electoral volatility that has occurred, even in some of Europe's most stable democracies, provides some clues to these tensions.[69] New political relationships and procedures for governance are in the offing. But these will not necessarily accommodate old shibboleths or conform to current expectations about the nature or direction of political change. Nor will they automatically lead to a promised land of cosy supranationalism underpinned by a new sense of European identity. Students of European integration need to be aware that we are indeed in a new and rapidly changing political landscape, one that calls for entirely new paradigms to explain its unique dynamics.

The search for the causes or stimuli of European regional integration has tended to focus on the political consequences of economic change. This causal equation was one of the principal legacies of those functionalist theories that made most of the early pace in the academic discourse on European futures. Economic factors have done much to determine the pace and shape of European integration, but this is clearly only one theme in a wider picture. Recent events, not least the unexpected and largely negative response of large sections of public opinion in the EU to the Maastricht treaty, suggest that we need to cast our theoretical net further afield. In future, those theorists searching for clues to the dynamics of the European regional process will need to trawl the largely uncharted waters of sociology. The most revealing evidence for the prospects or otherwise of an 'ever closer' union may well lie in what the behavioural sciences, other than politics or economics, have to tell us about changing cultural patterns and identity formation. These disciplines, with their focus on the linkages between value patterns and social and political structures, undoubtedly have as much to contribute to our understanding of this multifarious process as the policy sciences per se.[70]

It is not difficult to see why this should be so. After all, the affective under-pinning of those significant shifts in the aspirations of the national political elites who are charged with legislating these changes, and of the expectations of their citizens who legitimise them at the ballot box or in ratification referenda, are far from incidental to the direction of change or to its outcomes. On the contrary, as the Maastricht interlude showed, social attitudes, political values and cultural perceptions are, in the final analysis, the foundation on which the European project is either securely built or otherwise founders.[71] Public opinion, and the deeper perceptions of self, identity and place which continue to inform it, cannot be ignored or discounted in any attempt to account for the integration phenomenon, either by those politicians charged with making the project work, or those academics who set themselves the task of explaining it.[72] The success or otherwise of the project of European integration depends now, as it has always done, on gauging how much integration it is likely, and with what implications for the traditional political order of nation states, public opinion will countenance, and how quickly.[73] It depends for its success then – whether this is measured in maximalist or minimalist terms – on instilling a sense of common purpose across those still deeply entrenched barriers of historical myth, cultural difference, and linguistic or ethnic identity that continue to divide European states and, as the Yugoslavian fall out has revealed, occasionally divide Europe against itself. This sense of Pan European identity may well be, as Anthony Smith (**Document 46**) suggests, an easier prospectus to recommend as an abstraction, than it is to deliver in practice.[74] At the same time, we must never underestimate the novelty of the present European situation or the prospects it harbours for a real and permanent change in the patterns of economic and political decision making in the European Union.[75] What is patently clear from both the developments on the ground and the theoretical debate that has accompanied them, is the coexistence of radical and conservative options at the very centre of the European project. In that sense, little has changed from the outset of the quest for European integration.

This complementarity of opposites implies less an impasse than a creative tension at the heart of the Community project. This is the case in both the theoretical discourse and in the actual evolution of the Community's institutions and procedures. And, as we have seen in this book, these two aspects of integration remain closely connected. The extensive policy bargains and institutional accommodations that resulted from the debate over the limits or prospects of regional integration, reflect the EU's unique status as an international network. The momentous changes that have occurred in the Community's affairs during the past decade were too sudden and disruptive of the status quo to sustain the narrow intergovernmental account of the integration process. At the same time, these changes were by no means as extensive as those predicated in the federalist thesis.[76] There was, nevertheless, a kind of systemic momentum in this remarkable catalogue of events; an element of what neofunctionalists have identified as undirected change, alongside the directed change and structurally determined outcomes of the policy bargains struck between those functional and governmental, national and transnational elites who oversee the regional process and contribute most to its outcomes.

What is apparent, both from the way the European regional process has unfolded and from the way that academic theorists have tried to conceptualise it over the duration, is that the process is an endemically syncretic one. It harbours mixed motives and conflicting expectations.[77] In these circumstances, any appropriate theoretical explanation of this regional process needs to encompass the two fundamentally different purposes that reside within it. The continuities of nationhood as a source of identity, belonging and, thus, of political stability, need to be accommodated to the new demands of global interdependence which challenge and erode the sense of autarchy and insularity of the traditional politics of sovereign states. The syncretic model is best suited to explaining this coexistence of competing impulses alongside mutual interests that bind the EU's states in common endeavours, within a cogent theoretical framework. By starting from the implicit assumption that international change is driven by a mixed impetus rather than a singular impulse, and indeed that it thrives on the clash of competing expectations about the purposes, procedures and best outcomes of integration, the new syncretic model is much better placed to explain the patterning of variables that are at work in the regional process. During the past decade or so, those theorists who have been persuaded of this hybrid quality of the integration process have kept pace with the flux of events and, as such, given a more than useful account of those initiatives launched in response to them on the European ground.

We have begun, then, to navigate the currents and eddies of European integration with a degree of intellectual modesty and with a ready eye for the ambiguities which inhabit the process and continue to throw more confident and certain predictions off course. Contemporary commentators have at last assimilated what Suzanne Boddenheimer perceptively condemned as the futility of 'a rhetoric of absolutes'. She pointed out as early as 1967, when such a view was far from fashionable and the current integration discourse was dominated by paradigmic extremes, that 'to stake the future of Europe upon a choice between the decline of national structures and the permanent acceptance of absolute national sovereignty is to pose the question in absolute and somewhat irrelevant terms'.[78] European integration theory has finally come to terms with, and embraced, the common sense of this position. The European process is now widely recognised as a hybrid rather than a singular process; a composite of opposing tendencies rather than one driven by a unicausal dynamic. This is the sensible starting point for any plausible attempt to explain European integration. Indeed, it is the most we can expect from honest scientific endeavour. The acceptance of things as they are rather than as we might prefer them to be, distinguishes the pursuit of the social scientist from that of the ideologist, and separates the work of the theoretician from that of the mere polemicist.

Part III

Documents

Documents

Document 1: W. Lipgens, 'The major political consequences of the Second World War', from *A History of European Integration: Vol. One, 1945–1947* (Oxford, 1982), pp. 44–52

The major political consequences of the second world war

... The Second World War thus ended a process that had started with the catastrophe of the First World War. Up to then the European states had directly or indirectly dominated the world for at least three centuries; it was in Europe that military might, economic superiority, and intellectual progress were all concentrated. Under Europe's leadership between 1870 and 1914 the world, having undergone an industrial revolution, had experienced an unprecedented transformation of its mode of living and a vast increase in production, trade, and investment under the aegis of economic liberalism and internationalism. Within the monarchical state the doctrine of 'sovereignty', conceived in an earlier age as an antidote to the civil wars of religion, was now used by the conservative opponents of the liberal–democratic movement in order to break it up and divert it, and on both sides, as traditional Christian values lost their power, people came to accept hypercharged nationalism as a substitute religion; it had degenerated into the dogma of an eternal and absolute national sovereign state, responsible to no one and nothing except the policy of national imperialism and expansion. As a global concern Europe could only lose its hitherto unchallenged hegemony in the economic, financial and political spheres if the states which were partners in it were to wage a suicidal war against each other. It was their compartmentalized power politics – in contrast to their growing economic interdependence and the international character of world trade – which, once they had failed to resolve the tensions between them, drove them into four years of mutual destruction in the First World War.

In the most critical year of the war – 1917 – the United States and Russia, which had long since outstripped the Europeans and in the nineteenth century had colonized their vast open spaces, entered world politics with decisions of revolutionary significance ...

. . . But the direct influence of both powers was, as yet, short-lived; internal factors – which lie outside the scope of the present work – pulled them both back into isolation soon after the end of the war . . .

. . . Europe was given one more chance. This chance was indeed almost inexplicably squandered by the Europeans between 1919 and 1939. The balance sheet of the First World War was soon realized: Europe had lost its position as leader of the world; the independence movement had become active among the colonial peoples; Great Britain had to concede full freedom of action to her Dominions even in foreign policy; Europe's resources had been exhausted, victors as well as vanquished were impoverished and had become debtors to the new world creditor nation, the United States. Many European statesmen were well aware that their countries, lying between the rising continental-size states, had been granted only a temporary respite in which to come to their senses and to unite; but their wish for future peaceful close co-operation in Europe did not go far enough to make them will the necessary means . . .

. . . In this way Europe persisted in a situation which Carl J. Burckhardt had accurately defined in 1922: 'We shall have to wait a long time for nationalism to subside . . . Its hypnotic power continues to increase. In that respect we have long been in the position of the Greeks after the first Roman victories, perhaps we too shall have to experience occupation.'

The most serious direct results of this obdurate nationalism occurred in the economic sphere. The European states clung to the policy which they had adopted during the First World War of pursuing economic 'autarky' as a supposed remedy for their economic decline . . . Every attempt in the 1920s to restore a liberal world economy proved fruitless because the European countries reacted to their reduced ability to import from each other by throttling back trade inside Europe by raising tariffs along frontiers which the Treaty of Versailles had lengthened by about 20,000 kilometres. The national economies, fragmented and artificially restricted, stagnated; in consequence of economic nationalism they were unable to produce anything like the domestic prosperity they desired; while in the same period in spite of crises the United States and the Soviet Union opened up and industrialized their countries and thus developed their production and markets to a formidable size.

Economic, political, and intellectual developments, though not understood by the European peoples, were in fact working towards large-scale communities; the European nation states, already dwarfed in size, could not achieve the welfare they all sought. It was this very failure which, on the contrary, produced the reactionary movements that opposed the devaluation of the state and the repudiation of war, and sought to uphold 'national sovereignty' by every means in their power. Thanks to the misery caused by the world economic crisis, which led to a complete retreat into economic isolationism that in turn only aggravated the crisis, various forms of Fascism came to power in almost half the states of Europe, and saw in their countries' 'struggle for survival' a higher value than peace. The German form of Fascism, culminating in a last attempt of one nation to achieve hegemony in Europe, and intensified by Hitler's ruthless and total application of the slogan 'My country right or wrong' into a brutal late form of national imperialism, plunged Europe into the Second World War. By defeating all the other Continental states Nazi Germany imposed an effective economic and military unification of the Continent but by a dictatorship which provoked the opposition of every vital force still left in Europe, even though it took the intervention – this time a final one – of the two new world powers to bring the regime down. At the end of this war all real authority on the European Continent lay in the hands of these two superpowers, who alone made decisions about frontiers, political institutions, and economic affairs; who, in a formal sense – and this must be repeated – decided in favour of systematically restoring the national states, while in fact dividing the Continent between themselves into areas of control or spheres of influence. Whatever in subsequent years the two world powers in their respective spheres would – very differently – initiate, the 'Roman occupation' foreseen by Burckhardt had arrived. The European system of national states which had once dominated the globe had been replaced by a bipolar system of global hegemony jointly exercised by the United States and the Soviet Union . . .

Document 2: Alan Milward, 'Reconstruction and integration',
from *The Reconstruction of Western Europe 1945–51* (London, 1984),
pp. 491–8, 502

Reconstruction and integration

Few would dispute that the prosperity of the 1950s itself contributed to the durability of the western European reconstruction, seeming to confirm the wisdom of its principles. The process of integration, although explained and understood in a great variety of ways, has usually been regarded as making an important contribution to this durability also and the argument of this book supports that view. The nexus of economic and political ties between France and the Federal Republic was what held the second peace settlement together, just as the absence of these ties was a main cause of the ineffectiveness of the first. The various attachments which bound the other European countries into the settlement could not have been completed without those ties and would not survive their breaking. In that sense 'European integration', that phrase capable of so many meanings, depended on a central necessity, a Franco-West German economic association and alliance. But although a simple reassertion of this basic diplomatic reality explains more of the nature of European integration than much of the vague rhetoric on the theme, the concept of European integration was obviously always a larger one and more forward than backward-looking.

To a greater or lesser degree earlier treatments of this theme attribute the movement towards integration to human idealism fortunately triumphing at *against*

specific moments over the narrow, anachronistic realism of national governments. The strength of this idealism is usually related to the events of the war itself, as though the experience of National Socialism, of resistance, of the appalling bloodshed and terror and, at the end, of the relative feebleness and helplessness of the European nation state, particularly in the face of the two 'superpowers', had convinced a sufficient number of people that it was an inadequate, unstable basis for a durable reconstruction.

That view of the matter is flatly contradicted by this book. Here the interpretation is that the very limited degree of integration that was achieved came about through the pursuit of the narrow self interest of what were still powerful nation states . . . Previous writers have always entirely failed to show through what political mechanism the idealisms which supported western European integration actually influenced governmental policy-making in the nation states, unless it be through the vague suggestion that men like Adenauer, Schuman, Sforza, and Spaak, who themselves shared these enthusiasms, were able to override the massed cohorts of government and bureaucracy whose task it was and is to define and uphold the national interest before all else. Of these idealists Monnet has always been depicted as the most effective just because he deliberately stood outside this apparatus of national bureaucracy and government in order to persuade others of the higher ideals which it was necessary to espouse.

There is no intention in this book to deny a certain welcome leaven of idealism to these men, although the other political ideas which they stood for were not shared by many who also ardently desired a less divisive political framework in western Europe. But the policies from which a limited measure of economic integration did emerge were, so the evidence clearly indicates, created by national bureaucracies out of the internal expression of national political interest, not by the major statesmen who implemented them. The Schuman Plan, for example, was based on two and a half years of the evolution of policy in the French Ministry of Foreign Affairs . . .

. . . Those who explain the movement towards integration as essentially a victory of higher ideals see it also as a progression towards political virtue, reaching a high point between 1950 and 1952, falling back between 1953 and 1954, relaunched in a forward direction in 1955 until it reached the furthermost point of its advance in 1957 with the Treaty of Rome, holding that advanced position until the entry into force of the European Economic Community, and then being beaten back in a series of small but constant defeats, interrupted only by the election of a European parliament, as the nation states reasserted their misguided claim to be able to guarantee the European future. The interpretation of the EEC in this book[1] is quite different. The historical evidence is that it came into existence to cope with certain historically specific and well-defined economic and political problems and, those problems once resolved, there would be no further momentum from the national interest towards any further stage of economic or political integration . . . The obvious implication of this book is that the ECSC, the Common Agricultural Policy and the Common Market were indispensable pillars of Europe's reconstruction. But each was and is designed to resolve a particular and limited, not a generalized and universal, problem. There was no necessary implication in any of these carefully controlled acts of economic integration that the supersession of the nation state was an inevitable continuing process. The process of integration is neither a thread woven into the fabric of Europe's political destiny nor one woven into the destiny of all highly developed capitalist nation states.

This does not mean that integration has come to a stop, only that any further steps in that direction will have to be equally specific to the resolution of economic and political problems not otherwise resolvable. There may well be such problems; the theoretical possibility therefore certainly exists that the pattern of integrative activity of the reconstruction period could be repeated.

The historical evidence gives considerable support, in fact, to the theoretical proposition that the validity of the ECSC, as of other examples of sectoral integration, did not lie so much in their vaunted supra-nationality as in their extra-nationality – that they were created as an arm of the nation states to do things which could not otherwise be achieved.

Integration, as it evolved between 1947 and 1951, was a formalization of inter-dependence significantly different in form and final implication from anything previously seen. Even if the motive which compelled nation states to surrender aspects of the 'sovereignty' they had so jealously guarded over centuries was to prevent the uncompleted arch of western Europe's reconstruction from collapsing in ruins, this in no way diminishes either the importance of the specific acts of integration or their novelty. The durability of western Europe's reconstruction has in part depended on a new kind of international organization. But was that development specific to the time and circumstances of the reconstruction, a historical, rather than a political or economic problem? If the historical evidence will in no way support the theory that integration is the necessary and inevitable end of the nation state, is it possible to comprehend the role of integration in the reconstruction as anything other than a set of specific, unique historical events . . .

. . . In so far, therefore, as other theories of integration place the emphasis less on this progress towards 'community' and more on the primacy of major political actors, the political elites and the machinery of the state, in achieving integration (however it be defined), the history of the reconstruction gives them far more support. The role, for example, of political socialization, of the acquisition of new and more favourable attitudes towards the idea of European political integration by the national voters or populations as a whole, was negligible in producing the ECSC compared to the role of political elites, often concerned with matters of future national security about which the population at large was far from fully informed. Even when a wave of emotional sympathy for the ideas of a European federation welled up in 1947 and 1948 it was no more than a faintly disquieting and soon stilled disturbance for the ships of state, their officer governments and their crews of civil servants. For the populations of the nation states it was only a publicly experienced dream of a better Europe which could not long survive the baleful awakening reality of those years. The growth of political pressure groups advocating European unity which culminated in The Hague Congress, although an interesting study in itself, had very little effect on the major political actors, except when they wished temporarily to use such sentiments for their own ends . . .

. . . Much of the political theory which aims to explain how this type of supranational integration can come about tends to put the emphasis on the development in the modern world of economic, social or ecological trends which the nation state can no longer cope with inside its own frontiers. To continue to function adequately the powers of many of its institutions have to reach beyond the frontiers. The mechanism of integration is thus a functional one, depending not on the highest levels of governmental decision-making, but on the problem-solving activities of functional institutions at a lower level. This sort of theory is no better a fit with the historical evidence from the reconstruction period than the more generalized liberal equation of integration with progress and development as inherent tendencies in the nation state, and obviously has certain shared assumptions with it . . .

. . . More complex and interesting theories which would explain the process of integration are those which have been labelled 'neo-functionalist'. Here the emphasis is on the tendency of the interaction of political forces such as governments, parties, or interest groups, in promoting their own interests through the medium of international political institutions, to find, nevertheless, that in this pursuit their self-interest is best satisfied in an integrative solution. Thus, Haas would see the process of interaction by all these forces within the ECSC as leading to a gradual move to a new, supra-national centre of authority.

Whether this has in fact been the case seems extremely doubtful, but the historical evidence in this book[2] could be no test of such a theory because it would have to be tested by historical events subsequent to the forming of the Communities. The way in which the Schuman Plan emerged, its causes and motives, the course of negotiations for the ECSC, all suggest, however, that the major political actors have first to make the decisive political step and build the arena in which the neo-functionalist interplay of vested interests can push the process of integration further, if, indeed, they do. Many of those vested interests were firmly opposed to the building of that arena. To suggest, as Haas does, that the emergence of this neo-functionalist interaction of vested interests implies that there is no longer a distinct political function 'which finds its reason for being in the sublime heights of foreign policy, defence and constitution-making' is to attribute a formidable change of function and attitude over a very short period to an international institution such as the ECSC, which was created, against the strong opposition of many of those vested interests, to conquer those very heights.

Political theory, therefore, does very little to explain why the process of reconstruction was able to clinch its success by new forms of political and economic organization . . .

... The form of integration which did complete Western Europe's reconstruction was based on an attempt by the nation states to control and distribute the gains and losses which might arise in the particular sectors involved in such a way as to determine beforehand the extent to which the national interest of each party to the agreement would be satisfied. Monnet's own original conception of the High Authority would have left more scope to the neo-functionalist interaction of self-interest than Haas believes did actually characterize the ECSC once it began to operate. But this scope was drastically reduced in the negotiating process which set up the ECSC so as to determine as far as possible the extent and direction of national gain and loss before the High Authority began to function ...

... The appropriateness of the present Western European institutions to an enlarged EEC is not easy to see. For the first time the validity of the principles of western Europe's reconstruction is called into question on all sides. Its pillars tremble. The painfully constructed roof of interdependence shakes. The balance of power still depends on the thrust and counter-thrust of the nation states which sustain it. Adjustments of their positions are continually necessary, but even the smallest makes the two great buttresses of the super-powers start to slip and slide and those beneath to cower. Let all those who wish to reconstruct the roof on fundamentally new principles think first that never except beneath that roof has western Europe known so long a peace nor a life so prosperous and so humane ...

Notes

1 Refers to the publication in which this text originally appeared.
2 As above.

Document 3: W. Lipgens, 'The triumph of the supranational principle in the Resistance', op. cit. (1982), pp. 44–57

The triumph of the supranational principle in the Resistance

During the inter-war period European-minded writers had given prophetic warnings that, unless unity was achieved in time, the selfishness of national states would plunge Europe into a new war. And this war, unleashed by Hitler in 1939 in a bid for German supremacy in Europe, was now a cruel reality which brought suffering to millions of families and expanded into a global conflict ...

(A) The Resistance movement against 'Hitler's Europe'

The First World War, fought in trenches lying to a greater or lesser extent along national frontiers, was a war which (apart from the Habsburg Empire) did not bring about the wholesale collapse of states. Consequently at the European level its impact was felt chiefly by small groups of intellectuals. The six years of the Second World War, by contrast, were a harsh and unforgettable experience for the great mass of the population and caused the total collapse of almost every state on the Continent. The experience of the inter-war period had shown that Europe's states were too small to solve by their own efforts the problems of a modern economy, and the outbreak of a new war in 1939 proved the failure of all the attempts made since the First World War to set up a collective peace-keeping organization. Then for most Europeans came a still greater shock: by 1940–1 every European state north of the Pyrenees, with the exceptions of Great Britain, Sweden, and Switzerland, had been destroyed by Hitler's brutal lust for power, in a process which finally led to the destruction of the Italian and German states. All these governments had shown themselves incapable of guaranteeing their peoples the minimum of security and independence which it is the first duty of any government to provide.

During the war people had to put up with the effective domination of practically the entire Continent by the German occupation forces, the humiliation of their own governments, and the mobilization of all resources irrespective of existing frontiers. This was the day-to-day reality which lasted for four years. The object lesson provided by the collapse and conquest, and by the creation of a single centrally controlled economy, did more to accustom the public at large to think in Continental terms than the whole Coudenhove-Kalergi movement a decade earlier . . .

. . . For the Resistance groups which sprang into existence in Italy, Germany, and the occupied countries paramilitary resistance operations were impossible until the last few months before the Allied landings, at least in central and western parts of Europe, because of the efficient police system. Mental resistance was for a long time the only possible and in fact the most important form of resistance. The difficulties and obstacles in the way of even an adequate response to the challenge were inconceivably great; yet despite pressures of every kind the men of the Resistance (of course only a small minority) risked their lives not simply against something which already existed, but above all for something which they wished to put in its place. In a dangerous situation and facing a formidable challenge, they still succeeded in saying what a better future might look like.

The majority of the underground leaflets, distributed every week by the hundred, even by the thousand, contained accusations of coercion, injustice, and disregard for human rights perpetrated by the Nazi regime. But hardly ever in the non-Communist Resistance – which was the original and for most of the war the predominant type of resistance everywhere – did any underground newspaper or leaflet favour a return to the pre-war system of national states . . .

. . . Many Resistance pamphlets demanded, following the logic of their case, decentralization within national states, with more power placed in the hands of self-governing local communities of manageable size. By making people accustomed to a free kind of democracy in Europe (such pamphlets argued, using similar language despite their independent origins), by making the democratic principle of self-government from below a reality, 'effective guarantees would be set up against the creation of an absolutist, centralizing and bureaucratic power of the national sovereign state'. But, living as they did through a period of absolutist power, the authors of these pamphlets knew that interstate federation could not in itself overcome the totalitarian claims of existing states, but that a supranational authority must be established to safeguard peace, democratization, and human rights.

(B) The need for supranational authority

The attempt to answer people's first and most pressing question during the miseries of war and occupation – how to safeguard peace in future – led in the literature of the Resistance to the further question which was put in many different ways: Why had the organization for collective security set up after the First World War failed? So horrified had the statesmen been at the loss of their security and prosperity, and at the decline of Europe by comparison with the rest of the world, that they had tried through the Covenant of the League of Nations to create a law to prevent war that would have been unthinkable in the decades before 1914. Why was it that, only twenty years later, 'the first dream of world peace had dissolved in blood'? Men of the Resistance in every European country gave the answer independently of each other, indeed without even knowing of each other, in what turned out to be astonishingly similar terms. Two major reasons were identified:

1 The League of Nations failed not for this or that accidental reason, but because, as all the evidence quite plainly showed, it had been set up as an institution in international law consisting of sovereign states. Therefore it was inhibited by its very structure from performing the task assigned to it, whatever the nature of that task might be. The League had failed, as Léon Blum, at the time a prisoner of the Vichy government, wrote in 1941 in a passage that influenced the whole French Resistance: 'because it was not a sovereign power in its own right, independent of and superior to national sovereignties; because to implement its decisions it possessed neither the political authority nor the material power that would have prevailed over that of individual states'. It failed, wrote Einaudi, leader of Italy's underground liberals in 1943, like all mere alliances or confederations 'because it had no legislature and executive power of its own, but depended on the unanimous votes of its member states'. The same kind of arguments were used in the other languages of Europe, though there is no space here to go into detail.

2 The other reason why the League failed, as documents of the Resistance continually emphasize, is that it could neither meet what were supposed to be its global responsibilities on the one hand, nor concentrate on Europe on the other, but fell between two stools . . .

. . . Therefore 'a gradual and piecemeal solution must be tried', and a distinction drawn between two problems. 'One solution consists of forming unions or federations which would allow states with close territorial or cultural ties to abolish their currency, customs and defence barriers and to manage their resources in common', so that nationalism and war between them would in future be impossible.

The other solution was to strive for world-wide 'international laws, whereby clashes of self-interest between the federations could be settled and a common code worked out in the sphere of morality and law'. The final goal remained, in the words of the umbrella organization of all Resistance groups in the Lyons region, a definite outlawing of war and the 'unity of all nations in a federal world organization', but 'this immense and long-term task can only be undertaken with any prospect of success if in the first place a solution is found for the problem of Europe, which has been the starting-place of so many appalling catastrophes' . . .

. . . In this way the future voluntary European federation came to occupy a dominant position in the programme of the non-Communist Resistance groups in every country. There were countless descriptions of how this federation was to be created in detail. Within the Resistance there were, probably in every country, small right-wing groups which for special reasons were not in the collaborationist camp, such as the Goerdeler group in Berlin, the 'Organisation civile et militaire' in Paris, and others. These acknowledged the need for a binding international legal order and for economic unification, but they wished to preserve a degree of independence for individual states in their foreign policy. They spoke of a 'European directorate' and an 'economic council' which would need machinery to implement their decisions, but nevertheless sought solutions which would leave states their freedom to make basic decisions and would be confederal rather than federal in character. The great majority of Resistance writers, however, opposed any special consideration for national sovereignty in the sphere of foreign policy, economics, and defence. This time care was to be taken to avoid the chief mistake of 1919, which was the institutional weakness of the League of Nations. War between European states would have to be made absolutely impossible by the establishment of a strong European federal government . . .

. . . A test agreed by the umbrella organizations of all the Resistance groups in the Lyons region effectively summarized the views of many similar documents: 'The nation states ought to federate and transfer to the common federal state the right to manage the economic and commercial life of Europe, the sole authority over its armed forces and the right to take measures against any attempt to re-establish a fascist regime. The federation must also have the right to manage foreign relations and to administer colonial territories not ripe for independence, and the right to create a European citizenship in addition to national citizenship. The government of the federal state is to be chosen not by the nation states but by democratic and direct elections by the peoples.' It was in such terms that the basic insights of innumerable writers were expressed at a time when Continental Europe was lying prostrate. For them it was completely unthinkable that the old system of European sovereign states should be restored once again after the experience of Fascism and world war to which that system had led . . .

Document 4: Karl Kaiser, 'L'Europe des savants: European integration and the social sciences', *Journal of Common Market Studies* **Vol. 4: 1964, pp. 40–1, 43**

. . . No wonder then that American scholars have succeeded, where Europeans have failed, in making successful contributions in vital areas of political science: the former are not subject to the restraining forces of insecurities and traditional concepts present in European thinking.

Their first contribution lies in the attention they have paid to the roots and nature of the social and political changes transforming Europe, i.e. their attempt to sort out *political integration or community-building* as a relevant trend in modern Europe and to investigate it systematically, with the aim of organizing knowledge. As such, it represents the first stage in the development of theory. And that leads to their second contribution, perhaps the most important one American scholars have made. It consists of the attempt to approach the subject of change in the European system from the standpoint of the social sciences. They have set out on the basis of systematic empirical analysis to elaborate a number of conceptual frameworks which enable us to ask relevant questions, to orient future research, and to suggest a variety of working hypotheses which can be tested against reality, and if necessary, revised. They have thus made a serious effort to pursue some of the goals of the social sciences, namely to develop a theory that will enhance our understanding of reality and to advance a set of propositions which will eventually provide tools to solve concrete problems more effectively.

The effort of American scholars to apply the methods and purposes of the social sciences to European integration raises a second general point that might help explain the failure of Europeans to address themselves to some vital areas of change in modern Europe. The difference in concern and in scientific methods between European and American scholars is partly due to a difference in their disciplines of political science.

This branch of the social sciences was largely developed in its modern form in the United States, and this accounts for the higher degree of sophistication in American methods. But even more important: American political science starts from a much broader definition of politics than its European counterpart, whose notion of politics is more restricted and strongly legal. American political science, therefore, regards a wide range of problems as 'political' and incorporates large areas of neighbouring disciplines like sociology, psychology, or economics into its field. Political science in (continental) Europe, however, tends to allocate the same problems to other disciplines and defines its scope in much narrower terms, confining it to the study of phenomena defined by or relevant to the Constitution. Naturally, there are significant exceptions, but we are dealing with general trends. If this characterization of differences in political studies (and basically in their notion of politics) is valid, then it should help us understand why European political scientists have not turned their attention in a systematic way to the problems of political integration in Europe. They are less inclined than their American colleagues to regard them as an obvious subject of their discipline . . .

... These works, to which could be added a number of other studies, mainly in article form, have one characteristic in common: they address themselves to developments that tend to transcend socio-political structures centred in the nation-state and their underlying value systems. Uninhibited by the Europeans' feeling of uncertainty about the 'new Europe' or the imposing presence of traditional values, the American scholars (whose European origin, incidentally, is mostly not very remote) have felt more freely able to investigate and theorize about political and social changes in Europe that go 'beyond the nation-state'. To them, more than to Europeans, Western Europe represents a huge laboratory of change that offers unique opportunities to the social scientist of searching into the nature of modern society by observing the process of change, experimenting with and testing a set of hypotheses that could help to explain it.

In addition, it has been the broader definition of 'politics' that has made the study of European integration more imperative to the American than to the European scholar whose notion of politics is more narrowly defined.

Finally, mention should be made of the institutional facilities in the United States which create a uniquely favourable climate for research in the social sciences. The European University system is far less flexible than that of the United States, and the financial resources of universities and foundations in Europe are hardly comparable with those in America.

It goes without saying that theoretical propositions advanced by different authors should stimulate a scholarly discussion in which their findings are subjected to scrutiny and clarification. Although in Europe the adherents and opponents of a European federation have been discussing issues of European integration, the debate has been primarily a political one; the scholarly debate so far has taken place mainly in America ...

Document 5: R.J. Harrison, 'Integration theory: context, scope and method', from *Europe in Question – Theories of Regional Integration* (London, 1974), pp. 9, 14–18, 20–3

Integration theory: context, scope and method

... The object of this particular study is to examine this literature and determine whether it does provide the basis for a reliable 'general theory' of regional integration – a theory upon which expectations about the future development of the European Community may be based. A first step must be to outline the envisaged scope of the subject and show how it relates to explanations or theories in other subject areas in social science. ... The literature relevant to this concern has gone through a number of phases.

... Integration is evidently a process of political but also far-reaching social transformation. The integration process which has interested modern theorists and the one to which the six are ostensibly committed by the Rome Treaty may be further, though still loosely, defined then, as the attainment within an area of the bonds of political community: of central institutions with binding decision-making powers and methods of control determining the allocation of values at the regional level and also of adequate complementary consensus-formation mechanisms. This is the dependent variable on which this study focuses. Within the terms of this stipulative definition, successful integration means a balanced development of all these elements . . .

. . . At the heart of these problems is the general question of the applicability of scientific method in the study of human behaviour. A few observations should be made, therefore, about the approach to this question in the present work.

The concept 'science', denoting man's disciplined enquiry into the nature of his physical environment, is now widely used in the study of the social environment also. Since a body of explanatory theory relating to the social environment has been in existence for some time, built up by philosophers, historians, economists, through perceptive and intuitive observation of the social order, it is not surprising that there has been some controversy between those who prefer this 'classical' approach and the new force of self-styled 'social scientists'. Hedley Bull, for example, has criticised the 'scientific approach' in its application to international politics. He presents, as an alternative, the classical view that there is very little of significance that can be said about international relations; that general propositions cannot be accorded anything more than the tentative and inconclusive status appropriate to their origin. We must 'appreciate our reliance upon the capacity for judgment in the theory of international relations'. There are, for example, empirical questions, but of so elusive a nature that any answer we provide to them will leave some things unsaid. And, 'It is not merely that in framing hypotheses in answer to these empirical questions we are dependent upon intuition or judgement (as has often been pointed out, this is as true in the natural as in the social sciences); it is that in the *testing* of them we are utterly dependent upon judgement also, upon a rough and ready observation of a sort for which there is no room in logic or strict science, that things are this way and not that . . . the student whose study of international politics consists solely of an introduction to the technique of systems theory, game theory, simulation, or content analysis is simply shut off from contact with the subject, and is unable to develop any feeling either for the play of inter-national politics or for the moral dilemmas to which it gives rise . . . the freedom of the model builder from the discipline of looking at the world is what makes him dangerous.'[1]

Though this controversy has sometimes proceeded as though there were mutually exclusive methods at stake, both have, in fact, yielded valuable and, generally, compatible results. If it is a comment on current teaching, Bull's warning of the dangers of narrow training is scarcely justified even in the United States. Really at issue, are the respective merits of the two approaches in meeting the requirements of comparative cost and of logic. There can be no denying that the methods of social science are sometimes more costly than those of traditional research. The human and market resources used in the collection of data and in data processing for example. . . . But to conclude the debate in such terms would be very short sighted if scientific method can add something to the status of explanation relating to the social environment.

The question on which this is dependent is one Hedley Bull raises. Is social enquiry susceptible to logical rules applied in the scientific spirit of ethical neutrality? Of a completely negative answer one can only say that it must rest on some intuitive philosophical position, itself not absolutely susceptible, therefore, to logical refutation. A positive answer provokes the very practical question, whether the nature of the material, though it may not of itself preclude ethical neutrality, nevertheless raises insuperable barriers to the application of scientific procedures. A first answer to this question would be that it is impossible to equate the whole range of social phenomena in this respect. . . . The data peculiarities of each subject of social enquiry are different. Thus, though it is possible, and we shall now try, to generalise very broadly about the methodological difficulties of social science and the way they affect our enquiries, we must consider thereafter the special problems which arise for integration theory.

One fairly innocuous way of condensing and simplifying an account of the methodological difficulties which affect all social scientists is to suggest that they have to contend, more or less, with two basic difficulties. The first is one of terminology. Human behaviour, though it may be studied with ethical neutrality, is not itself ethically neutral. Explanation must, therefore, take account of such factors as prestige, loyalty, religion, legitimacy, terms which change their connotation in time and place, or, with little or no difference in connotation, produce quite different behaviour patterns in time and place . . .

. . . The second general problem is the absence of the experimental situation, and the consequent problem of bias. Essentially, experiment requires the isolation of variables to determine their causal significance. The answer of the social scientist is the comparative method, which has the same underlying logic as the experiment. Sets of variables are compared, to establish, by agreement and difference, the necessary connections between them. The difficulty for the social scientist is that control is virtually impossible and he must, therefore, select those variables for comparison which he considers significant. In selecting some and dismissing others, a value judgement is exercised in the initial comparison. So numerous are the concurrent factors which might be relevant in social phenomena, that subsequent repeated attempts to falsify the hypothesis can merely reduce the possibility that a wrong selection and a false hypothesis was made. However, as hypotheses formulated by other social scientists are tested and compared and a general theory begins to emerge, the problem of selecting which variables are relevant for comparison becomes less subject to the initial bias, more closely governed by the theoretical orientation.

Integration theory does not escape these difficulties of terminology and bias. . . . In the analysis of these developments, the terminological difficulty has been acute. The term 'political community' has been widely used in attempts to define the dependent variable – integration. It has been used to express the basic conceptual difference between the integration of the Six and other patterns of regional international co-operation. But the term 'political community' has itself proved confusing. In popular usage, as here, the component term 'community' connotes the existence of some common interests and some elementary sense of identity or fellowship among people. It is used indiscriminately, and without apparent confusion to imply these qualities of any group. . . . The problem extends to the use of the hybrid term 'political community' in integration theory . . .

. . . So far one cannot claim that a generally accepted meaning for the term has evolved in integration theory. With perhaps justifiable impatience, therefore, Siotis has insisted that 'the basic characteristic of a Community is that there exist between its members certain bonds of solidarity that distinguish them, and as a result the Community which they form, from the other members of the surrounding social milieu. This 'core element' of popular usage he does not find an adequate criterion for distinguishing between the EEC and other regional and international organisations and treaty arrangements. The confusion illustrates the danger of purloining, for stipulated use, a word with a generally accepted meaning in popular usage.

To the variety of terms borrowed from 'popular' usage in this specialised field must also be added a great host of neologisms, elite unit, lieutenant unit, identitive power, internationalisation, spillover, feedback, supranational. As with words imported from everyday use, stipulative definitions are always offered, but discipline in their use is much harder to attain in social science than in the natural sciences. Ohms, watts, and volts are quantifiable, and can be expressed in terms of other quantifiable phenomena. Indentitive power, spillover, supranationality are expressions for intangibles . . .

. . . The second general problem, the existence of bias in the selection of variables for comparative study, is also evident in integration theory.

. . . Another sort of bias derives from the historicist view that there is something inevitable about the demise of the nation-state in a world shrunken and exposed to new terrors of war by the technological revolution. In this view, international functional cooperation, conforming with the trend rather than trying to manipulate it, is the only really rational transformation response. Functional imperatives must be allowed to determine new jurisdictions. This 'functionalist' approach deliberately eschews any consideration of the integrative role of institutions for the expression and the binding revolution of conflicts over what states perceive to be vital interests. In contrast, federalists have tended to emphasise institutions and the formal powers to be allotted to them, because their primary concern is how to secure political expression for what are presumed to be existing and evolving patterns of social cohesion and diversity in the international community.

In addition to these general problems of social science, the importance of European Community integration both as intellectual stimulus and principal example of an experiment in integration has produced its own methodological problem . . . the process of European integration among 'the six' is widely claimed to be unique.

... Thus any explanatory hypothesis based on a study of European integration would appear to be a generalisation from the instance of a phenomenon. There are two mitigating features of this fundamentally unscientific procedure. First, European integration is not a single event. It is a term which refers to a variety of comparable decisions, actions, and reactions in a specific environment. Considered, further, as a process in time, it has suffered setbacks and advances and, therefore, may be regarded not as one continuous process but as a continuous series of processes which, though different, may be compared with each other. Second, even though the EEC experiment be considered unique, i.e. a unique series, it does present features which invite comparison with other experiments in international, regional and sectional cooperation ...

... There are thus methodological difficulties inherent in the European orientation of integration theory, but they do not of themselves proscribe the study ...

Note

1 H. Bull, 'International theory: the case for a classical approach', *World Politics* Vol. 5: 18, 1966, pp. 361–70.

Document 6: Charles Pentland, *International Theory and European Integration* (London, 1973), pp. 16–19

... Beyond a general notion of what the problem of integration concerns, these efforts are based on no central, organizing concept around which a macroanalytical framework might be fashioned. Contention, after all, may prove more productive intellectually than consensus. That is, at this stage in the development of the field, it would seem potentially more fruitful to identify, acknowledge and sharpen the fundamental differences between various approaches, so that they can be tested through confrontation in the empirical world. Through this procedure scholars may in time converge on the most useful approach, agreeing on its superior theoretical productivity. On the other hand, just as physics supports the existence of two conflicting theories of light – each useful within a certain context – so we may come to have two or more co-existing theories of integration. But by drawing the disorderly collection of approaches we now have into recognizable lines of battle, we can at least suggest where the most important points of contact will be.

What exactly is an 'approach' in this sense? According to one scholar, an approach performs three main 'intellectual functions'. In the first place, it acts as 'a rather systematic and consciously developed set of criteria and procedures to help with the problems of perception.'[1] That is, it guides the scholar in selecting his data, telling him what is of interest, and where and how to find it ...

... The second function of an approach is to provide a framework for the 'intellectual organization' of perceptions. It does this by establishing boundaries of relevance, emphasizing certain variables, ranking data in importance, and generating hypotheses. For example, Etzioni's 'paradigm' postulates that certain sets of variables are more important at one stage of the integrative process than at others. Similarly, Lindberg and Scheingold's systems-model provides a set of interrelated categories into which data about European political processes may be organized, and which, in so doing, incorporates certain prior judgements about the role of each variable in those processes.

These two functions comprise the purely psychological dimension of an approach. In this sense, an approach is a broad intellectual orientation, which may suggest or be associated with certain models, metaphors or analogies, and within which certain conceptual frameworks and methodological predispositions may be characteristic. It thus makes up the cognitive structure, or 'image', through which any individual scholar deals with the world around him.

The third 'intellectual function' of an approach, however, adds an important sociological dimension to the foregoing. An approach provides a common language or framework of communications for those engaged in research. In Young's words, there must be a 'minimal standardization of word meanings, concepts, categories and patterns of explanation' among those accepting a given intellectual orientation. In integration studies, the groups of scholars who draw their inspiration from the work of Deutsch or Haas respectively, seem to an increasing extent to be characterized by this sort of shared symbolic system. An approach, in short, is not simply one man's image of the world, but an intellectual outlook shared by a community of scholars who both cooperate and compete in developing it into a more systematic theory.

The theory to which these communities of scholars aspire is usually seen as some kind of logically interrelated set of general statements capable of empirical testing. It provides descriptions, explanations and often predictions about the empirical world with reference to which it is constantly being refined and reformulated. Whether such 'scientific' theory can or ought to be the sole aspiration and preoccupation of political scientists has been, and remains, a contentious issue. Most students of integration quite willingly leave the debate over a 'general theory' of politics to others, and simply assume that it is both necessary and possible to develop islands of 'middle range' theory in such areas as theirs. Whether we can build bridges between these islands and arrive at, say, a general theory of political change which incorporates, among other components, a theory of integration, is a question which ought logically to await the emergence of a body of falsifiable general propositions about integration. Each of the approaches discussed in the following chapters can therefore legitimately be assessed as to its potential in this respect.

Few integration theorists, however, would accept that explanation is the sole or sufficient purpose of theory. Indeed, normative positions are rarely, if at all, disguised in their writings. Integration itself is assumed to be a good thing – a proposition which is understandable if not exactly self-evident. From such general propositions and assumptions, numerous prescriptions flow, although theorists differ considerably as to the emphasis they place on policy-advice. In functionalist writings the advocacy of solutions for specific social and political problems is usually the main object of argument, but it does not necessarily follow that an explanatory theory of integration cannot be found there as well. Conversely, the most self-consciously 'scientific' approaches, such as those of Haas and Deutsch, do not preclude (and often in fact encourage) the derivation of policy-advice by those engaged in the politics of integration. In short, the normative foundations and prescriptive uses of theory are a part of the total fabric of an approach, and to examine them critically may aid an understanding of its explanatory components . . .

Note

1 O.R. Young, *Systems of Political Science* (Engelwood Cliffs, NJ, 1968), pp. 8–12.

Document 7: J.B. Priestley, 'Federalism and culture' (1940), cited in R. Mayne, J. Pinder and J.C. Roberts, *Federal Union: The Pioneers* (Basingstoke, 1991), p. 37

. . . If I thought federalism meant the cosmopolitan touch everywhere I would certainly oppose it. . . . But . . . I cannot see the slightest reason why the delegation of national sovereignty to a federal authority should blot out all regional influences, depending as they do not on political organization but on local climate, landscape, social traditions and the like. Indeed, it is possible that the removal of national barriers, many of which are purely artificial, and the disappearance of cunningly stimulated national feeling, might increase the natural attachment of all sensitive persons to the region in which they live.

It might do most of us good to have loyalties at once wider and narrower than the ones we have at present. Wider, because we substitute for the nation a great federation of peoples, with whom we co-operate instead of competing. Narrower, because once we are free of the age-long dog-fight of the nations, once we have no longer to attend to the horrible, cynical spectacle of the powers lying, cheating and arming, we can attend to what is in all truth our own bit of the world, our own hills and dales and woodlands, our own wind and rain, our own folk whom we know by name, the near magical world in which we spent our childhood . . .

Document 8: H.N. Brailsford, 'The federal idea' (1939), cited in R. Mayne, J. Pinder and J.C. Roberts, ibid. (1991), p. 81

What shall we have gained if we can realise anything resembling this project of Federation? Firstly and chiefly we shall abolish internecine war in Europe, the homeland of our civilisation. . . . In the positive sense we shall achieve vastly more: we shall rescue the priceless values of this civilisation itself. . . . If we abandon the old concept of the Sovereign State, it will not be because we have changed our views about a legal theory. It will be because we have reached an ideal of human fraternity that embraces our neighbours, who in other languages think the same civilised thoughts. We can end war only by widening. ... Our Federation will ... respect the rich variety of a Continent, that has preserved many stocks, many cultures, many tongues, through all the vicissitudes of its history.

Document 9: Lord Lothian, 'The ending of Armageddon' (1939), cited in R. Mayne, J. Pinder and J.C. Roberts, ibid. (1991), p. 35

'We are in the midst of the greatest race in armaments ever known, which if it continued can only lead to universal bankruptcy. And everyone feels that another world war, fiercer and more ruthless than the last, may break out at any time, either because it is deliberately provoked or because an accident or a fool may set in motion events which it is beyond the power of statesmanship to control. The real cause of our troubles is that the nations are living in anarchy ... the consequences of which have been intensified a hundredfold in recent times by the conquest of time and space ... anarchy cannot be ended by any system of co-operation between sovereign nations but only by the application of the principle of federal union.'

Document 10: W. Lipgens, 'Motives for European unity: the summing up by the Geneva Conference of Resistance Fighters', op. cit. (1982), pp. 53–7

The motives and theoretical arguments which the leaders of the Resistance put forward in favour of a European federation were surprisingly similar in all European countries, even though, if only for reasons of brevity, they were tersely expressed in underground leaflets and not developed in scholarly detail. In the following paragraphs they are arranged in order of the importance assigned to them by the Resistance writers themselves.

1 The basic and major justification for their plans for European unification in the case of nearly all the Resistance writers was defined as taking up an ideological stand against worship of the state, against the 'terrible compulsion towards total-iarian rule, as it is inevitably forged by nationalism'. The system of nation states which had brought on mankind so much suffering, and in its extreme form of Fascism had been carried to absurd lengths, was felt to be unworthy of preserva-tion. What was needed, instead, was to safeguard true values, personal freedom, religious and political rights, etc. against state nationalism by a European federation which should prevent the return of nationalism and Fascism in its member states.

This conviction was reinforced by the experience of a common struggle against injustice and slavery by the Resistance groups of all the occupied countries, a feeling of Europeanness . . .

. . . 2 An equally fundamental argument, and one which was put forward by almost every author during the ordeal of war, was that the unity of Europe would make it impossible for the nation states to plunge the peoples of Europe into war in generation after generation. If the first argument stemmed from the degeneration of the nation state, the second argument was based on the experience of the League of Nations, whose purely intergovernmental machinery was unable to prevent war between European nations. Only a European federal union could put an end for good to 'European Civil wars' and make peace secure once and for all. Not another loosely structured League, only a supranational federal authority could finally overcome nationalism and, being directly elected by the people and under their watchful eye, could exercise those common powers over foreign policy, security, and economic planning which could be effective only on a European scale . . .

. . . 5 The fifth argument emerged towards the end of the war: Europe would only be able to retain its own kind of civilization and make its political voice felt if it united as a federation . . .

. . . These themes were taken up by Resistance groups in country after country with an astonishing degree of unanimity, though without knowledge of what the others were doing. Yet even before the end of the war representatives of the Resistance in nine different countries managed to arrange a meeting on Swiss soil at which a large measure of agreement was seen to exist . . .

. . . Among them two names were specially noteworthy, those of E. Rossi and A. Spinelli, both of whom had escaped after spending years in Mussolini's political prisons. As will be seen later, they had founded the Movimento Federalista Europeo inside the Italian Resistance, and in the autumn of 1943 arrived already convinced that the Resistance all over Europe should accept a future programme of the same kind, and that the time had come to sum it up. From November 1943 onwards they tried to distribute an invitation to other refugee Resistance groups suggesting that the time had come in view of their common experience of resistance to work together for a 'United States of Europe', and appealing for help in co-operating for a 'preparatory congress' aimed at drawing up an agreed 'solemn declaration of our common aims'. The large number of contacts, often made with great difficulty, during the winter of 1943–4 led to the formation of a more closely knit group . . .

. . . clandestine meetings of a formal character were held on 31 March, 29 April, 20 May and 6–7 June 1944. The most important of these was the meeting of 20 May. It was then that the draft of a declaration of the European Resistance movement was drawn up and sent with an accompanying letter, preceded by a declaration of solidarity, to the Resistance groups of all nine countries so far as they could be reached. The draft dwelt with some emphasis on the need for a federal union of all the nations of Europe. An excerpt from this document will show the determination with which unity of a federal kind was demanded as an irreducible minimum, and the deliberateness with which it was described as a supranational statement of Resistance aims.

1 Resistance to Nazi oppression, which unites the peoples of Europe in a common struggle, has forged between them a solidarity and a community of aims and interests . . .

2 The lack of unity and cohesion which still exists between different parts of the world will not allow the immediate creation of an organization containing all the world's civilization in a single federal government. . . . At the end of this war it will be necessary to establish a world-wide organization of a less ambitious kind. . . . That is why, within that universal organization, the European problems must form the object of a more direct and more radical solution.

3 European peace is the key to world peace. In the space of one generation Europe has been the epicentre of two world wars, whose origins lay in the existence on this Continent of some thirty sovereign states. What is needed is to put an end to this anarchy by creating a federal union among the European peoples. Only a federal union will permit the German people to take part in European life without being a menace to other peoples. Only a federal union will enable frontiers to be drawn in areas of mixed population, which will thus cease to be the object of foolish national jealousies and will become simple questions of territorial delimitation, of pure administrative competence. The federal union will not be empowered to limit the right of each member state to solve its own problems in accordance with its ethnic and cultural characteristics. But in view of the experience and frustration suffered by the League of Nations, the states will have to surrender irrevocably to the federation those aspects of their sovereignty which concern the defence of their territory, relations with other powers outside the federal union, international exchanges and communications. Most importantly, the federal union will have to possess:

(i) a government responsible not to the governments of the various members states but to their peoples, through whom it will have to exercise direct jurisdiction within the limits assigned to it;

(ii) an army subject to the orders of this government and excluding any other or national army;

(iii) a supreme court for trying all questions concerning the interpretation of the federal constitution and for settling disputes that may arise between the states and the federation.

By means of clandestine frontier crossings and courier services this clear summary of 21 May 1944 was sent from beleaguered Switzerland to as many Resistance groups in as many countries as possible in order to get their agreement to the preparation of a European conference of Resistance leaders immediately 'after the end of hostilities' . . .

Document 11: J. Monnet, 'A ferment of change', *Journal of Common Market Studies* Vol. 1: 1963, pp. 204–8, 210–11

We are used to thinking that major changes in the traditional relations between countries only take place violently, through conquest or revolution. We are so accustomed to this that we find it hard to appreciate those that are taking place peacefully in Europe even though they have begun to affect the world . . .

. . . Yet we have only to look at the difference between 1945 and today to see what an immense transformation has been taking place under our very eyes, here in what used to be called the old world. After the war, the nations of continental Europe were divided and crippled, their national resources were depleted and, in most of them, the peoples had lost their empires. It might have been expected they would be further depressed by what many considered the loss of past greatness and prestige.

And yet, after all these upheavals, the countries of continental Europe, which have fought each other so often in the past and which, even in peacetime, organized their economies as potential instruments of war, are now uniting in a Common Market which is laying the foundations for political union . . .

. . . To understand this extraordinary change in all its basic simplicity, we must go back to 1950, only five years after the war. The whole French nation had been making efforts to recreate the bases of production, but it became evident that to go beyond recovery towards steady expansion and higher standards of life for all, the resources of a single nation were not sufficient. It was necessary to transcend the national framework.

The need was political as well as economic. The Europeans had to overcome the mistrust born of centuries of feuds and wars. The governments and peoples of Europe still thought in the old terms of victors and vanquished. Yet, if a basis for peace in the world was to be established, these notions had to be eliminated. Here again, one had to go beyond the nation and the conception of national interest as an end in itself.

We thought that both these objectives could in time be reached if conditions were created enabling these countries to increase their resources by merging them in a large and dynamic common market; and if these same countries could be made to consider that their problems were no longer solely of national concern, but were mutual European responsibilities.

Obviously this could not be done all at once . . .

. . . This profound change is being made possible essentially by the new method of common action which is the core of the European Community. To establish this new method of common action, we adapted to our situation the methods which have allowed individuals to live together in society: common rules which each Member is committed to respect, and common institutions to watch over the application of these rules. Nations have applied this method within their frontiers for centuries, but they have never yet been applied between them. After a period of trial and error, this method has become a permanent dialogue between a single European body, responsible for expressing the view of the general interest of the Community and the national governments expressing the national views. The resulting procedure for collective decisions is something quite new and, as far as I know, has no analogy in any traditional system. It is not federal because there is no central government; the nations take their decisions together in the Council of Ministers. On the other hand, the independent European body proposes policies, and the common element is further underlined by the European Parliament and the European Court of Justice.

This system leads to a completely changed approach to common action. In the past, the nations felt no irrevocable commitment. Their responsibility was strictly to themselves, not to any common interest. They had to rely on themselves alone. Relations took the form either of domination if one country was much stronger than the others, or of the trading of advantages if there was a balance of power between them. This balance was necessarily unstable and the concessions made in an agreement one year could always be retracted the next.

But in the European Communities, common rules applied by joint institutions give each a responsibility for the effective working of the Community as a whole. This leads the nations, within the discipline of the Community, to seek a solution to the problems themselves, instead of trading temporary advantages. It is this method which explains the dramatic change in the relations of Germany with France and the other Common Market countries. Looking forward to a common future has made them agree to live down the feuds of the past . . .

. . . Beyond the economic integration of our countries and the increase in our wealth which it will bring there remains the problems of achieving our political union which was our aim from the beginning. As you know, I have always felt that the political union of Europe must be built step by step like its economic integration. One day this process will then lead us to a European Federation . . .

What conclusions can we draw from all these thoughts? One impression predominates in my mind over all others. It is this: unity in Europe does not create a new kind of great power; it is a method for introducing change in Europe and consequently in the world. People, more often outside the European Community than within, are tempted to see the European Community as a potential nineteenth-century state with all the overtones of power this implies. But we are not in the nineteenth century, and the Europeans have built up the European Community precisely in order to find a way out of the conflicts to which the nineteenth-century power philosophy gave rise. The natural attitude of a European Community based on the exercise by nations of common responsibilities will be to make these nations also aware of their responsibilities, as a Community, to the world.

Document 12: A. Spinelli, *The European Adventure – Tasks for the Enlarged Community* (London, 1972), pp. 1–10, 13–17

The purpose of the European Community is to unite progressively the destinies of several nations by the development of a body of laws and institutions common to them all, obliging them to face certain great tasks with a common policy and to adopt a common position and responsibility towards the world outside. This purpose is not something new in the history of mankind; nations, initially divided, have constantly united to form greater nations. When there develops an intense relationship between several countries even if they differ in traditions, language, laws, institutions and politics; when powerful spiritual currents pass from one country to another; when in each country an increasing number of men who are enterprising, more adventurous and more curious recognise in the other countries kindred spirits, and realise the opportunities for action which appear there; when economic exchanges between countries increase in volume and interests become interwoven; when the policies of the great powers with which these people live oblige them to face similar challenges; when all or a major part of these circumstances exist, then, at a certain moment, the idea is born that these nations should in some way unite and reasons, real or invented, are duly discovered to justify such aspirations.

This has always happened. These unions, however, when they take place, are usually achieved through violence, even when there is a high degree of accord for the union among the nations concerned . . .

The origins

The special quality of the plan to unite the European Community is that it is proposed to achieve union not by means of force and conquest, but by the free consensus of the European nations. The Community is, for this reason, one of the most extraordinary adventures of the human spirit. It will be difficult, if not impossible, to appreciate its profound meaning if this particular characteristic of the union is not understood.

The adventure of the European Community is extraordinary, as there are practically no precedents for it. The United States of America, whose birth European federalists have studied closely in order to learn its precepts, were certainly created by a vigorous and courageous political imagination. The United States were, however, born as a community; while posing as sovereign states, they had always been purely autonomous provinces of the British Empire, and when they joined in federation they did nothing more than re-establish the political unity which had collapsed only shortly before . . .

. . . The nations which the European Community proposed to unite have never been united in the past and have been formed in the bitter conflict of delimitation or liberation, one against the other. They have all undergone that real brain-washing which made up popular education and which overwhelmed every citizen while he was still a child and continued to exert, in the most diverse forms, an implacable control over him for his entire life. All these nations have developed political and administrative policies which have been inspired constantly by the absolute priority of national interests and which have been powerful and penetrating in every field of activity, to the point where they have become technically capable of organising the entire society of a nation in a totalitarian way. Thus armed, spiritually and materially, these nations have generated, faced and suffered a senseless first world war. From this emerged a nationalism which, as a popular sentiment, was endowed with even more virulent power over men's minds, and which succeeded in producing the totalitarian tyranny of Fascism and Nazism, and in precipitating Europe, after 20 years of uneasy peace, into the second world war.

The war of 1939–45 was played out with the rigour of a classical tragedy, in which the actors are motivated more by fate than by their will, and which concludes with a catastrophe and with catharsis. The war consisted of the ferocious attempt by Hitler to unify Europe under the imperial dominion of the German nation, of the desperate resistance, openly nationalistic of all the other countries in Europe . . .

. . . Catharsis did, however, take place in Western Europe, where nationalism as a popular sentiment was given a death blow by the catastrophe, as it was felt to be both the underlying cause of the catastrophe and a useless instrument of rebirth for a democratic civilisation. If the concept of European unity was felt, by the nations returned to democracy, to be no longer an abstract rational ideal to be realised at some unspecified future date, but to be a task for the present to be faced and made reality in our generation, this was possible because the long nationalistic past had suddenly become repugnant and had ceased to be a crushing weight on the political conscience of the people. To believe in a process for unifying Europe, based on the free consensus of its peoples, would have seemed, before the catastrophe, highly ingenuous. But now, as well as unrealistic agitators, we find that professional statesmen are prepared to explore this unfamiliar and uncharted realm, and in a manner which will ensure that they have the confidence and following of their countries . . .

. . . Let us limit ourselves to a brief summary of the main obstacles that were encountered.

The obstacles

The first obstacle was the small number of people involved in the adventure. . . . The small number of those concerned does not mean in any way that there is a lack of contact between their feelings and those of their peoples. Many signs show that the idea of Europe is popular everywhere. Public opinion polls regularly show positive results . . .

. . . The fact is that Europe is popular and is believed in a rather confused but permanent way to be something desirable by the majority of the citizens of the

Community; the differences lie in the features which each person confusedly gives it, rather than in the idea itself. This dissolution of national mythology and an opening of the mind towards the new idea are becoming general in all the countries of Western Europe, even if they are not always manifestly evident everywhere with the same intensity at the same time . . .

. . . This pro-European attitude, which is widespread, permanent and tends to increase with the passing of time, reflects the permanence of a considerable number of serious political problems which should be treated more as European problems than as national ones . . .

. . . This widespread Europeanism remains, however, a passive participation, a guarantee of benevolent expectancy on the part of public opinion and of a lack of basic opposition; it will never take an active part in the enterprise.

How could it be otherwise? Europe already has feelings and interests in common, but it is not yet sufficiently articulate, politically, to translate them into action, nor does it have the fundamental institutions essential for popular participation – elections, parliament, a European government – which alone could make it possible for popular feelings and interests to give politics a direction, to oblige political parties to become involved on a European level and to develop European programmes; to choose politicians who have decided to express their ambitions in a European political career. The federalists saw this obstacle clearly from the outset and had asked for the construction to begin with the institutions of democratic participation. This step, however, seemed too daring and has not yet been taken. It was therefore inevitable that involvement in European action remained limited . . .

. . . Since its creation the Commission of the European Community has fulfilled to a large extent the function of inspiration which was formerly carried out only by individuals and private associations. Compared with these, the Commission has the advantage of preparing more accurately through its services the proposals which it makes, in the secure knowledge that they will be put before governments who are normally obliged to discuss them with the Commission.

It has the corresponding disadvantage that it is obliged to make its proposals within the framework of the treaties of Rome and Paris, which are only an incomplete and imperfect realisation of the European enterprise . . .

. . . The Commission has not yet been able to develop the constructive political imagination which the European adventure needs. To the extent that it realises this deficiency it will, however, still be able to fulfil this role – and it is difficult to see who else could do so with the same prestige. Finally, we come to those who have until now been the centre of the construction, the governments, or, more accurately, those among their heads and members who are most directly involved in European matters . . .

. . . It is within this restricted circle that the European adventure has moved from its very beginning until the present time. The most powerful protagonist, that is the feeling of the people expressing itself in a democratic political struggle at a European level, has not so far succeeded in making an appearance.

The second obstacle consists of the resistance of wide sectors of what may be called the national establishment – that is the aggregate of those who hold political, administrative and economic power in each country. They no longer hold the secure power which they held in the past. They either know or feel that behind them there no longer exists a profound belief in the supremacy of national interest and that the problems of supranational interdependence, especially in Europe, are on the increase. For these reasons they normally assume an attitude which is generally pro-European. They also feel, however, that to build European unity means, in the last instance, either nothing at all or the transfer of certain centres of political, administrative and economic power from the national level to the new European level, that is from their hands into other hands. It is not the end for any of them, but there is a prospect of a lessening of their power in many cases, of adapting their methods of planning, of decision-making and of execution in many other instances. The balance between the various components of the establishment will necessarily change. If it is easy to see immediately what will be lost, it is difficult to calculate what will be gained in the long run.

The capacity to resist which these people have is remarkable. One may no longer believe in the supremacy of the national perspective, but all traditions, laws, centres of command, habits of obedience, working habits and standards, and calculations of profit and loss are national in character; the majority of personal relationships, public or private, are with fellow nationals, who think and feel in a similar way. Once homage has been paid to the idea of Europe, profound national conservatism is easy. At times those who practise it are not aware of it and are offended if the fact is pointed out to them as they wish to be considered good Europeans.

Not all the establishment resists in the same way – indeed some sectors of it have already capitulated, adapting themselves to a greater or lesser extent to the new prospect . . .

. . . When faced with each of the problems which emerge with the passage of time, demanding a European solution, those politicians responsible rarely reply with a coherent 'yes' or 'no'. In principle they know that they should aim for European objectives which are more than, and different from, the sum total of the different national objectives. They recognise that to achieve them it will be necessary to have European institutions to ensure a consensus of opinion, to elaborate policy, to make binding decisions and to carry them out effectively. But they postpone as long as possible the creation of such political institutions and when they are obliged to take action they create them in as modest and limited a form as possible; there is a tendency to take away with one hand what is given with the other. But they are always ready to look for agreements between national governments which are shaped by national decision. Each government sees and desires the European objective above all from the national point of view and is disposed to accept it only in so far as it finds this point of view reflected there. The fact that such a procedure makes every agreement more and more difficult in relation to the increasing complexity of the material; that this procedure often makes agreements impossible; that even when an agreement is reached it is reduced regularly to the lowest common denominator of very limited importance – all this is understood with irritation and an uneasy conscience, but it is as difficult as ever to break out of the vicious circle. Yet, again and again, the governments and, in their turn parliaments and parties, attempt to square this circle; they seek European decisions which show continually, coherence and great potential, by means of an abortive combination of national decision-making procedures.

The tendency of the national political powers to move towards a confederated Europe – for confederation is nothing more than the vision of policies generated by inter-governmental agreements – is even further reinforced by the fact that there exist national administrations to prepare the decisions to a great extent and to implement them once they have been made . . .

. . . This brief description of the protagonists in the construction of Europe and of the obstacles which they encounter may help in understanding the pattern of development so far.

A union based on the free consent of the states implies that those who should give approval to every step forward are the legitimate representatives of the countries in the process of uniting – that is, their governments. These are induced to do so because they are pressurised both by great problems and by new ideas which make them consider these problems as European problems. But the governments represent and express also all the old ideas and requirements which maintain the form of the nation. The same men are, therefore, obliged by force of circumstances to be both conservative and innovators. In their normal daily activity they are the conservatives of the old national system, in that every day they must legislate, govern, make decisions and guide their peoples along well-known, traditional paths. From time to time, when they are confronted with this or that serious problem which weighs heavily on the life of the nation and cannot be kept under control by national measures, they become innovators of the new European system.

The moments of creative tension

Only in these moments of crisis do governments pay more attention to European-orientated proposals and become more inclined to feel the profound meaning of history. They are able to take a step to advance the European enterprise; sometimes they go beyond simple inter-governmental commitment and decide to create or reinforce some centre of common action to promote the realisation of the common task in the interest of all.

The critical moments of high European tension for national governments never last very long. The problem which caused the tension ends by resolving itself – it disappears or becomes less urgent, or the day-to-day concerns of national politics compel the governments to withdraw more or less rapidly from the sphere of the European adventure into that of the national routine.

Then the customs, interests and mental reservations of the nation re-emerge and begin to corrode the European sentiment which appeared in the moment of crisis. The European cause is then no longer in the hands of the governments, but depends on the vitality and solidity of the European sentiment which occurred briefly during the crisis and which must now resist the corrosive effect of national conservatism. The permanent uncertainty of the governments results in their European creations being on every occasion more limited than they need have been and in their dealing only with the most clearly urgent problems, and even then not thoroughly. If what emerged in the moment of creative tension did not go beyond inter-governmental or confederate action then there is little hope for it in the period of return to national conservatism. The commitments are usually formally respected but in reality they are more and more ignored, violated and finally forgotten, submerged by the procedures of decision-making which have remained national. There is no harmony between the nations and they are in agreement only during the fleeting moment of European crisis.

If, instead, a centre of common action is established, or strengthened, in order to reach a common objective, it will by its nature act with continuity to achieve the common aim and head the resistance to national conservatism. It will be weakened a little by the conservatism, but will try to heal its own wounds, rise again after its defeats and, in its turn, will corrode and weaken a little national resistance, since by its very existence it arouses support for its aims and gives strength to the European feeling existing in each country. Against the resistance of national conservatism the strength of the European centre of common action can be used and this will help to ensure that the European commitments do not dissolve into nothing. The sphere of competence of such a centre, and its authority and independence will reflect the degree of unity which has been progressively achieved. The Commission of the Community has been until now the most authoritative and effective of such centres of common action. It is due to its existence that the Community has survived the long winter of de Gaulle and may be considered today as the original nucleus to be reinforced and developed later, if new moments of creative European tension arise . . .

. . . Such is the present condition of the Community which, with its institutions, is able to make progress by jumping forward at exceptional moments. These moments alternate with periods of ordinary administration and even of deterioration. This situation will last until the Community gains control over such a variety of relations and problems of European society that it will have action centres nourished directly on such intensive participation by European political and social forces that to develop subsequently it will need no further pushing from the governments, as is now the case. The Community will then grow on its own, itself taking the initiative on the necessary tensions and the necessary compromises to be made with the various national governments.

It is not inevitable, however, that the Community will reach this point. Before reaching it, it could well happen that the complex of relations and problems which until now have nourished the idea of European unity fall apart; this could be due to a return to a more introverted way of life, more suited to a rebirth of nationalism.

Document 13: M. Burgess, 'The European Community's federal heritage', from *Federalism and European Union* (London, 1989), pp. 24–8

This chapter seeks both to underline and to reinstate the importance of the European Community's federal heritage. It does not assume, however, that the Community owes its existence solely to federalist pressures and aspirations. Indeed we must guard against unchallenged assumptions which often lead either to over-simplified or outright erroneous conclusions. The origins of the European Community remain complex at the levels both of political ideas and policy formation. Further research is still needed in order to understand more fully and appreciate the complicated relationships which existed between several long and short-term factors: the role of key elite individuals; the relevance of intellectual thought; the intrinsic motives behind particular decisions; the reactions and responses to events; and the changing international environment. And the temptation to impose a consistent, almost teleological, pattern upon what might be a set of unconnected events must be resisted. This would be to distort – and even to rewrite – history . . .

. . . Certainly it is true that the ultimate goal of Monnet and Schuman was a European federation but we should not underestimate the size of the gap between the rhetoric and reality, nor that between intention and consequence. Any attempt to link political ideas with political actions is fraught with immense pitfalls. Efforts to relate political influence to political impact and to connect political strategies with political effectiveness are equally difficult. When we make claims for the Community's federal heritage, then, we must proceed cautiously. It is an assumption which needs to be proved . . .

. . . Intergovernmentalism has commonly been accepted as the dominant operational mode of Community relations since around the mid-1960s, however. The mainstream academic literature bears testimony to this development. . . . And one danger of a bland intergovernmentalist concept of the Community is that it tends to become the only reality. It is blind to rival perspectives. In consequence it not only underestimates actions and energies directed towards different goals but it also seriously limits the real possibility of policy and institutional renewal.

Tudgendhat, however, is correct to acknowledge the continued presence of federalism and supranationalism in the Community.[1] These ideas, influences and strategies have varied in strength over time but they have always been a perfectly legitimate part of the Community's mixed political tradition. The precise nature of this federal heritage, like the Community itself, is complex with many tantalising theoretical twists and turns which stretch back, paradoxically, much further than the Community's own history . . .

... Europe's growing self-awareness 'should not be construed as simply a continuation of earlier European plans for unification'. Such schemes and plans for political unity had been drawn up repeatedly in past centuries but remained, with few exceptions, mere paper projects with no real chance of policy implementation. However, the intellectual self-examination 'initially begun ... during the First World War', which led eventually to a cultural and political revival of ideas advocating European unification, 'arose from a passionately renewed awareness ... of the centuries-old unity of European civilisation and values'. In short, the movement for European unification in all of its cultural and political manifestations was both a highly self-conscious and a uniquely twentieth century phenomenon.

Naturally, the intellectual and historical lineage of this movement can be traced back many centuries, probably at least to the Enlightenment, but for practical reasons in terms of an embryonic self-conscious political movement Lipgens' emphasis upon the impact of war in the twentieth century seems incontestable. The compelling drive to reorganise European state relations after 1918 possesses both a qualitative and a quantitative distinction from previous public expressions and sentiments for closer European union. ... It is clear that among the long and short-term factors assisting the centripetal forces towards unification were: the horrors of what military technology could inflict upon human beings; the rise of the United States of America; the impact of the Russian Revolution; the spread of fascism; and a myriad of economic and social changes. Together these ideas and events amounted to a crisis of European values which provided fertile soil for the nourishment of the unification movement.

But why and how did federalism acquire such a prominence as the solution to Europe's future? Much recent research has been devoted to the examination of plans for European union during the years between 1939 and 1945 and we are now in a better position to understand both the origins and the influences of such ideas. Both the threat of war and the Second World War itself spurred political elites and intellectuals to reconsider ways and means to prevent Europe from tearing itself asunder at regular intervals. Government elites by and large sought merely the destruction of totalitarian states but there was also a formidable body of European intellectual opinion whose vision transcended this immediate priority. It was among the members of the anti-fascist European Resistance that the federal idea was largely nurtured as the answer to Europe's destiny. For them the defeat of Hitler was only the first step. It offered a golden opportunity for Europeans to return to fundamental questions. The Franco-German conflict was only the most visible and persistent manifestation of nation-state rivalries in Europe. In order permanently to remove the very basis of military conflict, Resistance thinkers directed their intellectual challenge towards the perceived cause of war itself: the nation-state ...

... Using broad brush strokes, we must of necessity paint the federal idea on a large canvas. It comprises radically different conceptions of Europe and divergent political strategies. What does seem common ground among rival federalist conceptions and strategies, however, is shared experiences of war. Among the intellectual Resistance this factor runs continuously throughout their agonising journey towards the new reconstructed Europe . . .

. . . They learned that just as the Fascist juggernaut had demonstrated how supposedly immutable European structures could be swept away, so the defeat of Hitler and Mussolini could open the way for their vision to become reality. Old state structures and petty sovereignties were not part of God's law for the universe. At the end of the War almost anything must have seemed possible.

The Resistance belief in man's capacity to control events and to shape his own destiny ensured that former national loyalties and the obedience to the old state would not be integral to their ideas about the reconstruction of Europe. Reverence for the old state seemed inappropriate. It had collapsed everywhere in continental Europe in the face of the Nazi Blitzkrieg. In their quest for a better and peaceful society the Resistance had fought Hitler not for the old nation states but rather for a new European society. The consensus of opinion which emerged among Resistance groups, then, was that the defeat of totalitarianism and the creation of a 'United States of Europe' in its place went hand in hand. To allow the old nation states to recover and regain their former positions in a world of international rivalry would be to recreate the very conditions for war and totalitarian rule.

Written by a small nucleus of Italian federalists led by Altiero Spinelli and Ernesto Rossi, these views and assumptions were lucidly expressed in the famous 'Ventotene Manifesto' of 1941, which was one of the first Resistance declarations devoted to European unification. In it Spinelli observed that the collapse of most European states had already 'reduced most peoples of the Continent to a common fate' but that public attitudes were 'already much more favourable towards a new, federative European order'. The brutal experience of the previous decade had 'opened the eyes of the unbelievers' . . .

. . . The Ventotene Manifesto thus elaborated the idea of a federal Europe as the panacea for virtually all the outstanding problems which would confront post-war statesmen. And Spinelli, who became the leading spokesman of the federalist cause, always retained the Resistance-based capacity to argue that the common people, if allowed to determine themselves, would inevitably gravitate towards unity in co-operation. It was obsolete state structures and the selfish, anachronistic values of states' elites and interests which impeded this natural movement. People's basic needs, whether in Italy, France or Denmark, were fundamentally the same. And contemporary problems were essentially common problems necessitating common solutions. All that was needed was a solid institutional structure to allow this common elaboration to develop and determine itself.

This brief outline of the emergence of the federal idea in European Resistance thought does not, of course, do justice to the various nuances of opinion and real differences existing among those federalists who sought to rebuild Europe after 1945. But their agreement on basic principles remains more striking and more significant than their personal controversies . . .

... Leaving aside the strategic and doctrinal controversies which ruptured the early federalist movement in the mid-1950s, we should not forget the pervasive influence of federalist thought upon practical policy-making at this time. If we look closely at the eventful years between 1952 and 1954 it is clear that the attempt to launch the project for a European Political Community (EPC), building upon a European Defence Community (EDC), was made 'largely as a result of federalist pressure'. Moreover, 'federalist ideas also contributed a great deal to the content of the proposals' ...

... The failure of this federalist strategy – built upon giving a major role to a parliamentary assembly in drafting a new treaty for Europe – enabled interested observers to earmark 1954 as the end of the federalist phase in the Community's early political development. Journalists, politicians and scholars helped to shape a conventional wisdom which appeared to vindicate Monnet's approach to Europe and, correspondingly, to downgrade federalist ideas and strategies. The so-called 'constitutional method' was thereafter dismissed as unrealistic and impracticable. Monnet's Europe seemed an unassailable citadel during the late 1950s as first Messina and then Rome became symbols of what could be achieved via elite bargaining over primarily economic issues.

Spinelli accepted that Monnet's elite-led functional strategy for Europe had paid dividends. He could hardly have denied its successes. But he remained convinced that Monnet's conception was fundamentally flawed. It did not provide Europe with the effective means to go beyond what existed. National governments would always prevent the Community from developing the capacity to strengthen its own corporate personality independent of the member states ...

... This personal perspective would have encountered serious objections from many academic quarters. One can imagine what inconsistencies an incisive political economy approach would have exposed in Spinelli's federalist beliefs today. But Spinelli was an intellectual activist in politics, not merely an intellectual studying politics. Practitioners do not usually have the luxury of testing their beliefs for theoretical symmetry. In retrospect, the ideological ambiguities apparent in this notion of 'democratic radicalism' can be explained by examining the intellectual origins of Spinelli's federalism. One might also add, moreover, that Spinelli's federalism was itself a new overarching political ideology which committed its adherents ultimately to nothing less than a European federation.

... Let us conclude this section of our discussion on the European Community's federal heritage by recapitulating very briefly the logic implicit in federalism for the building of Europe: it offered the means by which the various elements and forces extant in the daily practice of European social, economic and political life could be effectively canalised and co-ordinated into an organic whole. The new political society would emerge only gradually, in piecemeal fashion, but it would evolve naturally from solid European structures. This was to be, we must remember, a new beginning. The federal idea was not to be shackled by the ideological conditioning of the past.

The federal heritage: past, present and future

The European Resistance movements gravitated towards the federal idea as the basis for a new Europe from a mixture of motives. The reasons for Spinelli's adoption of this idea are especially interesting because his own point of departure and his turbulent journey towards Ventotene in 1941 conveniently demonstrates both the general and the particular aspects of the wider conversion to federalism across Europe. We must not forget that many other groups in different countries had, via separate routes, arrived at the same conclusion independently. What stands out in the general resistance literature is the personal experience of war; this trauma gave the burgeoning support for federalism its strong moral content . . .

. . . Given the peculiar contexts and circumstances within which the various resistance movements found themselves during the war, their fervent belief in federalism is now perfectly understandable. We can appreciate both how and why it emerged. But is the idea of a federal Europe still relevant today? After all, the Europe of the late twentieth century has changed dramatically from the wartime realities so familiar to Resistance minds. And why is it important to emphasise the Community's federal heritage? What purpose does its reassertion serve?

In our introduction to this chapter we noted Christopher Tugendhat's observation about the two rival concepts of Europe which continue to compete for attention and legitimacy in the Community's political development. But he also warned against too great a use of federalist rhetoric in the Community today. He argued that the Community owed its existence to the imagination and determination of the federalists who endowed it with moral inspiration and authority, and whose ideals generated a resistless energy enabling it to take root and maintain an unwavering sense of purpose. However, he also claimed that federalist aspirations had 'turned out disappointingly' and that both the tone and the style of their rhetoric had lent a 'scale of values and criteria for measuring progress' which today is unrealistic and damaging because it suggests that 'the whole array of concrete achievements has not lived up to expectations'. With the eclipse of the federalist dream 'no new intellectual or moral framework has been constructed to enable the general public to make sense of what is going on and no new objectives have been set with which they can identify and towards which they can aspire'. His conclusion is simple, the Community will never be the first step towards the United States of Europe because 'now . . . it looks . . . unlikely to be realised'. Accordingly, federalist ideas and federalist rhetoric should be sensibly jettisoned because they propose what today and tomorrow is unattainable . . .

. . . His underlying argument is that the stark contrast between federalist rhetoric and intergovernmental reality is harmful to the Community because as the language and the actions of the Community and its member states increasingly diverge so public confusion and misunderstanding about the Community and its objectives intensifies and 'attitudes in its institutions . . . often appear to be theoretical and unworldly'. . . . It should also be added that such views are typical of a traditional British mentality towards European unification. Terms like 'realistic' and 'pragmatic' feature prominently in the vocabulary of British commentators on the European Community's future political development, as if rival conceptions of Europe were illusory and chimerical. Nonetheless, these hardened, insular national conceptions must be confronted and rebutted. They either underestimate or completely dismiss the Community's enduring federal heritage as irrelevant today . . .

. . . Much of the hostility towards the idea of a federal Europe derives from fears and anxieties about the loss of national sovereignty. And some of these worries may be legitimate concerns. Most of them, however, are based upon outmoded conceptions of national independence and upon a fundamental misunderstanding of the Community's federal heritage. . . . Federalism is consigned to history. 'It could never have endured as a guide and stimulus to political action'.[2] This is both to distort and to impoverish the federal idea. It overlooks the crucial problem which our brief examination of the Community's federal heritage has already pointed up, namely, the need for an institutional system which has the capacity to develop an autonomous European political life without threatening the Jacobin destruction of the nation state.

The Community's federal heritage must be neither forgotten nor jettisoned. It is the important continuing theme in the Community's past, present and future . . .

. . . It is important both to underline and to reinstate this federal heritage because it serves to emphasise the legitimacy of the federal idea in the Community's political and constitutional development. It must not be pushed to the margins of Community activity. On the contrary, our discussion suggests that federalism retains its significance for European integration both as a process and as an end to be attained . . .

Notes

1 C. Tugendhat, *Making Sense of Europe* (London, 1986), p. 71.
2 C. Tugendhat, ibid. (1986), p. 81.

Document 14: Samuel Brittan, 'Let fools contest about the forms', *Financial Times* 21 November 1991

The British political and business classes have been victims of a self-imposed confidence trick. They have allowed themselves to believe that the European Community is mainly concerned with free trade and economic co-operation, and that political union has suddenly been sprung on them by other member countries.

They have no excuse other than wishful thinking. The first sentence of the 1957 Rome Treaty speaks of 'an ever closer union among the people of Europe'. To remove any ambiguity, the first Commission president, the formidable German jurist Walter Hallstein, used to repeat: 'The Community is in politics, not business.'

The Single Market Act of 1987, signed by Margaret Thatcher, not only recalls that the objective of Economic and Monetary Union was accepted at a Euro Summit as long ago as 1972. Its preamble starts off with the aim of 'transforming relations among states into a European Union in accordance with the solemn declaration of Stuttgart on June 19, 1983'.

Where the Euro-enthusiasts have not played fair is in their failure to state clearly why a European political union of any kind is so important. It would help to have a complete ban on transport metaphors such as catching trains, missing buses, and being left behind at the post.

The poet Alexander Pope once wrote: *'For forms of government, let fools contest/What e'er is best administer'd is best.'*

This quotation puts too much weight on the question-begging word 'administration'; but it does make the point that governments are workaday organisations to provide those services which are better secured by collective action than by either the profit motive or by voluntary co-operation. The Eurofederalists and the nationalists have in common a hang-up over state power. But if we have a utilitarian attitude to government we shall neither worry about the shedding of national sovereignty, nor actually desire to do so just for the fun of creating new institutions.

The original European motive was stated most explicitly in relation to the Coal and Steel Community, the earliest of all the Community organisations. It was to make it impossible for France and Germany to go to war again. Its 1951 preamble talks of 'peoples long divided by bloody conflicts . . . establishing a destiny henceforth shared'.

Until the Berlin Wall came down in 1989 one might have said that this motive was noble, but out-of-date. Since then, some people have revived fears of the power of a united Germany. Those who share these fears have responded in diametrically different ways. Mrs Thatcher became more suspicious of everything to do with the Community, while President Mitterrand wanted to bind Germany more firmly into a Community structure.

Nevertheless, the existing Community has become quite unsuitable for containing Germany, if that is seen as a need. The threats to Continental stability which might involve Germany stem from the central and eastern parts of Europe. The Inter-Governmental Conference on Political Union, concerned with strengthening links among the existing Twelve, has become obsolete, as some of the shrewder foreign ministry officials attending it realise. Unfortunately, their governments were too committed to call the whole thing off. Despite the slogan 'There is no conflict between widening and deepening the Community' we know that there is.

Enlargement is, however, very tricky territory for proponents of a wider Europe including the former communist countries. For there is no way a community of 20 or 30 states can function without some qualified majority voting. The solution is to make such voting acceptable by limiting the functions of a European authority to those of a 19th-century night-watchman state.

A completely different motive for European political union is the desire of declining powers such as the UK to play a role on the world stage. In Britain it has come to the surface whenever the spuriousness of the 'special relationship' with the US has become apparent. But it is not self-evident that such a world role is desirable or will be exercised for good purposes.

Yet another motive is the Big Business one. We are told that only large political units can afford to back industries such as aerospace and advanced electronics. There is no evidence of a link between national size and prosperity. Whether one thinks of income per head, or rates of growth, some of the most thriving countries such as Switzerland, Singapore or Taiwan, have been of modest size, and outside the main blocs. The interests of large flagship companies that depend on state support are not necessarily those of the citizen or consumer. It is no accident that the British Labour Party, which still sees the state as a source of economic growth, is now keener to see a European super-government than those who see the main streams of growth in the discovery processes of the market.

There is a more modest case to be made that a large single market is neither sufficient nor necessary, but at least helpful, to economic prosperity. Moreover, such a market will be more successful if it goes beyond dismantling tariff barriers to common action on state aids or monopolies which distort competition, and if a single non-inflationary currency prevails. These conditions require a degree of supranational power. Under the 1987 Single European Act, accepted by Mrs Thatcher in her prime, issue after issue is decided by varying forms of qualified majority. And rightly so. For a single market can hardly function if each country can protect its own producer privileges by veto.

In an article on this page[1] three weeks ago, I suggested that the real enemy in the European Community negotiations was not federalism but centralisation, and that national sovereignty was a thoroughly mistaken banner under which to fight. Moreover, I fear that economic commentators such as myself have been fobbed off until almost the last moment into writing articles and giving lectures on Economic and Monetary Union when the real threat to a liberal free market order comes not from Emu – which is thoroughly sensible – but from the economic and social moves which have been attempted in the political inter-governmental conference.

Meanwhile the battle against harmful *dirigiste* interference has to be fought in a peculiar way. For the foreign ministry types in Brussels are not arguing about whether hours of work or environmental standards in roads or railway *need* to be harmonised in a Single Market; the issues are being argued through the back door of Community competence and decision rules; for example, when majority voting can be used or the European parliament can initiate proposals.

The Maastricht summit is unlikely to be a victory either for a free market, limited Europe or for a so-called 'social Europe'. It is more likely to be a mass of small print about competence and voting rules, the meaning of which will take many years, and a good few court actions, to discover. If there were a referendum on a single currency, I would vote 'yes'. But if there were an earlier referendum on

Maastricht, I would be quite inclined to vote 'no', thus depriving me of the chance of a later 'yes'. Thus I might reluctantly have to put in two 'yeses'.

The true dividing lines are between different ideas on the role of the state rather than between countries or between federalists and nationalists.

Note

1 Refers to an earlier *Financial Times* article.

Document 15: E. Wistrich, 'A federal democracy', from *After 1992: The United States of Europe* (revised edn, London, 1988), pp. 97–105

As a result of the technological revolution ever more rapid change has become the norm. Since the last world war modern industrial society has become much more complex and its management has led to a massive increase of government involvement in people's daily lives. Economic management, physical planning and environmental control, transport and communications, and social, health and welfare provisions are all relatively new concerns of government. They require a vast and complex machinery to administer. And so in modern industrial countries public sector expenditure accounts for nearly half of their gross national product. Most of these new responsibilities and powers have gone to national governments and central administrators.

This centralization leads to functions and resources being accumulated in relatively small geographic locations, usually within easy reach of metropolitan areas especially around national capital cities. These dominate the rest of the country, relegating vast parts to a peripheral and subsidiary role. Such concentration is not confined to government functions but inevitably extends to commerce and industry, to culture and centres of excellence, all of which want to be close to where power and money reside.

Within the European Community such concentration of functions and resources has occurred in the triangle between London, Paris and the Ruhr . . . The trend has had serious consequences.

The peripheral areas remain underdeveloped, culturally deprived, and increasingly depopulated. The metropolitan conurbations, congested and expensive, have turned into maelstroms of feverish activity. City centres have become increasingly dehumanized centres where mental illness, drugs and crime have escalated.

Many local communities have lost their sense of identity. With decisions about their lives taken, usually far away, by faceless bureaucracies, people have become increasingly alienated from their governments. Democratic accountability of national governments to their citizens through elected representatives has become tenuous. Parliaments find it ever more difficult to check the activities of burgeoning administrations. Representative democracy, meant to give ordinary citizens a say over their lives, is becoming discredited through growing cynicism about politicians. A sense of community has been replaced by a general feeling of 'them and us' as the gap between government and governed has alarmingly widened.

One consequence has been the proliferation of single issue politics, campaigns and demonstrations. Traditional methods of democratic control through elected representatives have been increasingly marginalized. Representative democracy is being undermined and questioned as people demand direct participation in the decision-making process.

In most of the modern industrialized countries existing institutions are failing to respond to the needs and demands of ordinary citizens. Rapid change in our technological society and the massive increase in governmental responsibilities clearly require that our institutions adapt to the new circumstances if democracy is to survive. What is needed in particular is much greater flexibility and the diffusion of over-centralized powers . . .

The European dimension

Against this background of a general diffusion of powers from the centre to regional and local tiers in most European countries, except for Britain, a new dimension to the issue of the distribution of powers has arisen with the creation of the European Community. As the story of its evolution, recounted in chapter 2,[1] has demonstrated, the Community's institutions are continually evolving as they acquire new responsibilities. Each stage in its evolution from the very first European Coal and Steel Community has been seen as yet another step in what Robert Schuman in 1950 described as, 'laying the foundations of a European federation', referred to by others as the European Union.

What is often not realized by protagonists of federal devolution within nation states is that the federation of such states into larger entities is merely the other side of the same coin. It is part of a coherent system concerned with the whole range of interdependent levels of government, each democratically accountable to its own elected representative councils, assemblies, or parliaments with constitutionally guaranteed powers. Thus the attempt to federate Europe can be seen as the response to the changing nature of society, brought about by its growing interdependence and complexity in the wake of the technological evolution, which is echoed by demands for devolution of powers within nation states towards democratically accountable and autonomous regional and local authorities.

Semantic arguments about the description to be given to the process of European integration are in themselves not very important. Its substance is, as Edward Heath, in the inaugural Lothian Memorial Lecture in November 1987, put it: 'the Community was created by the founding fathers as an institution *sui generis*'. He did not believe that it was very productive to spend time arguing about federalism and its many different definitions. The final form of the Community's political organization will be *sui generis*, and he urged that one should instead concentrate on making the Community a success in all its different forms . . .

. . . British hostility to the federal idea was fomented by establishment figures who opposed British participation in the building of the European Community after the Second World War. Since Britain joined the Community, those who want to resist the development of its institutions have played on the belief that British cultural values would be submerged within an alien continental European tradition.

The fear that we would all become foreigners is a major public misconception of federalism in its application to European unity. In a recent speech to the European Parliament, the Queen of The Netherlands pointed out that it is a common mistake to regard the political development of the European Community as a 'development comparable to the evolution of a nation state'. Social homogeneity and cultural standardization are not part of the Community's purpose. On the contrary the whole history of European integration since the 1950s clearly demonstrates that the aim of the Community is to preserve and enhance Europe's social and cultural diversity. Indeed, the very essence of federalism is a federal constitution that safeguards the autonomy and integrity of its component states. This is to prevent the cultural identities of individual countries being subsumed, as they surely would, were they to merge into a super-state without constitutional guarantees.

Part of the confusion is generated by the uncertainty about the form a future European federation might take. Many people imagine that advocates of the United States of Europe wish to replicate the system operated within the USA. Yet there are many different federal systems in existence in other parts of the world, each with its own distinct structure, adapted to the needs and wishes of its founders . . .

. . . The diversity of federal systems stems from the historical origins and distinctive cultural backgrounds of each federation and none can be regarded as the correct model for the European Community to follow. It is in this sense that Edward Heath was right to claim that Europe's political organization will be *sui generis*, but there is little doubt that its development will be on federal lines.

The European Community has many federal features already. Its constitution consists of the treaties which set it up and the many institutional reforms introduced during its existence. The latest among them is the Single European Act. The guarantor and interpreter of the constitution is the European Court of Justice whose judgements are binding on all member states as well as on its citizens. The Community's Council of Ministers has the power to pass laws that override national legislation and are binding on all. It has a directly elected Parliament with supervisory powers over the European Commission, the governing organ of the Community; it has the final say over the Community's budget and, increasingly, it participates in the legislative process.

Nevertheless, the Community's institutions are still some distance from providing a European government with real democratic accountability and real, if limited powers, which would transform the Community into a federation or union, to the creation of which member countries have repeatedly declared they are committed . . .

Note

1 Refers to the publication in which this document originally appeared.

Document 16: D. Mitrany, 'The prospect of integration: federal or functional', *Journal of Common Market Studies* **Vol. 4: 1965, pp. 119, 125–7, 129–31, 134–7, 139, 141–2, 144–5**

The line between what is actually happening today and what is hoped will be happening tomorrow is frequently obscured by those people who have been most closely involved in the 'making of Europe'; partly it may have been due to enthusiasm, but in part 'a deliberate tactic' designed to generate the support that success or complete confidence in success attracts . . .

. . .To build up a cohesive loyalty national movements have often had to disinter or invent all sorts of historical, social and emotional affinities, above all to keep alive the fear of some common external danger. Regionalism, starting with more differences than affinities, would have to go even further in that . . .

. . . Western man used to pride himself on his humanistic cosmopolitan outlook, but now even men of standing have come to talk of the need to develop a 'European personality'. It would not be fair to saddle them with the aberrations of the Count Coudenhove-Kalergi, the first recipient of the Charlemagne prize, but what is that 'European personality'? Does it begin and end at the limits of the Common Market . . .

. . . If there is a unique characteristic of European civilization, in contrast with Eastern and other civilizations, it is that it always has been an open civilization . . . [and so] able to permeate the whole world with her political, social and cultural outlook and experience . . .

. . . The very concept of a closed regional union is a contradiction of the historic European idea; and the farther it moves from the sheer material sector, the more does its synthetic nature stand exposed. But even if these inbreeding efforts and devices – closed economic planning, exclusive political institutions, the cultivation of a regional patriotism – even if all this were to serve the goal of a (limited) European union, it can hardly bear the argument that it also is the highway to a wider international unity . . .

The federal fallacy

Of the many assumptions which have gone into the making of the 'European' creed the most persistent has been the idea of federation; and the federal idea in fact traverses most aspects and issues of European union, both in its internal organization and in its relation to the wider international problem. It is an old idea which has appeared often in plans and literature, but all that has little to say on the substance of the present appeal; except that it always expressed some antagonism . . .

... The European federalists have been so fascinated by a readily convenient formula that they have neither asked how it works where it exists, nor whether its origins bear any relation to the problem of uniting a group of states in the present social ambience. It is this question of sociological fitness which is at issue here ...

... A new union or association is not conceivable without some formal compact, whose main purpose is precisely to delimit the competence of the various organs. ... The very purpose of any such written compact or statute is precisely to introduce the factor of fixity in the index of power; and nothing is so fixed as a federal constitution. It is intended to withstand the constant pressures from the ordinary claims of government as from sectional interests, and so 'hold together' the whole ...

... The original intent of the democratic idea was the Government should be kept to a minimum, and that minimum was to be guided by an informed and sensible electorate and controlled by its independent representatives. In all these respects we have gone far towards the opposite pole, even in democratic countries. Government now tends to be omnipresent and, where present, almost omnipotent, if we accept, as we must, Sir Ernest Barker's definition that government authority is 'the sum of its functions'. For any new federal experiment, if meant to be free to develop the modern attributes of a welfare society, the working prototype is likely to be not the US Constitution of 1787 but something nearer to the federal system of the USSR. ...

The functional alternative

... So much of what precedes had to be given to a critical examination of the federal idea because what matters here is not its theoretical virtues but its fitness for multi-national association – even within the arbitrary limits of a region. That people should have turned to it is not unnatural: it seemed the only available formula, because our political thinking has been so long rooted in the notion that every authority must be linked to a given territory. For the rest, it is plain that European federalism has been a blend of myth and some very mixed sentiments ...

New and original phenomena demand as at other crossroads in history suitable changes in the government of societies, and three such phenomena may be singled out as governing the present problem of international peace and development. (i) The new scientific inventions and discoveries have raised political, social and moral issues which can be dealt with only on their own global scale. Not one of them is peculiar to Europe; in the nuclear field all that Western Europe can do is to add its own pile of nuclear bombs, but not to halt their fearful menace. (ii) At the same time we face the contrary prospect of twice the number of independent states entitled by their sovereign status to follow their own will, and many tempted by a revolutionary mood to do so. (iii) The third factor, cutting across the other two and confusing their relation, is the trend to neo-mercantilist 'planning'. It has injected the political element into well-nigh all the manifold international activities and relations which formerly grew freely across most frontiers. That is the given equation. The key we have to find is how in these conditions 'to harmonize the actions' economic and social, in the words of the UN Charter, 'in the attainment of common ends'. To have lasting effect the solution must be global. In the theory it could be done through a world state or federation, but even if desirable such a monstrous construction could hardly come about except through conquest. Or it can be done by making use of the present social and scientific opportunities to link together particular activities and interests, one at a time, according to need and acceptability, giving each a joint authority and policy limited to that activity alone. That is the functional way.

Let it be said at once that there is nothing new in that. It has been the natural mode of Western international relations, some public and many private, before the two world wars, but since then we have moved backwards from the liberal nineteenth century. Before 1914 world integration was proceeding steadily by means of firm treaties and relationships, open-door arrangements and so on. In addition, a great number of pre-1914 agreements created what might be termed 'abstract regions' through multi-lateral contracts under the authority of international law. Now, as in former autocratic times, economic, social and even cultural relations have fallen under the control of the state – the State has almost become an organization for the prevention of free international intercourse and the growth of a normal human society . . .

. . . That is the new world which somehow has to be brought back into working relationships, to open up a prospect and provide the elements for international government. We do not know what kind of international government will work. But we do know that as government is only a framework which enables a social community to live its life well, international government can have little sense or body without a living international community. One new phenomenon at least opens up a positive and remarkable prospect in that direction. As was said before, the immediate impact of planning, with its spreading concern for social welfare and rights, is nationalistic. But in its external aspect one central characteristic is that it is universal. I believe this to be a novel, a unique historical situation . . . If this reading is correct, two practical factors are already at work, and on a world scale, to which strands of functional co-operation could be made fast. One is the indispensable factor of a common outlook and purpose, which in this case puts into strong relief an evident identity of everyday social aims and policy. The other is the useful factor of close similarity of ways and means. Administrative law is implicitly 'functional' law, and so is administrative practice. Every functional link helps to build up a common legal order – as the ILO well exemplifies – specific but also concrete and cumulative, one which does not stay aloof in the atmosphere of diplomatic and juridical pacts but which enters everywhere into the daily life of the peoples themselves . . .

. . . Considerations such as these show why one can find both opportunity and promise in working arrangements as a way of building up an international community. But it also is a natural, not a contrived idea pressed into an existing political mould. Generically speaking it represents a general turn grown out of the living complexities of twentieth-century society. Both devolution and integration tend to go that way, within states as between states . . .

. . . This is not the place to restate the political philosophy which informs the functional idea beyond saying that to prefer it to the constitutional approach is not to be timid, much less to be haphazard. It rests indeed squarely upon the most characteristic idea of the democratic liberal philosophy, which leaves the individual free to enter into a variety of relationships – religious, political and professional, social and cultural – each of which may take him in different directions and dimensions and into different groupings, some of them of international range. Each of us is in fact a 'bundle' of functional loyalties; so that to build a world community upon such a conception is merely to extend and consolidate it also between national societies and groups. . . . The functional approach does not offend against the sentiment of nationality or the pride of sovereignty. Instead of a fictitious formal equality it offers even to the weakest of countries the assurance of non-domination and of an equality of opportunity in the working benefits of any functional activity in which it participates . . . Internationally speaking, political self-determination in this way is translated into functional co-determination . . .

. . . The question of membership provides one final point of comparison. A federal system is bound to be closed and exclusive; a functional system is as naturally open, as changes in membership can be absorbed without doing violence to policy and administration. A federal constitution is a balancing act in regard to a whole range of social and political factors: with any change in membership the whole structure may have to be re-organized and probably to be re-negotiated . . .

. . . On a minor scale the contrast stands out clearly even within the existing Communities. The ECSC and Euratom are straight functional bodies and can get on with their allotted task without offending the position of other countries, while remaining open to link up with them. The scope of EEC is by comparison diffuse and subject to a continuous temptation to self-inflation (which the 'Europeans' deem a virtue); with a bureaucratic tendency because it is diffuse, and an expansionist tendency because it is bureaucratic. The more fields of activity it actively enters, e.g. agriculture, the more acquisitive it tends to become, and in the degree to which it is rounded out it also hardens into a segregated entity . . .

Federation was an advance on empire as a way of joining under a common government a group of separate territorial units. But federation is not only inadequate but irrelevant when the general task is not to consolidate but to loosen the hold of the territorially sovereign conception of political relations, and find a way to world peace through the revolutionary pressures of the time . . .

. . . As a student I have sought an answer to two questions: What kind of political construction was a European union likely to be, and what would be its temper – for if, as I think, function determines structure, this also means that structure must affect practice. And therefore, in the second place, what would be its relevancy to the prospects for a general international system? Admittedly, to try to examine the 'European' idea thus is like trying to hold a line on a political rainbow with its many fleeting hues – a rainbow with one horizon among those who are clear that they were not seeking 'a new fatherland' and wanted Europe united that it may work the better for international union, and the opposite horizon falling in Dr Hallstein's camp. For Dr Hallstein is no less clear that they were after 'awakening a new European patriotism'; and that – while the old nations may be left to dream their national dreams (and after dismissing any idea of supplanting the national with the supranational as 'another illusion') – 'perhaps it is true that only States can act politically. Then let us create the European State – or is Europe finally to abdicate?'

If the aim is political union, a 'United States of Europe', Dr Hallstein's picture, with all its tactical tergiversations, is clearly nearer the mark. Both lines of inquiry have led to the same point, that by its nature and tendency a political union must be nationalistic; and that as such it must impede, and may defeat, the great historic quest for a general system of peace and development. Under the pressures of a planned and radical social transformation it is bound to shape towards a centralized system – closed, exclusive, competitive; and whatever else it may do, such a system would hardly be suited to mediate between the new ideological divisions, or temper the raw nationalism of the new states so as to steer them towards the greener pastures of a mutual international community.

More likely it is that it will cause the tentative 'blocs' that have already confused policy at the UN, out of distrust of the old world, to harden into other 'unions' in emulation of it. Could a European union, in the long run, benefit its own peoples if it tends in the least to split the world afresh into competing regional sovereignties? Is not breaking through that dour barrier of sovereignty the ultimate test? In a world of a hundred and more states sovereignty can in simple fact never be dismantled through a formula but only through function, shedding national functions and pooling authority in them; unless we are to give up all purpose of wide all-round international sharing in the works of peace.

Document 17: D. Mitrany, 'A working peace system' (1943), reprinted in P. Taylor and A.J.R. Groom (eds), *The Functional Theory of Politics* (London, 1975), pp. 123–9, 131–2

When this short study was first published in the summer of 1943 there was great confidence in the unity which had grown up during the war, and students of international organisation were thinking mainly of how to consolidate that unity and expand it. Many of them felt that a definite constitutional framework was needed within which the world society would grow of itself, and they naturally looked upon the ideas of this pamphlet as politically inadequate; others felt with the writer that a world society was more likely to grow through doing things together in workshop and market place rather than by signing pacts in chancelleries. Since then we have moved fast but not well . . .

. . . For to prefer a functional to a constitutional approach is not to be timid, much less to be haphazard. The argument has grown out of a definite view of the historical problem of our time, the chief trait of which is the baffling division between the peoples of the world. . . . That is all the more strange as in its material life the world has moved far towards a common unity. When the sense of unity was still alive in the Middle Ages, social life was a mosaic of small and largely self-sufficient local units; now social life has a highly integrated organic unity, but politically our outlook is bound to a mosaic of separate national units. Much depends on our understanding of this paradox, now that we stand at a historical turning point. How has it come about, what does it signify in terms of world politics? Very broadly, it was bequeathed us by the dynamic nineteenth century, which internationally moved on two separate and opposite lines. Politically it saw the rise of national states, a trend solemnly recognised when in 1919 the Paris conference took 'national self-determination' as its guiding principles. . . . With a new social era before us we find national states a hindrance, but historically the trend was sound in itself. It had its roots in the same currents – the Renaissance, humanism, anti-authoritarianism – which inculcated respect for the individual personality and so, by a natural extension, also for the group or national personality. And as the first led politically to the enfranchisement of the individual, the subject becoming a citizen, in the wider society, the second led to the enfranchisement of national groups through states of their own. Let us call that broadly the cultural side of Western civilisation. But side by side with it the same period produced a rapid and growing division of labour. The economic self-sufficiency of the individual and of the local group was broken up by the development of communications, of new sources of power, of new materials, the opening up of new lands and the rise of mass production, all factors which have bound peoples increasingly together. That is the material side of Western civilisation; and again the trend was the same nationally as internationally. To reconcile these two trends is the task which history is setting us. Both are legitimate, both must be satisfied. To ignore the deep-rooted loyalties of nationality in the search for material efficiency, or to deny the swelling cry for social betterment for the sake of a fictitious independence, is to perpetuate the unrest which is the spring of perennial conflict. It is in the light of this task of how to achieve unity in diversity (and in the domestic sphere too the problem is how to have planning without breaking too many individual liberties), that we must look at the various ideas for international organisation. These have followed in the main three lines of thought.

1 An association of nations, like the League, which would leave the identity and policy of states almost untouched; though comprehensive, it would be a loose association merely suggesting the need for a measure of material integration.

2 A federal system, favoured because it is thought to provide the cohesion lacking in a league; but this would be so only within the limits of some new continental or regional group, and so would tend to divide the world again into a number of potentially competing units.

3 The functional approach, which by linking authority to a specific activity

seeks to break away from the traditional link between authority and a definite territory (perpetuated by either an association or federation of nations). This approach resolves the dilemma of creating either too loose or too narrow an international organisation by building up authorities which would be both comprehensive and solid, in selected fields of common life . . .

The point that matters is that whatever the form and the manner, international organisation must do the same things which national governments do in modern society, only with a difference in scale – it must do those things which cannot be done well, or without friction, except on an international scale. That would mean something very different from the scope of the League of Nations. It was in keeping with our former outlook that international law in general and the Covenant in particular were concerned primarily with defining the formal relationship of states, in a negative sense, and only vaguely with initiating positive common activities. The economic, financial and other sections of the League were mere secretariats, and so in fact is the ILO. The functional bodies contemplated here would be executive agencies with autonomous tasks and powers; they would not merely discuss but would do things jointly, and that would be in keeping with the needs of the time. The trend at present is to enlarge and co-ordinate the social scope of authority, but national planning cannot work in harness with laissez-faire in the international field. The Charter of the United Nations has at least come near to recognising the true nature of the problem . . .

. . . This new approach towards the goal of international collaboration is free from dogma and avoids the cramping limitations of a more nicely designed but hard and fast system. It is an attempt, after looking squarely at the lessons of history, to offer a practical line of action that might overcome the deep-seated division between the needs of material unity and stubborn national loyalties; a division which explains why appeals to world unity have so far remained barren and why the task is essentially one of practical statesmanship. The two obvious tests for any step towards an international order are, first, the means by which we bring about the change, and secondly, the fitness of the change for the communal needs of the time. Historically two ways have been known for adapting the range of government to changing needs and aspirations – conquest or consent . . .

If the new international experiment is to be effective it must have real tasks of government entrusted to it. But at the same time it must in its make-up accept the present reality of a world that is divided into many national states. The most one could hope for during the period of transition is that national governments should act as willing agencies of the incipient international authority; for even if it were possible to deed formal authority in full to an international body, the elements which go to the making of power – raw materials and manpower, industrial potential and strategic positions – would in the nature of things, until national boundaries and authorities are done away with altogether, still remain in the grasp of particular national groups. Nothing could be more barren and confusing, therefore, than the habit of mind which, in the words of Dr Reinhold

Niebuhr, 'thinks that we lack an international government only because no one has conceived a proper blue-print of it. Therefore they produce such blue-prints in great profusion. These pure constitutionalists have a touching faith in the power of a formula over the raw stuff of history'.

The ultimate ideal is simple and universal. But the prospect of the first steps towards it depends not a little on whether we struggle for a formal or constitutional idea – in regard to which there are many creeds – or work for a practical achievement towards which we might strive together. Some of the issues of constitutional principle and structure which have been discussed of late show how serious can be the difference if we choose one way or the other. There is no better illustration of this than the frequent plea for a 'surrender of sovereignty'; and no issue has strayed farther afield from practical needs and possibilities. Sovereignty is a legal concept, a status; it cannot be surrendered unless the units which form the political community, whether individuals or groups, abdicate their political rights.

. . . If a new world authority is to come into being by consent and not by conquest, its status will depend on how far the transfer of sovereignty from national groups is both willing and continuous. To such willing transfers of sovereignty – or abridgement of national sovereignty – there is no limit except that set by our political maturity. But there is an effective minimum, which must include some essential functions now performed by national states. Security is first among them. There can be no real transfer of sovereignty until defence is entrusted to a common authority, because national means of defence are also means of offence and also of possible resistance to that common authority . . .

. . . An editorial in *Nature* (December 1943) suggested that 'functional cooperation may be a means of persuading the Powers ultimately to make the wide sacrifice in national sovereignty which the preservation of peace will demand'. That is historically true and politically sound. In any normal evolution the change has been gradual – a gradual transfer of sovereignty from the ruler to the people, the people in their turn gradually entrusting its exercise to a central authority. Therefore the democratic tests have all along been expressed in a selection of policy and of ultimate control of its execution, and not in any grandiose juridical gesture. Sovereignty cannot in fact be transferred effectively through a formula, only through a function. By entrusting an authority with a certain task, carrying with it command over the requisite powers and means, a slice of sovereignty is transferred from the old authority to the new; and the accumulation of such partial transfers in time brings about a translation of the true seat of authority. If that has been the considered process in the domestic sphere, is it not still more relevant in the international sphere, where even the elements of unity have to be built up laboriously by this very process of patient change? It would indeed be sounder and wiser to speak not of the surrender but of a sharing of sovereignty: when ten or twenty national authorities, each of which had performed a certain task for itself, can be induced to perform that task jointly, they will to that end quite naturally pool their sovereign authority insofar as the good performance of the task demands it.

That may seem a limping way towards world community. Yet the eagerness for a finished constitution may actually hold up progress. It is too often overlooked that written constitutions have in the main served as a check to authority; and federal constitutions, while they serve to bind, also serve to divide. A federal system is by its nature both rigid and limiting. It arranges a few things to be done in common, but limits them strictly and also lays down the many things which must remain separate . . .

. . . The two main objects of government are the organisation of stability and the organisation of change. As regards the first it would not be difficult constitutionally, if the political will were there, to translate the instruments and experience of national life into the needs of an international order; but with regard to peaceful change the problem in the two spheres is utterly different. All the efforts to devise an international system, all the demands for restraining national sovereignty, centre upon this issue of how to bring about the voluntary and progressive evolution of world society. The weakness of the League of Nations lay in the fact that it was limited to the task of organising stability; in this respect the United Nations Charter shows a great advance, and it is significant that the changes which at San Francisco were made in the original draft all tended to add weight to the economic and social functions of the new international organisation. But in a field which is so vast and complex, and in which the participants are so different in outlook and levels of organisation, common ways of thinking and of doing things will not be easy to achieve. Here again the demand for equity tribunals and such devices has only served to confuse the problem; even the legislative process to which we are accustomed in the West may prove at first an uncertain instrument. The choice we shall have to make at every step will be between a gratifying form and the effective working of the international experiment. If for instance the immediate problem is how to bring power under some common control, it is as well to admit that it cannot be done without the willing partnership of the Great Powers themselves. Their preponderance is inevitable; the only choice is between power exercised within a common organisation – for defined common ends and under a measure of common control – or independently and arbitrarily from without . . .

Certain it is that power cannot be restrained except within an effective world system; and to be effective, indeed to come about at all, such a system will have to be built up not on tenets of formal equality but on such as would satisfy the one crucial question: how can we make this organisation work and last? The transition from national to international control of power is bound to be stubborn.

Document 18: E.B. Haas, *The Uniting of Europe: Political, Social and Economic Forces 1950–1957* (Stanford, Cal., 1968 edn), pp. 16–19

We can now state a formal definition of political integration, as used in our ideal type. Political integration is the process whereby political actors in several distinct national settings are persuaded to shift their loyalties, expectations and political activities toward a new centre, whose institutions possess or demand jurisdiction over the pre-existing national states. The end result of a process of political integration is a new political community, superimposed over the pre-existing ones.

Before a formal analysis can be made, however, it is essential to specify who the political actors are. . . . It suffices to single out and define the political elites in the participating countries, to study their reactions to integration and to assess changes in attitude on their part. In our scheme of integration, 'elites' are the leaders of all relevant political groups who habitually participate in the making of public decisions, whether as policy-makers in government, as lobbyists or as spokesmen of political parties. They include the officials of trade associations, the spokesmen of organised labour, higher civil servants and active politicians. The emphasis on elites in the study of integration derives its justification from the bureaucratised nature of European organisations of long standing, in which basic decisions are made by the leadership, sometimes over the opposition and usually over the indifference of the general membership. This gives the relevant elites a manipulative role which is of course used to place the organisation in question on record for or against a proposed measure of integration.

A further important justification for the elite approach to the study of integration lies in the demonstrable difference in attitudes held at the leadership levels of significant groups, as contrasted with the mass membership . . .

. . . Having so far focused on the perceptions and activities of politically significant groups and their elites, it remains to state the role assigned to institutions and structured belief patterns in our ideal type of political integration. Groups put forward interdependent sets of values – ideologies – in their struggle with other groups for political prominence. In a given political community, these ideologies merge and overlap to permit the existence of a set of beliefs held by almost all citizens. But since group action at all levels of political activity hinges around action by governmental institutions, the relationship assumed between beliefs and institutional conduct must be made explicit. During the initial stages of any process of political integration, the nationalism established in each of the participating countries is still supreme. The decision to join in or to abstain from the proposed steps of integration is defended in terms of national values by each interested group. Once the institutions associated with the step of integration are established, however, a change is likely to take place. The ideologies defended by national groups are likely to influence and perhaps shape the values and ideology of the officials manning the new institution. Certainly no effort will be spared to make the attempt at shaping. However, a reverse process of gradually penetrating national ideologies can also be supposed to get under way. Decision-makers in the new institutions may resist the effort to have their beliefs and policies dictated by the interested elites, and advance their own prescription. Or the heterogeneity of their origins may compel them to fashion doctrines and develop codes of conduct which represent an amalgamation of various national belief systems or group values. A two-way process is likely to result in any case: influence originating from national sources seeking to shape 'federal' or 'supranational' decisions and efforts to make national groups conduct themselves in accordance with doctrines originating from the new central institutions. If permitted to operate for any length of time, the national groups now compelled to funnel their aspirations through federal institutions may also be constrained to work within the ideological framework of those organs. Eventually, the transformed doctrines will again be utilised to influence the federal decision-makers, who in turn will have to react in one or both of the approaches sketched above.

It is evident, therefore, that a complex pattern of interaction between national ideologies on the one hand and the beliefs of the office-holders in the central institutions on the other will come about. The eventual changes produced at the national level will constitute one of the indicators of the degree of integration as the process continues, while the analysis of this interaction is one of the crucial problems of this study, and of any study of political integration. Hence the contemporary doctrines and institutions relating to European integration must be examined more closely.

Document 19: E.B. Haas, ibid. (1968), pp. 286–9, 291–4, 296–9, 317

. . . There can be little doubt that broad similarities in the social values entertained by the dominant elites of the ECSC countries explain in large part why the Treaty was accepted and successfully implemented. Such reasoning, further, goes a long way in explaining why certain groups see in supranational institutions a technique for systematically realising their specific values. However, the literal application of this scheme would impute far more ideological cohesion to groups only nominally united by religious or secular norms than seems warranted by the facts of political behaviour. It would permit projections of pro-integration sentiment merely on the basis of religious or party affiliation, without raising questions about the qualifications and special demands voiced constantly in the integration framework. . . . Integration there has been in Europe since 1950 even if it cannot be meaningfully delineated with a few central concepts. To do justice to the multiplicity of aspirations involved in the pluralistic setting provided, we must return to the ideal type stated in Chapter 1. There is no circumventing the need for stating the initial demands and expectations of relevant elites, and to sort them with respect to identities, opposition and convergence. Our basic finding was that the acceptance of ECSC is best explained by the convergence of demands within and among the nations concerned, not by a pattern of identical demands and hopes. Further, there is no circumventing the need for exploring the changes in demands and expectations which developed after the supranational institutions began their work, and there is no avoiding the task of projecting the future pattern of integration in terms of the hopes and demands set free by unification of the coal–steel sector. The success of integration must thus be assessed in terms of the perceptions of the crucial actors. To what overall identities did the common market give rise? To what convergences of group and national aspirations? If there is a spill-over, is it explained by identical hopes or by another accidental convergence of separate aspirations? And, finally, have the identities given rise to a pattern of unified ideologies cutting across national boundaries or has the common market resulted merely in ad hoc group alliances along supranational lines, devoid of ideological unity? If the latter is the central finding, the basic conclusion must then be that continuing integration can well rest on progressive convergences of expectations without any significant central ideological underpinnings.

If it seemed extremely difficult to state any general proposition summarising the pattern of evolution, it became evident, nevertheless, that crucial changes did take place: opponents of integration became supporters, initial supporters became neutral or disinterested, while still other initial supporters developed even stronger motives for continuing integration. It is now our task to state four categories of evolution under which all these developing aspirations can be subsumed . . .

Types of political expectations

Long-run positive expectations
Short-run positive expectations
Short-run negative expectations
Long-run negative expectations

Ideology and political expectations

Intensities of ideological convictions associated with each of these types of expectations vary distinctly. We are here concerned not with the committed 'European', be he Liberal, Conservative or Socialist, but with permanently functioning elites for whom 'Europe' is one of several important symbols, but not necessarily the dominant one. Groups with long-range expectations, for example, are likely to possess well-developed bodies of doctrine, whose implementation is closely associated with the positions taken toward further integration. Those with positive expectations look to supranationalism to achieve their goal, having decided that the national framework is not up to the task. The 'spill-over' is real for them, since basic ideological tenets even in the coal–steel sector seemingly cannot be attained without expanding the supranational task to additional fields. The demand pattern of ECSC labour and of the Socialist Parties is the most striking case in point. Conversely, groups marked by clearly negative long-range expectations, notably the Communists and small businessmen in high-cost countries, have an equally well-structured and staunchly defended body of ideology at their disposal, whose very firmness commits them against integration . . .

The 'spill-over' and political expectations

Only the convinced 'European' possessed long-run positive expectations with respect to ECSC in 1950, and among the elites directly concerned with coal and steel there were few such persons.

The crucial evolution of such expectations among the bulk of ECSC labour leaders both Socialist and Christian – is one of the clearest demonstrations of the role of a combined social welfare–economic democracy idealogy, seeking realisation through the medium of new central institutions. These groups as well as the Socialist and left-wing segments of Christian-Democratic Parties associated with them are now in the vanguard of more integration – through ECSC as well as in the form of Euratom and the General Common Market – because they see in supranational rules and organs the means to establish a regulated large-scale industrial economy permitting the development of permanent worker influence over industry. Thus a 'spill-over' into new economic and political sectors certainly occurred in terms of expectations developing purely in the national contexts of the elites involved. Yet these expectations were reinforced along supranational lines not only because action was demanded of the High Authority but because continuous joint lobbying with labour leaders from other countries became both necessary and possible. The same, of course, is true of the Socialist Parties, whose national aims found supranational support in the formation of the Socialist political group in the Common Assembly. Hence the true impact of integration can be appreciated only after a study of joint supranational activity on the part of these groups. The evolution of industrial attitudes and of parties sympathetic to business interests is much more difficult to classify . . .

. . . Trade association activity in the six countries fails to support any hypothesis of the evolution of a prevalent and unified industrial ideology in favour of a common market under the direction of central public authorities. Instead, there developed a series of opportunistic and frequently anti-competitive demands for specific measures of integration designed to benefit a specific national industry, though supranational action is commonly invoked for such purposes. Conversion to 'Europe' is therefore short-range, limited and 'tactical' in nature. Yet it is of the greatest significance for a study of integration processes to isolate even these instances of changed attitudes, because permanent loyalties may still develop from these initial faltering steps, if long-range expectations are identified with them . . .

The more important index, however, is the readiness of industrial groups to accept integration if accompanied by supranational institutions possessing powers of direction and control, potentially 'dirigistic' in nature. In 1951, all groups without exception opposed such an approach and were compelled by national legislative action to accept the ECSC rules. Four years later this unqualified opposition had changed to a demand for more supranational powers and control if specific benefits were expected from this . . .

. . . even the consistently negative-minded may be persuaded to adjust. . . . But responsive to the threat of the Council of Ministers' approving the High Authority programme of freight-rate equalisation, the shippers adjusted to the extent of admitting the principle of non-discriminatory, competitive and public pricing of all hauls – provided the actual administration of the system were left to voluntary international arrangements among shippers, subject to supervision by intergovernmental organs like the Central Rhine Commission. This, certainly, is far from welcoming supranationalism. But it implies tentative adjustments toward an integrated economy in order to head off supranational 'dirigisme'. Similar opinions and expectations may be found among Dutch and German shipping interests. The 'spill-over' thus takes place despite long-term negative expectations. Sector integration, however, begets its own impetus toward extension to the entire economy even in the absence of specific group demands and their attendant ideologies. Thus, ECSC civil servants speaking for national governments have constantly found it necessary to 'harmonise' their separate policies in order to make it possible for the integrated sectors to function, without necessarily implying any ideological commitment to the European idea . . .

The practical need for co-operation in other international economic organisations is especially striking. The six countries had to act in unison in being recognised as a single contracting party in GATT and in being exempted from extending liberalisation requirements in OEEC . . .

. . . It was only in 1956 that Jean Monnet's doctrine of a strong, united Europe, revitalised by a progressive industrial economy resting on a large common market, came into its own. Among the early supporters of ECSC and general economic integration there had always been individuals who saw in economic unity the only means of survival in a global setting of Soviet-American dominance and rising Asian and African nations. The lesson was driven home in a much more direct fashion by the Suez Canal crisis and the isolation of a weak Europe in the face of Afro-Asian, Soviet and American opposition. Economic integration – with its evident political implications and causes – then became almost a universal battle-cry, making complete the 'spill-over' from ECSC to Euratom and its promise of independence from oil imports, from sector common markets to the General Common Market. Certainly the process of extending the integrated sector had been under way since the recession of 1953–1954 when the first industrial demands for supranational market regulation were heard. It came into its own with the patent demonstration of political weakness and the desire to unite economically to constitute a power centre independent of both Moscow and Washington. This consciousness now seems to form part of the expectations of most European elites, though supranationalism is not necessarily the technique universally agreed upon to realise unity . . .

. . . A geographical spill-over is clearly taking place. In its unique British form it rigorously rejects any federal trimmings and continues to rely on intergovernmental 'association'. But it grants not only the need for more and more intimate economic contacts in areas of activity until recently considered the sacrosanct preserve of national governments, but even the necessity for decision by majority vote among ministerial delegates. All other things being equal, it is as inconceivable that this form of co-operation should not result in new patterns of profound interdependence as it is unlikely that the General Common Market can avoid a species of political federalism in order to function as an economic organ.

Document 20: L.N. Lindberg and S.A. Scheingold, 'Alternative models of systems change', from *Europe's Would-Be Polity: Patterns of Change in the European Community* (Engelwood Cliffs, NJ, 1970), pp. 135–40

A new classification of outcomes

Broadly speaking, the European Community has involved two kinds of commitments or obligations: on the one hand, to carry out specific, agreed functions or to obey specific rules, and on the other hand, to institute an ongoing Community decision-making process which was to translate general goals into specific rules and policies. The former represents a commitment to execute agreements already arrived at, that is, to make decisions that administer a previously agreed area of joint action. The latter implies a commitment to seek such agreements by means of joint processes and institutions, that is, to make new policy. Thus, in a sense what we are talking about here is different kinds of bargaining to which actors are committed. Community institutions are typically assigned more or less routine enforcement and 'housekeeping' functions in the first case. In the second, they may become the focus of potentially far-reaching processes of a collective legislation in which they intensively interact with national political leaders, interest groups, and other political actors. And it is this sort of process that is central to the neofunctionalist theories of integration. These theories argue that once the governments and a supranational agency become involved in such an open-end process, a number of 'politicizing' forces are set in motion that may lead to increases in the authority of the supranational agency and to the assumption by the governments of more joint tasks than were originally specifically envisaged. . . . The commitment to engage in such a process is thus the chief method whereby the scope and authority of this European Community system can be increased over time. As such it represents a key to the dynamics of integration. This is not to imply that obligations of the first type, that is, obligations to implement rules or execute specific agreements already arrived at, are necessarily substantively less important. The agreement to establish and administer the customs union is of this type and yet is perhaps the single most important act in the history of the Communities. But these commitments do pertain to different stages of the integrative process and they do have different implications for the future development of this system. As such they should be subjected to a separate analysis, for the variable factors that account for 'success' are likely to be different. When we combine our present three-fold categorization of outcome patterns with this two-fold categorization of types of obligation, we get the alternative process model [shown in Figure 1] . . .

Forward linkage describes a sequence whereby commitment to participate in joint decision-making has initiated a process that has led to a marked increase in the scope of the system or in its institutional capacities. In terms of the growth of the system this model yields potentially high benefits but at considerable risk of failure.

	Fulfilment	Retraction	Extension
To participate in a joint decision-making process (i.e., to make new policy)	Forward-linkage model	Output-failure model	Systems transformation model(s)
To implement agreements, and the routine enforcement of specific rules (i.e., to administer a previously agreed area of joint activity)	Equilibrium model	Spill-back model	

Obligations   *Outcomes*

Figure 1 Alternative process model

Output failure refers to a situation in which such a commitment was accepted but where the system was unable to produce an acceptable set of policies and rules and where the capacity and scope of the system hence were not enhanced. In fact, scope and authority could both be decreased, since the failure is one that might be generalized as due to a lack of will or leadership to go on with integration as such.

Equilibrium occurs when an area of activity is routinized or institutionalized. Rules are established and recognised, and there is little need for new inter-governmental bargaining. Nor is there any increase in scope or institutional capacity, although the original commitment may involve important joint tasks in both regards. In terms of growth, the gains are very modest, but so are the risks.

Spill-back refers to a situation in which there is a withdrawal from a set of specific obligations. Rules are no longer regularly enforced or obeyed. The scope of Community action and its institutional capacities decrease. Spill-back may occur in an area that had once been in equilibrium or enjoyed forward linkages. While spill-back does entail risks for the system as a whole, it is likely to be limited to the specific rules in question.

Systems transformation means an extension to specific or general obligations that are beyond the bounds of the original treaty commitments, either geographically or functionally. It typically entails a major change in the scope of the Community or in its institutions, that often requires an entirely new constitutive bargaining process among the member states, entailing substantial goal redefinition among national political actors. The signing of the EEC and Euratom treaties represented a successful systems transformation. The failures of EDC, of the Fouchet Plan negotiations, and of British entry are examples of unsuccessful systems transformation. Implications for growth are of very high benefits and risks.

The systems transformation and forward linkage models are both growth models. They differ in that the latter refers to incremental growth and the former to what economists call 'step-function' or 'step-level' growth. The essential difference is that incremental growth involves changes in amounts and dimensions that are already established; the changes are quantitive, not qualitative. Incremental change can be predicted by projecting well-established trends, whereas this is often not possible with step functional change, for it may involve large and unexpected variations and the introduction of wholly new variables.

Even though the 'real world' rarely fits logical models exactly, they are useful because they highlight certain crucial theoretical dimensions and thus help to 'make sense' out of the infinite complexity of that real world. Several things must be kept in mind as we use these models, however. First of all, they refer basically to parts of the Community system, not to the whole. This is dictated by our decision to direct our attention to within system variations. Thus our focus is predominantly on change within the sectors or issue-areas delineated in Chapter 3. This is not to say that our models do not touch on dynamic relationships among a number of different issue-areas. Indeed, one of our major findings is that incremental growth (forward linkages) is unlikely to occur in one area if it is not accompanied by some growth in other areas too. It also seems implicit in the concept of systems transformation that what we are talking about is system-wide. We admit to some difficulties with that concept, and these will be fully discussed in Chapter 7. Nevertheless, we will hold to our distinction until then and will not turn to cross-system analysis per se until the last chapters.

Our analysis is also temporally limited. We are trying to find out what happens to an empirical integration system once it is launched. We assume 'take-off' as a 'given' and we have no concept for a termination state for the Community. Thus, we are not trying to make statements about all of the presumed successive stages of the integration process . . .

Finally, what we are categorizing in our process models are decision sequences at particular points in time that lead to particular patterns of outcomes, that in turn have consequences for system change. We are not categorizing the issue-area within which that activity is taking place. Any given area can over time be characterised by very different outcomes, and the study of the circumstances of change from one type to another will be most instructive for an understanding of the Community. In other words, the process models lead into each other over time. Thus if governments succeed in living up to a prior obligation to make joint policy decisions in a particular area, we refer to this as forward linkage. To the extent that these decisions in turn set up a system of specific rules and machinery for their enforcement, the area will become either an equilibrium or spill-back area depending on whether or not the rules are regularly obeyed. An issue-area might then be partly in equilibrium and partly in forward linkage, as, for example, is the case with agriculture. Should governments decide to include entirely new areas of activity within the Community system or drastically alter the authority structure governing joint decision-making, a systems transformation would occur. We would then in a sense be back at the beginning again in that a new set of obligations would have been undertaken. The question would be to see whether these new obligations would in turn be fulfilled, that is, would there be forward linkage or output failure, equilibrium or spill-back. Of course, the cumulative effect over time of these different patterns of change would be reflected in fluctuations in scope and in institutional capacity.

Thresholds and momentum effects in integration

Since our process models are bounded by both issue-area and time, we must next inquire whether they lead into each other in any regular and predictable fashion, either sector to sector or over time or both. Having achieved (or being stabilised at) a particular level of integration (i.e., of system growth defined in terms of scope and capacities) as a consequence of forward linkage, systems transformation, or equilibrium outcomes, what happens to the chances of moving to another level or to another sector or sectors? Do the chances for future growth increase the more the system has already grown? Does rapid growth conduce to more rapid growth? Does equilibrium in some sectors conduce to growth in others? Is systems transformation more likely to result from successive forward linkages or from imaginative manipulation of crises set off by output failure or spill-back? Or is it that most impulses for change come not from the system itself, but originate outside as a result of the operation of some kind of extra-system or external variable? It is not that we are prepared (or inclined) to specify precise causal relationships between change in one area or at one point in time and change at other points in time or in other areas. We do not see any necessary sequence in our models. On the other hand, it is clear from our basic model of system change in the European Community that each of our outcome patterns affects the system itself (or parts of it) and also the environment, and that they will in that measure condition other parts of the system or the future of the system (or parts of it). If outcomes increase the scope of the system, or its capacities, or systemic support, or demand flow, or leadership, then future growth possibilities would appear to be enhanced. The converse would hold if outcomes were seen to have negative effects . . .

. . . If we directly confront the broader problem of the implications of changes in discrete sectors or issue areas for changes in the parameters of the total system . . . we will have to confront (if not resolve) a new set of questions. Is system change in some areas more important than change in others as far as the total system is concerned? Are increments of functional scope more important or less important than increases in capacities? Is there some sort of 'point of no return' beyond which the chances for disintegration diminish drastically? Has the Community reached such a point? Or conversely, is there something about the system or the environment that puts a ceiling on the potential growth of the Community? The conclusions we draw from the following case studies[1] provide some of the building blocks for this analysis.

Note

1 These case studies can be found in the publication in which this document originally appeared.

Document 21: E.B. Haas, 'The study of regional integration: reflections on the joy and anguish of pretheorizing', in L.N. Lindberg and S.A. Scheingold (eds), *Regional Integration: Theory and Research* **(Cambridge, Mass., 1971), pp. 23–4, 26–32**

The neo-functional approach

Neo-functionalists have their own troubles. True, neo-functional theorizing is consistently phenomenological; it avoids normative assertion and systematic generalization. Neo-functionalism stresses the instrumental motives of actors; it looks for the adaptability of elites in line with specialization of roles; neo-functionalism takes self-interest for granted and relies on it for delineating actor perceptions. Moreover, neo-functionalists rely on the primacy of incremental decision making over grand designs, arguing that most political actors are incapable of long-range purposive behavior because they stumble from one set of decisions into the next as a result of not having been able to foresee many of the implications and consequences of the earlier decisions. Ever more controversial (and thus system-transforming) policies emerge, starting from a common initial concern over substantively narrow but highly salient issues. A new central authority may emerge as an unintended consequence of incremental earlier steps. Most neo-functionalists have not explicitly recognized, however, the crucial question of whether even this incremental style is not 'foreseen' and manipulated by certain heroic actors (Jean Monnet, Sicco Mansholt, Walter Hallstein, Raul Prebisch) – and eventually checked by certain equally prescient national actors (Charles de Gaulle).

The neo-functional theory is therefore a highly contingent one. One limitation is embedded in the source of the approach – modern pluralistic–industrial democratic polity. That source offers a rationale for linking the separate variables found in the neo-functional model in Western Europe; but application to the third world has so far sufficed only to accurately predict difficulties and failures in regional integration while in the European case some successful positive prediction has been achieved. Another limitation, however, involves the very question of what constitutes a successful prediction. Neo-functionalist practitioners have difficulty achieving closure on a given case of regional integration because the terminal condition being observed is uncertain: Neo-functionalists do not agree on a dependent variable and therefore differ with each other on the point in time at which a judgement of how much successful integration is to be made. Thus, specific processes, specific cases of spillover, specific styles of accommodation and increasing mutual responsiveness among actors have been successfully predicted. But whether this adds up to achieving closure or the attainment of some kind of 'community' in the region remains a matter of how we define the dependent variable. As of now the theory has not been falsified in the sense that a successful community has been achieved by virtue of processes not contained in the theory. . . . Nor has the theory been fully validated as long as it cannot explain how and why a postulated condition is attained . . .

Toward a dependent variable

Our reflections have led us to two somber conclusions: First, the lessons we have learned from the study of regional integration have been imperfectly 'integrated' because they coexist at several levels of abstraction, thus making it difficult to engage in conceptually focused evaluation and projection; moreover, a primary cause of imperfect conceptual integration is the nonadditive character of the pretheories which have inspired our research. Second, one major reason for the lack of fit between the major theories is disagreement on what constitutes the dependent variable. A giant step on the road toward an integrated theory of regional integration, therefore, would be taken if we could clarify the matter of what we propose to explain and/or predict.

Ideal types and terminal conditions

Federalist theory has been the least ambiguous in telling which end product it seeks to explain or predict: The terminal condition of the process of integration is the achievement of a federal union among the units being studied, nation-states. Communications theorizing has used the construct of a security community as its terminal condition, recognizing the possibility that such a condition may be of the 'amalgamated' or the 'pluralistic' variety. This terminal condition, of course, is wider in scope than the federalists' though it is able to subsume the notion of a federal union. Neo-functionalists have worked with the idea of a political community or a political union, a concept which also subsumes a federal union but is less sweeping than a security community because it makes specific assumptions about central institutions and the progressive centralization of decision making among the members. One of the more bothersome aspects of these efforts at speci-fying a dependent variable was the tendency to mix its imputed characteristics with those of independent and intervening variables.

The nagging thought persists that we lack clear dependent variables because we have followed the practice of erecting these terminal states by treating them as ideal types reconstructed from our historical experience at the national level and then of observing the types of behaviour that contribute – or fail to contribute – to the attainment of that condition. These ideal types are not true dependent variables since they cannot yet be observed or measured in nature. The postulated conditions have not yet come about anywhere, at least in the contemporary world. At best we have a putative dependent variable. It is sobering to take a glance at some real-life dependent variables. The European Economic Community in 1962 seemed on the point of a break through to a political community de facto because of an attempted expansion in the scope and level of its decision making capacity; instead it settled down into the uneasy equilibrium state of continuing its established role until 1969. . . . The examples could be multiplied. They suggest that the variety of possible outcomes is considerable, that unions may settle down into a stable system without reaching any of the stages we defined in the earlier phases of our research. Yet these stages still represent higher degrees of 'integration' than was true of the member states at an earlier point in time.

Scales as dependent variables

But why the insistence on a single ideal type as the terminal condition? The terminal condition envisaged could very well be more than a pluralistic security community and less than a political community, defined as the successful pluralistic-democratic state writ large; in fact, this is likely to be the case. Hence I suggest that we follow the approach of deliberately positing end states that could reflect extensive system transformation leading toward centralization or decentralization or the achievement of a new integrative plateau. The verbally defined single terminal conditions with which we have worked in the past political community, security community, political union, federal union – are inadequate because they foreclose real-life developmental possibilities.

Efforts have indeed been made to get away from the ideal typical definition of end states. They have taken the form, predominantly, of specifying separate dimensions or conditions which would constitute a higher degree of integration as compared to a previous point in time. In addition, scales are provided in some instances to observe and measure how far a given union has moved along the specified dimension. The end state, then, is a quantitatively specified 'point' on a scale; when several scales are used for several salient dimensions, the end state is a specified convergence of separate curves.

But the quantitatively phrased multidimensional definition – usually rendered as an 'integrated community' – also presents problems. It suggests that if the union being studied scores 'high' on a number of salient dimensions, particularly if it scores progressively 'higher' over time, some theoretically relevant outcome is being attained; yet the total shape of the outcome is not given. This approach has the virtue of papering over the disagreement over the appropriate mix of independent and intervening variables that are embedded in the various theoretical approaches to regional integration studies. It recognizes that we do not know what the mix is, nor whether it is the same for all situations. But it stresses simple observation for the careful development of hypotheses justifying and linking various independent variables – which in turn requires some kind of theory. Nor does this approach overcome the difficulty of foreclosing the future to a variety of possible integrative outcomes since it posits progressively 'higher' scores instead of making a disciplined effort at imagining various future conditions. In short, the quantitative definition of progressive integrative developments is best seen as a methodological help in making accurate observations and at limiting recourse to overly restrictive verbal definitions; but it cannot alone provide the dependent variable. Scales of separate dimensions of integration are useful descriptively because they capture a process; but without hypothetically linked variables they are not explanatory of an outcome which, itself, remains unspecified. When used in lieu of descriptive or schematic images of end states they substitute premature operationalization for theory and vision.

This truth is firmly recognized by Leon Lindberg and Stuart Scheingold. They posit three possible outcomes: The fulfilment of a postulated task on the part of practices and/or institutions created for integrative purposes; the retraction of such a task (i.e., disintegration); and the extension of such a task into spheres of action not previously anticipated by the actors. Models are provided for explaining the sequence of action made up of events created by actors. These three terms sum up and interpret independent variables into recurrent patterns yielding one of the three possible outcomes . . .

. . . I should like to propose three different dependent variables, all of which are heuristic in the sense that they do not have any real-life counterparts. They provide orienting terminal conditions on which our thoughts and efforts can focus. Nor are they really 'terminal'; we can posit them as provisional points in the future on which we fix our analytical attention. . . . Nor are the three dependent variables exhaustive of possibilities. They provide rather an invitation to imagine still different outcomes which involve a higher degree of unity among the particip-ating units than existed at a previous time. In short they are illustrations of possible temporary results of the processes we sum up under the label regional integration, so designed as to stretch our imagination of what the future may hold. I shall label the three 'regional state', 'regional commune', and 'asymmetrical regional overlap'. The processes associated with all of our pretheories could, in principle, result in the attainment of any of these terminal conditions. Minimally, they all must meet the attributes of a security community. The three differ in how the main resource – legitimate authority – is diffused. Hence normative questions of some moment are implied. A regional state is a hierarchically ordered arrange-ment resembling states familiar to us. Political authority is concentrated at the center; resources are marshalled and distributed from it. The centralized authority is legitimate in the eyes of the citizens, voluntary groups, and subordinate structures. To the extent that the political culture of the region is 'participant' in character the legitimacy bestowed upon the central authority represents a sense of 'regional nationalism'.

There is nothing unfamiliar about this construct. But its opposite, a regional commune, is a much stranger beast. It assumes the kind of interdependence among the participating units which does not permit the identification of a single center of authority or perhaps of any clear center. It is an anarchoid image of a myriad of units which are so highly differentiated in function as to be forced into interdependence. Authority is involved primarily in the sense of having been taken away from previous centers without having found a new single locus. Legitimacy, however it can be imagined, would not take the form of a loyalty akin to nationalism.

Asymmetrical overlapping involves a much more complex arrangement. Many units depend on many others but the pattern of interdependence is asymmetrical: For some purposes all may be equally interdependent, but for others a few of the units cohere closely with a few others while for still other purposes the pattern may again be different without involving all units equally. In short, while authority is certainly withdrawn from the preexisting units, it is not proportionately or symmetrically vested in a new center; instead it is distributed asymmetrically among several centers, among which no single dominant one may emerge, though one might imagine subtypes of this dependent variable involving various degrees of centralized authority. The ensemble would enjoy legitimacy in the eyes of its citizens though it would be difficult to pinpoint the focus of the legitimacy in a single authority center; rather, the image of infinitely tiered multiple loyalties might be the appropriate one. Perhaps the now existing Western European pattern approaches this image.

What about the vexing question of dependence on extra regional centers of influence, if not authority? How significant is it to talk about such end states of regional integration processes when the resulting structure may be autonomous in a rather fictitious sense? It is possible to describe a variant of each type which locates the regional cluster within a larger system and specifies the degree of subservience to it. Moreover, other variants or subtypes will readily come to mind. I emphasize again that nothing exhaustive is being attempted at this stage: My concern is to provide some generalized images of outcomes before we get lost in operationalization.

One final advantage of using heuristic multiple variables is the emancipation thereby provided from our pretheories. Neo-functional efforts stress case studies of decision making within a region and in regional organizations, an interest justified by the neo-functionalist assumption that decision makers are the true heroes and villains of the integration process. Transactionalists counter that a great deal of relevant activity goes on outside of organizations and decisional encounters, an argument based on the assumption that anybody who 'transacts' or 'communicates' anything is potentially relevant to the creation of integrative/ disintegrative trends. Obviously, these two approaches are far from mutually exclusive. Linking them, however, requires articulate hypotheses about presumed relationships between decisional outcomes and communication patterns. Since the multiply defined dependent variable, in turn, implies different scopes of collective decision making and varying strength of interunit dependence, such hypotheses can be usefully linked with the presumed attainment of one or the other of these outcomes. This, in turn, requires a specification of what mix of which independent variables is likely to lead to a given outcome – something clearly not achieved by our pretheories or our empirical generalizations – and raises questions as to what kinds of studies ought to be tackled next . . .

Document 22: E.B. Haas, 'Turbulent fields and the theory of regional integration', *International Organization* Vol. 30: 1976, pp. 177–80, 208, 210–11

Obsolescent but not obsolete

Theories of regional integration thus retain a good deal of relevance wherever and whenever the setting they were designed to describe and explain continues to exist . . .

. . . Obsolescence is a gradual process, not a sharp break. Federalist theories of regional integration retain relevance whenever a group of actors profess a commitment to the introduction of a specific set of objectives and plans which herald a new order and when a deep and abiding consensus on such a new order prevails for some time. Other theories of regional integration retain their relevance whenever a group of actors retains a commitment to the enhancement of a set of common values – security, equity, efficiency, harmony – and does not reexamine or question these values, or the means of action for attaining them. The agreement on these values then continues to define the manner of exercising choice, and the manner is incremental. If, therefore, the functionalist, neo-functionalist and transactionalist theories are to remain relevant, two conditions must hold: (1) institutional outcomes must be open in the sense that various end states are possible, provided only that the collective decision making mode adopted will be more centralized than was true at the beginning of the process: (2) the pressure for including common tasks and programs directed against external forces and states must not be resolved in such a manner as to detract from regional centralization. Failure to adhere to these conditions in regional integration processes will result in the creation of interdependence patterns with extra-regional forces and actors. While this may be both likely and desirable, it is not the condition which regional integration theories were designed to explain.

It follows that the assumptions, methods, and concepts found in theories of regional integration may apply to some activities and institutions in a given regional organization, but not to all. I shall argue in the next section that the logic of incrementalism and regional self-containment no longer holds for certain activities of the European Community. This, however, does not imply that such activities as maintaining the customs union and the common agricultural policy also fall outside the theory. If a common monetary policy is agreed upon as a result of the pressure for maintaining the customs union, we would have a classical case of spillover. If however, a common monetary policy is not devised, or if that policy is part of a more general agreement in OECD or the Group of Ten, the results cannot legitimately be attributed to the spillover mechanism but to imperatives of an external nature not captured in regional integration theories. Consider also the possibility that a new task, not part of the original value commitment (e.g. environmental protection) is added to the prior commitment relating to the customs union. Again regional integration does retain relevance here if the member states then proceed to treat the new task in the same old incremental manner. But perhaps they won't. Obsolescence comes in parts, not in wholes . . .

Turbulent fields

For those who are preoccupied with analyzing and predicting the future fate of specific regions, then, the group of pre-theories to give them their accurate labels, continue to serve as heuristic aids of some value. Undoubtedly, the fit among the three incrementalist pre-theories can be improved.

But I doubt that it is a good investment of our time and ingenuity. Integration theories, I believe, are becoming obsolete because they are not designed to address the most pressing and important problems on the global agenda of policy and research. They do not and cannot capture a pervasive condition that characterizes the entire earth and the whole range of international relations, because they are inspired by a sense of orderly process and by the assumption that states manage to cope collectively according to the rationality of disjointed incrementalism. This inspiration is not wrong; it is merely incomplete. Global politics and the so-called search for a new world order are akin to what planners have called a 'turbulent field'. And this calls for a different conceptualization if we wish to make sense of it.

Turbulence is the term we bestow on the confused and clashing perceptions of organizational actors which find themselves in a setting of great social complexity. The number of actors is very large. Each pursues a variety of objectives which are mutually incompatible: but each is also unsure of the trade-offs between the objectives. Each actor is tied into a network of interdependencies with other actors which are as confused as the first. Yet some of the objectives sought by each cannot be obtained without cooperation from others. A turbulent field, then, is a policy space in which this type of confusion dominates discussion and negotiation. It can be sub-national, national, regional, inter-regional, and global – and all at the same time.

In such a policy space it is very difficult for organizational actors to develop stable expectations of mutual behavior and performance. If one is not sure of one's own goals, it becomes very hard to adjust one's behavior to the goals of negotiating partners who are no more certain of their objectives. This condition implies the erosion of such interorganizational patterns of consensus, reciprocity, and normative regularity . . . The questioning of older norms and values then accelerates and problem solving machinery which had been accepted earlier falls into disuse. New organizations are then devised in large numbers in the attempt to cope; but they change form and purpose almost as fast as they are created. As old rules fall into disrepute the new rules lack legitimacy and efficacy and are soon discarded. Everything is 'up for grabs' . . .

. . . The control of turbulent fields is emerging as the political task in what remains of this century. The search for world order is nothing but an attempt to conquer turbulence. Theories of regional integration have a lot to teach us still about non-violent methods for collectively solving international problems, for coping. They can find a place in the intellectual armory of studying alternative world orders. But this armory must be stocked with new concepts as well. I shall suggest that this process has begun in the European Community at the level of policy, and that these policies and the institutions devised to implement them illustrate the attempt to deal with turbulence rather than achieve regional political integration . . .

Integration or interdependence?

The paradox of all this is that as we increasingly subordinate the discussion of regional integration to the consideration of overall interdependence, we undermine the theoretical and ideological tenets which in the past seemed to point towards increasing regional integration. This is what makes regional integration theory obsolete in the European setting. While it is not yet obsolete elsewhere, the same logic suggests that eventually obsolescence will set in there as well. In the meantime, however, much of the theory remains relevant for analytical purposes because not all aspects of European activity are equally infected with the syndrome of more complex linkages. Integration processes clearly continue, diffused and sidetracked by the competing process of growing extra-regional enmeshment which may not be integrative in the same sense, or which may lead to a different focus for integration. Hence, there is every reason why the study of regional integration should be both included in and subordinated to the study of changing patterns of interdependence . . .

. . . interdependence and integration cease to co-vary . . .

When we talk of social and economic 'integration' as contrasted with 'interdependence', no very sharp and meaningful distinctions can be drawn. Differences become very apparent, however, when we talk of 'policy interdependence' and 'policy integration' (as we have done in this essay). Policy interdependence, substantively speaking of course concerns itself with activities and events which can be described as economic and social. Policy interdependence is a condition both physical and perceptual under which governments are so sensitive and vulnerable to what their partners may or may not do that unilateral action becomes unwise and dangerous to their survival. It is possible and even helpful to draw up continua of this condition which run from 'autarky' at one extreme to 'interdependence' on the other by way of 'interconnectedness' and 'dependence'. The notion of 'integration', however, refers to institutionalized procedures devised by governments for coping with the condition of interdependence; coping, it must be stressed may take the form of increasing, decreasing, or maintaining interdependence. Policy interdependence, then, need not necessarily lead to progressive policy integration at all. These institutionalized procedures reinforce interdependence only under the special and possibly marginal conditions associated in the past with welfare objectives tied to a political program of unification. Regional integration theory is therefore properly seen as a component of a larger analytic framework, dealing with a special case within the overall scheme.

Patterns of interdependence are changing everywhere, not just in Western Europe, Central America, or East Africa. The emergence of new political objectives stressing new approaches to human welfare is not confined to these regions. New knowledge is not the private property of any regional elite. Dependence of regional elites on events and demands outside each region seems to be increasing. We have noted the manifestations of rising external cogency in many instances of Community policy making. The implication must be that – barring an ideological resolution of all cognitive uncertainty in favour or regional unions – the growth of interdependence is incompatible with the orderly march of regional integration. But it is not incompatible enough to reverse in all sectors the distance already covered. The moral of the story is: not integration or interdependence, but integration and interdependence, in an unpredictable mixture . . .

Document 23: S. Hoffmann, 'The European process at Atlantic cross purposes', *Journal of Common Market Studies* Vol. 3: 1964, pp. 85, 87–92, 94–5

The studies devoted to Western European integration have reached a remarkable level of sophistication: thanks in particular to the work of Ernst B. Haas we dispose of an empirical theory of considerable analytic power and predictive ambition . . .

. . . A look at the European 'subsystem' today shows both the merits and the limits of Haas' theory of integration.

1 The 'spill-over' process has continued to operate in the realm of welfare. Recent discussions over common agricultural policies and over a common stand on tariffs at the GATT conference have shown that, just as before, the Six manage to reach compromises which further integration in the double sense of promoting joint policies and of strengthening the common organs. In particular, the Commission of the EEC continues to play the role of the shaper of and spokesman for the common interest to which the governments are willy-nilly obliged to turn for elements of solution so as to avoid the alternative of deadlock and failure . . .

However, even within this realm, a number of difficulties have appeared.

(a) In some sectors, 'the 'spill-over' has turned into a trickle'. The failure of the Six to agree on a common energy policy.

(b) On the whole it has been easier for the Six to agree on 'negative' than on 'positive' policies, i.e. to eliminate tariffs, quotas, obstacles to competition or to mobility, than to take measures that require a more painful, deliberate and persistent transformation of existing practices (for instance, against inflation).

(c) The more the communities progress, the more difficult agreement tends to become. The difference between the two types of agreements which Haas calls 'splitting the difference' and 'upgrading the common interest' tends to vanish. The reasons are as simple as they are serious. The whole spill-over process is a fiduciary operation: 'You and I accept today a measure that gives us less than you and I have hoped for, because each of us expects our concession of today to be repaid tomorrow on another issue'. Now, a day must come when the reckoning has to be done and the credit is exhausted. First, the more each partner has already obtained through past measures – i.e. the more the gains expected from integration have already been cashed in – the less he will be incited to make new concessions in anticipation of further gains. . . . Success may be the worst enemy of spill-over, even within the realm of welfare. Secondly, the more the process develops, the less likely it is to affect only or mostly sectors in which all parties have convergent expectations of gains: this is clearly not the case in agriculture. Consequently compromises have to range over a variety of sectors, and conform increasingly to the pattern of *do ut des* (sometimes rechristened 'synchronization') – and such compromises are likely to involve exchanges of immediate benefits rather than expectations of future gains. Thirdly, both of the difficulties I have just mentioned are aggravated once the process reaches issues which affect inextricably the realm of power and high politics as well as the realm of welfare: here again, 'spill-over' com-promises may be capable of delaying choices for a while, but there must be a time when ambiguities have to be cleared: at which point agreement becomes much more difficult, and progress may stop or fizzle out altogether . . .

. . . None of this suggests that economic integration will fail. But it indicates that, contrary to a famous French proverb, the first steps may be the easiest ones: the bigger the functional scope of integration, the more interests members tend to see as vital are likely to be at stake – and the less smooth the process may become . . .

. . . Thus the two realms remain very different. In the welfare area the new framework modifies traditional state politics: vetoes are rare or disguised, bargaining is more frequent than (or the preferred form of) blackmail, reliance is more likely than rupture, the lions have to behave as foxes. This is due to two kinds of pressure on the governments. The organs of the Six are manned by skilful operators who know how to lead states toward joint policies, and the states have a generally convergent interest in the development of a process which brings overall advantages to all because of the very nature of the subject matter: economics, where inter-state competition is curbed by solidarity (at least when the competitors have interlocking economies). Transnational interest groups and parties re-enforce those two pressures. But they operate only because the governments have set up the institutions and created the conditions thanks to which the states can thus be penetrated; and this the governments did because of both the background circumstances of the 1950s and the nature of the subject matter. But in the area of high politics, the subject matter is composed of discrete issues, among which there may be discontinuity and which show no or little solidarity among the contenders. Thus here politics as usual – Machiavellian or Bismarckian or Gaullist – prevails without any of the subtle tributes which vice elsewhere is forced to pay to virtue . . .

. . . Today, economic integration proceeds under its own steam, and the creation of a Political Community depends on whether the nations of Western Europe will be capable of agreeing in defining a policy toward the US.

. . . Indeed, Western Europe's relation to the US is at the heart of all the important issues discussed among the Six at the present time . . .

It is in the area of political integration that the problem of the relations with the US dominates the scene most imperatively. Here, we are faced with a paradox: all the statesmen of the Six agree on the need to 'crown economic integration' with some kind of political association; and yet no progress had been made since the fiasco of EPC in 1953, repeated in 1962 by the failure of the 'Fouchet plan'.

It has to be said that the movement toward political integration has been delayed by General de Gaulle's obstinate rejection of supranationality, but that forces that push toward 'regional government' are so strong that supranational institutions will ultimately spillover from the economic into the other spheres . . .

. . . This thesis appears to me to be essentially mistaken, for many reasons. First, in no industrial society . . . has the distinct political function disappeared: if the welfare calculus prevailed, the defence budget, the space race, foreign aid would not have reached the astronomic heights they are . . . no statesman – and certainly no statesman of a nation that can pretend to a significant role in world affairs or that is forced by events to be either a major actor or a major stake . . . can afford to act on the basis of welfare calculations alone . . .

Secondly, not only is welfare not only the single criterion of political action, but welfare often tends to be a means towards other goals. . . . Precisely because there is a distinct political function, the economic wealth accumulated thanks (in part) to the Common Market may find itself used up for power purposes – a reverse kind of spill-over. And precisely because the Six remain politically disunited, this exploitation of resources may feed diversity rather than unity. . . . Indeed, I would argue that there was more of a European 'sense of community' in the 'pre-industrial' days of post-war dejection and humiliation; prosperity has strengthened the nation-states along with the common enterprise . . .

. . . Thirdly, the style of collective bargaining is sharply limited: on the one hand, it hardly extends to that sphere of 'high politics' whose autonomy strikes me as evident; on the other hand, even in the economic and social sphere, where the various interest groups and the 'technocrats' have undoubtedly played a major role in the process of integration, it is a mistake to forget that some of the actors are neither of the same kind nor at the same level as the others; I refer to the states . . . for their decisions during the process are not explainable only in terms of pressures and counter-pressures from interests; often, political calculations lead governments to take positions to which powerful groups are hostile . . . 'welfare solutions' negotiated by the governments are likely to be more balanced and complex – thus the states are quite unlikely to leave the field to interested parties and experts alone. Moreover, the states' decisions are at the origin of the process itself . . .

. . . Finally, both the welfare calculus and collective bargaining, even when they operate without inhibition, cannot fail to reach a stage at which 'high politics' again takes over: the question of the geographical dimensions of the enterprise. The point must come (indeed, for the Dutch and for many Germans it has come) when the interest groups themselves wonder whether the geographical framework makes sense, whether they would not gain more by enlarging it (or on the contrary by making it absolutely clear that their competitors within the enterprise cannot hope for any enlargement). If welfare alone had been the goal the limitation of the experiment to the Six would have been rather absurd. Nor are proposals for geographical extension based on economic calculations alone; once again we find unacceptable either the image of the irresistibly rising tide, or the idea of the necessary spill-over. Thus, within well-defined limits, Haas's theory is valid; beyond those limits, it becomes an act of faith in a kind of modern *saint-simonisme*, as appealing and as erroneous as Saint Simon's gospel in his days.

. . . The proponents of supranationality operate on two assumptions: first, the obsolescence of the nation-state, i.e. the irrelevance of 'independence' and sovereignty if not for all nations at least for those of Western Europe; secondly, the belief in the capacity of the supranational procedure to solve problems on which governments cannot agree if they are left to themselves (i.e. in 1957 no inter-governmental agreement on a farm policy would have been possible; in 1962–4 such an agreement has become possible through the very process of the Common Market). Both assumptions could be called reasoned acts of faith.

Document 24: S. Hoffmann, 'Europe's identity crisis: between the past and America', *Daedelus* Vol. 93: 1964, pp. 1271–4, 1278–82, 1290–6

To be sure, we find an effort toward unity, directly inspired by the example, and encouraged by the policy of the United States . . . Is it not here that the Europeans have succeeded in turning prosperity into a statecraft, in breaking with their past without evasion, in shaping a *projet* for Europe? And yet, the answer must be: no. The enterprise has not fully succeeded, because the model was not relevant and the *projet* was not drafted. Aron is right. 'It is not sufficient to create a European state. Rather, one must ask: What would be the object of a European state? To have a sense of vocation, Europe would have to discover a goal.'[1] It is the search for a common goal which has not yet succeeded ... Let us imagine some European publicist, in a coma since 1914, who suddenly wakes up and looks at the new world picture. He finds the air buzzing with clamours about Europe's new strength and new claims. His curiosity is aroused. What is it that the Europeans have to say? His astonishment begins. He finds them talking to Americans. ... They acknowledge dependence in what constitutes the alpha and omega of foreign policy – the area of survival – and merely ask for a greater part in the definition of the mode of protection. ... The Europeans also say: 'Twenty years have passed since the end of the holocaust, and we want to be heard on all the issues that matter.' So our publicist listens. But all he hears is a strange cacophony tantamount to silence ... To this, the first reaction of our publicist is a sharp flash of familiarity. Isn't that what it has always been?

... Hasn't Europe always failed to speak with one voice only? But then he sees that there is something abnormal in the situation. Shouldn't the very new fact of dependence for survival incite the dependents to get together and snatch their destinies back? At this point, and with the help of some background briefing, a third reaction sets in: he realizes why there is no European project. It is not just the absence of a precedent, it is also the avalanche of rocks that have battered and buried Europe's pride and ambition. They have not just bruised Europe as a whole; they have bloodied each European state in a different way. A common fate has created a unity of concern in this little 'cape of Asia', but there is no unity of reaction. For each nation's fate has been slightly different, and the common fate is not perceived alike ...

... Our publicist cannot remain discouraged very long. For undoubtedly his eyes will come across the evidence of European integration. Here there is a common enterprise. It has its institutions, it has given Europe a single voice in matters of tariffs and trade, of industry and (soon) agriculture. There is one Europe of welfare and wealth – no mean achievement, to be sure. And yet, how much of an achievement is it? It does not amount to a common world design for Europe. There is a striking contrast between the concrete, down-to-earth, toughly bargained results obtained by the economic communities and the often nebulous and usually divergent expectations of the governments and nations engaged in the enterprise. Europe is a divinity which means different things to the different faithful, as well as a business that brings tangible gains to many. For the Germans Europe is both the mast to which they find it wise to tie themselves in order to resist any new siren's temptations, and the new backbone that replaces the cancerous nationalistic one. To the French it is an opportunity for leadership – the only one left. It is the elevator that will lift them to the floor of rank, prestige and power. To the Italians it is a pump of economic development and an alibi for absence on the world scene. Such ambiguity, to be sure, has its merits; indeed, it has its champions. As long, they tell us, as all those divergent aims fasten on the same techniques and institutions, this very diversity of expectations will feed and foster the new entity. As the entity has been endowed with bodies that exploit ably and diligently that convergence of the many on one, it is true that the entity has grown. And yet it is just at this point that our publicist stumbles upon those illusions that abound in the European void. Indeed, it is in the area of integration that illusions have most seductively lulled and dulled European and American minds . . .

Restraints and recriminations

Limited in its scope, confused in its ambitions, the choice for integration has been based on three factors. First the Europeans took into account the situation of Europe in the postwar years: the economic collapse of the nations, the felt threat of Communist invasion and subversion. Then there was American policy, determined to unify what had been a zone of wars and what was now a zone of weakness, so as to produce a peaceful and strong entity capable of helping (the French word *seconder* is indispensable here) America carry its world load, as well as of accelerating the hoped for 'thaw' of Soviet policy. Finally there was the 'Europeans'' own desire to overcome the poison of nationalism, and to regain a sense of self-respect for Europe. These are well-known factors. Today, if we look at what inhibits Europe's choice of a unified role in the world, we find again three forces, not too different from the first three: the new situation in the world, the policies of the United States and the reactions of the Europeans to General de Gaulle. The new situation in the world puts money back into the once empty bank account of separate European nations. This is true quite literally: prosperity, although connected with unification, has removed some of the sense of urgency which animated the drive for integration . . .

. . . Today's world is still dominated by the risk of war – hence the role of the superpowers, which in the nuclear age no one can deny. But the expectation and likelihood of war appear to have decreased, and the very change in the nature of the mobilizable potential has made its actual use in emergencies by its unhappy owners quite difficult and self-defeating. As a result, nations endowed with infinitely less can behave in a whole range of issues as if the difference in power did not matter. The very lightness of their rucksack facilitates their roaming on the world scene, whereas the superpowers are often immobilized by their unwieldy baggage. It is the extraordinary convergence of two quite independent series, the emergence of two poles of power only, and the discovery of nuclear weapons, that has made of a bipolar world a stable one for the first time in history. This stability magnifies the influence of lesser states – which may ultimately impair stability itself. While those developments could help a united Europe, in the meantime they enable the separate European states to avoid or postpone the choice of a goal and role for Europe . . .

In today's Europe, it is discord that exists. Here the responsibility of the United States is real, although – one must be careful – there is a crucial distinction between responsibility and blame. Good intentions often produce unintended consequences. America's relationship to Europe has been and remains dual. On the one hand it is the relation of the leader in a hegemonical alliance to the lesser states – not satellites, given their considerable freedom of external manoeuvre and domestic action, but nevertheless dependents. On the other hand there is a relation of adviser to client: the United States has supported the kind of supranational integration that Monnet advocates . . .

The combination of these two relations has inhibited in three ways the emergence of a new European sense of identity. First, America's relationship of domination has undermined the policy promoted in its capacity as an adviser. For it is of the essence of any relationship of dependence, be it a hegemonical alliance or a genuine empire, not only that the leader be convinced of the broader gauge of his concerns and of his superior understanding of his dependents' true interests, but also that he succeed in so convincing many of the dependents. Through his wealth, his better expertise, his network of official and semiofficial organizations (which in the American case involves the formidable establishment of foundations and centers and councils) the leader is able to develop a perfectly honest and respectable clientele of 'friends' who see their nations' interest in exactly the same light and from the same perspective as he. Now, this would not be necessarily an obstacle to European unification. But it is necessarily an obstacle to the appearance of a united European entity capable of acting in any way but that of a junior partner in the American firm. And it happens to be an obstacle to any unification in this particular instance, for two reasons: in matters of diplomacy and strategy the United States has continued to deal with the separate nations of Europe . . .

. . . Secondly, America's advice and promotion of supranationality have also had evasive and delaying effects on Europe's search for a new mission. Inevitably, people resentful of dependence were bound to be suspicious of any scheme of unity so ardently embraced by the leader: Europeans especially expect no state ever to act selflessly, and Americans tend to be seen as far more cunning and scheming than a careful examination of their policies warrants. This suspicion could not but be strengthened by the fact that the procedure supported by the United States might be legitimately thought of as damaging to European interests if applied prematurely in the sensitive areas of military and foreign policy. Not only the Gaullists happen to note that enthusiasm for such procedures is greatest among those European statesmen for whom dependence on the United States has become a dogma, among those leaders who see in supranationality a cushion to protect them from the direct influence and impact of their more powerful European partners, and among civil servants and economists with little understanding of the complexities of strategy and diplomacy.

Finally, America's impact on Europe has been inhibiting because of the ways in which the United States reacted when it discovered – in the areas of tariffs, agriculture and strategy – that European unification could lead to conflict, not harmony, in the Atlantic world. American reactions have been fourfold. First, there have been offers of 'partnership', but so vague and so circumscribed (since they exclude the military realm) as to disconnect America's friends and to feed fuel to America's critics. Second, there has been a reassertion of the policies designed to consolidate America's domination, even at the cost of undermining the drive toward unification among the Six. The two best examples here are the wooing of West Germany by the United States in economic and military areas, and promotion by the United States of the MLF [Multilateral Force] . . .

It strengthens America's hold on the other participants, thus tying them to the United States directly in a network of bilateral agreements much like Soviet-satellite agreements after the war. It makes the emergence of a joint European will and policy in the military realm far more difficult, since it diverts the participants' financial resources from such a goal, and even more because it chooses for defense a geographical framework entirely different from that of economic integration. The third United States reaction has consisted of veiled threats of return to isolationism and unilateral self-protecting or retaliatory action should the Europeans continue to mistake prosperity for power and to harm United States interests. These threats are divisive and regressive because they are used in Europe both by America's friends and by America's critics . . .

. . . The final United States reaction, which somehow embraces all the previous ones, consists of stating that as long as Europeans remain divided it is indeed impossible for the United States to share control and to limit its freedom of action . . .

. . . It makes little sense to negotiate a common defense so long as the combined forces would be unable to serve, not merely a common doctrine, but a common foreign policy. Thus the solution to the military problem presupposes an agreement on Europe's role in world affairs. Only then will it be possible to arrange either a coordination of national forces effective enough to give all participants a share in the control if not in the possession of the European deterrent, or a genuine merger of national forces under a single authority endowed with the formidable power to threaten the use of and to use nuclear weapons: a power which presupposes a sense of identity and a certainty about aims and strategy that exist no more today among the Europeans than they exist between them and the United States.

Finally, the task of those who would like to use United States-European military divergences as a reason for reducing intra-European ones is complicated by the detente. True, peril parity, which led the United States to revise its strategy in Europe, has shocked the Europeans. But this same parity combines with internal Communist dissensions to lessen the risk and the fear of war. Thus, European champions of unity are squeezed between two facts: when the peril is highest, as long as Europe is militarily weak a separate European establishment (by contrast with a specialization of Europe's military contribution as often suggested by the United States) makes no sense. When the peril declines, the sense of urgency recedes and the prevalence of national calculations resumes . . .

. . . Thus the trends can be interpreted as either suggesting a joint European enterprise or as removing the need for it altogether. There is choice – and a question of will. A joint European undertaking at this point, is not likely to be supranational or federal, for all the reasons mentioned before. There is not yet any agreement on goals and directions; such an agreement would take time to emerge. But the enterprise out of which such agreement should come presupposes at least a common intention to find the goals and the directions. In other words, the prerequisite to common policies (and to institutions capable of carrying them out and of sharpening them) is a determination to define a new role in the world for Europe; behind such a determination there is a postulate: that Europe is not only a geographical expression but an entity capable of overcoming its divisions and of bringing its own contribution to world affairs. Out of the postulate of a possible European identity would gradually arise the policies realizing this identity. Should the European statesmen of the near future behave in such a way, two consequences would follow. First, the European entity would obviously be playing the game of world politics. Here and there some writers suggest that it should not behave as a superpower; this can mean only that it either ought to behave like someone else's dependent, or that it ought to give the world the example of abnegation or of observance of the Golden Rule (or the Rule of Law). Europe, alas, can hardly define its identity either in subservience or in what amounts to self-sacrifice. The alternatives to a sort of collective European nationalism are a set of separate ones or a kind of despondency, not a world government or a world ruled by love and charity. Second, the European entity, if it becomes a going concern, is likely to pursue policies closer to de Gaulle's than to those of the United States. The precedent of the realm of welfare indicates this, as well as the divergence of interests discussed before. Moreover, any definition of common policies entails of necessity a deliberate distinction between the new entity and the powerful senior ally . . .

. . . In international relations, the possession of power is to be sought not only for the sake of prestige or domination but also because only the mighty create; the influential can manoeuvre and advise, convince or set examples; they can dig in and defend their place in the sun, but the mighty alone set the course of the sun. De Gaulle has understood this well. This is why, should no European common will emerge, he may remain in history, not as the gravedigger of a unity that was never there to bury (had it been there, he would not have tried or succeeded), but as the last European statesman with a world-wide vision. The 'new Europe' would then fall back into the habits of its past, but in the context, both happier and more bitter, of an economic intertwining that would limit its self-destructive atavism, and of a world in which the relative importance of the European nations would – for all their possible freedom of action – be far less considerable than in the past . . .

. . . Under Roman rule the Greek cities satisfied with the peace and order brought from the outside, saw no reason to coalesce, and congratulated themselves on the degree of rationality they had achieved in the mastery of social problems, for internal complacency and dependence breed and feed each other. In that fertile desert of Europe, which now spurns adventures and savors the delights of production and consumption, and which wavers between a cursed past, a protection increasingly less adequate, and a future so far more happening than chosen, how long will one have to wait until economic vigor is matched by political and intellectual inventiveness – long the chief glory and the only pride of the Old Continent?

Note

1 R. Aron, *Paix et guerre* (Paris, 1962), Introduction.

Document 25: S. Hoffmann, 'Obstinate or obsolete? The fate of the nation-state and the case of western Europe', *Daedelus* Vol. 95: 1966, pp. 863–4, 908–11

Statesmen have invented original schemes for moving Western Europe 'beyond the nation-state,' and political scientists have studied their efforts with a care from which emotional involvement was not missing. The conditions seemed ideal. On the one hand, nationalism seemed at its lowest ebb; on the other, an adequate formula and method for building a substitute had apparently been devised. Twenty years after the end of World War II – a period as long as the whole interwar era – observers have had to revise their judgments. The most optimistic put their hope in the chances the future may still harbor, rather than in the propelling power of the present; the less optimistic ones, like myself, try simply to understand what went wrong.

My own conclusion is sad and simple. The nation-state is still here, and the new Jerusalem has been postponed because the nations in Western Europe have not been able to stop time and to fragment space. Political unification could have succeeded if, on the one hand, these nations had not been caught in the whirlpool of different concerns, as a result both of profoundly different internal circumstances and of outside legacies, and if, on the other hand, they had been able or obliged to concentrate on 'community-building' to the exclusion of all problems situated either outside their area or within each one of them. Domestic differences and different world views obviously mean diverging foreign policies; the involvement of the policy-makers in issues among which 'community-building' is merely one has meant a deepening, not a decrease, of those divergencies. The reasons follow: the unification movement has been the victim, and the survival of nation-states the outcome, of three factors, one of which characterizes every international system, and the other two only the present system. Every international system owes its inner logic and its unfolding to the diversity of domestic determinants, geo-historical situations, and outside aims among its units; any international system based on fragmentation tends, through the dynamics of unevenness (so well understood, if applied only to economic unevenness, by Lenin) to reproduce diversity . . .

. . . A second set of remarks concerns the meaning of integration. It has become possible for scholars to argue both that integration is proceeding and that the nation-state is more than ever the basic unit, without contradicting each other, for recent definitions of integration 'beyond the nation-state' point not toward the emergence of a new kind of political community, but merely toward an 'obscur[ing of] the boundaries between the system of international organizations and the environment provided by member states'.[1] There are two important implications.

(a) The first one is, not so paradoxically, a vindication of the nation-state as the basic unit. So far, anything that is 'beyond' is 'less': that is, there are cooperative arrangements with a varying degree of autonomy, power, and legitimacy, but there has been no transfer of allegiance toward their institutions, and their authority remains limited, conditional, dependent, and reversible. There is more than a kernel of truth in the Federalist critique of functional integration: functionalism tends to become, at best, like a spiral that coils ad infinitum. So far, the 'transferring [of] exclusive expectations of benefits from the nation-state to some larger entity'[2] leaves the nation-state both as the main focus of expectations, and as the initiator, pace-setter, supervisor, and often destroyer of the larger entity: for in the international arena the state is still the highest possessor of power, and while not every state is a political community there is as yet no political community more inclusive than the state. To be sure, the military function of the nation-state is in crisis; but, insofar as the whole world is 'permeable' to nuclear weapons, any new type of unit would face the same horror, and, insofar as the prospect of such horror makes war more subdued and conquest less likely, the decline of the state's capacity to defend its citizens is neither total nor sufficient to force the nation-state itself into decline. The resistance of the nation-state is proven not only by the frustrations of functionalism but also by both the promise and the failure of Federalism. On the one hand, Federalism offers a way of going 'beyond the nation-state', but it consists in building a new and larger nation-state. The scale is new, not the story, the gauge not the game. Indeed, the Federalist model applies to the 'making of Europe' the Rousseauistic scheme for the creation of a nation: it aims at establishing a unit marked by central power and based on the general will of a European people. The Federalists are right in insisting that Western Europe's best chance of being an effective entity would be not to go 'beyond the nation-state', but to become a larger nation-state in the process of formation and in the business of world politics: that is, to become a sovereign political community in the formal sense at least. The success of Federalism would be a tribute to the durability of the nation-state; its failure so far is due to the irrelevance of the model. Not only is there no general will of a European people because there is as of now no European people, but the institutions that could gradually (and theoretically) shape the separate nations into one people are not the most likely to do so. For the domestic problems of Europe are matters for technical decisions by civil servants and ministers rather than for general wills and assemblies (a general will to prosperity is not very operational).

The external problems of Europe are matters for executives and diplomats. As for the common organs set up by the national governments, when they try to act as a European executive and parliament, they are both condemned to operate in the fog maintained around them by the governments and slapped down if they try to dispel the fog and reach the people themselves. In other words, Europe cannot be what some of the nations have been: a people that creates its state; nor can it be what some of the oldest states are and many of the new ones aspire to be: a people created by the state. It has to wait until the separate states decide that their peoples are close enough to justify the setting up of a European state whose task will be the welding of the many into one; and we have just examined why such a joint decision has been missing. The very obstacles which make the Federalist model irrelevant to nations too diverse and divided also make all forms of union short of Federalism precarious. Functionalism is too unstable for the task of complete political unification. It may integrate economies, but either the nations will then proceed to a full political merger (which economic integration does not guarantee) – in that case the federal model will be vindicated at the end, the new unit will be a state forging its own people by consent and through the abdication of the previous separate states, but the conditions for success described above will have to be met – or else the national situations will remain too divergent, and functionalism will be merely a way of tying together the preexisting nations in areas deemed of common interest. Between the cooperation of existing nations and the breaking in of a new one there is no stable middle ground. A federation that succeeds becomes a nation; one that fails leads to secession; half-way attempts like supranational functionalism must either snowball or roll back.

(b) But the nation-state, preserved as the basic unit, survives transformed. Among the men who see in 'national sovereignty' the Nemesis of mankind, those who put their hopes in the development of regional superstates are illogical, those who put their hopes in the establishment of a world state are utopian, those who put their hopes in the growth of functional political communities more inclusive than the nation-state are too optimistic. What has to be understood and studied now – far more than has been done, and certainly far more than this essay was able to do – is, rather than the creation of rival communities, the transformation of 'national sovereignty': it has not been superseded, but to a large extent it has been emptied of its former sting; there is no supershrew, and yet the shrew has been somewhat tamed. The model of the nation-state derived from the international law and relations of the past, when there was a limited number of players on a stage that was less crowded and in which violence was less risky, applies only fitfully to the situation of today. The basic unit, having proliferated, has also become much more heterogeneous; the stage has shrunk, and is occupied by players whose very number forces each one to strut, but its combustibility nevertheless scares them from pushing their luck too hard. The nation-state today is a new wine in old bottles, or in bottles that are sometimes only a mediocre imitation of the old; it is not the same old wine. What must be examined is not just the legal capacity of the sovereign state, but the de facto capacity at its disposal: granted the scope of its authority, how much of it can be used, and with what results? There are many ways of going 'beyond the nation-state,' and some modify the substance without altering the form or creating new forms. To be sure, as long as the old form is there, as long as the nation-state is the supreme authority, there is a danger for peace and for welfare ... An examination of the international implications of 'nation-statehood' today and yesterday is at least as important as the ritual attack on the nation-state.

Notes

1 E.B. Haas, *Beyond the Nation State* (Stanford, Cal., 1964), p. 29.
2 E.B. Haas and P.C. Schmitter, 'Economic and differential patterns of political integration', *International Organization* Vol. 28: 1964, p. 710.

Document 26: M. Forsyth, 'Federation, federal union, federal state', from *Unions of States: The Theory and Practice of Confederation* (Leicester, 1981), pp. 2, 4–8, 10–16

Federalism, federal union, federal state

It will be clear already that the kind of federalism that this book investigates is different from the federalism which has formed the subject of so many studies in the past few decades. It is different, for example, from the 'federal government' that K.C. Wheare investigated in his influential book, first published in 1946, and from the 'modern federalism' that G.F. Sawer examined in his more recent work ...

... Now the interest of these two writers on federalism is clearly focused upon the governmental structure of a state. The question they wish to answer is: when can such a structure be called truly federal? ...

... We will be concerned, as we have already indicated, not with federal government as a mode of organizing a state, but with federal government as a type of government founded upon a foedus or treaty between states. It is the process by which a number of separate states raise themselves by contract to the threshold of being one state ...

... In Western Europe today, where old established states have already constructed a limited but in many ways remarkable union based on a treaty, it is this viewpoint, and this perspective which seems most profitable and illuminating. Confederations or federal unions of states enable us to understand more clearly what is now happening, what can happen, and perhaps even what has to happen ...

... The European Economic Community is the most significant, though not the only example, of such a union in the twentieth century. Professional economists have of course not been slow to develop theories about the working of customs unions and common markets. However, in so far as such organizations have attempted to transform the relations between several distinct state economies into relations analogous to those that pertain within a single state economy, and to weld the external economic relations of these states with the rest of the world into a single policy, that is, in so far as they represent the creation by mutual agreement of a new acting, corporate being, enclosing its members, they go beyond the phenomena susceptible to the analysis of economic science and demand a political interpretation as well.

What then is the political theory of economic union? It does not seem unfair to say that at the present time it lacks clear contours. There has been a strong tendency for political analysts of the European Economic Community, for example, to stress over and again that it is sui generis, a completely new and peculiar form of political life, which is hence either unsusceptible to theory – for theory is by definition concerned with what is typical or normal or demands a completely new and peculiar form of theory, usually called 'integration theory'. There has been an unfortunate tendency too, to apply paradigms and models to the Community in which reference to the state is either completely avoided, or kept to an absolute minimum. Even the word 'supranational', which has so often been used to differentiate the European Economic Community from other, merely 'international' organizations, is scarcely conducive to clear thinking because it deflects the eye from the main constituent elements of the Community.

It is one of the main theses of this study that economic union, of the kind represented by the Zollverein and the European Community, is a subspecies of the genus confederation. Its development as a distinct form alongside confederations for defence and security is largely explicable in terms of the profound changes that have taken place in the structure and needs of the state with the development of the industrial revolution and the concomitant intensification of economic exchange over the boundaries of states. These changes provide a strong added impetus to the 'welfare' motive for confederation, sufficient to sustain it on its own. Defence and security confederations are by no means replaced by this new form; they remain the deepest and most fundamental type; but they are no longer the only type. The political theory of economic union is hence the classical or traditional theory of confederations transposed and adjusted to the particular arena of economics . . .

The thesis that the study of federalism as a mode of government for a single state requires to be supplemented by the study of federation as a mode of linking states together in a bond that takes them to the brink of being transformed into one state has something in common with the arguments of those writers who have maintained in recent years that federalism should be understood not as a particular structure of government but as a 'process', 'continuum' or 'spectrum'. It differs from these arguments to the extent that it insists that there is a particular spectrum, bounded on the one hand by what may be called normal interstate relations, and on the other by what may be called normal intrastate relations, which forms a discrete area of investigation . . .

. . . It is this area, the area of the 'half-way house', that deserves special attention. This is not to deny that it is natural and inevitable that the word 'federalism' should be used in a very wide overarching sense that spans both the spectrum of federal union and that of the federal state, and can be used in a hundred other contexts as well. In this wide sense federalism would seem to mean basically 'association', 'co-sociation', 'reciprocity', 'mutuality', and to be contrasted with 'rule', 'empire', 'dominance', 'monarchy'. It may be said to stand for one of the two great organizing principles of political and social life, which in the well-ordered state should fit together harmoniously. Precisely because of its all-pervasive character however, federalism in this sense makes a dangerous object of study. With sufficient effort it can be detected almost everywhere, and endless pursuit can take the place of hard analysis. To become significant it would seem to be almost essential to differentiate it by relating it to the other basic concepts of political life, and above all, it may be suggested, to the concept of the state. 'Federal union' – as the spectrum between interstate and intrastate relations and 'federal state' – as the spectrum between federal union and the unitary state – would seem to be the two critical categories of federalism when it is differentiated in this way.

In so far as they represent the intermediary stage between the interstate and the intrastate worlds federal unions or confederations have a particular fascination. They open a new perspective on these two worlds. In making such a union, individual states place themselves within a totality which has its own distinct representation, its own external policy and its own internal policy. It is tempting to say that they agree to present a common face to all other states, while retaining their independence internally, a definition which has, for example, the authority of the historian Freeman to recommend it, as well as the official text of at least one historical confederation. A moment's reflection, however, shows that this is an incorrect way of putting it. It is impossible to present a common face externally if relations between the states concerned remain 'external'. These relations must therefore become 'internal' at the same time as a common exterior is constructed. By forming a union, therefore, states, in seeking to promote their own interests by way of treaty become a part of something which has its own 'inner' and 'outer', its own state-like interests.

Yet this new body is not a state, it is not a union of individuals in a body politic, but a union of states in a body politic. Despite the many undoubted analogies and parallels between the original social union of individuals into civil society, and the political union of states into a confederation, states and individuals are different kinds of 'personality'. A social union of individuals may well emerge from a political union of states, and historically has so emerged, but the incubator is not the same as the thing that is born.

The problems and paradoxes involved in the formation of federal unions are evident. What is the nature of the pact or agreement by which states transcend the classic or normal modalities of interstate relations? How far can states go in voluntarily alienating statehood? When and how do confederations change into full and complete states? Problems such as these have provoked a theoretical literature concerning the union of states which has often reached a very high level . . .

Interstate and intrastate relations

. . . Federal union, we have suggested, represents the intermediary stage between normal interstate relations and normal intrastate relations. But what is meant by these two types of relationship? It seems essential, before entering into a discussion of federal union, to make some effort to define them. At the same time it has to be recognized that space does not make it possible to undertake a complete survey of these two vast areas, but only to indicate certain fundamental and relevant features of them. This will be the task of the remainder of the chapter.

We will begin with relations between states. States, it may be suggested, are inherently 'social' beings, not in the sense that they are particularly amiable or warm-hearted creatures, but in the sense that they define themselves in relation to one another. This appears most clearly if we consider the actual territorial boundary of a state, which simultaneously defines the state's own area of activity, and positively excludes other states from action upon it. The first question to be asked therefore, in attempting to construct the logic of normal interstate relations, appears to be this: how does stability, order, and right come to manifest itself in the process of mutual repulsion and exclusion which seems to be implied in the very definition of the state? At what point does bare struggle become transmuted into a regular interchange? The answer to this question – not the whole answer, but the clue to the whole – would seem to lie in the act by which states recognize one another initially as states. It is through this act of recognition that the process of possession and exclusion, that is inherent in the concept of the state, is transformed into right. The act of state recognition, however one-sided it may often appear, is in essence a mutual pact . . .

. . . The pact itself is a paradoxical one, and may perhaps be best defined as a 'coming together to stay apart', or as a 'joint agreement to be independent'. It signifies in other words the renunciation by each of the communities concerned of the right to rule or possess the other, and simultaneously the acknowledgement by each community of the other's right to rule and possess itself . . .

. . . This second aspect of sovereignty, the right to be treated as independent or self-determining, is, for all its formality, of crucial importance. It signifies that the normal mode of interaction between states, after they have recognized each other, is one in which the identical free status of each is acknowledged. It means that states can normally bind one another only by treaty, agreement, or convention, that is to say only by a mutual, reciprocal procedure, in which, whatever the actual content of the agreement that is finally made, the will of each is respected. Obligations, or specific rights and duties, can arise solely through a concurrency or parallel action of wills, not through one will commanding another, or legislating for another . . .

. . . It is because the foundation of right and order between states is so fragile that they take every measure to insure and guarantee their status as sovereign beings . . .

... At the foundation of normal interstate relations therefore there lie the original – often long forgotten and historically obscured – acts of recognition by which the equal sovereign status of states has been acknowledged. On the basis of recognition there rises the superstructure of treaties, agreements, and conventions which have been made to guarantee and secure sovereign existence, on the one hand, and to enhance welfare on the other. The third and final tier of normal interstate relations may be said to be provided by interstate organizations, which have multiplied so remarkably during the past one hundred years ... Organizations of this kind are founded by interstate treaties ... They often have considerable freedom as organizations to lay down the rules that determine their own internal structure. With very few exceptions, however, they cannot as organizations make general rules or measures which are directly binding upon the states that create them ... Interstate organizations are hence essentially standing agencies at the disposal of states; they supplement but do not fundamentally alter, the substructure of interstate relations already described, the substructure of self-determination ...

... Once again the contrast between the normal interstate and the normal intrastate worlds strikes the eye. At the root of the former is a pact between two wills by which they agree to treat one another as equal in status. At the root of the latter is a unilateral constitutive act by which the people, acting usually by way of a majority, establish a superior power capable of making and applying law. Mutual recognition established right on the one hand; popular constitution on the other.

It is between these two worlds, the interstate and the intrastate, that the phenomenon we have called union or confederation exists. It is based on a treaty between states, that is to say, on the normal mode of interstate relations, but it is a treaty the content of which goes well beyond that of the normal treaty, even those which establish international organizations. Thus a treaty of union founds a body that possesses personality, but it is more than merely the technical, 'legal' personality of the typical international organization, with its capacity to own property, to sue and be sued, and so on. The 'personality' formed by union is an original capacity to act akin to that possessed by the states themselves. It is a 'real' personality. Similarly the permanence accorded to a confederation is more than merely the standing 'disposability' of the institutions of the typical international organization, it is a profound locking together of states themselves as regards the exercise of fundamental powers. The same words may thus be used to describe the two kinds of body – the typical international organization and a union of states – but their meaning is quite different.

Conversely – seen from the viewpoint of normal intrastate relations – a confederation manifests itself as a constituted unity capable of making laws for its members; however it is not the constituted unity of one people or nation, but a unity constituted by states. The contract which lies at its base is not a contract to abide by the will of the majority regarding the government to which all shall be subordinate, but simply a contract between equals to act henceforth as one. To borrow the words of the American statesman James Madison, spoken at the Federal Convention in 1787, we are not to consider a 'federal Union as analogous to the social compact of individuals: for if it were so, a Majority would have a right to bind the rest, and even to form a new Constitution for the whole'. A confederation hence is far more directly a contractual creature than the normal state and for this reason – it need hardly be said – far more fragile.

It is to a closer consideration of the history and theory of this curious treaty-constituted political body, this 'half-way house' between interstate and intrastate relations, that we wish now to turn our attention . . .

Document 27: J. Pinder, 'Why the single market is a step towards federal union', in J. Lodge (ed.), *The European Community and the Challenge of the Future* (London, 1993), pp. 61–3

Why the single market is a step towards federal union

. . . There are two contrasting views of the EC's future. One is that its essential task is to establish a single market and that any political implications should be confined to the minimum required for this. The other is that the Schuman Plan was rightly seen as the first step towards a European federation and that, even if the process of taking the remaining steps is lasting half a century or more, that is indeed the process in which the EC is engaged. There are of course many views that lie between these two. But the reader should be warned that this author takes the latter view, and sees the completion of the single market as a step towards a federal union and then a federation.

Since the term 'federal union' and 'federation' are often used loosely, the meanings they are given here will be explained. A 'federation', following the many existing examples of which the most venerable European one is the Swiss, has federal institutions with powers over trade, money, the environment, enough tax for its budget, and finally over armed forces and external relations. The federal institutions include a legislature comprising a house of the people and a house of the states, an executive which can be called a government and a federal court. Whereas in international organizations the relationship of the international institutions with the citizens passes through the states, the federal institutions deal direct with the citizens. While in a unitary state the central government exercises all the powers under the constitution, even if it chooses to delegate some to provincial or local authorities, in a federation the member states hold their powers by right under the constitution, and powers are reserved to them except where it can be shown that the larger size and resources of the federation are required to perform the functions effectively.

The essential powers of a federal union, as defined here, are similar to those of a federation apart from the control over armed forces; and its institutions are similar to a federation's institutions. Thus a federation is a state whereas a federal union, although its federal institutions have essential economic and environmental powers, falls short of that. The single market is a big step towards federal union because it gives the EC, with SEA added to the existing EC treaties, full powers over both internal and external trade. The Maastricht Treaty gives the Community federal monetary powers. But the budgetary and environmental powers fall short of those required for a federal union; and the EC institutions would likewise have to be reformed beyond what is provided in the Maastricht Treaty in order to be able to exercise their powers effectively and democratically. External policy depends on security as well as economic instruments; and the Maastricht Treaty, establishing what it calls a Union (though not a federal one), gives the Community a more substantial basis for its external policy by adding a measure of cooperation in security matters, including defence policy. The SEA provided not only for the completion of the single market but also for the development of EC competences in the monetary, technological, environmental, social, regional and external policy fields as well as for some reforms of the EC institutions. It was not, it will be argued, by chance that these measures accompanied the single market programme: if the single market is to become and remain complete and to bring its full benefits to EC citizens, the EC will have to develop along such lines so as to become at least a federal union. Maastricht takes it a few more steps down the road, but a number of essential steps remain . . .

. . . With monetary union this function of social solidarity, which is a normal expression of citizenship in a federal system, will have to be further developed. The Maastricht Treaty provides for a strengthening of the cohesion policy; and that is not apt to be the end of the story. The budget is likely to move closer to the size and shape of a federal budget, with more resources and a better articulated redistributive function . . . The Single Market programme and the SEA have thus not only given the EC an impulse towards monetary union, social solidarity, foreign policy and security cooperation, budgetary and institutional reform but also an impulse towards a federal union which many see as the prime political project for the present stage of the EC's development. The EC also has the chance, if it moves in this direction, to become a powerful agent for unifying the increasingly interdependent world. None of this is easy, let alone assured. Positive integration may prove to be beyond the present political capacity of Europe, let alone the world. Even negative integration may be too hard, although the EC has already made much progress with it. But this writer's view is that a federal union in a uniting world is desirable; it is possible; and the Community's single market can be seen as an important step towards it.

Document 28: W. Wallace, 'Europe as a confederation: the Community and the nation-state', *Journal of Common Market Studies* Vol. 20: 1982, pp. 57, 59–68

The collapse of integration theory does not necessarily carry with it the collapse of European integration. In spite of oil crises, economic recession, and political instability, the European Community remains a functioning political system. Certainly, it does not function well; but few political systems have functioned well under the difficult circumstances of the 1970s, even those equipped with a full range of policies and a strong central administration. Certainly, too, it has disappointed the hopes of the more idealistic of its founders, and failed to achieve the most ambitious of its objectives. But – as will be argued below – those hopes were founded upon two linked illusions: that politics could be tamed within the European enterprise, and that national governments would allow themselves to be bypassed and undermined. Grand and rhetorical objectives are the stuff of summit conferences . . . without necessarily committing their authors to reach their ultimate destination.

European cooperation is a profoundly political process, best understood in the familiar terms of political analysis, not in the arcane language of functionalism or the loose concepts of regime theory. It is not only 'today's reality' that is 'complex and messy'; the realities of politics were always so. In heroic times, perhaps, men created new federations out of a clear sense of purpose, supported by a public that shared that purpose. The myth of the making of the American constitution, in its popular form, portrays the founding fathers as men of wisdom and vision. . . . The mythology of European integration has similarly endowed the statesmen of the 1950s and the electorates they led with a vision and a purpose which their successors are sadly seen to lack . . .

. . . A balanced assessment of the state of European politics and European cooperation must start from a recognition of the common predicament which the advanced industrial states have faced, uncomfortably, since the end of the 1960s. The dismantling of barriers to trade and to international financial flows, negotiated under American leadership, had led to an increasingly integrated international economy. The impact of economic interdependence on national politics and national economies was heightened during the 1960s by advances in transport and communications, and complicated by the emergence of the first significant non-Atlantic economy, in Japan . . .

In Washington as in London, Paris and Bonn, prime ministers and presidents struggled to reconcile the demands of domestic political survival and the necessities of international collaboration; playing very different games simultaneously on two complicated boards, and occasionally making – not surprisingly – ill-considered moves.

In such adverse political and economic circumstances, the record of European cooperation in the 1970s is not a total failure. It has not, of course, been a startling success . . .

The federal analogy

The second reason for pursuing the analogy with the United States, I wish to argue, is that the concept of federalism offers a perspective for understanding the nature of the European political system far more appropriate to the patterns we observe than approaches drawn from the literature of international relations. At first sight this may seem paradoxical. The functionalist strategy for integrating Europe sector by sector was, after all, adopted as a second best after the failure of the first post-war attempts to move directly towards a European federation. Given the very limited progress made towards integration even in those sectors covered by the Treaties of Paris and Rome, how can the resulting fragile and stunted system be usefully described as a federation?

If we start out with the disappointed hopes of those who wanted to create a United States of Europe, confining the federal label to such a fully fledged system of European Union, the case is of course hopeless. But if we start out with a disillusioned and realistic appreciation of the difficulties of building a framework for close collaboration among independent states, not long past waging war against each other, it becomes much easier to distinguish this relatively developed system of politics and government above the level of the nation-state from the loose and limited patterns of international interaction which are conveniently labelled as regimes . . .

. . . The crucial dividing point between an international regime and a federation, I would suggest, lies in the presence or absence of authority and resources at the centre which effectively limit the behaviour of the member states and which impose obligations on them which are generally accepted.

A comparison of the Community in its current 'half-starved limping' state with the powers of the American Congress under the Articles of Confederation may help to register the progress made so far. That association of states lacked any taxing powers, even customs revenues accrued to the treasuries of the states in which the goods were landed. Though it had moved a little beyond the principle of unanimity, it still observed the principle of sovereign equality: each state, whatever its size, had one vote. There was no federal system of law, nor any direct contact between the Congress and the citizens of the separate states. The central concern of the Congress at its formation was with defence and with foreign policy: but though it maintained an army, its authority over it was not complete, and its activities in foreign relations were paralleled by independent actions by its more powerful member states. An international regime, perhaps, with an unusually strong defence component? We would not now dismiss it so easily – because we are aware of what it has developed into, after another two hundred years, after many internal crises and a bloody civil war.

Joseph Weiler's paper, above,[1] makes clear the importance of the legal framework of European integration, as marking out the Community system from other intergovernmental networks. Community law operates, within the confines of Community competence, directly on the citizen throughout the Community; accepted as authoritative in national courts, interpreted and extended by the

European Court in a process of judicial intervention and judicial review which the student of federal governments will instantly recognise as familiar ground. True, the Community authorities have few means of enforcing judicial decisions, and compliance with Community decisions and Community law is not perfect. But federal law and federal court decisions have not been uniformly or instantly recognized throughout the United States for much of its history. What is remarkable in Europe, as Weiler notes, is the high level of compliance, the automatic acceptance of Community supremacy and Community obligations in almost all cases, even against the interests of the governments concerned.

The Community commands resources, distributes benefits, allocates markets and market shares, and adjudicates between conflicting interests – all on a modest scale, within limited sectors, but all taking it into the central issues of politics. Unlike conventional international organizations, it is also a highly visible forum for politics, in which national politicians perform for both domestic and international audiences. National governments make valiant efforts to impose coherence and coordination on their activities at the European level, but the operation of trans-governmental coalitions among both ministers and officials is a long-accepted aspect of Community politics. Transnational groups have mushroomed, representing the interests of European steel-producers and pig-farmers, trade unionists and environmentalists. The belated establishment of a directly-elected European Parliament with the consequent added incentives to form effective parliamentary groups and to campaign during elections on more than a national stage – has increased the transnational dimension of party politics. The number and proportion of national elites drawn into the network of discussions and debates in Brussels, Strasbourg and Luxembourg has continued to rise as the 1970s have passed; partly in response to the continuing recession and the intractable problems of industrial adjustment and economic recovery which the recession has imposed, partly in reaction to the heightened external tensions which the response of the United States and of other third countries to international recession have created for the Community . . .

. . . A European federation, if it were to develop into fully-fledged form, would unavoidably take a different shape from that of the United States, or Canada, or Australia. Multiplicity of languages – above all, the absence of a single generally-accepted dominant language – cultural diversity, highly differentiated patterns of national law, administration, economic management and economic structure, all make the combination of the separate European states into a federated whole a more complicated task. The European confederation which has emerged so far is also highly distinctive from other and earlier attempts at federation in its exclusion of defence and the central issues of foreign policy from its field of competence: historically, in other federations, the engines of federal aggrandizement and the justification for rising federal revenue and expenditure.

I do not intend to imply by the label 'confederation' that the current state of European cooperation is satisfactory or stable. In the adverse conditions of the last decade it may, perhaps, be a matter for modest satisfaction that the Community has survived, with so little damage to its basic structure. One can discern contradictory trends of integration and disintegration. The member states have made considerable advance, outside the strict framework of the Treaties, in coordinating foreign policy, most of all since the beginning of 1980. Some halting progress has been made in the concertation of industrial policy, particularly in the 'crisis sectors', where external bargaining and the allocation of shares within a reduced internal market have gone together. The establishment of the European Monetary System in 1979, after a great deal of intricate politicking, took the Community a little way down the road towards economic union on which it had started out – and faltered – ten years before. Against which, the impact of national industrial policies and the deliberate actions of governments responding to domestic pressures have re-erected barriers within the common internal market. The effectiveness and prestige of the Community's institutions has declined, despite the achievement of a directly-elected Parliament and the establishment of the new 'quasi-institution' of the European Council. Most fundamentally, the rumbling and linked disputes over the distributional consequences of the Community budget, the reform of the Common Agricultural Policy, and the application for membership of Spain, have demonstrated a worrying rigidity in the structure; the Community's capacity to adapt its policies and institutions to changing circumstances appears to be low.

Federations and confederations do not follow unilinear paths from disunity to unity. They rise and decay, in response to internal and external developments, to the wisdom or unwisdom of the men who direct them, and to the changing loyalties and expectations of their citizens. The European Community may not survive the slow erosion of its authority and prestige now evident in most member states, the gradual crumbling of the single internal market, the domestic distractions of its member governments and the uneven pressures exerted on European economies by the United States and Japan. The progressive disintegration of the Belgian state is an ever present example to the Community's policy-makers of what may happen if economic grievances and political discontents cannot be satisfied. There is nothing inevitable in politics, for all the attempts to build predictive theories; the paths both to union and to collapse are liberally strewn with incentives and with obstacles . . .

Sovereignty, integration and the nation-state

The idealist tradition of international relations has long wished to discover evidence of the withering away of the nation-state, the transfer of loyalties to international authorities, and the growth of world society. The optimistic vision of an integrated Europe, with power progressively transferred away from national governments to the new supranational authority, was firmly within this idealistic tradition. Scholars more firmly rooted in the study of domestic politics, like Stanley Hoffmann, were never deceived; they noted the recovery of national distinctiveness, the resilience of the nation-state, and the inertia of national bureaucracy, even during the first flood of enthusiasm about European integration.

Disappointment at the failure of the European authority to replace national authorities in major areas of policy is at the heart of academic and political disillusionment with the Community. To some extent this reflects the disappointment of hopes and expectations which were unreal from the outset. The success of the neo-functional approach depended upon national governments not noticing – in effect – the gradual draining away of their lifeblood to Brussels. The mixture of description and prescription, of academic analysis and idealist commitment, which marked the literature on European integration in the 1960s encouraged observers to focus on the development of the Brussels authorities, rather than to investigate the response of national governments to the process of integration . . .

In the legal domain, as Weiler argues above,[2] integration is an 'all or nothing' process . . . In the political domain the position is never so clear cut. Those who cling to a unitary model of the sovereign state may find it difficult to accept the concept of the division of sovereignty, or of the distribution of power among different levels of government. But federal government rests upon that principle. Looser federations, such as Switzerland, with its model of cooperative federalism, operate more through concerting the powers of the separate states than through transferring those powers to a new decision-taking centre . . .

As John Pinder has argued, we risk misunderstanding the process through which member states have begun to concert their actions through the framework of the Community if we insist on seeing the Community either as 'above' or 'below' the nation-state: either as an established supranational authority, or as a useful but non-authoritative international regime. In complementing, but not displacing, national activities in regional policy, in research and development, international development policy, and industrial restructuring the Community is neither supra- nor international, but 'extranational'; neither above nor below the nation-state, but 'alongside'. As Hoffmann argues . . . Community politics and national politics can thus be mutually reinforcing, rather than the one necessarily undermining the other . . .

. . . The temptation at this point is for the academic observer to conclude, as international relations scholars so often do, that we are in 'a period of transition', and that the Community is moving in one direction or another – towards further integration or disintegration, according to one's preferences. It seems more realistic to conclude that the Community is stuck, between sovereignty and integration, as Ghita Ionescu put it some years ago: recognising the necessity of closer collaboration in a still-widening number of fields, anxious not to jeopardise what has been achieved so far, but unable to mobilise the imagination or the coalition of political forces needed to supply the central authority needed . . .

. . . The reasons for this apparent paralysis are not hard to seek: they lie first and foremost in the domestic preoccupations of the member governments, in their lack of spare resources, political or financial, to invest in the European dimension. But continuing failure to do so – to accept that there are further limitations on sovereignty which have to be granted, further transfers of authority which must be made – will gradually undermine the prestige, the legitimacy and the effectiveness of what has so far been achieved. The European Community is more than another international regime; but it is not impossible that it will drift towards an international regime, as recession at home and uncertainty abroad progressively undermine its authority.

Notes

1 J. Weiler, *Supranationalism Revisited – Retrospective and Prospective* European University Institute Working Paper Two (Florence, 1981), p. 4.
2 See note 1 above.

Document 29: M. Forsyth, *Unions of States: The Theory and Practice of Confederation*, op. cit. (1981), pp. 171–81, 183–7

. . . It is hardly surprising . . . that it was the smaller states of Europe, those that felt their lack of size even within Europe itself, that provided the prototype of modern, twentieth-century economic confederation . . .

. . . It is notable that none of these new European organizations and communities resembled a confederation either defensive or economic. The most far-reaching project, the proposed European Defence Community, might seem to believe this, and to suggest an effort to establish a classic defensive confederation. . . . Like the European Coal and Steel Community, the European Defence Community was devised essentially as a means of solving the problem created by the concrete and imperative need, at the end of the 1940s, to transform Germany from a defeated and subordinated enemy into a powerful and loyal ally . . .

. . . It can be seen that the proposed European Defence Community was not genuinely a confederation, for confederations are not basically techniques for preventing a particular state from having an army at its disposal, by pooling the armies that the other states have at their disposal, in order that a wider hegemonical alliance can operate. Confederations are rather communities made by a group of states in order to assert a common policy of peace and war for all time in the future. The very attempt that was made in 1952–3 to create yet another community – the European Political Community – to 'control' the European army that was to be created by the European Defence Community demonstrates how technical, and lacking in true confederal elements the latter was. The Coal and Steel Community, for its part, lacked the elements of a genuine economic confederation because it too was essentially a technique for solving a specific political problem, namely the need to end the controls imposed upon Germany's war industries after the country's defeat. Neither the main aspirations nor the main achievements of the movement towards European unity in the first phase from 1945 to 1954, therefore, can be said to have reflected the idea of confederation . . .

. . . General de Gaulle reiterated his opposition to the European Defence Community, and proposed instead the formation of a European defensive confederation of the classic type, to be founded on a popular referendum in each country. General de Gaulle's proposals are worth pursuing a little further, for it is one of the striking features of the whole post-war period, when viewed by the student of confederation, that the strongest, clearest, and most consistent call for a classic defensive confederation for western Europe has come from de Gaulle and the Gaullists. This call was made with particular force between 1951 and 1953, and again in the period from 1960 to 1962, indeed the first draft of the so-called Fouchet plan of November 1961 may be said to represent the nearest approach to the founding text of a classic confederation that has been made in post-war Europe . . .

. . . The Fouchet plan of confederation was not of course successful. It has indeed been one of the continuing ironies and tragedies of European history since the Second World War that the proponents of defensive confederation have been deeply suspicious of the proponents of economic confederation and vice-versa. Instead of an overlap and mutual strengthening – defence union providing the framework for economic union, and economic union providing the material basis for defence union – there has been tension and antagonism between the two conceptions . . .

. . . In the 1970s, it is true, steps were taken to establish co-operation between the members of the EEC within the realm of traditional foreign policy. Foreign ministers have held regular meetings, a political committee has been established to prepare these meetings, and joint declarations have been issued on critical issues of world politics. Meetings and joint communiques, however, still remain a long way from the permanent commitment to united action with regard to all questions of war and peace that is implied in the making of a confederation.

It is time to complete our account of the development of the idea of a European economic confederation . . .

. . . That the European Economic Community is an economic confederation, standing in line of descent from the economic provisions included in the Constitution of the American Union 1789, the Zollverein established in 1834, and the Benelux Union of 1948, is clear from both its content and its form. Thus, as regards content, the Community represents essentially the transformation of the external economic relations between a number of states into an internal market. To see it merely as a technique for liberalizing the external trade of a number of states, to be placed on the same level as other techniques aimed at liberalizing external trade, and to be judged by the degree to which, in liberalizing external trade in one direction, it does not liberalize it in another, but 'discriminates', is, as Walter Hallstein pointed out with exemplary clarity during the ill-fated efforts to create a general European free trade area in the late 1950s, to judge it by the wrong yardstick. It overlooks the very element of constituting one 'unit of production', of internalizing external markets, which is at the heart of the operation.

The transformation of external markets into an internal market is effected in the first instance by a process of enclosure: the creation of a common external tariff and of a common commercial policy towards third countries. This enclosure has incidentally nothing to do with the degree to which the common external policy of the Community may be liberal or protectionist; the crucial change is that external trade policy itself, or the decision as to whether to be liberal or protectionist vis-à-vis the outside world, is made the preserve of common institutions making common regulations. In the same way the creation of a defensive confederation does not necessarily imply the ending of all alliances, but solely that the decision to ally or not is a joint and common one.

The enclosure of markets is accompanied by the removal of the barriers to the free movement of goods, services, persons and capital within the new common boundary. At the same time the attempt is made positively to promote and guarantee such internal exchange by the establishment of a common transport policy, the establishment of a fund to ease the redeployment of labour, and the adoption of a collective approach towards economic policy in general and monetary policy in particular. The provisions regarding monetary and exchange-rate policy have long been recognized as one of the weakest links in the EEC Treaty, and repeated efforts were made during the difficult decade of the 1970s to give them a substantive content, the latest being the creation of the European Monetary System. Whether the European Community, pursuing this path, will proceed to the point of having a 'parallel currency' – as the Zollverein did – remains to be seen.

Alongside the creation of a common external policy, and the freeing, promotion, and guarantee of internal exchange, stand the policies for improving and stimulating what List would have called the 'material productive powers' that lie within the common boundary of the Community: agriculture, by means of a common agricultural policy; and industry by means of competition policy and through the activities of the European Investment Bank. In all these complementary ways the Community represents the replacement of external economic relations between its members by economic relations similar to those that obtain within a single state. The economy of each state has not ceased to exist, but it has been placed within a new economy – that of the Community as a whole.

As regards the form of the European Economic Community the confederal elements are again conspicuous. The Community is based on a treaty which is more than a conventional interstate treaty. It is a constitutive treaty which, in the act of creating a new body politic, alters the constitutions of the partners to it. The treaty establishes common institutions which are capable of passing laws that are directly binding throughout the territory of the community, and which are also endowed with considerable discretionary power to fulfil the general objectives of the union. The treaty is concluded for an 'unlimited period'.

It is true that the institutional structure of the Community is unusual in that the distinctive notion of 'supranationality' that was embodied in the European Coal and Steel Community, and also in the proposed European Defence Community, has been carried over into it. This notion, based on a deeply rooted belief that the only way to transcend the traditional 'intergovernmental' institutions of the international world is to create common bodies which are not only – like those of the classic confederation – possessed of real legislative power over the citizens of member states, but which are also completely independent of the member states, finds expression in the European Economic Community in the special position of the Commission, with its treaty-based independence vis-à-vis the member states, and its monopoly of the law-proposing power. Such independent, or as Huber expresses it, such unitary as distinct from federative organs, are unusual in confederations, but are certainly not unknown, as the example of the United Provinces plainly demonstrates.

Moreover this difference between the European Economic Community and many confederations is lessened by the fact that from the start the Community institution that has held the final power of legislative decision has been – in the more usual confederal fashion – the Council of Ministers, in which are gathered the representatives of the member states. During the development of the Community, and more especially since the Luxembourg Compromise of 1966, the position of the Council of Ministers, and of the body that is responsible for preparing the decisions of the Council, the Committee of the Permanent Representatives of the member states, has strengthened in relation to that of the Commission. The current pivotal role of the Committee of Permanent Representatives deserves particularly to be noted. Because of its permanency, its close links with the member states, and the 'instructions' which pass to it from them, it is in some ways more analogous to the governing body of the customary confederation than any other body in the European Community. The procedure by which the Council of Ministers makes its decisions also conforms closely to confederal practice. Since the Luxembourg Compromise unanimity has been the accepted norm for matters affecting the vital interests of a member state, with majority voting possible otherwise.

The factor which today most seriously obscures the Community's status as an economic confederation is not the special power of the Commission, but rather the increasingly fragmented and uncertain character of the Council of Ministers. On the one hand it now conspicuously lacks continuity of membership, and hence coherence of decision-making. On the other hand, a new body, the European Council, has developed over and above it. This new body, which came into existence in 1975, is perhaps best described as an institutionalized summit conference, bringing together the heads of governments and foreign ministers of the Community three times a year. As a result of these developments the Council of Ministers of the Community cannot be said to possess the unequivocal representative status of the usual confederal diet or congress.

The Court of Justice of the European Community is entirely in keeping with the confederal character we have ascribed to the Community. A confederation implies the establishment of a 'supremacy' or law-making power, acting within the area set out by the founding treaty, and existing alongside the 'supremacy' or law-making powers of the member states. It implies the establishment of some kind of judicial machinery to ensure that when this new law-making power acts within its proper treaty-based competence its laws are uniformly observed. Perhaps above all it implies the existence of machinery whereby disputes between the member states pertaining to the scope of the treaty and to the acts taken under it can be settled by 'due process of law'. In fulfilling these functions therefore the Court of Justice of the Community stands fully within the logic of a confederal system.

The last major organ of the European Community, the European Parliament, stamps the new confederation as a democratic one in the double sense that it has been made between democratic countries, and is intended itself to embody democratic principles. The difficulty of organizing a confederation of democratic states was indicated by Seydel in the late nineteenth century. On the one hand a confederal congress of states, with the power to decide upon laws, cannot act if its participants are controlled too closely by their national parliaments. To this extent a confederation is 'anti-democratic'. On the other hand, there is a limit to the extent to which the government of a confederation can be made democratic by way of a joint confederal parliamentary assembly. A fully democratic form of government presupposes a deep-rooted underlying sense of oneness or nationality, a trust binding together government and governed whatever the outcome of the ballot box. A confederation, by contrast, is formed by communities that feel one in some respects but not in others. The parliamentary assembly of a confederation hence cannot be expected to occupy a position identical to that of the conventional parliamentary assembly of a democratic state. Its most appropriate status, and the one to which the European Parliament approximates, would seem to be that of a critical body set over as a distinct whole against, or alongside the confederal government, rather than as a body in which a government elected by the people faces the criticisms of an opposition that itself awaits election to government by the people.

This is of course not to say that such a role can or ought never to change. Confederations – as our historical survey showed – provide the framework within which the sense of oneness and nationality concomitant with democracy in the fullest sense, can gradually develop. This development is, however, a slow process, even amongst peoples that speak the same language, and it ends often with a bitter struggle in which the constitutional form of the confederation, based on a treaty between states, is pitted against the emergent will of the majority of the population of the confederation. In the European Community, where cultural differences are many and deep, and are indeed likely to grow wider as the number of members increase, these somewhat sombre historical realities deserve to be remembered.

In 1979 a major step was taken when the European Parliament, in accordance with the provisions of the Rome Treaty, became a body directly elected by the people of the member states. The roots of the Community became significantly deeper. The creation of one European people, however, which is the prerequisite simultaneously of a fully democratic European union and of the transition from a confederal structure to a federal state, remains a matter for the future. Progress in this direction is likely to be slow unless and until the European states decide, as a result of convergent self-interest, to establish a security confederation to complement the existing economic confederation . . .

Document 30: P. Taylor, 'The confederal phase', from 'The politics of the European Communities: the confederal phase', *World Politics* April 1975, pp. 336–48, 350–1, 354–5, 357–60

. . . The present essay does not consciously follow any of the established modes of theorizing about international integration, but concentrates upon the contemporary or Confederal phase of the process.

The approach is to follow three major interrelated themes which summarize the major qualities of contemporary integrative politics.

1 They are, first, the broadly defensive stance of the governments in their conduct of relations with the Brussels institutions;
2 Second, the appearance of a system of political interaction which may be called a 'managed Gesellschaft' and
3 Third, the oscillation between advanced schemes for integration and retreats into nationalism which can be seen in the stated intentions of governments . . .

. . . It is implicit in this essay that the Confederal phase is a mature one in the European context and that it represents a culmination of earlier phases . . .

. . . The working methods of the European Communities have tended to fragment the idea of national interest and to weaken a government's claim to be its spokesman. A more cautious approach by governments to the work of the Communities has thereby been encouraged; in addition, the development in the European Communities of an extensive range of economic, social, and cultural interdependencies has led them to adopt an increasingly defensive attitude in the face of a potential or actual threat to their powers, which could, it is felt, challenge their sovereignty. As was to be expected, as integration proceeded governments became more defensive in the face of an increasing range of regional constraints . . .

. . . It must not be concluded that the extent of the fragmentation of the idea of the national interest is a measure of the decline of national governments in the European Communities. The point is rather that the Community method of decision making, by fragmenting the idea of national interest, has placed governments on their guard. They have lost something; compared with the general pattern of relations between governments in the 1930s and before, when raisons d' état, Realpolitik, and the zero-sum game mentality were the rule, they have lost a great deal. But the process of losing this much has encouraged a watchful defensiveness rather than posing a fundamental challenge to their existence.

It is arguable that governments constructed the institutions of Europe and defined their roles and their specific tasks within the Rome Treaty so as to make it easier for them to defend their interests as integration proceeded than it had been in the Federalist phase of 1950–1954 . . .

. . . There are numerous examples of governments dragging their feet in the development of the European Communities. That is not unusual in diplomacy in international institutions. It is, however, perhaps paradoxical that the granting of unusual powers and the right of initiative to an independent body of international civil servants should be part of a deliberate strategy for making it easier for governments to reduce their level of cooperation or to resist further integration. It is not surprising though that, faced with a broadly uncooperative or defensive posture on the part of members, some governments become impatient and tried more desperate remedies . . .

. . . The most powerful pressure toward the adoption of a defensive posture in the Confederal phase, however, probably derives from the very success of the integration process. Governments in the European Communities no longer preside over states whose various 'functional' tiers are largely coextensive. In many respects, states have been economically, legally, and politically penetrated by systems which extend throughout the area of the European Communities and, occasionally, beyond them. One result is that governments are now unable to take decisions which refer to their own territory without taking into account a range of influences, pressures, and sometimes rules which originate outside their own frontiers, and which they are unable to control . . .

In member states, the law of the Communities has a status comparable with municipal law . . . Within the Communities, according to one commentator, are to be found about three thousand nongovernmental international organizations, including some powerful multinational companies – by far the largest concentration in the world. It is hardly surprising that governments, when faced with these developments have been pushed toward a more defensive posture . . .

. . . It should be added that it is partly because of the development of higher levels of international interdependence that national cohesiveness increases; in reacting to increasing levels of international interdependence, governments seek to involve themselves in larger areas of national economic and social life. This reaction derives from their urge to defend themselves against international functional encroachment on their traditional domain; it is not just another example of governments asserting their traditional powers.

These developments can be related to certain arguments about Functionalism: opponents of that approach to international organization have noted the tendency of an increasing range of activities within the state to become politicized; governments are becoming more involved in activities within the state, and more questions seem subject to political controversy. Functionalists have said that integration would occur most easily in noncontentious and nonpolitical areas (which no one would deny) and, further, that as integration proceeded, a greater range of such noncontentious areas would manifest themselves . . .

It is readily accepted that governments have indeed become more involved in a greater range of issues within the state. But they have become involved in this Confederal phase of integration in part because of the earlier success of the Functional approach to integration; in part because of the practical requirements of integration which frequently demand decisions of governments about matters with which they were not previously directly concerned . . . It may be that Functionalism as a strategy for integration is less useful in the later phases of regional integration because governments have become increasingly sensitized to the political implications of integrative ventures. But they are so sensitized because of the past success of the Functional approach . . .

. . . To what extent, then, has the condition of the Europe of the Confederal phase been affected by the defensive postures of member governments? (It is necessary to distinguish at this stage between the scope and the level of integration: scope refers to the horizontal extent of integration, the number of functional areas which are linked together in some way within the larger territory; level refers to the manner in which the areas are organized – in particular, the extent to which they are ruled from new centers which can act independently of governments.) A salient feature of Confederal Europe is that the scope of integration is extensive (a wide range of matters has been brought within the integrated area), but the level of integration is low. It is very difficult to show that there has been any significant transfer of authority to the Brussels institutions . . .

These powers are exercised within the framework of policies, agreed on by national governments and only with their approval. Another outstanding feature is that the low level of integration, the fact that national governments retain ultimate control has to be balanced by the habits of cooperation on a significant range of questions and of using established procedures, and by the development of pressures toward agreement in cooperative arrangements . . .

Pressures toward agreement derive from public expectations, the high level of interdependence, and the range of regional constraints. The Europe of this Confederal phase of integration is therefore decentralized but highly inter-dependent, potentially autarchic but in practice united by entrenched practices of consultation.

A second theme which emerges from an examination of the Confederal phase of integration is that of the 'managed Gesellschaft'. The central features of this system are the undermining of the hierarchy of actors and interests, both at the national, and the European level and, as a corollary, the legitimization of an increas-ing range of interests which are fed into the political arena. The development of mechanisms for the management of relations between existing actors of more or less equal status, whose interests are generally seen as having more or less equal validity, is increasingly the condition for stability . . .

A large number of interest groups, the activities of which cut across national frontiers, have emerged in the area of the European Communities. There is also an increasingly dense range of international interdependence and interaction. Compared with developments at the level of organizations and transactions, there has been but a weak development of positive identification with the institutions of Europe . . .

. . . It is hard to escape the conclusion that international interdependencies make it more difficult for national governments to control their economies. As the Nine have a greater range of interdependencies with each other than with outsiders, it might be argued that the development of the European Communities has added to the difficulty. The importance of this development for the status of governments cannot be overstressed: it means that they are now removed from that position of command over the levers of economic power which was one of the hallmarks of government. And this has happened precisely at a time when economic success – the ability to deliver the goods – has been the main test of political virtue. In this sense, they have been reduced in status. It means also that, in trying to compensate for the loss of mechanisms of control, governments are increasingly pushed toward what might be called government by alliance. The condition of successful government is the arrangement of an effective alliance or set of alliances with other governments in order to achieve specific objectives. Furthermore, governments may enter into arrangements with other organized groups, involving negotiations and concessions on their demands in return for help with the running of the economy . . .

. . . Two developments which affected the status of governments adversely have now been identified: they are each partly attributable, though not exclusively so, to membership in the European Communities. Membership has contributed to the weakening of the Gemeinschaft in the nation-state, has helped to undermine the hierarchy of values and attitudes, and has reduced the authority of governments. Membership has also exacerbated the problem of control over national economies and has disposed governments to seek alliances with other organized groups in an attempt to regain control. The weakening of agreed values in the state, the declining authority of governments, and the reduction of the effectiveness of their mechanisms for control have encouraged organized groups to increase their demands on governments, and to view their own and the governments' interests as possessing an equal validity. The Community links have certainly contributed to these developments.

There is, however, no tendency for governments to be eliminated as actors from the European Gesellschaft. In fact, their right to remain as actors has, if anything, been reinforced by developments in the Communities over recent years. The absence of a Gemeinschaft at the European level means that there is no means of establishing the priority of any one set of interests and no way of deciding whether any actor should be eliminated from the system. As has been implied, it is accepted that satisfaction of any one interest depends upon the construction of appropriate alliances of power and influence between groups, including governments, rather than upon a government's ability to relate specific demands to a general interest. This is as true at the Communities level as at the national one. The Commission of the European Communities – the main independent, active element in the Brussels institutions – has in effect renounced its claim to be a rival center of authority, a putative European government. It has accepted the role of actor, like any other in the European Gesellschaft, with the specific task of encouraging European arrangements and encouraging alliances to solve particular problems. In other words, it no longer sets out to challenge national governments. In helping them to define their interests and to form alliances, it reinforces their right to exist. The total effect has been an equalization of the hierarchy of actors both at the national and at the European level.

The character of the Commission and the major features of decision making in the Communities have come to reflect the abandonment of the ambition to build at Brussels a centralized European government – a development which mirrors at the European level the changing status of governments at the national one. It can be said that before 1965, the Commission was self-consciously defining a European interest, and that it was active in initiating policies for European integration and creating the norms of the European would-be polity. That was the period of optimism in the Commission about the building of a more centralized Europe. . . . The crisis later in 1965 marked the deflation of this optimism: the resistance to the Commission's proposals of March 1965 for expanding the powers of the institutions, and the confirmation of the powers of European governments in relation to Brussels.

During that time, the dominant features of the Commission's method were a relatively passive involvement in the process of mediation between the governments, and the execution of agreed policies. The Commission of the European Communities had been recreated in a more traditional style of international bureaucracy.

After the Hague Conference of the Heads of States and Governments of the Six, in December 1969, a third style of Commission involvement in decision making in Europe began to emerge. It combined the greater energy of the first period with the purpose of the second: the Commission began more actively to seek the reaching of agreements between governments; it began to see its role as the bringing together of actors the separateness of which it recognized, and it accepted the status of 'interest group', as governments were having that status in the Communities thrust upon them. In addition, the Commission actively sought to coordinate the work of Europe's institutions, even those strictly outside the framework of the Communities, and to mange the Gesellschaft. The Commission's ambition to transcend the other actors in defining Europe seemed to weaken, but there was no loss of energy in attempting to build agreement among them. This role of the Commission is another of the features of the Confederal phase of integration . . .

. . . Thus, the Commission, in relation to developments at the European level, has in some ways become more like governments at the national level. It has found itself unable to sustain its claim of being a putative European government which would accede to an unusual authority and power as national governments lose some of their traditional functions within the state . . .

The Commission and governments have in a way become more like each other as actors, seeking alliances with other actors as one condition of success, and attempting to extend their presence in striving for proper coordination and management . . .

. . . In this Confederal phase of integration, what are the implications of the 'managed' Gesellschaft for proposals for improving the European institutions and the quality of integration? Despite pessimism about prospects of centralization, there are considerable opportunities for improving the quality of coordination between the various actors and for tackling specific problems, such as those of obtaining greater representativeness and greater responsibility in decision-making institutions. The earlier institutional fundamentalism of the Commission has in practice been gradually abandoned over a number of years. This is in line with the undermining of the hierarchy of actors both at the national and at the European level . . .

. . . The third theme in this account of the Confederal phase of integration in Europe is the oscillation between advanced schemes for integration and retreats into national independence which may be found in the stated intentions of governments. That such oscillation exists is not difficult to demonstrate; the reasons for its existence are more difficult to uncover. It does, however, have implications for the chances of increasing the scope, as distinct from the level, of integration . . .

But there is also a sense in which the Hague meeting began the oscillation effect which became so evident later on. In questions which affected the scope of integration there was, in the main, success; but in matters which seemed to threaten to change the level of integration there was much less progress . . .

. . . One reason for this oscillation effect is the confusion in the minds of European statesmen between questions about the level of integration and questions about the scope of integration. On the one hand, there is the awareness of advantages to be gained from further integrative measures; there are problems to be solved and also, of course, prizes to be won. In summit conferences, statesmen are liable to be particularly impressed by the advantages of working together; the accession of Great Britain has been the occasion of several such meetings. Once generated, a particular set of diplomatic initiatives acquires a dynamic and creates an ethos of its own, working through national bureaucracies and Community institutions, and is added to the material temptations and more idealistic promptings of the summit. Furthermore, as the Neofunctionalists have suggested, some technical problems in relations between integrating states can undoubtedly be solved by further integration.

Once away from the conference table, however, different factors may swing the pendulum to the side of doubt: a reassertion of what is conceived as the special interest of governments takes place. It is, of course, possible to argue that the proposals for integration were thwarted by practical considerations, by the world economic crisis of 1971 and the world energy crisis, and by the mundane factor of disagreement about means rather than ends. There have also been occasions when doubts were reinforced by electoral considerations . . .

. . . The reassertion of the separate interests of governments has also been bound up with the peculiar vulnerability that intensive interdependence creates. States which are interdependent are exposed to exploitation by each other because of the very high cost which severing the relationship would entail. . . . The oscillation effect is the result of a very complex set of diplomatic pressures which are characteristic of relations between governments involved in close interdependencies. It revolves around the paradox that interdependence involves a capacity for independence. However, these pressures are only partly based on the reality of the political situation which now prevails in the European Communities. The difficulty is that statesmen have become convinced that it is now virtually impossible to act in Europe without transferring greater authority to the center, that the scope of integration cannot be increased without significantly increasing its level. In this view, statesmen and the Commission are probably wrong: they are the victims partly of their own rhetoric in more euphoric moments and partly of a mistaken strategy by the Commission which has not yet been entirely abandoned. Statesmen have been taken in by their own assertion of being 'one', and believe that this must mean the birth of some transcendental European entity; the Commission, in continuously reminding statesmen of the relevance of practical questions to political unity and in arguing that a particular question is indeed political and that it must necessarily be transferred to the center, has succeeded only in warning statesmen of possible dangers and of frightening them into confusing questions about the level with questions about the scope of integration. In discussing this danger, Ralf Dahrendorf has particularly blamed the Functionalist approach to integration and the Commission's acceptance of it. He criticizes the strategy of integration which poses a necessary link between one level of integration and the next, and which maintains that governments are led inevitably from a Common Agricultural Policy to monetary union, and thence to 'political union by 1980'. He labels any such gradualist strategy 'Functionalist'.

Individual governments and the Commission seem to be equally responsible for this impasse; it is surely incorrect to blame Functionalism in general for some of the errors in the strategy of integration which have been suggested mainly by interpretations of one of its offsprings, namely, Neofunctionalism. It should be recalled also that governments were tempted into extravagant and unfulfilled ambitions in the early fifties without any help from Functionalists or Neofunctionalists . . .

. . . These then are the major features of the Confederal phase of European integration. Each theme illustrates characteristics of the actors, the system, and the behavior of governments. The themes also link with particular kinds of proposals for changing the nature of integration and for tackling specific problems in the present phase. It is essential that the proposals and any theory which is explored as the source of strategy of further integration be related to this specific phase of the process.

Document 31: S. Bulmer, 'Domestic politics and European Community policy making', *Journal of Common Market Studies* **Vol. 21: 1983, pp. 353–5**

This article examines the links between domestic politics and the European Community and seeks to explain how the former may have a vital impact on the policy-making output of the EC . . .

. . . Too much literature has concentrated on the upper tier – the formal institutional framework of the Communities – without examining the domestic sources of national negotiating positions. We may think of the European Community in the manner adopted by Stanley Hoffmann for defining the term international system.

> An international system is a pattern of relations between the basic units of world politics ... This pattern is largely determined by the structure of the world, the nature of the forces which operate across or within the major units, and the capabilities, pattern of power, and political culture of those units.

These basic units are the nation states.

The term 'domestic politics' also underlines the fact that the lower decisional tier of the EC is rooted in policy environments which differ between member states and within them, according to the policy area concerned. For the purpose of illustrating the different environments, the concept of 'policy style' is utilized as an analytical framework. Apart from its value in examining national policy-making, it remains neutral as regards integration theories. Supranationalism and the 'Community method' are inextricably linked with a neo-functionalist view of integration. However, it should be clear – without resorting to concepts such as 'spillback' – that the policy-making process does not follow the logic of integration but rather that integration follows the logic of decision-making processes. These processes have their roots in the power structures of the nation states.

A third dimension to the domestic politics approach concerns the nation state's position in the interdependent world of today. International monetary instability, oil supply and pricing matters are, as the transnationalist school of thought indicates, phenomena which are outside the control of individual EC member states or interests. These states do, however, have the ability to decide at which level to defend their interests: at the national level, the EC level or in other international regimes. The domestic political tier thus has an important function in determining whether the EC is an appropriate forum for responding to international economic uncertainty.

Assumptions of the domestic politics approach

There are five assumptions in the domestic politics approach.

1 The national polity is the basic unit in the European Community. It is the level at which governments, interest groups, parliamentary bodies and political parties derive their legitimacy, their power and at which they may be called to account.

2 Each national polity has a different set of social and economic conditions that shapes its national interests and policy content. Each state has different ideological cleavages which determine the extent of consensus. In more structural terms, policy instruments differ as does the extent of centralization in the state. Finally, each state's relationship to the outside world differs (reflecting Haas' idea of 'differential enmeshment of the member states in the world economy').

3 European policy only represents one facet of a national polity's activity. It is somewhat artificial to separate a member state's European policy from its other domestic behaviour. Not only are national EC policy making environments similar to those obtaining for domestic policy decisions but the subject matter is overwhelmingly similar, too. Thus the EC's concern with regional, agricultural and monetary affairs is in tandem with the nation states' domestic policies. Katzenstein and others have explored the relationships between domestic economic and political structures, on the one hand, and foreign economic policy strategies, on the other. Thus an adaptation of this approach to European policy should be possible.

4 In formal terms the national governments hold a key position at the junction of national politics and Community politics. Whether the governments are really as powerful as the intergovernmentalists would have us believe must depend on specific examination. Governments may be 'captured' by domestic interests and by the transnational forces inherent in an interdependent world. This would restrict their manoeuvrability greatly. On the other hand, national governments may have considerable powers to impose a policy on affected domestic interests so that they can derive power both from their formally authoritative position in domestic politics and from their important position in the Council of Ministers.

5 The concept of policy style is employed to analyze the relationships between government and other domestic political forces vis-à-vis European policy.

These assumptions can now be examined in more detail, in particular to highlight the distinctions from the more familiar EC policy-making models of supra-nationalism and intergovernmentalism . . .

Conclusion

. . . The above examination of the domestic politics approach suggests an approach for examining member states' attitudes and interests in the EC. It is not bound up with integration theory which makes it more neutral, although less dynamic. Its complexity, however, makes it somewhat unwieldy for applications to policy-making from an overall EC perspective.

It corresponds most closely to the transnationalist approach of international relations theories. It looks at the power structures within member states in a general manner similar to the transnationalist study of the international political economy. There is thus a certain congruence between the two approaches that perhaps deserves further investigation than is possible here.

The domestic politics approach might be accused of having somewhat mixed intellectual parentage but is arguably more embracing and/or more realistic as a device explaining Community negotiations than the alternatives on offer. There is scope for further elaboration, too. The welfare economist may be able to append a public choice model on to the assumptions made. However, whether the language of economics can best express a political process is only answerable on the basis of evidence. In whatever way the domestic politics approach is developed or applied, it surely indicates that the study of EC policy-making – perhaps unlike that of integration theory – is not obsolescent until the Community itself is.

Document 32: H. Nau, 'From integration to interdependence: gains, losses, and continuing gaps', *International Organization* Vol. 33: 1979, pp. 139–46

What is missing?

The discovery that regional integration is an epiphenomenon, a subset of larger global phenomena, is not a new or surprising one. Regional integration activities and theories were always a function, in part, of larger global events. As Tsoukalis points out in his brief discussion of approaches to European integration, the power politics approach consistently emphasized the external factor. With the help of hindsight, we can now see that it was in part because of the external confinement besetting Western Europe in the 1950s that broad consensus prevailed on security issues and internal economic issues could be separated and treated, at least initially, as 'low' political issues. The 'low/high politics' distinction was never a matter of substance but of priorities. Today, the external context is more fluid, agendas are expanding and, to the extent that governments fail to set new priorities – either because hesitancy is rational in the face of uncertainty or because interdependence undermines the ability of governments to influence outcomes – few fixed parameters exist to permit the decomposition or limited handling of issues. Instead, everything is politicized and is or can be linked.

It is less important, however, that the power politics approach, as well as other criticism of early integration theory, was ultimately right about the significance of external factors than that, in the period when external factors remained relatively constant, these critics completely missed the exciting events that occurred in the European Community, particularly from 1958–1963. Indeed, functionalist and neofunctionalist thought applied to the European Community have provided students of international organization, in my view, with most of the novel insights we have achieved in the post war period concerning the role and potential of international institutions. Interdependence themes clearly de-emphasize central-ized institutional processes. These studies therefore are, in one sense, less relevant to the study of international organizations than to the study of international politics as a whole. It may be objected, of course, that a centralized institutional focus is too narrow and confining for international organization studies. Nevertheless, it becomes increasingly difficult to identify a subfield of international organization without this focus.

Neofunctionalist theorists, therefore, are to be chastised, in my view, less for belatedly recognizing the significance of external factors and now perhaps for overemphasizing their significance (see below) than for abandoning too readily the most important distinguishing and analytically powerful features of their theory. To clarify this view, let me list and then discuss briefly the major relative differences, as I see them, between the integration and interdependence approaches and finally suggest what factors have been lost in the transition or which factors have never been adequately considered by either approach.

1 Integration theory stressed a certain voluntarism and field of manoeuvre in expanding the mandate and authority of central institutions; interdependence approaches emphasize the complexity and hence constraint of modern circumstances affecting the performance and growth of all institutions.
2 Integration theory depended upon the logic of competitive markets to establish substantive links among issues; interdependence approaches tend to look to new knowledge to suggest the partial (Haas' fragmented issue linkage), or holistic (Club of Rome) association of substantive issues.
3 Integration theory posited a definite hierarchy of issues (high/low), interests (non-governmental groups followed governments to Brussels not vice versa), and institutions (supranational over national outcomes); interdependence approaches stress the absence of hierarchy of issues (economic as important as military issues), interests (transnational and transgovernmental actors as important as central governmental ones), and institutions (all outcomes possible).
4 Integration studies relatively de-emphasized the role of global and national compared to regional factors; interdependence studies tend to weight global over both regional and national factors.

The voluntarism of regional integration theory expressed itself chiefly in the organizational leadership of supranational bureaucrats . . .

. . . Cox criticised these neofunctional views for overestimating the freedom of action of the international executive. Other critics doubted the efficacy of organizational leadership altogether, particularly at the supranational level and looked instead to dramatic/charismatic initiatives generated by national elites. Interdependence studies see organized bureaucrats acting more through horizontal alignments and coalitions across bureaucracies than through vertical planning and programming within bureaucracies as is stressed by neofunctionalists. From an interdependence perspective, hegemonic leadership from any source, national or international, is constrained, while effective initiatives are those which are shared among a number of actors and exhibit exemplary or stabilizing, rather than assertive or transformational aims. International organizations might nurture and even participate in such 'multiple leadership' initiatives, but these actions are neither a consequence primarily of organization variables (such as organizational ideology stressed by neofunctionalists) nor a cause of significant expansion of international organizational authority.

Neither of these perspectives inquires into the origins of supranational or international organizations. Integration studies never sought to explain the original decision to establish the Common Market. In fact, it is astonishing that, except for memoirs, we have few studies that seek to account for the remarkable events in Europe from 1955 to 1958. As part of the acceptance of supranational institutions, integration studies also assumed as given the priorities reflected in these institutions. The Common Market clearly implied a distinction between security and economic objectives in Europe; this distinction made possible the high/low issue dichotomy adopted by integration theory. Interdependence approaches, as we have noted, de-emphasize the role of institutions generally, giving greater attention to elites operating outside or beyond, as well as within, specific organizational settings. Interdependence studies further hesitate to assume or assert any priorities.

Admittedly, the analysis of leadership, organization innovation, and priorities is a complex task. Nevertheless, a repeated phenomenon of past and contemporary international politics is the exercise of consequential initiatives, the setting of new priorities, and the creation of new international organizations . . .

. . . To what extent is institutional innovation a function of intellectual vision, bureaucratic spill-over or spill-back (i.e., disillusionment with existing institutions), substantive needs, etc? These are issues that David Mitrany contended with, when he concluded that 'form follows function'. But we have not progressed very far, it would seem, since his rather deterministic and largely unacceptable answer. And while the study of leadership and organizational innovation is extraordinarily complex, is it any more complex than the situational turbulence celebrated by interdependence perspectives?

The key to leadership, to the extent that it can be patterned and is not just a function of random, psychological phenomena, would seem to lie, as Haas believes, in learning processes. As he writes, 'learning processes can be thought of as resulting from the availability of new types of knowledge, or the uninformed recognition of new objectives may trigger 'learning' which deliberately seeks new knowledge'. In the case of integration theory, learning involved relating the unintended consequences of competitive utilitarian forces (i.e. the functioning of competitive markets) to the expansion of central institutional tasks and authority. In the case of fragmented issue linkage, learning involves relating new scientific findings and techniques to the satisfaction of quality of life concerns, even if necessary at the expense of the growth of central institutions.

But how and why do new objectives and new knowledge arise? Is there a linearity in the evolution of objectives from pre-industrial to industrial to post-industrial societies? Are post-industrial concerns as widely shared in Europe, as Haas assumes? . . .

. . . One thing is clear, I think: We have paid far too little attention to the shifts in domestic political forces, both between and within parties, affecting government objectives and policies toward integration. For example, socialist parties in France, Germany, and Italy may have originally supported the European Community as a means of reducing the influence of capitalism in their national systems. After making substantial progress during the 1960s toward achieving this objective at the national level, however, they were in no mood to surrender these gains to Community institutions in the 1970s. Similarly, it is probably the pervasive shift from conservative to progressive governments in Europe that accounts for the decline of market objectives noted by Haas. To be sure, these political changes may also reflect more fundamental social and intellectual forces cutting across domestic societies, as Haas believes. But, even so, to grasp the rise and decline of objectives in Community processes, it is probably worth spending more time, as Puchala recommends in the Wallace volume,[1] looking at intragovernmental or intrasociety processes as well as community ones. This has to be done in some consistent theoretical framework, however, perhaps combining the insights of comparative politics and some new perspectives on the dynamics of customs unions.

Similar questions might be raised about new knowledge. Does this knowledge emerge according to a logic of its own or does it depend on a particular constellation of social and political interests, reflecting decisions to fund and pursue certain types of technical activities over others? Even if knowledge ultimately progresses and diffuses according to a cumulative, cross-cultural process, when and how it arises sometimes makes a great deal of difference. Causality becomes so complex that answers to these questions seem to remain, at least in part, articles in faith. Haas reminds us of this when he notes that rejecting the likelihood that a centralized institutional scheme will develop for mastering the future follows only if we lack faith in man's ability to plan for complexity in holistic terms.

In the end, understanding the complexity of situation and analysis can only be overcome through the setting of priorities and the making of assumptions. No action is possible without priorities, and no action is possible without assumptions. What we have lost, most unfortunately, in the transition from integration to interdependence theories is the hierarchy of issues, interests, and institutions that guided earlier integration studies. Integration studies have been accused of ignoring or down-playing certain issues, such as strategic relations, certain interests, such as transnational groups, and certain institutions principally national governments. But integration studies have not ignored governmental, transgovernmental, and transnational actors so much as they have analyzed the interplay among these actors (together with Community actors) within a specified hierarchy of empirical variables (supranational actors being the primary focus) and an explicit teleology of normative purpose. This was and remains the source of explanatory power of these studies. They may be faulted for focusing on the wrong actors, a critique that is especially valid after the Gaullist challenge to the Community in 1965. But they cannot be faulted for the fact that analysis requires some choice and hence some rank ordering of actors. Further, no one would quarrel today with the observation of interdependence studies that multiple channels and elite interactions characterize contemporary international relations. But these channels are more multiple compared to what – intrasociety interactions? From one point of view, as some have argued, it does not matter because increased domestic interactions only mean that the same number or even fewer international interactions may have stronger reverberations within a society. But it would seem to matter if governments are increasingly, in terms of the Wallace volume, the gatekeepers, that is, the point at which expanding domestic and expanding or declining international transactions meet. Governments are then in a position to divert, temper, or otherwise modify the content and meaning of incoming transactions or, what is even more important, they are potentially able to mobilize greater domestic resources to influence or initiate outgoing transactions. The number of actors or interactions involved horizontally may be less important than the structure or set of vertical relationships within which these interactions occur . . .

. . . The key to interdependence, it is being belatedly recognized, is not its existence but how governments respond to it. The latter depends on the size, speed, and costly effects of transactions (sensitivity) and on the relative availability and costliness of alternatives to these transactions that various actors face (vulnerability). Alternatives in turn are a function of capabilities (power) and objectives (purpose). As I note below, assessments of interdependence may change because of a shift in objectives . . . as well as a shift in capabilities, and capabilities include more fundamental social and political structures affecting a government's capacity to mobilize resources, as well as the more immediate policy (e.g., bureaucratic leadership) or material (e.g. size of economy) variables with which capabilities are usually identified.

Interdependence perspectives will not begin to acquire the explanatory power of early integration studies until these variables are ranked in more explicit judgments about what is important or what is not. Ordering variables in times of great flux and uncertainty must be done cautiously. One way to start is to develop alternative models applicable to different issues and circumstances . . .

. . . Thus, we need to continue the search for broader explanations, something more than eclecticism but less than all-encompassing global designs. We could use, for example, some guidelines to tell us when issues tend to (should) be decomposed and handled at lower levels or within partial frameworks and, in other cases, when these issues tend to (should) be treated globally. In this way, we avoid the temptation to conclude that they are always partial or always global.

Note

1 H. Wallace, W. Wallace and C. Webb (eds), *Policy-Making in the European Community* (London, 1977 edn).

Document 33: C. Webb, 'Theoretical perspectives and problems', in H. Wallace, W. Wallace and C. Webb (eds), *Policy-Making in the European Community* (London, 1983 edn), pp. 1, 32–9

The European Community (EC) has posed problems for political scientists since its inception. Its institutions and legal capacity have confounded traditional distinctions made between nation states and international organizations. Attempts in the 1960s and 1970s to fashion political concepts to suit the particular characteristics and pretensions of the EC raised expectations too high and left the theorists stranded or inadequately equipped to deal with a far from fully integrated, but nevertheless functioning, European Community . . .

Interdependence and integration

. . . The failure of the EC to move decisively towards a recognizable form of political union had undermined confidence in the application of the term 'integration' to the political processes of the Community. Equally the difficulties preventing the transformation of the customs union into a fully-fledged economic union have encouraged some economists to question the relevance of existing theories of economic integration in the light of extensive governmental involvement in economic management. In the midst of these doubts and uncertainties the concept of interdependence has been thrust into the foreground. Indeed, for some, it is clearly preferred to integration as the term better suited to describe the network of relations and collaboration represented in the European Community.

Does it actually help to substitute interdependence for integration as the major organizing concept of European integration? What is gained and lost by such a substitution? According to the proponents of the interdependence approach, the answer seems to be twofold. Firstly, interdependence refers to a condition (of intensive economic exchange) which may influence political relationships but does not necessarily elicit an integrative response from those most affected. It does not, therefore, assume a positive linear relationship between economic needs and political cooperation; rather the concept of interdependence emphasizes the loss of control and sense of hopelessness which complex economic interactions can trigger, especially in governments whose fate turns on their ability to safeguard the welfare of their electorates. Thus focusing on interdependence directs the student to the problem of the political management of economic exchange without assuming that, in the context of Western Europe, this necessarily will lead overall to a more centrally integrated regional system.

Secondly it follows that interdependence theorists are relatively unconcerned with the fate of particular institutionalized forms of cooperation, since they have no a priori basis for preferring one form over another. Thus there is no readily available institutional model offered by adherents of the interdependence approach to match the Commission-centred focus of neo-functionalists or the gladiatorial imagery adopted by intergovernmentalists. Indeed, interdependence analysts tend to eschew institutional studies on the grounds that they may mislead or mask the truly important changes in policy cooperation amongst governments which may not be represented in a highly institutionalized form. For most students, the concept of interdependence has been used to explain the conditions under which governments and other economic actors have to contemplate some form of collaboration; but, unlike the approach of integration theory, it does not necessarily help to define the outcome very precisely. Interdependence seems to be the answer for scholars and politicians who wish, for different reasons, to keep their options open on the evolution of the EC . . .

. . . In its most straightforward application in the literature of international relations, interdependence refers to the close and persistent relationship between two or more states or international actors, based on mutual reliance and therefore carrying a cost to one side or the other, or both, if the relationship were to be ended. Interdependence has, in fact, been invoked to describe a wide range of relationships . . .

. . . In its specific application to the European Community the concept of interdependence has been used variously to describe the conjuncture of economic conditions in Western Europe which gave rise to the EC initiatives; to the economic and political consequences of policy collaboration; to indicate the limits of regional cooperation and as a justification for maintaining the EC in spite of disagreements amongst its member states about its ultimate political purpose.

In addition, advocates of the interdependence approach argue that it enables the student to locate the EC in the mainstream of international politics. That is to say that the EC is seen as one example (albeit a particularly intense one) of trends that affect all governments and societies, especially in the advanced industrialized part of the world. From the perspective of policy studies, the attempt to 'globalize' the phenomenon of European integration has some merit. It encourages the analyst to focus on the policy issues first and foremost rather than be diverted by the particular and frequently parochial institutional problems which infiltrate and obscure the policy debate in Brussels. It may also help to underline the fact that for some governments the European Community does not offer the best hope of retrieving a sense of control, or pursuing a preferred outcome, in policy areas where the network of interests and sense of interdependence extends well beyond the regional frontiers of the EC.

Although interdependence analysts do not see much point in concentrating on institutional studies per se they, nevertheless, do have something to contribute to an understanding of the political setting within which policy is made, both in the national capitals and at the Community level. They have been unhappy both with the supranational bias of neofunctionalism and with the exaggerated monolithic image of national governments presented by intergovernmentalist analyses of the EC. Interdependence scholars have emphasized the diffusion of power within the Community; this they see as the result of the erosion of national government authority and the inability of the Commission to command sufficient political and economic resources within and across the most significant policy areas to constitute a counter force. Their explanation for the erosion of national authority lies partly in the impact of the rising volume of transnational and transgovernmental activity which has accompanied the intensification of political, economic, and administrative exchanges within the common market and customs union in Western Europe.

Transnational activity – that is the external representation and mobilization of non-governmental or intragovernmental interests – is a function of the structure and organization of interests within particular policy sectors or issue-areas. Especially powerful and well-equipped transnational groups such as multinational companies and banking interests can be identified . . .

. . . It is not just private, or semi-private, non-governmental groups which can assume transnational proportions. A consequence of interdependence is the need for continuous monitoring of the links established amongst governments and within policy sectors to maintain a minimum of coordination and supervision of policy in order to avoid disruptive and costly clashes. This requires substantial bureaucratic contact amongst governments, leading to the build-up of sets of vested interests in the stabilization of particular relationships. Keohane and Nye have identified this kind of sustained bureaucratic contact as the breeding ground for 'transgovernmental coalitions' and suggested that such coalitions are capable of undermining or complicating centralized state control when, and where, an assertion of central authority is seen to conflict with the pursuit of departmental objectives. In a policy-making context the identification of various kinds of transnational actors and interests is not in itself significant unless the relevance and influence of these can be established with respect to policy outcomes. The European Community constitutes an almost purpose-built laboratory for examining the impact of transnational actors and relations on policy processes. The network of economic relationships and scale of bureaucratic interpenetration necessitated and sustained by the EC's policy responsibilities suggest a hotbed of transnational activity. At the non-governmental level opportunities exist for cross-national alliances amongst interest groups . . .

. . . Thus the preference for underlining the multiactor characteristic of international politics is carried through in interdependence-oriented studies of the EC. The Commission is not seen as necessarily possessing the most effective resources in the policy-making process; it has to compete or seek to ally with a variety of groups in an elaborate exercise of coalition-building which may in fact be orchestrated from different parts of the Community depending on the policy issues at stake. The prevailing image projected through a transnational and interdependence focus is one of an increasingly fragmented and less controllable political process. Governments are seen to be losing some of their power to determine outcomes but they are still far from being eclipsed by international institutions.

It is not yet clear how accurate or widespread is the picture presented by interdependence theorists of the EC's policy-making process, particularly in terms of the leverage and durability of transnational interests. This is an area where the policy case-studies in this volume have something to contribute . . .

. . . It is difficult to undertake a proper evaluation of the transnational-interdependence approach as a framework for analysing Community politics, for two reasons. Firstly, the approach still lacks sufficient empirical support to enable a proper assessment to be made of its general propositions. Secondly, there has been a pronounced tendency among some of its adherents to play down the distinctiveness of the Community framework and to question the wisdom of attempts to explain its political features in terms of the specific conditions in Western Europe. Nevertheless, what the interdependence school does provide is a perspective on the EC which focuses directly on its very incompleteness as an integrated regional system, and its incipient tensions as a policy-making forum, stemming from the combination of external pressures and internal divisions. Thus in a conscious back-tracking from the neo-functionalists' 'integrated political community', interdependence analysts have suggested that the modest formula of an 'international regime' may be a more appropriate label for describing the rules and commitments of the EC. Puchala, for example, has suggested that the EC can be adequately explained as a 'system of managed interdependence' since it rests in mutually rewarding economic interdependence and the members adhere to a regime of rules and prescribed practices which is normally observed.

The concept of an international regime may in fact be usefully applied at a sectoral level within the EC to compare and contrast the rule-making environment in different policy areas. There is a great deal of scope here for determining exactly what combination of economic and political factors, together with the structural features present in particular policy areas, is sufficient to induce or inhibit policy collaboration. At the same time there are dangers in too wholehearted an adoption of the 'regime' concept as a means of describing the aggregate level of Community activity. It could be tempting to underestimate the significance and influence of the EC's legal framework and the normally high rate of national compliance with frequently detailed Community legislation, especially when political attention is concentrated on an area like monetary policy where the degree of commitment to common policy-making is variable.

Towards a synthesis

Neo-functionalist, intergovernmentalist, and interdependence images of policy-making in the EC are each imperfect and distorting. If applied in isolation they are most unlikely to account for the variations in the policy-making process and the combination of factors which are responsible for particular policy outcomes (or, equally important, the lack of them) even in the sectors covered in this volume. Indeed, the political scope of the Community's policy-making process is dauntingly wide. At the very least, as we have seen, the politics of resource allocation, bargaining and interest mediation has roots deep inside the domestic political systems of the member states. On the other hand, attempts by national governments to dominate the policy channels linking the states with the Community, and the absence of direct references to, and serious consideration of, explicit political values as yardsticks by which to determine policy (because there is still nowhere in the Community's institutional framework where such values can be effectively articulated) push the political process as a whole closer to the patterns characteristic of international politics.

The search for a suitable political model to fit Community politics may not, perhaps, be the most effective way of solving the political scientist's dilemma over the EC. One of the most noticeable consequences of the shift from the integrationist to the interdependence perspective is the extent to which the policy effectiveness and relevance of the EC – in other words its policy salience to the member states – has assumed a central significance in the literature. This is also echoed in the real world of politics. As the political and the more optimistic of the economic objectives of European integration articulated in the 1950s have waned, or been usurped by a much less favourable economic climate, so member governments have increasingly narrowed their horizons and begun to weigh the EC more critically and openly in terms of its policy effectiveness. This is not meant to imply that the ties between the member states and the Community are of such an instrumental kind that they could be easily snapped as a result of a failure to agree on appropriate policy in one sector or another. But in the absence of a substantive consensus on the long-term political objectives of the EC, the Community, given its structure, functional bias, and clientele, has to look to its policy performance to win support and stature. Whereas early neo-functionalists look to the transfer of authority to a new decision-making centre as the dependent variable of a process of regional integration, it could well be argued that the policy salience of the regional framework would constitute a more appropriate, albeit a more modest, measure of the significance of the EC. From this perspective the institutional pretensions and long-term political aspirations of the Community are less crucial than the Community's ability to convince governments and their electorates that it has, or can mobilize, resources which are relevant to the problems of the member countries.

The virtue of a policy-making approach is that it makes possible an explanation and evaluation of the variables which determine whether, and under what conditions, the Community is seen as a relevant, effective (indeed even a legitimate) body by its membership. The jostling for position and influence, and the articulation of demands and interests, take policy studies into the heart of Community politics. Above, all, they underline the extent to which the EC is a multilevel political system which, overall, lacks a clearly defined and universally accepted hierarchy for policy-making . . .

. . . Neo-functionalism and 'pure' intergovernmentalism have been shown to be too static, narrow, and therefore unconvincing in their institutional focus and their understanding of the political context for Community policy-making. The interdependence approach has rightly concentrated on the conditions which erode governmental authority in regional systems like the EC but is less helpful in specifying the factors which determine the policy responses of governments and other political and economic actors. There is considerable room here for both political and economic analysis of the domestic and structural factors which constrain the abilities of governments to adapt to the requirements of interdependence and the choices it forces upon them. On the political front this implies the need to take into account the complexities of the domestic environment both within and, especially, across the member states.

More fundamentally, the possibility of refining political analysis of the EC depends crucially on a better informed understanding of the relationship between economics and politics which the interdependence approach assumes rather than makes explicit. To the extent that neo-functionalism depended on the narrow and relatively unexplored theory of economic integration based on customs union theory, it lacked the means to explain the persistent lack of progress from negative to positive integration. It has become clear that trade liberalization and policy measures designed to intensify economic links cannot be isolated from more persistently uneven and politically contentious features of national economic systems such as the distribution of wealth and income, and the consequences of government intervention in the economy. A comprehensive political theory of European integration will continue to elude the grasp of the despairing analyst unless some account is taken of the complex interlocking of these factors at the Community and the national levels.

Document 34: S. Bulmer, 'The European Council's first decade: between interdependence and domestic politics', *Journal of Common Market Studies* Vol. 24: 1985, pp. 91–8

Keohane and Nye (*Power and Interdependence*, 1977) have identified 'complex interdependence' as having three main characteristics. Firstly, the many channels of contact between states no longer concern only the traditional diplomacy of the past. Foreign ministers can no longer supervise all foreign relations. Within the EC, this had been the case since the 1950s. For the EC's relations with the outside world, however, this situation became increasingly applicable during the 1960s and 1970s . . .

. . . The response of national governments to the growth of interdependence was two-fold. On the one hand, they wanted to assert their authority over non-governmental actors such as interest groups and currency speculators. On the other hand, they sought better intragovernmental cohesion to ensure that coherent policy signals would be picked up by the outside world. In both contexts, the heads of government saw themselves as well placed to take the appropriate action. Thus, the European Council may be seen as an EC response to the widening networks of foreign relations.

A second characteristic of interdependence – as identified by Keohane and Nye – is the absence of a fixed hierarchy of issues. In their view, in the 1970s, defence and security were no longer the dominant issues of foreign relations. This argument has also been advanced by Hanrieder (1981): 'the bulk of today's global political processes are of a kind that are typical of and approximate domestic political processes, leading to the 'domestication' of international politics . . .' (p. 135).[1] Clearly, this statement is particularly applicable to the EC which has no defence policy component. In comparison to other international regimes, such as the International Monetary Fund (IMF) or the General Agreement on Tariffs and Trade (GATT), the EC deals with a vast range of economic issues. Thus, the EC's potential for tackling the multi-sectoral problems of interdependence was (and still is) significant.

The third characteristic of interdependence is the decline of military force as a means of resolving international disagreements. If military means were the only ones with impact on international relations, the EC would have no influence at all on the external world. (Defence and security issues have increased in importance in the 1980s but they were less significant during the 1970s when the European Council was created.)

A final component of the external challenge to the EC was the decline in the influence of the United States in the international economic order of the 1960s and 1970s. The collapse of the Bretton Woods monetary system, one of the pillars of post-war American foreign economic policy, was symptomatic of this. Indeed, it presented the heads of government with a continuing problem of managing international monetary turbulence.

The combined impact of external and internal stimuli − of interdependence and instability in national economic well-being led heads of government to take measures to re-assert their authority. The creation of the European Council was one such response; the holding of Western economic summits was another. Putnam (1984)[2] summarizes the situation in the following terms:

> For a chief executive whose political fate hung on his electorate's well-being, international economics by the mid-1970s could no longer be considered 'low politics', left to bloodless diplomats, to cunning central bankers, to distant international organizations, or to the haphazards of the market. (p. 44)

The external and national stimuli pointed to the need for action at the EC level. But why should this be through the European Council? The answers to this question are fairly well-trodden territory. The EC was suffering from a number of difficulties in the early 1970s. It lacked direction and dynamism. The tariff reductions had largely been completed; the treaty provisions for such 'negative integration' had been met. However, as regards the establishment of new, co-ordinated, active EC policies ('positive integration'), the prospects were bleak. A cause of this lack of dynamism derived from the Commission's loss of status as the motor of integration. The Commission's supranational authority had suffered at the hands of the increased intergovernmentalism which the 1966 Luxembourg Compromise had ushered in. The Luxembourg Compromise also had a major impact on the Council of Foreign Ministers. This body became so preoccupied with unblocking decision-making and with its increasing work as a 'technical' Council responsible for external affairs that it could no longer cope with its function of policy co-ordination.

Two further problems confronted the EC's institutional structure: the absence of a body for controlling the EC's progress in goal-attainment; and the continuing absence of an EC institution with democratic legitimacy. The creation of the European Council in 1974 aimed to counteract these deficiencies in the institutional structure of the EC. However, this objective was subservient to the primary goal of making the EC an effective actor for coping with the impact of interdependence on the economies (and the politics) of the EC Member States.

The European Council was thus seen as a means of rendering the EC a more effective actor in the changed circumstances of the 1970s. Two further factors encouraged the specific involvement of heads of government in EC policy. The inter-relationship between national and international developments in technical areas outside the remit of foreign ministries necessitated a stronger co-ordination of national governmental policy. This was especially necessary in the dense network of relations between the Member States and the EC. In the absence of such co-ordination, the member governments would be less effective at policy articulation, because of a piecemeal, 'sectorized' approach (Bulmer, 1983, pp. 361-2).[3] The centralization implicit in this increased co-ordination would not be easy to achieve, however, because of pre-existing decentralizing tendencies. These included such factors as the weak constitutional and political authority of some heads of government; various tendencies of 'bureaucratic politics', and the vast amount of knowledge which a head of government would require in order to have technical and political superiority in cabinet discussions. The other force leading to increased involvement on the part of the heads of government was the increased personalization of politics at that level in the media, especially by television.

The European Council: games and bargaining

The European Council must be understood as an exercise in coalition building within the EC in order to increase the member governments' influence on international affairs. In a recent essay on Western economic summitry Robert Putnam put forward some ideas on a political theory of international economic co-operation, drawing on the theory of games and bargaining. As in the collective bargaining application of this theory, international economic co-operation involves four separate processes. The intention here is to apply this theory to the functioning of the European Council.

1 Distributive bargaining ('fixed-sum game')
The participants at the negotiating table (the heads of state or government, the foreign ministers, the president of the EC Commission and one vice-president) are involved in various agenda items where conflict arises. This happens specifically where a fixed sum has to be distributed among the participants . . .

. . . 2 Integrative bargaining ('variable-sum game')
The European Council's agenda is not merely a matter of conflictual items, however, despite the media's infatuation with the 'gladiatorial struggles' of EC negotiations. In the case of integrative bargaining there is normally a 'variable-sum' game in operation. In other words, all the participants at the negotiating table can benefit from adopting a co-operative position . . .

. . . 3 Attitudinal Structuring
Putnam (1984, p. 47)[4] argues that overall relations between the participants – i.e.

trust or hostility, co-operativeness or competitiveness – are of great importance for the functioning of Western economic summitry. This is much more import-ant for the European Council, however. The agenda items of a single session of the European Council are important to the overall pattern of relations amongst the Ten. An abortive session of the European Council, such as that in December 1983 at Athens, can have a negative impact on EC policy-making as a whole. This is an important distinction from the seven-power economic summits which are not attached to a permanent international organization.

This argument must not be pursued too far, however. Whilst good relations between the heads of government are vital for the strengthening of European integration, a single abortive session of the European Council will only have a negative impact in the short term. This is because there are numerous other bodies where the member governments and the European Commission continue their co-operative/conflictual relations, namely in the various incarnations of the Council of Ministers, in COREPER and other such committees. Moreover, beyond the specific framework of the EC, there lie the many multiple bilateral contacts between the Member States. These can also play a part in attitudinal structuring . . .

. . . 4 Intra-organizational behaviour

The three previous component parts in this model of negotiations between the EC heads of government have assumed that the participants have a considerable amount of flexibility in their actions. This is far from the case. Indeed, the difficulty in the 1970s of maintaining the momentum of increasing living standards greatly heightened the domestic electoral political stakes and thereby provided the national stimuli for the intervention of heads of government. This is precisely where Walton and McKersie's[5] approach comes into its own because it recognizes that the participants are not unitary actors; each represents a multitude of differing views on each agenda item.

Putnam (1984, p. 48) argues that the problems of intra-organizational bargaining are much more intractable in the context of international political–economic negotiations.

> First, the costs of failure to reach agreement internationally are likely to be more obscure to most constituents than the costs of rejecting a contract are to most workers, so the 'strike threshold' is probably lower in the case of inter-national political economy. Second, and even more important, in any modern society the diversity of interests that are affected by international economic trends is immensely greater than the diversity of interests within a single union or firm.

This means that the European Council is a 'two-level game', just as Putnam argues that economic summitry is. In this game, the heads of government seek to weld together the forces of the national and international political economy in order to satisfy domestic constituencies (the electorate generally and socio-economic interest groups in particular). One could perhaps argue that the European Council is a three-level game: the EC itself being an intermediate tier. There are two reasons why this idea is rejected here. First, the idea that integration in the Community is an objective which must be pursued regardless of the national costs no longer has validity in an era of international recession. This neo-functionalist argument was always somewhat exaggerated and it played no significant role in the decision to create the European Council. Second, only the Commission representatives are likely to favour such a dynamic as an over-riding priority. They are greatly outnumbered in the European Council, however, thus rendering such a strategy impractical. Hence, their role is to try to convince the other participants that the EC level is appropriate to the welding together of the national and international games. The Commission representatives are playing a kind of national game which is best seen along these lines.

Intra-organizational bargaining explains the behaviour of heads of government in two ways. Their objective is to use the European Council to increase their domestic manoeuvrability . . .

. . . The second way in which intra-organizational bargaining explains the behaviour of the participants is by drawing attention to the way the heads of government try to use the European Council to satisfy some of their domestic constituencies. Political parties, parliamentary bodies, interest groups, sub-national government, institutional interests (e.g. nationalized industries) are all involved in lobbying the governments, at whose apex sit the heads of government. Moreover, it must not be forgotten that the Commission is lobbied by similar forces organized at the European level. All these groups are 'players' in the lower tier (or domestic-level) game of the European Council. Even if they are not lobbying directly, they act as a constraint on the heads of government/Commission president in summit negotiations; they limit the respective participants' freedom of manoeuvre.

The European Council's ability to achieve a bargain at both the national and international games is by no means easy. It should be clear that distributive issues, such as those concerning the EC Budget, are likely to be particularly troublesome. However, this merely underlines the importance of having an agenda containing both distributive and integrative bargaining. Without the latter, the European Council will take on an overwhelmingly conflictual nature which is likely to reduce its effectiveness. Nevertheless, as Putnam (1984, p. 50) notes:

> . . . each national leader has made a substantial investment in building a particular coalition at the domestic (game) board, and he will be loath to try to construct a different coalition simply to sustain an alternative policy mix that might be more acceptable internationally.

Notes

1 'Dissolving international politics: reflections on the nation state', in M. Smith *et al.* (eds) *Perspectives on World Politics* (London, 1981).

2 R. Putnam, 'The western economic summits: a political interpretation', in C. Merlini, *Economic Summits and Western Decision Making* (London, 1984).
3 See Document 31.
4 See note 2.
5 R.E. Walton and R.B. McKersie, *A Behavioral Theory of Labor Negotiations* (New York, 1965).

Document 35: W. Wallace, 'Less than a federation, more than a regime: the Community as a political system', in H. Wallace, W. Wallace and C. Webb (eds), *Policy-making in the European Community* (London, 1983 edn), pp. 403, 406–10, 424–5, 429–34

... What sort of animal is the Community: a federation in the making, an unusually well-developed framework for the management among governments of complex interdependence (or, as international relations scholars might now prefer to title it, a diffuse formal regime), or some sort of hybrid the like of which cannot easily be identified either in the contemporary international system or in earlier times? ...

... *The federal analogy*

... The crucial dividing line between an international regime and a confederation, I suggest, must be drawn between the presence or absence of authority and resources at the centre which effectively limit the behaviour of the member states and which impose obligations on them which are generally accepted. The range of issues over which that authority exists need not be comprehensive, the size of the resources at the federation's disposal need not be large ... The Community incontestably represents a new level of government. Whether it is 'above', 'alongside', or 'outside' the nation-states which are its members is a matter for semantic disputation; the governments and political processes of those nation-states are so closely enmeshed in its operations in particular sectors of policy as to make all of these terms oversimplifications. The conceptual mistake of the most enthusiastic supranationalists was to assume that the Community would succeed in entirely displacing the actions and authority of national governments, and that it would displace their actions and authority over a steadily widening range of issues ...

... The Community has virtually displaced national governments in a very few areas, as the acceptance of the Cassis de Dijon ruling on particular national barriers to internal trade demonstrated. But the characteristic feature of federal government, as in the United States, in Federal Germany, in Canada, is that authority is shared between the different levels of government in a great many sectors. Thus in competition policy, Community and national actions continue side by side, the overlap of authority managed by formal and informal rules and consultations. In agriculture, national governments come together to bargain within the framework of Community policy, with the Commission responsible for managing and monitoring, and with national administrations acting as Community agencies in implementation ...

... It will, however, be equally clear from the case-studies that the extent of the authority exercised by the Community is still actively contested, and the balance between Community and national authorities unsettled . . .

... The student of federal government will not have been surprised at the role which interpretation of the Treaties has played in this process, or at the extent to which the European Court has substituted in its judicial process for the failures and inadequacies of the political sphere. The successful establishment of the principles of direct effect and of the supremacy of Community over national law created an integrated legal system appropriate to a federal structure of government. The distinction between political and legal integration, Joseph Weiler has argued, is that the locus of political authority can remain blurred or contested without the system necessarily breaking down; but legal integration is an 'all or nothing' process. Either Community law is accepted as superior to national law within the competences of the Treaties, or it is not; once it is so accepted, then the Community is 'endowed with sovereign rights, the exercise of which affects Member States and also their citizens' . . .

The almost unquestioning acceptance by the member states of the supremacy of Community law and of the gradual extension of the Court's influence through judicial interpretation is one of the most remarkable developments of European integration. It is remarkable also in that it has continued to develop during the 1970s, while the pace of political and economic integration has slowed: clear evidence of the reluctance of member governments to challenge the framework of the Community system, even while they obstructed its policy-making process and attempted to bend its rules . . .

... The Community is thus more than an international regime, but less than a fully-developed political system. It lacks full legitimacy, in the eyes both of its member governments and of their citizens. Its capacity for handling complex issues and for promoting discussion, bargaining, and decision-taking on them is extremely limited. It remains, for its member governments and for the over-whelming majority of their citizens, a secondary and subordinate framework for political activity. Indeed, the degree to which national publics and national interest groups still see the Community policy process refracted through the spectrum of their national governments, looking to those governments to promote and defend 'their' interests against those of other countries without more than a passive and undefined acceptance of any wider 'European' interest, must raise the question of how far the Community can be described as a political 'community' in the widest sense. The Community may be a new level of government, over a limited range of issues; but it is not yet a fully developed political system . . .

... From one perspective the Community system as operating in 1982 represents the successful transformation of West European politics since the 1950s. In spite of the failures of the first ambitious attempts at European Union between 1950 and 1954, the gradualist approach represented by the three functional Communities had created a sense of common interest and common identity which had spread out from economic and technical issues to the political sphere.

Even the most sensitive issue of defence was again being raised within the Community framework, through the indirect approach of the Genscher–Colombo proposals. But from another perspective, the most striking aspect of the Community has been its failure to adapt the initial compact, enshrined in the Treaties and developed in the early years of the EC's operation. The prevailing response to an increasingly turbulent international economy, to American demands for changes in transatlantic economic relations, to the challenge of Japanese competition, was not to develop new policies but to cling to the status quo. The first enlargement from six members to nine did not lead to any major adjustments of the original compact to accommodate the new members; and the question of a second enlargement on the Community agenda since 1975, remained unresolved seven years later in the face of the difficulties of adapting policies and priorities to accommodate Spain . . .

. . . The growth of informal meetings of ministers outside the 'constraints' of the Community structure was one of the most significant – if seldom remarked – developments of the 1970s; covering not only foreign ministers (and later interior and justice ministers) within political cooperation, but also ministers of employment, trade, industry, education, and finance. It would be too simple to regard this as a return to intergovernmentalism. One great advantage of such meetings, for the participants, was their transgovernmental basis, talking about common interests within their fields without having to subject themselves to the rigours of the coordination of national policy maintained in the preparation of Council Ministers meetings. But their cumulative impact was to reduce the Community system proper, with its formal structure and legal basis in the Treaties, from 'its original function as a point of crystallisation for all integration activity' to become at most 'one element in European unity among many'.

The community in the 1980s

Integration theory aspired to prediction in its presentation of a model for the Community's future development. In the less confident and certain conditions of the 1980s, not only political scientists but also economists have become more modest about the predictive qualities of their models, or the universal validity of their assumptions. The analysis we have offered here throws light on some particular dimensions of the Community policy-making system, and points to a number of crucial variables affecting the system's maintenance and development. It would be rash to claim more.

The Community as an established system of policy-making and management has considerable weight and momentum to maintain it in operation. Conversely, the national governments and administrations which constitute its members carry their own momentum, maintaining existing structures and patterns of policy, resisting the innovating efforts of the Commission and the occasional interventions of ministers and heads of government. The safest prediction is therefore that the system is likely to continue, barring acute internal or external crisis. Yet neither the

Community nor the international environment are unaffected by unanticipated developments. The illusions of the 1960s, when Community leaders spoke of Europe as an island of stability in an increasingly turbulent international economy, were shattered by the events of 1969–73. Two further questions for the reader to consider in reaching his own assessment of the Community's likely future development are, thus: what are the internal and external developments most likely to disrupt the established balance of the Community, and what is the Community's capacity for further adaptation – or even, eventual transformation – under the pressure of such developments?

Some seasoned observers of the Community have seen the existence of crisis (or, as a necessary tactic in approaching major decisions, the creation of crisis) as an unavoidable and essential element in the Community policy process. One may anticipate a number of internal and external pressures which will push an unwieldy system towards adapting and developing policies. The continuation of international recession, with its complement of high unemployment, represents a chronic problem demanding attention, consultation, even adaptation, but not – unless it were to turn down into depression – presenting deadlines or enforcing choices. Relations with the Community's major economic and political partners, the United States, the Socialist states, Japan, the Middle East oil producers, do, however, contain the potential for provoking change. The relationship with the United States has, after all, been a crucial factor in the Community's development since the outset . . .

. . . The experience of the last decade has not provided conclusive evidence of its capacity for further adaptation – or for its transformation into a more highly developed political system. There have been significant developments in the structure and framework of the system, notably in the creation of the political cooperation framework and in the direct election of the European Parliament, even though successive attempts to reform the Commission and to rationalize the procedures of the Council have made little progress. There have been new initiatives in the policy sphere, notably in the establishment of the European Monetary System and in the acceptance of Community action in crisis industries. But these are modest successes in comparison to the number of items on the agenda, and to the importance of such unresolved issues as energy or dollar policy to the member states. It is possible to discern, in the shifting attitudes of the German and British Governments, in the potential exhaustion of the Community budget, in the deteriorating Atlantic relationship and in the increasing uncertainties over Eastern Europe, a combination of pressures capable of forcing decisions on the redistributive and constituent issues which the Community has so far pushed to one side . . .

. . . Without such a transformation, is continued adaptation possible and likely? That depends upon the external and internal pressures which face the Community, and the capacity of its existing institutions to operate more effectively through coordination and consensus rather than through central authority . . .

. . . It depends, too, upon the changing pattern of domestic politics within the member states, the political weight of those who directly benefit from the current acquis and the political representation of those who would benefit from a different balance of policies . . .

. . . Paul-Henri Spaak remarked, in 1952, of the Eden Plan for European defence cooperation, that 'half-way houses were not good enough for Europe'. Thirty years later, the European system for policy-making which has been established is very much of a half-way house – between sovereignty and integration, between the management of interdependence and the acceptance of central decision-making, between an international regime and a federation. It was characteristic of integration theorists to see such a position as inherently unstable, likely to lead either on towards the establishment of a clear central authority or back towards intergovernmental cooperation. But the Community system has been marked in the 1970s by its stability – even resistance to change – under conditions of rapid change in its internal and external environments. Its stability rests upon the perception by member governments and by their interested publics that the existence of such a new level of government, whatever its limitations and internal contradictions, continues to serve a number of established interests and objectives; that its collapse or weakening would create risks and uncertainties which none would wish to take; and that the autonomy of national political systems (and economies) would be threatened by further progress towards integration. Perceptions may change, priorities may alter – in more than one direction. It will be hard for the Community to continue to resist pressures for a reopening of the underlying issues buried in the Treaties, or to ignore changing demands from outside. But the student of the Community would do well to appreciate that 'it is a common criticism of federal government that it is too rigid, too conservative, too difficult to alter; that it is consequently behind the times'. If that is true of more highly developed systems of multilevel government, it is hardly surprising that it should be characteristic of the European Community.

Document 36: F. Scharpf, 'The joint decision trap: lessons from German federalism and European integration', *Public Administration* Vol. 66: 1988, pp. 241–4, 265, 267–71

. . . In short, the history of the European Community has not confirmed the hopes of 'Europeanist' politicians and 'neo-functional' theorists alike, for dynamic processes of deepening and widening functional integration, culminating in the creation of a full-fledged federal state; but the European enterprise has proven much more resilient than the 'realist' school of international relations and the political and scholarly promoters of an Europe des patries would have predicted. Paradoxically, the European Community seems to have become just that 'stable middle ground between the cooperation of existing nations and the breaking in of a new one' which Stanley Hoffmann (1966, p. 910)[1] thought impossible.

It is tempting to ascribe the paradox of European integration – frustration without disintegration and resilience without progress – to historical accidents or to the interventions of certain powerful individuals.

Instead, I will try to argue in this paper that the European malaise may be systematically explained as the consequence of a characteristic pattern of policy choices under certain institutional conditions. This pattern, the 'joint-decision trap', was first identified in the institutional setting of federal-Lander relations in West Germany. It can be shown that similar decision patterns are being produced in the European Community.

Two models of federalism

When Europeanist politicians and social scientists were considering processes of integration that might lead to a United Europe, what they had in mind was a federal system fashioned after the American model. What was created, however, were institutional arrangements corresponding more closely to the tradition of German federalism. The fundamental difference between the two models is often misunderstood in Anglo-American treaties on federalism which tend to dismiss the German variant as little more than a camouflage for de facto centralization. Even William Riker (1964, p. 123),[2] who recognized the unique characteristics of the German model, finds it hard to fit into his conceptual scheme which classifies federal systems according to the relative weights of the spheres of independent authority of central and constituent governments, respectively. What is missed is the possibility that authority might not be allocated, in zero-sum fashion, to either one or the other level of government, but that it might be shared by both. This is what distinguishes the German model from American federalism . . .

In both models, the powers of the central government are limited, and constituent governments (the 'states' or the Lander) continue to exercise original governing powers legitimated by democratic elections. In the American model, however, the central government's authority is derived entirely from direct elections of the President and of both houses of Congress, and the federal government is able to rely upon its own administrative infrastructure at regional and local levels whenever it so chooses. In other words, the exercise of federal government functions is formally independent of the governments of the American states, and those functions that have been taken over by the federal government are effectively nationalized. Whatever sharing of functions is going on, is voluntarily granted, and may be withdrawn again by the federal government, as is illustrated by successive waves of the 'New Federalism'.

In the German model, by contrast, only one house of the federal legislature (the Bundestag) is based upon direct, popular elections, while the other one (the Bundesrat) provides for the representation of Lander governments. In practice, all important federal legislation does require concurrent majorities in the Bundestag and the Bundesrat and does depend, therefore, upon the agreement of Lander governments. In addition, the federal government is severely limited in its executive powers, having to rely upon the administrative services of the Lander for the implementation of most federal legislation . . .

. . . In short: the exercise of most governing functions is shared between the federal government and the Lander governments in West Germany. More specifically, for my present purposes, Lander governments have a significant share in the exercise of many of the important functions of the federal government. It is in this regard that German federalism is most comparable to the European Community.

It is probably fair to say that, even in the heyday of political enthusiasm for European integration in the 1950s, a European union along the lines of the American model of federalism was never a realistic possibility. The Community was created by the action of national governments at a time when their own continuing viability was no longer considered precarious (as it had been immediately after the war). The potentially most powerful motive for federation, common defence, was satisfied by the separate organization of the NATO alliance under US hegemony. What remained was the opportunity pull of economic integration whose attraction was certainly not sufficient to persuade national governments of the need to commit institutional suicide. While recognizing the advantages of a common European market, they also had every interest in retaining as much control as possible over the substance, direction and speed of future steps towards political integration.

The primacy of national control is reflected in the limited authority of the European Parliament, even though it is now elected directly, and in the fact that the European Commission, the executive body of the Community, does not derive its authority from either the Parliament or from direct elections. Instead, the centre of power has remained in the Council of Ministers, representing national governments, and in the periodic summit meetings of the European Council. In both bodies, the principle of unanimous agreement has prevailed in important matters, providing each member government with an effective veto over policy decisions affecting their own vital interests. Furthermore, the European Community is without administrative agencies of its own at the regional and local level; it must rely entirely upon member governments to execute its policies. And, of course, the Community has not been invested with its own powers of taxation, depending primarily upon import levies and upon contributions from the revenues of the member states.

This is not to suggest that there are no significant differences between European institutions and German federalism. In fact, the European Community is much weaker in relation to its member governments than the German federal government is in relation to the Lander. Nevertheless, institutional arrangements are sufficiently similar to suggest that the difficulties of European integration might be illuminated by reference to some of the problems of German federalism which have been studied more systematically. The parallelism between European and German institutions appears to be particularly close in those areas of joint policy making which were added rather late (in 1969) to the existing structure of the German federal constitution. In these areas, which have been the subject of empirical and theoretical studies under the label of 'Politikverflechtung' federal policy making is operating under the same requirement of unanimous consent which prevails at the European level. It is here that the 'joint-decision trap' was first identified . . .

. . . To summarize a perhaps overly involved line of argument, unanimity is a decision rule which can claim welfare theoretic optimality, most plausibly, for single-shot decisions. In ongoing joint-decision systems, from which exit is precluded or very costly, non-agreement would imply the self-defeating continuation of past policies in the face of a changing policy environment. Thus, pressures to reach agreement will be great. The substance of agreement will be affected, however, by the prevailing style of decision-making. In its ability to achieve effective responses to a changing policy environment, the bargaining style is clearly inferior to the 'problem-solving' style. But the preconditions of 'problem-solving' – the orientation towards common goals, values and norms – are difficult to create, and they are easily eroded in cases of ideological conflict, mutual distrust or disagreement over the fairness of distribution rules. Thus, reversion to a 'bargaining' style of decision-making was characteristic of German federalism during the 1970s, and it seems to have been characteristic of the European Community ever since the great confrontations of the mid-1960s. The price to be paid is not simply a prevalence of distributive conflicts complicating all substantive decisions, but a systematic tendency towards sub-optimal substantive solutions. In short, it is the combination of the unanimity rule and a bargaining style which explains the pathologies of public policy associated with joint decisions in Germany and in Europe.

Joint decisions and the dynamics of European integration

At this point, we can return to the concerns raised in the introduction. Why is it that real developments since the mid-1960s – the frustration without disintegration and resilience without progress – have disappointed hopes for a dynamic deepening and widening of European integration and invalidated predictions of an inevitable return to the intergovernmental relations of sovereign nation states? An explanation has been derived from the decision logic inherent in the particular institutional arrangements of the European community . . .

. . . Given this premise, the two most powerful institutional conditions affecting the process of European integration are, first, the fact that national governments are making European decisions and, second, the fact that these decisions have to be unanimous. The 'joint-decision trap' set up by these two conditions is responsible for the pathologies of substantive public policy described and analyzed above.

But joint-decision systems are a 'trap' in yet another, and more important sense. They are able to block their own further institutional evolution. This possibility has been overlooked by functionalist and neo-functionalist writers . . .

. . . The situation is even more one-sided in the European Community. In the absence of a European government with a popular political base of its own, all possibilities of institutional transformation are entirely determined by the self-interests of national governments. And even those among them which most vigorously support activist and expansionary European policies are likely to hedge their bets when it comes to relinquishing their veto powers. Conversely, the 'reluctant Europeans' among member governments have been much more willing to accept disagreeable compromises on substantive policy than to weaken their own institutional control over the substance of future decisions. As a consequence, the jurisdiction of the Community has expanded, and Community law has achieved the effectiveness of the legal order of a federal state – but the price has been 'an ever closer national control exercised in the decision processes' (Weiler 1982, pp. 42–7).[3] . . .

. . . If that is so, two of the crucial spill-over mechanisms, which neo-functionalist theory expected to create external political pressures for more integration, seem to be blocked or seriously weakened. First, the reorientation of economic, social and political interests toward the European level remains incomplete. As long as European decisions continue to be made by national governments, the interests affected by them will be mediated by national governments, as well. Of course, interest groups will also operate at the European level, but ultimately it is still national governments which they will have to persuade. As a consequence, nationally specific definitions of group interests, and of party-political ideologies, will be maintained and reinforced, rather than amalgamated into European interest associations and European political parties. In that regard, the tendencies toward the segregation of interests and ideologies inherent in federal, as compared to unitary, states are even more pronounced among the member states of the Community. By the same token, there is less reason to expect a transfer of the demands, expectations and loyalties of political elites from the national to the European level.

Second, there is much less reason to expect that 'goal frustration' should lead to politicization and, ultimately, to a redefinition of goals and the 'transcendence' to a higher level of political integration. If the iron grip of national governments cannot be broken, the decision logic of European institutions will continue to reproduce the substantive pathologies discussed above. Beyond a certain point, surely, political frustration and exasperation over the inefficiency and inflexibility of European policy making, and over its structural inability to respond to crises creatively, may not lead to renewed demands for a more perfect union but, rather, to cynicism and indifference or to a renewed search for national remedies, however imperfect and limited, for the problems which the Community seems to handle so poorly. As was the case with joint policies in West Germany, the dynamic movement toward greater European integration may have been retarded and, perhaps, reversed, not by the ideological strength of nationalism or by the obstructions of a Charles de Gaulle or a Margaret Thatcher, but by the pathological decision logic inherent in its basic institutional arrangements. But why is it, then, that the Community didn't disintegrate long ago? As in the case of

German federalism, an adequate explanation of its continuing resilience needs to consider two levels of interest, functional and institutional. At the functional level, it is clear that at least some of the benefits predicted by the economic theories of integration have in fact been realized. This tends to be more true for the benefits of 'market integration' than of 'policy integration' or of 'negative', rather than 'positive' integration. But as it is uncertain, even in the industrial sector, whether the common market could be maintained in the absence of a substantial commitment to common (and compensatory) policy measures in such areas as the Social Fund, the Regional Fund and Industrial Policy, one probably could not have the one without the other. In other words, to the extent that joint policies are addressing, however inadequately, real problems which could not be handled at the level of member governments, these problems would simply reassert themselves if the joint-policy system were to be dismantled . . .

. . . At the institutional level, the Community is unequivocally supported by the self-interest of the vertical alliances of policy specialists – interest associations, national ministries and parliamentary committees, and the large contingents of specialized lobbyists, bureaucrats and politicians operating at the European level. They all profit from the availability of additional resources, and of additional points of access to political decision processes, providing additional opportunities for playing the game of influence and obstruction which is their raison d'être. Of course, they also must cope with the political frustration, among their clienteles or electorates, over the impact of sub-optimal or even counter-productive European policies. But as in German federalism, the political effect of voter frustration is largely neutralized by the very diffusion of responsibility and accountability which is characteristic of joint-decision systems.

Similar cost–benefit calculations tend to stabilize the Community from the perspective of national policy generalists – heads of government, finance ministers and parliamentary budget committees – if their countries are among the net beneficiaries of the Community budget. Net contributors, on the other hand, find themselves locked into an ongoing decision system whose direction they could only hope to change significantly by either assuming the burdens and costs of hegemonic leadership or by threatening to leave the Community altogether. As it is, the only pretender to hegemonic status, West Germany, is too weak or too egoistical to assume the burdens of leadership, while confrontation strategies are unlikely to work for countries whose interest in, and attachment to, the Community is known to be very great. Thus, the Community is likely to remain secure as long as care is taken to concentrate net contributions to the Community budget upon those countries which would have most to lose economically and politically by its dissolution and, in particular, by the disintegration of the common market.

By way of summary, it is now possible to define the 'joint-decision trap' more precisely. It is an institutional arrangement whose policy outcomes have an inherent (non-accidental) tendency to be sub-optimal – certainly when compared to the policy potential of unitary governments of similar size and resources.

Nevertheless, the arrangement represents a 'local optimum' in the cost–benefit calculations of all participants that might have the power to change it. If that is so, there is no 'gradualist' way in which joint-decision systems might transform themselves into an institutional arrangement of greater policy potential. In order to be effective, institutional change would have to be large-scale, implying the acceptance of short term losses for many, or all, participants. That is unlikely, but not impossible. And, of course, the system might be jolted out of its present equilibrium by external intervention or by a dramatic deterioration of its performance which would undermine even its local optimality for crucial participants. Thus, I have not described a deterministic world, even though the logic of the 'joint-decision trap' may provide as close an approximation to structural determinism as one is likely to encounter in the social sciences.

Notes

1 S. Hoffmann, 'Obstinate or obsolete? The fate of the nation-state and the case of western Europe', *Daedelus* Vol. 95, 1966.
2 W. Riker, *Federalism: Origin, Operation, Maintenance* (Boston, 1964).
3 J. Weiler, 'Community member states and European integration. Is the law relevant?' *Journal of Common Market Studies* Vol. 21: 1982, pp. 42–7.

Document 37: M. Burgess, *Federalism and European Union* (London, 1989), pp. 1–8

The idea behind this book[1] arose from a growing belief that the study of federalism in the specific context of European integration has been the victim of a strange paradox in scholarly thought among social scientists in the Western world. While there has been no shortage of intellectual theorising and pretheorising about the conditions deemed necessary for effecting a closer, more binding, union among the states and peoples of Western Europe, no attempt has been made in recent times to demonstrate both how and to what extent federal ideas, influences and strategies have been an ever-present, indeed integral, part of the European Community's continuous political and constitutional development. At the very least this book is intended to fill this gap. In a very general sense it seeks to restore the importance of federalism to the study of the European Community's past, present and future. Almost without exception, most of the recent mainstream political science literature on the European Community, published in English, depicts it as little more than an intergovernmental grouping of independent states. There is no real sense of an evolving organic whole. The whole, when it is acknowledged, is deemed no greater than the sum of its aggregate parts. The Community's central institutions, particularly those, like the Commission, the Parliament and the Court of Justice, which have supranational, federal propensities, are tolerated but rarely applauded. Recognition of their important potential for the future of the European Community is particularly grudging . . .

. . . The European idea to this extent is impoverished. A wholly intergovernmental perspective of the European Community while firmly grounded in the
constituent state reality, both obscures and devalues an important rival conception
of Europe. It is this federal European conception – which for many extends
beyond what is Western Europe – that has suffered from an understandable, if
undue, obsession with what governments say and do. This overriding concern
with inter-governmental relations arises in particular out of the academic focus
upon policy-making in the European Community. Since it is member state
governments and the associated paraphernalia of elite hierarchies which dominate
most of the policy sectors of the Community, political scientists using this
approach to Community affairs repose in the safe knowledge that their research
is empirically verifiable. But a policy-making approach has many limitations. It
is singularly unhelpful when dealing with questions about the future of the
European Community. It is myopic about institutional reform and it may actually
be detrimental to the vision and work of those who strive to widen the range of
practical options for reform even within an accepted intergovernmental framework. Finally it is uncomfortable with theoretical issues. As Carole Webb once
remarked, a policy-making approach is a coward's way out of a theoretical
dilemma.

But for our purposes in this book the overloaded concept of intergovernmentalism has a particularly damaging and distorting impact upon the relevance
of federalism to the European Community. Not only does it by implication
overlook federalism but it also serves ipso facto both to misrepresent and devalue
it. Federal ideas, influence and strategies appear only as an intermittent not a
continuous pressure in the Community's life. They are relegated to the sidelines
as a laudable but unrealistic force and the widespread impression conveyed is one
of minuscule support for an abstract utopian goal. Here the past is conveniently
forgotten and the eye is deflected from what are deemed marginal influences and
activities compared to the gladiatorial combat of intergovernmental rivalries and
conflicts. Federal ideas, by contrast, fade into insignificance.

The main purpose of this book is to challenge the prevailing conventional
wisdom of intergovernmentalism by reasserting and reinstating the relevance of
federalism in the politics of the European Community. I do not wish to imply
that federalism has in some sinister, covert sense replaced intergovernmentalism
as the dominant guiding concept of the Community's political future. Nor do I
impute to it some notion of moral superiority over its conceptual competitors.
My intention is to demonstrate that there has been a fundamental continuity of
federal ideas, influence and strategies in the political development of the
Community during the years between 1972 and 1987. Moreover, this continuity
of federalism has been the main impulse behind the attempt to flesh out the meaning of European Union since the early 1970s. It has been neither an intermittent
nor a fragmentary impulse but, on the contrary, a persistent and continuous
struggle to achieve qualitative and quantitative change in the relations both
between states and among the peoples of Europe.

One of the underlying assumptions of this study is that ideas are important in politics. They not only inspire individuals and groups to act – to do something about what they believe in – but they also provide a constant source of discussion and debate about the goals of political activity and the strategies required to achieve them . . .

. . . The federal idea is one of these and it constitutes a perfectly legitimate part of that mixed tradition. It also acts as a solid antidote to that complacent instrumentalism so characteristic of intergovernmentalism and commonly revered as pragmatism. The word 'pragmatic' figures prominently in the language of inter-governmentalism largely as an apologia of pedestrian progress but it often carries with it the silent disapproval of forward, progressive political strategies designed to accelerate the pace towards 'an ever closer union'. The boundary between being pragmatic and being chimerical is thus tightly drawn . . .

. . . What, then, do we mean by federalist influences in the European Community? Where is the evidence for this and how is it brought to bear upon political integration? The concept of political influence is difficult to grasp but I would suggest that we are entering the uncertain world of political communication where successful influence means shaping and changing people's perceptions of what exists and what can happen. This indicates a capacity to affect human behaviour. The institutional framework and the policy-making processes of the European Community both furnish appropriate sites for federalist influences to act upon national and supranational elites, as well as mass publics, in a significant way. By regular contact and political intercourse federalist influences can be spread widely and often imperceptibly across a network of Community activities so that the policy and decision making environments become more receptive to alternative options and strategies . . .

. . . Federalist influences flow through several channels both inside and outside the formal institutional and policy frameworks of the European Community. Individuals, groups and professional organisations exert such influence in many ways . . .

. . . The European Parliament, especially after the first direct elections in 1979, also played a leading role in this debate and has long been an important repository of distinct federalist influences . . .

. . . And we cannot of course overlook the role of political and administrative elites working in the Commission in Brussels. Many Eurocrats will have been socialised into federalist thinking if only because of the institutional dilemmas confronting a supranational body operating within a predominantly intergovern-mental framework. These are not ideological preconceptions but rather rational conclusions. Federal practice would seek to overcome the Commission's perceived impotence by reinstating it at the centre of Community affairs. Outside of the formal Community framework there also exists a myriad of European groups and organisations which are either openly federalist in their aims or tacit federalist sympathisers . . .

. . . We must not forget, too, that particular nation state leaders and elites have also contributed to forward movement in the Community at different periods in their history. This is not to imply that such elites and individuals have necessarily been convinced federalist but the impact of their actions has often coincided with movement in a federal direction. Most interested observers of Community affairs would doubtless point to the Benelux countries which have often been associated with progressive, and sometimes bold, initiatives. Some might interpret the Paris–Bonn axis with concrete policy achievements facilitating further incremental steps towards a more binding European union . . .

. . . For a variety of intellectual, historical and political reasons Italy played a particularly prominent role in recent efforts to translate European Union into a practical form . . .

. . . This study suggests that there is a basic continuity of federal ideas in the European Community's political development and it is important to recognise this if we are to understand the consistency of purpose which characterised attempts to give the idea of European Union both meaning and content during 1972–1987. The context of federal ideas and influences provided a platform for the testing of rival political strategies to flesh out European Union. It would be erroneous to claim that the period surveyed here witnessed a unanimous agreement among federalists as to the correct political strategy to adopt towards European Union. However, there was a convergence of opinion of sorts during the 1980s sufficient to mobilise a significant movement in support of institutional reform. This centred around Spinelli and the European Parliament, but it was a quite different political strategy from that which Tindemans was forced to shoulder in the mid-1970s. The federalist inspiration was the same but the strategy was different.

What, then, should we say about political strategy? If influence is a difficult concept to grasp and to operationalise, strategy is much more tangible although it generates more controversy. Agreement about the goal of a federal Europe does not automatically stretch to consensus about the strategy required to achieve it. And federalists have furnished a rich diverse literature about approaches to this goal which is as prolific as the numerous diversities which they themselves cherish. In this study, however, we shall reduce the complexities of this literature about federalist strategy by dividing it broadly into two categories: those strategies which focus primarily upon policy changes and policy innovations and those strategies which concentrate upon institutional reform. These rival approaches are not necessarily mutually exclusive. Indeed the political and constitutional development of the European Community indicates their lively coexistence . . .

. . . These two simplified categories of political strategy – policies and institutions – also harbour additional implications for federalist practice. Some policy strategies may be legitimised in the simple sense that they are merely fulfilling commitments already adumbrated in the Treaty of Rome while others are actually breaking fresh ground as new policies absent in the original treaty. Similarly institutional reform meant support for direct elections to the European Parliament, fulfilling Article 138 of the Rome Treaty, but it could also mean more far-reaching proposals necessitating either treaty amendments or a new treaty. These strategies are sometimes juxtaposed as the big leap forward versus incremental change. They have been the source of heated disputes among federalists and considerable misunderstanding among even informed observers of European Community politics. They also have major theoretical implications for the study of federalism.

Note

1 Refers to the publication in which this document originally appeared.

Document 38: J. Pinder, 'European Community and nation-state: a case for a neo-federalism?', *International Affairs* Vol. 62: 1986, pp. 50–4

Neo-federalism?

Thinking other than that of the federalists has had relevance to the Community experience. But the 'realist' and the 'regime' and 'system' schools have been too reductionist about the possibilities of movement in the direction of federal institutions with substantial competences. The neo-functionalists took, on the contrary, too facile a view of such possibilities, without clarity about the conditions under which integrative steps would be possible and without appreciating the strength of the nation-state. Federalists are less inclined to err in either of these directions. But, although they have acted in support of the Community's step-by-step development, they have not thought deeply enough about 'the intermediary stage between normal interstate relations and normal intrastate relations' or about the concept of constitution-building as not just a single act, but also 'an evolution-ary development'. If it is to help us assess the prospects for development of the Community, federalist theory needs to refer both to a federalizing process and to a federal end which implies substantial transfers of sovereignty. Its scope needs to incorporate steps in the development of European institutions and in their assumption of functions and competences; the resistance of member states to this process and the pressures that may induce them to accept it; and the perspective of possible 'qualitative breaks' involving a 'constitutional redistribution of powers'. Existing theories do not seem to deal adequately with these things.

The neo-functionalists appeared strangely uninterested in evaluating how far any particular functions needed to be performed by supranational institutions. The assumption that such institutions would come to assume all important functions begged the critical question of the circumstances in which states would establish institutions with federal characteristics, or transfer competences to them, as they did when they launched the ECSC, the Treaties of Rome and, to some extent, the EMS, and as they will do if they decide on significant amendments to the

Treaties following the European Parliament's Draft Treaty initiative. Nor did the neo-functionalists seem much concerned about the form of democratic control by European institutions that can be seen as a corollary of the most far-reaching transfers of competence. The classic federalists were clearer about this, proposing democratic federal institutions to accompany the transfer of the more basic competences such as money, taxation or armed forces. But because they did not consider any process of establishing federations other than through a single act transferring to them coercive and security powers, their thinking was not directly applicable to the transfer of less fundamental competences. Thus the political problem of transferring particular competences or instruments from the member states to the Community has been neglected by the various schools of thought, and much the same can be said of the political problem of securing the Community's institutional development, from the original addition of the Parliament, Court and Council to the High Authority mentioned in the Schuman declaration, through the establishment of the European Council, the European Parliament's budgetary powers and the direct elections, to the point where the Draft Treaty had only to propose majority voting and legislative co-decision to convert the Community institutions into a federal form. A useful contribution to evaluating the prospects for the main elements in European Union proposals would be greater understanding of the circumstances which have enabled such increments of federal institutions or competences to be decided in the Community up to now.

One circumstance which stood in the way of such increments in the 1960s was, as we have seen, de Gaulle's leadership of France. He was doubtless unusual in the consistency with which his 'supreme value' remained the nation-state . . .

. . . The background conditions which favour steps towards community or integration have been fairly extensively studied. Prominent among them are the degree of similarity or difference in certain attributes among members of the group. Economic and political systems and culture are usually regarded as sufficiently similar among West European countries to facilitate a substantial degree of integration. But the divergence in economic performance grew in the 1970s to be seen as an obstacle . . .

. . . The intensity of interdependence and communication among the member countries is also held to condition the prospects for integration. There has, however, been surprisingly little effort to link measures of economic interdependence with constraints on national policies and with readiness for policy integration, in view of their potential significance for European integration . . .

. . . The conclusion of a study of various transnational links between the (then) six member countries in the late 1960s was that 'if . . . India is seen as a nation, then Europe may well be described as an emergent nation'. Some writers have tried to encapsulate the conditions that make federal institutions feasible in the formula that there must first be a single 'people' or 'nation'. Yet this remains too vague an assertion unless the concept of a 'people' or 'nation' is defined and related to the characteristics of the population of the countries in question. It has indeed been observed that, in the field of theory, 'no positive definition of the nation exists', and that national behaviour is linked with 'the situation of power, and probably depends on it'. Is the assertion that a European nation is a pre-condition of a 'fully democratic European Union' perhaps either tautological (a European nation being defined as a population which can uphold a European federal system), or merely another way of saying that we need to study the similarities, links, differences and divergences between member states in order to judge how far they can move towards federation?

However favourable the conditions may be for steps towards federal institutions and competences, such steps are not likely to be taken without adequate political leadership. The neo-functionalists were too little concerned about the political efforts required to secure such steps; and they were justifiably criticized for concentrating on the Commission as the political motor for integration. The European Parliament has the electoral base that the Commission lacks; but the political leadership which the Parliament has shown with its Draft Treaty could hardly secure major reforms, as distinct from public support for such reforms, without corresponding leadership from among the member states. The roles of Monnet and of Schuman, Adenauer and de Gasperi in relation to the ECSC have been noted above[1] . . .

. . . The argument of this article suggests that the British, in order to play a more constructive and successful role in future discussions and negotiations on European Union, will need to take more seriously the possibility of developing the Community's institutions, as well as its competences, thus continuing a process which, thanks mainly to the initiatives of the founder members, is already fairly far advanced in the form of the Community as it exists today. The tendency to identify federalism with a great leap to a federation with military and coercive power inhibits practical thought about the prospects for taking further steps in a federal direction, whether in the form of a system of majority voting to complete the internal market, developing the EMS in the direction of monetary union, an increase in the powers of the European Parliament, or a package of such reforms that could deserve to be called European Union. Such thought would be helped by a systematic study of the specific steps that could be taken and of the conditions that favour or impede them. If the term 'neo-federalism' would help the British to come to terms with the process of incremental federalism, the neologism would be a small price to pay for a major advance in our capacity to play our proper part in contemporary European and international politics.

Note

1 Refers to the article from which this document has been extracted.

Document 39: D. Muttimer, '1992 and the political integration of Europe: neofunctionalism reconsidered', *Journal of European Integration* Vol. 13: 1989, pp. 78–82, 99–101

... The neofunctionalist approach would seem to provide the most useful theoretical context for discussing integration in 1992 for several, interrelated, reasons. The most important is the focus on the process of economic integration and its relationship to an ill-defined political end-product. This allows us to derive the likely results of the process of economic integration, without being burdened with an overriding teleology. Neofunctionalists have, in fact, explicitly argued that this is a necessary element of their project. Haas has written: 'The verbally defined single terminal conditions with which we worked in the past – political community, security community, political union, federal union – are inadequate because they foreclose real life possibilities.'[1] Thus the relationship between economic and political integration differentiates neofunctionalism from federalism in useful ways. Stated simply the advantage of neofunctionalism, for the purposes of this discussion, is that the end products that federalism and other theories have proposed seem consistent with neofunctionalist theorizing concerning the integrative process.

While the neofunctionalist end-product is ill-defined, it is clearly intended to be institutional. As Jane Sweeny has written, for the neofunctionalist 'institutions are an important outcome of the integration process, that is, they are a measure of the success of the integration project'.[2] It is on the question of the form these institutions will take that neofunctionalism makes no firm commitment. This being said, however, neofunctionalism would seem to priviledge federalist institutions as the solution to the integration problem, but only because federation has tended to be the manner in which independent units have historically been joined. A neofunctionalist integration can lead to integrated structures short of a supranational state, or to a state of a non-federal character, but it is not theoretically limited to any particular level or kind of political integration.

While neofunctionalism would seem to be the best theoretical choice, the portrayal of neofunctionalism provides, as yet, an insufficient guide for a discussion of 1992. There are two elements of the neofunctionalist approach to international integration which are central to this discussion. The most famous, and the most important, is 'spillover' ...

... Spillover assumes that the various elements of the political economy of states and regions are interconnected in such a way that problems in one area will raise problems or require solutions in another. In this way, the expectation is that when certain economic functions are placed in the hands of central bodies, a demand for increased power at the centre will result from the need to look beyond the originally integrated area for solutions. As Harrison noted, these solutions do not require the complete agreement of states, but rather a general convergence of similar interests around the goals of the original common undertaking.[3] In the case of Project 1992, this weakened requirement for common action is enhanced by the adoption of qualified majority voting on the European Council, in place of the former requirement for unanimity, in order to implement measures associated with the completion of the internal market. This suggests that decisions with spillover implications may be reached, even in the face of fairly substantial division among states.

It is assumed that, at the outset, such spillover will occur only among different functional tasks, but that, as the centre grows, more politically salient areas will begin to be affected . . .

. . . This is the necessary result of the neofunctionalist move to reconnect the economic and the political. If economic integration is not completely separable from political, then, as the areas of economic integration expand, points of over-lap with the political will be reached. Economic integration, it is assumed, will gradually accelerate, spilling over further and further into the political sphere, until a 'take-off' point is reached. After the take-off point, the central institutions will spill over at a dramatically increased rate, and community building will begin in earnest.

An important shift in neofunctionalist thinking has eliminated much of the determinism that was originally included in this formulation of spillover, primarily as a result of the problems the EEC confronted in the late 1960s. In this new view, the probability of spillover increases as the salience of the issue involved increases to the community at large. In addition, to the degree that automaticity is eliminated from the spillover logic, it allows for the inclusion of the all-important element of political will. Regardless of the pressures for increased centralization within the community, the position of the member states is still sufficiently strong that substantial transfers of authority will depend upon the will of the governments involved.

Such a non-deterministic spillover conception can be useful in considering the potential political consequences of Project 1992. It suggests that in examining the programme to complete the internal market, what is of greatest concern is those elements which explicitly or implicitly encroach upon areas of high political salience, and which tend to create demands on the centre for problem resolution. Of at least equal importance is the existence of the requisite political will to achieve increased integration in face of these pressures. This still leaves, however, the question of what spillover means when applied to the more overtly political elements of integration. When applied to functional organizations, the result is not difficult to conceive – the central institutions gain greater decision-making competence. However, political institutions, particularly those at the heart of a political community, require more than simply an increase in the scope of their decision-making power.

It is here that the second key element of neofunctionalism becomes relevant. The neofunctionalists realize that having an increasingly powerful set of central institutions does not necessarily make for a political community. The missing essen-tial ingredient is the political identification of the peoples of that community. Put in another way, this means that the central institutions must be granted political legitimacy by the community's population before a true political community can emerge. The assumption of the neofunctionalists is that this identification will also spill over. As the central institutions increase their authority in areas salient to the community's population, the people will increasingly turn to these institutions for satisfaction. At this point, functional spillover becomes political spillover.

Before the neofunctionalist insights – spillover leading to increasing institution-alization and to shifting political identification – can be applied to the development of the European market, there are several possible objections that must be addressed. First, despite the expressed purpose of neofunctionalism to be a non-normative theory, there clearly is a normative bias. Neofunctionalists not only see functional spillover as the manner in which integration is proceeding, but as the best way to reach a preferred end – an integrated international political community – in the case of Europe, a European Union. This bias must be recognized in any attempt to use neofunctional theory to examine European integration, but there are two considerations which tend to alleviate the problems such a bias raises. The first is that the purpose of this paper is to examine the political integrative effects of the 1992 project. Were it simply attempting to consider the likely effects of the move to complete the internal market in some less focused way, the normative push to political union would inevitably bias the results. Secondly, the neo-functionalist argument and goal are explicitly part of the EEC project. There is a commitment (however weak and extended) to eventual European Union. Thus the bias built into the theory has been explicitly adopted by the Community.

The second problem, as anyone familiar with the integration literature will realize, is that the above exposition of the neofunctionalist thesis has required a degree of logical extension of the original positions. The neofunctionalist thesis was developed and articulated for the early stages of an integration process; that is, it is concerned with a very low level of integration which establishes a central power that can later become a political community. In at least one definition of the logic of the process, for example, there is an injunction against the inclusion of vital state interests in the integrative project. This is because the end point is perceived to be the establishment of an embryonic political community, the first stage of political community. 1992 is a different phenomenon. The central political institutions are in place, and the issues concerned are vital to the state, and so the rigorous application of neofunctionalism is inappropriate.

Despite this clear difference from the stage for which neofunctionalism was originally proposed, the underlying logic of the approach still provides useful insights. Project 1992 can thus be examined with these insights, though treated as informative and illustrative suggestions as to the possible course of European politics, rather than as hypotheses grounded in a potentially general law . . .

Conclusion

While a discussion such as this is, of course, both tentative and incomplete, there are conclusions which can be drawn. As a preface, however, it should be noted that any such conclusions are contingent upon the reasonably smooth unfolding of Project 1992, which is by no means a certainty. The political difficulties surrounding the Project's implementation have generally been excluded from this paper, for they unnecessarily complicate its argument . . .

. . . This being said, it is possible to suggest some conclusions which may be drawn from this discussion. First of all, it seems clear that Project 1992 does raise profound implications for the political future of Europe. A number of the proposed measures touch directly on the sovereignty of the member states, and seem destined to create tensions between the national prerogatives of states and the demands of a single European market. Clearly the most important of these are the measures that affect the foundations of the state's economic policies: control of revenue and of currency. The state's ability to control both of these is likely to be reduced in the aftermath of 1992. Indirect taxation seems certain to be increasingly centralized in order to facilitate a truly open single market, and the completion of that market, even its partial completion, will increase the already great pressures for monetary union

It is this latter possibility that holds out the greatest promise for political union. The creation of a central bank and common currency would put intense pressure on states to exercise political control over European monetary policy, which could only be achieved from the centre . . .

. . . While these are the most politically potent of the measures of Project 1992, fiscal and monetary changes are by no means the only ones with implications for continued national sovereignty. In each of the three areas of the White Paper, a number of the measures can be seen to have important political consequences. This suggests that 1992 is a useful test case of the validity of the neofunctionalist insights into the links between economic and political integration. The blatantly political implications of so many of the economic measures being taken make them perfect candidates for spillover. If, for example, the removal of internal borders with the consequent need for a common immigration policy is effected but does not result in substantial centralization of decision making, then it is reasonable to conclude that there are problems with the spillover hypothesis.

While neofunctionalism will prove a useful tool for assessing the political effects of the market completion, it is not sufficient for understanding the progress of political integration. To begin with, the possibility of a European Congress suggests that neofunctionalism should be amended to allow for the extension, as well as the transfer, of political legitimacy. In addition, the institutions of the EC, particularly the Commission and the European Parliament, are actively promoting enhanced political integration. Thus, there is an institutional framework already in place into which political authority can spill, and to which political identification can shift. This paper has suggested that the most likely result of this process is a political authority empowered not so much by a transfer of legitimacy, but by an extension of the legitimacy of the member states. However, to examine the process of constitution building which is taking place in tandem with the economic market completion, neofunctionalism, even in amended form, is not sufficient.

1992 promises to be a profoundly important date. Not only will a new economic entity emerge, with the potential to alter the balance within the international political economy, but a new political entity may well follow it . . .

. . . In the 1950s Ernst Haas promised that international integration would lead beyond the nation state, but subsequently he argued that the lessons of the 1970s were that the nation state was not yet ready to be surpassed. It is at least possible that 1992 will act the midwife to the birth of the world's first truly trans-national political organization.

Notes

1 E.B. Haas, 'The study of regional integration: reflections on the joy and anguish of pre-theorizing', *International Organization* Vol. 24: (1970), p. 631.
2 J. Sweeney, *The First European Elections: Neofunctionalism and the European Parliament* (Boulder, Col., 1984), p. 25.
3 R.J. Harrison, *Europe in Question* (London, 1974), pp. 76–7.

Document 40: R.O. Keohane and S. Hoffmann, 'Conclusions: Community politics and institutional change', in W. Wallace (ed.), *The Dynamics of European Integration* (London, 1990), pp. 277–81, 285, 287–9, 293–6

. . . We accept the assumption of this project that the politics of European integration can only be understood within the context of these changing economic and social dynamics. The Community is part of a larger complex of activities, including those, such as Western European Union, which are outside the Community structure . . .

. . . We seek first to characterize observed patterns of decision-making. The European Community, we argue, is an experiment in pooling sovereignty, not in transferring it from states to supranational institutions. Nevertheless, the concept of 'supranationality' that Ernst Haas developed 20 years ago remains relevant, although it has so often been stereotyped, misinterpreted or ignored. The European Community can best be viewed as a set of complex overlapping networks, in which a supranational style of decision-making characterized by compromises upgrading common interests, can under favourable conditions lead to the pooling of sovereignty.

Next, we move from statics to dynamics, seeking to provide some clues to the dramatic and unexpected extension of Community policies and strengthening of Community institutions that has occurred in the 1980s. In particular, we investigate whether 'spillover' has taken place as posited by neofunctionalist theory. We contend that the expansion of Community tasks depends ultimately on the bargains between major governments; but that after such a bargain has been made, Community tasks can be further expanded as a result of linkages among sectors, as envisaged in the theory. However, such an expansion is by no means automatic; there are limits on spillover. More unexpectedly, a sort of institutional spillover has occurred: enlargement of the Community to 12 members set in motion a process that strengthened Community decision-making institutions.

Finally, in our conclusion we speculate about the future of the Community in the light of changes taking place in world politics, particularly in relations between West and East Germany, and between Western and Eastern Europe in general. The crucial question that we briefly address, but do not pretend to resolve, is that of the degree to which the European Community can meet the aspirations of West Germany, its strongest member, while making those aspirations acceptable to its neighbours, both within the Community and to the east. Europe proved that it could create institutions to promote cooperation, even without a hegemon in its midst; now it must test whether this system of cooperation can adapt effectively to rapid changes in world politics, especially within Europe itself . . .

. . . Unlike international organizations, the European Community as a whole has gained some share of states' sovereignty: the Member States no longer have supremacy over all other authorities within their traditional territory, nor are they independent of outside authorities. Its institutions have some of the authority that we associate with institutions of sovereign governments: on certain issues individual states can no longer veto proposals before the Council; members of the Commission are independent figures rather than instructed agents. Especially when it is led by a statesman with a vision and a method, such as Jacques Delors, the Commission is an indispensable fount of proposals and prodding; under the complex provisions of the Single European Act, furthermore, its recommendations can only with great difficulty be amended by the Council. Yet national governments continue to play a dominant role in the decision making process . . .

. . . The European Community operates neither as a political 'market' characterized by arms-length transactions among independent entities − nor as a 'hierarchy', in which the dominant mode of regulation is authoritative rule. Rather, the EC exemplifies what sociologists refer to as a 'network form of organization', in which individual units are defined not by themselves but in relation to other units. Actors in a network have a preference for interaction with one another, rather than with outsiders, in part because intense interactions create incentives for self-interested cooperation and for the maintenance of reputations for reliability . . .

. . . The notion of a network is more a metaphor than a theory. It helps to emphasize the horizontal ties that exist among actors and the complexity of their relationships, but it does not elaborate clear hypotheses about behaviour . . .

. . . At the core of the dynamic theory of political integration devised by Ernst Haas and the neofunctionalist school was the concept of 'spillover'. Haas was interested in what he called the 'expansive logic of sector integration', which followed an initial bargain, such as that between the French desire for a common agricultural policy and Germany's search for a common market in industrial goods.

Spillover for the neofunctionalists was not a manifestation of enthusiasm for the ideology of Europe, but a more prosaic result of 'swapping concessions from a variety of sectors' . . .

. . . If spillover and pressure from the European institutions had been sufficient to create such a step-level change, it would have occurred much earlier. After all, the members had repeatedly committed themselves to full economic union, but it had been accomplished neither through spillover from the earlier bargains nor through mere pledges. A large part of the explanation for these major changes must, we think, be found elsewhere. For these events, an emphasis on inter-governmental bargains will probably be more fruitful. It is much more plausible to conjecture that spillover leads to task-expansion in the wake of a major inter-governmental bargain, than to hold that such bargains are themselves explained by the changing incentives coming from past policy change. As we have seen, the 1992 programme was much more strongly affected by events in the world political economy outside Europe – especially by concern about international competitiveness – than it was driven by the internal logic of spillover.

Our hypothesis is that successful spillover requires prior programmatic agree-ment among governments, expressed in an intergovernmental bargain. Such a bargain is clearly important in accounting for the Single European Act. Without the turnaround of French economic policy in 1983, and the decision by the British government to accept treaty amendment in order to institutionalize deregulation, no consensus could have been reached on a programme to dismantle barriers within Europe. The British government was very clear that it was entering into a bargain, and not acting on the basis of an ideology of unity or solidarity with Europe . . .

. . . Focusing on intergovernmental bargains, i.e. on governmental decisions, leaves out one actor: the Commission. The role of the Commission in preparing the White Paper on the creation of a single market by 1992, presented to the European Council in Milan in June 1985, was crucial in defining the agenda which governments had to decide. Still, it can be argued that Delors and his fellow Commissioners did no more than focus the states' attention on the one issue – the single market – that was acceptable to the three major actors, Britain, West Germany and France . . .

. . . Thus we end with a tentative conclusion congruent with regime theory: the existence of a 'regime' – in this case, the EC – affected these states' calculations of incentives, and made it possible for them to see a policy of European reliance as advantageous.

Spillover is an important concept, but it can only be usefully employed within a carefully delimited sphere. Before it is used effectively in research, different meanings of the concept of spillover will need to be distinguished, as above, and the conditions under which spillover can be expected to operate must be kept in mind. The 'theory of spillover' has, therefore, not been discredited: in the wake of an intergovernmental bargain based on subjective similarity and a common policy orientation, actors can have incentives to promote task expansion into new sectors in order to protect gains already achieved. But it remains to be seen, from empirical research, how much this theory will explain of the institutional developments under way in the European Community at the end of the 1980s.

Bargains that cover only certain sectors, omitting to provide for sectors linked to those, can stimulate a spillover process either on an interstate basis (as incentives facing states change) or on a transnational one. This core idea of the neofunctionalists is consistent with much of what we know about how changes in the international political economy affect incentives for states. It leaves open for investigation, however, the question of how fast and how far spillover from an initial bargain will extend . . .

Conclusions

. . . As we have seen, the Community political system can be viewed as a network. But networks can be curses or blessings. Their proponents regard them as particularly adaptive and well-suited to coping with changes in complex, information-rich environments. Critics of networks, by contrast, question whether such forms of organization can act decisively at all: if sovereignty corrupts, loss of sovereignty may corrupt absolutely!

To what extent has the sovereignty wrested from individual Member States been acquired by identifiable Community institutions, and to what extent lost in what often appears as a vortex of competing forces – or perhaps even a 'black hole' from which coherent authority can never emerge? The Community has its share both of centrifugal and centripetal forces: the former are not only national but sectoral, characterized by bureaucratic coalitions, poorly coordinated with one another; the latter are centred on the Commission, the Court, and to some extent the Council of Ministers. From this perspective, the relative power of Commission and Council may be a less important issue, despite the decades of debate about supranationalism, than their joint ability, along with the Court, to keep the decentralized coalitions of bureaucrats and interest groups – Europe's parallel to America's 'iron triangles' (bureaucrats, interest groups, and congressional committees or subcommittees) – in line. Indeed, to ask whether sovereignty is being 'transferred' from nation-states to a community may be quite misleading; more relevant may be the question of whether the sovereignty being lost by individual states can be focused at all – or whether Europe will become simply a network without a decisive or accountable centre of authority . . .

. . . The process characterizing the European Community in its most dynamic periods, the early 1960s and the late 1980s, is probably the only one that allows for integration despite the opposition of the states to outright transfers of power and loyalty to supranational institutions. The Single Act was both a rélance and a way of sidestepping the Federalist political union treaty advocated by Spinelli with the support of the European Parliament. But a heavy price has to be paid for this: the paradox of integrated economies and separate politics, the paradox of an elaborate process of multinational bargaining coexisting with an obstinately 'national' process of political life and elections, the paradox of the emergence of a European identity on the world scene coexisting with continuing national loyalties.

This identity remains hindered by the weakness of the Community in world affairs. Foreign policy and defence are activities that often require great domestic sacrifices, if only in the form of resources taken away from internal welfare and development, for such tasks as national defence and aid to other countries. In democracies, these sacrifices can be obtained by institutions that claim popular legitimacy and support. European Community institutions, dominated by bureaucrats and national ministers, with a parliament that has very narrow budgetary powers and a procedure of foreign policy cooperation that is intergovernmental, can draw on no such legitimacy.

Our analysis of the dynamics of the Community and of spillover suggests that despite the revival of supranationality and the emergence of a Community wide political system in which state sovereignty is both pooled and shrunk, what matters most are the bargains among the major players. The two indispensable ones remain France and West Germany, whose alliance continues to provide the political motor of the enterprise. Suspicion of 'Europe', even of supranationality, has dramatically declined in France, especially in the present generation of elites. But some fear that the resurgence of the economic and financial power of the Federal Republic, its new eminence in East–West relations, and the economic and, above all, national opportunities provided to it by the breakdown of communism in Eastern Europe, and by reunification, may make Bonn less committed to the Community. Competing demands and interests may make its government less willing to pay large sums to the Community budget, its industrialists and bankers less open to cooperation or alliances with others, its diplomats less eager to seek a European legitimation, once the single market – a major opportunity for the Germany economy – is achieved: a situation comparable to that of de Gaulle as we described him in 1965. Will France and the other continental members be willing to pay a price in order to make a further development of the Community – in effect, of controls and limits on German autonomy – more attractive to a German government preoccupied with managing reunification and its consequences? . . .

. . . At a more abstract level the issue is the degree to which even the European Community (which was established without a hegemon and which is stronger than ordinary international regimes) can adapt to a newly fluid pattern of European politics in which its strongest member plays a strategically pivotal role – and in which that power's national identity is involved. Especially in a set-up where the power in question does not provide military security to its partners in exchange for economic preponderance, can the Community's existence and policies help to dampen a rising hegemon's national aspirations so that they remain acceptable to the less powerful states, without at the same time appearing too burdensome to the hegemon? This is, obviously, a very different case from those which recent arguments about American hegemony, and cooperation 'after hegemony', have considered.

At present, one can only note that the evolution of world politics still favours the strengthening of ties among the partners of the Community. In such an environment, ties of European networks will deepen as habits of pooling sovereignty develop. Spillover will lead to incremental deepening of joint decision-making, and European organizations will – like all organizations – seek to extend their authority. Thus, barring a major slump in the world economy, or catastrophic events in Eastern Europe and the Soviet Union whose international fall-out cannot be predicted, there are reasons to be at least moderately optimistic about the Community's future prospects.

Document 41: A. Moravcsik, 'Negotiating the Single European Act: national interests and conventional statecraft in the European Community', *International Organization* Vol. 45: 1991, pp. 19–21, 42–8, 54

The European Community (EC) is experiencing its most important period of reform since the completion of the Common Market in 1968. This new impulse toward European integration – the 'relaunching' of Europe, the French call it – was unexpected. The late 1970s and early 1980s were periods of 'Europessimism' and 'Eurosclerosis', when politicians and academics alike lost faith in European institutions. The current period is one of optimism and institutional momentum. The source of this transformation was the Single European Act (SEA), a document approved by European heads of government in 1986 . . .

. . . What accounts for the timing and the content of the reform package that relaunched Europe? Why did this reform succeed when so many previous efforts had failed? As a first step toward answering these questions, this article presents a history of the negotiations that led to the approval of the SEA by the European Council in February 1986, formulates and evaluates two stylized explanations for their unexpected success, and relates the findings to theories of international cooperation.

The findings challenge the prominent view that institutional reform resulted from an elite alliance between EC officials and pan-European business interest groups. The negotiating history is more consistent with the alternative explanation that EC reform rested on interstate bargains between Britain, France, and Germany.

This 'intergovernmental institutionalist' explanation is more consistent with what Robert Keohane calls the 'modified structural realist' view of regime change, a view that stresses traditional conceptions of national interests and power, than it is with supranational variants of neo-functionalist integration theory. For the source of state interests, however, scholars must turn away from structural theories and toward domestic politics, where the existence of several competing explanations invite further research . . .

Explanations for the success of the SEA

Journalistic reportage, academic analysis, and interviews with European officials reveal a bewilderingly wide range of explanations, some contradictory, for the timing, content, and process of adopting the White Paper and the SEA. The various accounts cluster around two stylized explanations, the first stressing the independent activism of international or transnational actors and the second emphasizing bargaining between leaders of the most powerful states of Europe . . .

Interpreting the negotiations

Assessing supranational institutionalism

. . . The historical record does not confirm the importance of international and transnational factors. Let us consider each element in turn.

European institutions

The supranational model stresses the role of EC institutions, particularly the Parliament. Yet after Fontainebleau, government representatives, abetted by the Commission, deliberately excluded representatives of the Parliament from decisive forums . . .

. . . The fact that the member states parried parliamentary pressure with ease certainly casts doubt on the argument that the SEA was necessary to co-opt rising demands for even more thoroughgoing institutional reform. In the end, the Parliament overwhelmingly passed a resolution protesting that the SEA 'in no way represent[s] the real reform of the Community that our peoples need,' but it had little alternative but to accept the fait accompli.

Transnational business interest groups

The internal market program, like the EC itself thirty years before, appears to have been launched independently of pressure from transnationally organized business interest groups . . .

. . . The activities of the Roundtable of European Industrialists focused primarily on the concerns of its non-EC European membership. Before 1985, its chief involvement was in European infrastructure projects such as the Channel tunnel. The Roundtable was based in Geneva and did not move to Brussels until 1988, when Dekker assumed its presidency. Most transnational business lobbies got involved late . . .

International political leaders

Cockfield's boldness and Delors' extraordinary political skill are not in question. Cockfield and Delors acted on the margins to broaden the White Paper and the

SEA, and they may have contributed to the remarkable speed of decision making at the intergovernmental conference. Nevertheless, the broader outlines of both documents were proposed, negotiated, and approved, often in advance of Commission initiatives, by the heads of government themselves. Indeed, the breakthrough in the relaunching of the EC had already occurred before Delors became president of the Commission. The causality of the supranational explanation is thus reversed: the selection of a prestigious politician for the presidency was merely a symptom of mounting trilateral pressure for reform. In this regard, ironically enough, Delors' actions as Finance Minister of France may have contributed more to the SEA than those as president of the Commission . . .

. . . Delors' most important contributions to the process resulted not from his role as an initiator of unforeseen policies but instead from his keen awareness of the extreme constraints under which he was acting. A re-examination of his memoirs reveals that his arguments (as distinct from his tone) stress intergovernmental constraints rather than personal influence . . .

Supranational institutionalism and neofunctionalism

None of the three supranational variables – European institutional momentum, transnational business interest group activity, and international political leadership – seems to account for the timing, content, and process of negotiating the SEA. Moreover, governments did not bargain by 'up-grading' the common interest or by linking issues but, rather, by accepting the lowest common denominator, backed by the threat of exclusion. The resulting bargain places major obstacles in the path of attempts to extend the reform to new issues, such as monetary policy.

In this regard, one striking aspect of the negotiations for the SEA is their parallel to the negotiations for the ECSC and EC in the 1950s. Even regional integration theorists are inclined to accept that the founding of the ECSC was an extraordinary act of political statecraft, but they contend that once it occurred it sparked a qualitatively different and potentially self-sustaining process of spillover. The negotiating history of the SEA, however, suggests that three decades later the factors encouraging a greater commitment to European unity are essentially the same: the convergence of national interests, the pro-European idealism of heads of government, and the decisive role of the large member states.

The importance of interstate bargains in the SEA negotiations is consistent with the broader experience of the EC since the mid-1960s. European integration did not proceed steadily and incrementally; it proceeded in fits and starts. Moreover, since the Luxembourg compromise in 1966, the EC has moved toward inter-governmental ('state-to-state') decision making centered in the Council and summit meetings, rather than toward increasing authority for international bodies such as the Commission and Parliament. One detailed study concluded that the systems change in the EC has in fact proved to be more political and less technical than Haas predicted.[1] While spillover and forward linkages may in some cases suffice to prompt the intensification of international decision making under a specific mandate within a given sector, they play a minimal role in the processes of opening new issues, reforming decision-making procedures, and ratifying the accession of new members. Movement in these areas requires active intervention by heads of state and a considerable amount of non-technocratic interstate bargaining.

The SEA negotiations suggest, furthermore, that in the 1980s, just as in the 1950s, pan-European business groups were relatively ineffective at influencing policy. Business, at least on the supranational level, was mobilized by the emerging interstate consensus for reform, rather than the reverse. This casts doubt on at least one mechanism underlying the long-term historical prediction of neofunctionalism – namely, that over time, growth in the autonomy and responsibility of supranational actors and organizations will facilitate further integration.

Assessing intergovernmental institutionalism

The historical record confirms the importance of the three elements of inter-governmental institutionalism. Again, these elements can be considered in turn.

Intergovernmentalism

Heads of government and their direct representatives carried out the negotia-tions. The result represents the convergence of domestic policy preferences in the largest member states. The dominance of the three largest states is revealed most clearly by the lack of cases (with the possible exception of the Danish stand on workers' rights) in which a smaller nation either initiated or vetoed a central initiative . . .

Lowest-common-denominator bargaining

The only major exception to lowest-common-denominator bargaining concerned whether to amend the Treaty of Rome to promote majority voting on internal market matters. On this point, the British yielded to Franco-German pressure to convene an intergovernmental conference, at least in part because the Franco-German position was backed by the threat of exclusion . . .

Protection of sovereignty

The steady narrowing of the institutional reform to a 'minimalist' position in which majority voting is restricted to internal market policy, the power of the Parliament is limited, and the future spillover to areas such as monetary policy is blocked confirms the enduring preoccupation of all three major states with maintaining sovereignty and control over future changes in the scope of EC activities.

International institutionalism and domestic politics

While the intergovernmental approach, based on the relative power of member states and the convergence of their national policy preferences, offers a satisfactory account of the SEA negotiations, it raises a second, equally important question: Why did underlying national policy preferences converge at this point in time? As indicated earlier, part of the answer can be found in the domestic politics of France, Germany, and Britain. Four paradigmatic explanations can also be identified: autonomous action by political leaders, pressure from state bureaucracies, support from centrist coalitions, and pressure to replace failed economic policies. Each offers a promising starting point for analyzing the domestic roots of European integration, but none is entirely satisfactory . . .

Conclusion: the SEA in perspective

Neofunctionalism remains the sole attempt to fashion a coherent and comprehensive theory of European integration. The standing of neofunctionalist theory among political scientists is a lagged function of the standing of the EC in the eyes of Europeans. When the EC stagnates, as in the 1970s, scholars speak of the obsolescence of regional integration theory; when it rebounds, as in 1985, they speak of the obsolescence of the nation-state. Regional integration theory, we read today, has been 'unjustly consigned to the dustbin'.

This article challenges the notion, implicit in these statements, that progress in the EC necessarily supports all the claims of neofunctionalists. It does so by testing and rejecting a particular variant of neofunctionalism, supranational institutionalism, which rests on the argument that international institutions and transnational interest groups play a vital and increasing role as integration progresses. The approach proposed here, intergovernmental institutionalism, accords an important role to supranational institutions in cementing existing inter-state bargains as the foundation for renewed integration. But it also affirms that the primary source of integration lies in the interests of the states themselves and the relative power each brings to Brussels. Perhaps most important, the inter-governmental approach demonstrates that even this explanation is incomplete, thus clearing the ground for further research into the international implications of European domestic politics.

Note

1 L. Lindberg and S. Scheingold, *Europe's Would-Be Polity: Patterns of Change in the European Community* (Englewood Cliffs, NJ, 1970).

Document 42: A. Moravcsik, 'Preferences and power in the European Community: a liberal intergovernmentalist approach', *Journal of Common Market Studies* Vol. 31: 1993, pp. 473–4, 482, 517–19

Introduction

The European Community (EC) is the most successful example of institutionalized international policy co-ordination in the modern world, yet there is little agreement about the proper explanation for its evolution. From the signing of the Treaty of Rome to the making of Maastricht, the EC has developed through a series of celebrated intergovernmental bargains, each of which set the agenda for an intervening period of consolidation. The most fundamental task facing a theoretical account of European integration is to explain these bargains. Today many would revive neo-functionalism's emphasis on sui generis characteristics of EC institutions, in particular the importance of unintended consequences of previous decisions and the capacity of supranational officials to provide leadership.

This article joins the debate by reasserting the self-critique, advanced almost two decades ago by Ernst Haas and other leading neo-functionalists, who suggested that European integration can only by explained with reference to general theories of international relations. The basic claim of this article is that the EC can be analysed as a successful intergovernmental regime designed to manage economic interdependence through negotiated policy co-ordination. Refinements and extensions of existing theories of foreign economic policy, intergovernmental negotiation, and international regimes provide a plausible and generalizable explanation of its evolution. Such theories rest on the assumption that state behaviour reflects the rational actions of governments constrained at home by domestic societal pressures and abroad by their strategic environment. An understanding of the preferences and power of its Member States is a logical starting point for analysis. Although the EC is a unique institution, it does not require a sui generis theory . . .

This conception of rationality suggests that parsimonious explanations of international conflict or co-operation can be constructed by employing two types of theory sequentially: a theory of national preference formation and a theory of interstate strategic interaction [see Figure 2]. Unicausal explanations of European integration, which seek to isolate either demand or supply, are at best incomplete and at worst misleading. 'Demand-side reductionism' – the narrow attention to variation in domestic preferences while ignoring the strategic context in which states interact – or 'supply-side reductionism' – exclusive emphasis on interstate bargaining or international institutions without considering the underlying distribution and variation in preferences – risk omitting essential variables and encouraging misleading inferences about those that remain. Explaining the emergence in 1978–9 of the European Monetary System, for example, requires that we understand both the convergence of macroeconomic policy preferences, which led European governments to favour monetary co-ordination, and the determinants of the outcomes of the tough interstate bargaining that took place over the precise terms under which it would take place.

Thus liberal intergovernmentalism integrates within a single framework two types of general international relations theory often seen as contradictory: a liberal theory of national preference formation and an intergovernmentalist analysis of interstate bargaining and institutional creation . . .

Conclusion: beyond liberal intergovernmentalism

The liberal intergovernmentalist view seeks to account for major decisions in the history of the EC by positing a two-stage approach. In the first stage, national preferences are primarily determined by the constraints and opportunities imposed by economic interdependence. In the second stage, the outcomes of inter-governmental negotiations are determined by the relative bargaining power of governments and the functional incentives for institutionalization created by high transaction costs and the desire to control domestic agendas. This approach is grounded in fundamental concepts of international political economy, negotiation analysis, and regime theory.

The net economic interests of producers and popular preferences for public goods provide a solid foundation for explaining agricultural policy and industrial trade liberalization, as well as socio-economic public goods provision, within the EC. These preferences tell us the goals of states, their alternatives, and – through the level of societal constraint on governments – the extent to which governments are willing to compromise. The distributional outcomes of intergovernmental negotiations are shaped by the unilateral and coalitional alternatives to agreement, as well as the opportunities for compromise and linkage.

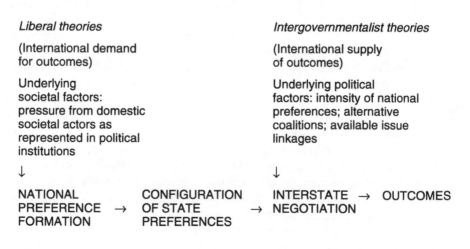

Figure 2 The liberal intergovernmentalist framework of analysis

Like other international regimes, EC institutions increase the efficiency of bargaining by providing a set of passive, transaction-cost reducing rules. But EC institutions cannot be explained entirely on the basis of existing regime theory. Instead, at least two other functions of international institutions need to be taken into account. First, EC institutions delegate and pool sovereignty, taking key decisions about linkage out of the hands of national governments. The delegation and pooling of authority in the EC can be explained by extending existing functional regime theory, which focuses on the reduction of transaction costs. Governments delegate authority and provide for qualified majority voting in order to increase the efficiency of bargaining at the expense of slightly increased political risk for domestic groups. While existing regime theory focuses on the risk of defection, the major concern of EC states tends to be the risk that the consequences of the agreement, even if all comply, will turn out to be less advantageous for key domestic groups than expected. Thus governments weigh the potential gains from co-operation against the domestic political risk.

Second, EC institutions structure a 'two-level game', which increases the initiative and influence of national governments by providing legitimacy and domestic agenda-setting power for their initiatives. To explain this function, regime theory must be supplemented by theories of domestic politics and two-level games.

By bringing together theories of preferences, bargaining and regimes, liberal intergovernmentalism provides plausible accounts for many aspects of the major decisions in the history of the EC in a way that is sharply distinct from neo-functionalism. Where neo-functionalism emphasizes domestic technocratic consensus, liberal intergovernmentalism looks to domestic coalitional struggles. Where neo-functionalism emphasizes opportunities to upgrade the common interest, liberal intergovernmentalism stresses the role of relative power. Where neo-functionalism emphasizes the active role of supranational officials in shaping bargaining outcomes, liberal intergovernmentalism stresses instead passive institutions and the autonomy of national leaders. Ironically, the EC's 'democratic deficit' may be a fundamental source of its success.

Moreover, liberal intergovernmentalism provides explanations for some nagging anomalies inherited from neo-functionalism. Variation in the tightness of domestic societal constraints is employed to explain the disruptive role of dramatic–political actors and the distinction between those issues where linkage or compromise is possible and those in which log-rolling or lowest common denominator solution prevails. The distinction between positive and negative externalities helps explain which issues generate common solutions and spark geographical spillover, and which do not. The introduction of a 'two-level game' analysis explains why France sought industrial trade liberalization with Germany in the 1950s, despite the unilateral openness of the German economy at the time.

Critics may challenge the approach proposed here in three ways. First, they may dispute the basic framework, arguing that state behaviour is not purposive and instrumental, that preference formation does not precede the formulation of strategies, or that national preference and intergovernmental bargaining are so completely manipulated by supranational officials as to be meaningless categories. Second, they may challenge the liberal understanding of state preferences employed here, which draws on contemporary theories of economic interdependence to explain national preferences. Alternative conceptions of economic interest are certainly possible, as are (liberal and non-liberal) explanations based on ideology or geopolitics. Third, they may question the intergovernmental theory of bargaining, with its stresses on bargaining power rooted in unilateral alternatives, competing coalitions, the possibilities for linkage, and the controlled delegation of power to supranational institutions under conditions specified by functional theories of regimes and 'two-level' games views of domestic polities. Such debate is to be welcomed.

Yet few would go so far as to deny the importance of preferences and power altogether. Indeed, a strong liberal intergovernmentalist theory is widely seen as a precondition for the development of more complex theories of integration, such as neo-functionalism. Without explicit theories of state interests, interstate bargaining, and international regimes, it is impossible to determine when consequences are truly unintended, the common interest is truly being upgraded, or supranational officials are truly acting autonomously. This vindicates Haas's judgement that debate between general theories of domestic and international politics is necessary. Such a debate is surely preferable to a clash between 'intergovernmentalist' and 'supranationalist' ideal-types, without any specification of the conditions under which each might be expected to apply.

It is certainly true that liberal intergovernmentalism accords supranational institutions and officials less weight and prominence than neo-functionalism once did. Committed integrationists typically read such conclusions as a disparagement of the unique achievement and future potential of the EC. Yet the real achievement and hope of the Community may lie not in the transcendence of traditional state preferences and power, but in the underlying domestic and international forces that have shaped national preferences and power in the direction of greater co-operation. Liberal intergovernmentalism assimilates the EC to models of politics potentially applicable to all states, thereby specifying the conditions under which a similar process of integration may occur elsewhere.

Document 43: W. Sandholtz and J. Zysman, '1992: recasting the European bargain', *World Politics* Vol. 42: 1989, pp. 95, 97–103, 126–8

Under the banner of '1992', the European Communities are putting in place a series of political and business bargains that will recast, if not unify, the European market. This initiative is a disjunction, a dramatic new start, rather than the fulfilment of the original effort to construct Europe . . .

. . . In this article, we propose that changes in the international structure triggered the 1992 process. More precisely, the trigger has been a real shift in the distribution of economic power resources (crudely put, relative American decline and Japanese ascent). What is just as important is that European elites perceive that the changes in the international setting require that they rethink their roles and interests in the world . . .

Explaining 1992: alternative approaches

Analysis of the 1992 project in Western Europe could follow any one of three broad approaches, each with a different focus. One approach would look to the internal dynamics of the integration process itself, as in integration theory. A second would concentrate on the domestic politics behind the regional agreements. The third approach, for which we argue, focuses on elite bargains in response to the challenges and opportunities posed by international and domestic changes. The analysis of elite bargains incorporates the strengths of the other two approaches while avoiding their major weaknesses. Although we have no intention of elaborating three different theoretical frameworks, we will briefly describe what appear to be the chief short-comings of the integration theory and domestic politics approaches.

Consider integration theory. Instead of a single theory, there were numerous permutations, each employing different concepts and definitions. But what distinguished integration theory from other, traditional analyses of international politics was that it assigned causal significance to the process of integration itself. Indeed, a genuine integration theory would have to posit some specific political effects stemming from the internal logic of integration. This was the contribution of neofunctionalist integration theories, which were in turn partly inspired by the functionalist theory of David Mitrany.

Integration begins when governments perceive that certain economic policy problems cannot be solved by national means alone and agree to joint policy making in supranational institutions. Initially, therefore, experts in the supra-national organization apply technical solutions to (primarily) economic problems. Integration proceeds through the 'expansive logic' of spillovers. Spillovers occur when experience gained by one integrative step reveals the need for integration in functionally related areas. That is, in order to accomplish the original objectives, participants realize that they must take further integrative steps . . .

. . . For a number of reasons, we do not believe that integration theories are well suited for analyzing the 1992 movement. The major weaknesses were recognized by the integration theorists themselves; two of their criticisms are most relevant to the concerns of this paper.

1 The internal logic of integration cannot account for the stop–go nature of the European project. One possibility, suggested by Lindberg and Scheingold, is that the Community attained many of its objectives, which led to 'the disappearance of many of the original incentives to integrate'. The question then becomes, why did the renewed drive for the single internal market emerge in the mid-1980s and why did it rapidly acquire broad support among governments and business elites?

2 Even where the Community did not meet expectations or where integration in one area pointed out problems in functionally related areas, national leaders could frequently opt for national means rather than more integration. That is, even in issue areas where the pressure for spillovers should have been strong, national means appeared sufficient and were preferred . . .

. . . The national option always stands against the EC option and frequently wins. An explanation rooted in the domestic politics of the various European countries is a second possible approach to explaining 1992. Certainly the shift of the socialist governments in France and Spain toward market-oriented economic policies (including privatization and deregulation) was essential for acceptance of the 1992 movement. The Thatcher government in the UK could also support measures that dealt primarily with reducing regulations and freeing markets. Thus, the favourable domestic political context was one of the necessary conditions that produced 1992.

But domestic politics cannot carry the full analytical burden, for three main reasons.

1 An argument based on domestic politics cannot answer the questions, why now? Such an argument would have to account for the simultaneity of domestic developments that would induce states to act jointly. Attention to changes in the international context solves that problem. International changes posed challenges and choices to all the EC countries at the same time.
2 The political actors that figure in analyses of European domestic politics have not yet been mobilized in the 1992 project, though perhaps that is now beginning. Although the political parties and the trade unions now talk about 1992 (and will act in the future as the social dimension moves to the top of the agenda), they were not involved in the discussions and bargains that started the process. Governments (specifically, the national executives) and business elites initiated and defined 1992 and have moved it along.
3 An argument based on domestic politics cannot explain why domestic political changes produced the 1992 movement. The project did not bubble up spontaneously from the various national political contexts. On the contrary: leadership for 1992 came from outside the national settings; it came from the Commission.

The third approach to analyzing 1992 is the one we advance in this paper. It focuses on elite bargains formed in response to changes in the international structure and in the domestic political context. The postwar order of security and economic systems founded upon American leadership is beginning to evolve after a period of relative US decline and Japanese ascent. These developments have led Europeans to reconsider their relations with the United States and within the European Communities. The international and domestic situations provided a setting in which the Commission could exercise policy entrepreneurship, mobilizing a transnational coalition in favour of the unified internal market.

The 1992 movement (as well as the integration of the 1950s) can be fruitfully analyzed as a hierarchy of bargains. Political elites reach agreement on fundamental bargains embodying basic objectives. The fundamental bargains agreed upon for 1992 are embodied in the Single European Act and in the Commission's White Paper which outlined specific steps toward the unified internal market. The Single European Act extended majority voting in the Council and cleared the way politically for progress toward unifying the internal market. Endorsement of the Commission's proposals in the White Paper represents agreement on the fundamental objective of eliminating barriers to the movement of persons, goods, and capital. The specific measures proposed by the Commission (some 300 of them) can be thought of as implementing bargains. Further implementing bargains have yet to be considered in areas like the monetary system, taxation, and social policy.

The original European movement can be seen in terms of this framework. The integration movement was triggered by the wrenching structural changes brought about by World War II; after the war, Europe was no longer the center of the international system, but rather a frontier and cushion between the two new superpowers. Political entrepreneurship came initially from the group surrounding Robert Schuman and Jean Monnet. The early advocates of integration succeeded in mobilizing a transnational coalition supportive of integration; the core of that coalition eventually included the Christian Democratic parties of the original Six, plus many of the Socialist parties.

The fundamental objectives of the bargains underlying the European Coal and Steel Community (ECSC) and the expanded European Communities were primarily two:

1 the binding of German industry to the rest of Europe so as to make another war impossible; and
2 the restarting of economic growth in the region.

These objectives may have been largely implicit, but they were carried out by means of a number of implementing bargains that were agreed upon over the years. The chief implementing bargains after the ECSC included the Common Market, the Common Agricultural Program, the regional development funds, and, most recently, the European Monetary System (EMS).

The fundamental external bargain made in establishing the Community was with the United States . . .

. . . The European bargains – internal and external – were made at the moment of American political and economic domination. A bipolar security world and an American-directed Western economy set the context in which the European bargain appeared necessary. Many expected the original Community to generate ever more extensive integration. But the pressures for spillover were not that great. Economics could not drive political integration. The building of nation-states remains a matter of political projects . . .

. . . The basic political objectives sought by the original internal bargain had been achieved: the threat of Germany was diminished and growth had been ignited. When problems arose from the initial integrative steps, the instruments of national policy sufficed to deal with them. Indeed, the Community could accommodate quite distinct national social, regulatory, and tax policies. National strategies for growth, development, and employment sufficed.

Several fundamental attributes of the economic community that emerged merit emphasis, as they prove important in the reignition of the European project in the mid-1980s. First, the initial effort was the product of governmental action, of intergovernmental bargains. Second, there was the partial creation of an internal market; that is a reduction, but not an elimination, of the barriers to internal exchange. The success of this initiative was suggested by the substantial increase in intra-European trade. Third, and equally important, there was toleration of national intervention; in fact, in the case of France such intervention was an element of the construction. There was an acceptance of national strategies for development and political management. Fourth, the European projects were in fact quite limited, restricted for the most part to managing retrenchment in declining industries and easing dislocations in the rural sector (and consequently managing the politics of agriculture) through the Common Agricultural Policy. There were several significant exceptions, including the European Monetary System that emerged as a Franco-German deal to cope with exchange-rate fluctuations that might threaten trade relations; however, the basic principle of national initiative persisted. Fifth, trade remained the crucial link between countries. Joint ventures and other forms of foreign direct investment to penetrate markets continued to be limited. Sixth, American multinationals were accepted, if not welcomed, in each country.

When the global context changed, the European bargains had to be adjusted for new realities. Wallace and Wessels have argued that 'even if neither the EC or EFTA had been invented long before, by the mid-eighties some form of intra-European management would have had to be found to oversee the necessary economic and industrial adjustments' . . .

Conclusion

. . . Europe is throwing the dice. It is confronted with a change in the structure of the international economy, with emerging Japanese and dwindling American power and position. It feels the shift in Asian competitive pressure in industry and finance. The problems are no longer those of American production in Europe, but of Japanese imports and production displacing European production. More importantly perhaps, Europe also feels the shift in rising Japanese influence in the monetary and technology domains. The industrial and governmental presumptions and deals with which Europe has operated are changing or will change. Indeed, Europeans may have to construct a coherent political presence on the global stage in order to achieve the most attractive accommodations to the new order.

We hypothesize that change in the international economic structure was necessary for the revival of the European project. A full-fledged test of this proposition will require detailed analysis of the perceptions and beliefs of those who participated in launching the 1992 movement. We have mentioned other analytical approaches – based on integration theory and domestic politics – that appear logically unsuited to explaining 1992. Of course, these approaches are not really alternatives. There are functional links among some of the bargains being struck, and domestic factors clearly shaped governmental responses to the international changes. But tests of alternative explanations often create a false sense of scientism by setting individually weak explanations against each other and finding 'confirmation' by denying the worst of them. Competing explanations often represent different types of explanation, different levels of analysis. In the end, it is not a matter of which one is better, but of whether the right questions are being asked. This article is an effort to frame the proper questions and propose analytical links among them.

We argue that structural situations create the context of choice and cast up problems to be resolved, but they do not dictate the decisions and strategies. In other words, the global setting can be understood in neo-realist terms, but the political processes triggered by changes in the system must be analyzed in other than structural terms. The choices result from political processes and have political explanations. In this case, the process is one of bargains among nations and elites within the region. The political process for implementing these bargains is labelled 'Europe 1992', a complex web of intergovernmental bargains and accommodations among the various national business elites.

In the first half of this essay, we showed why 1992 has so far been a project of elites; in the second half, we suggested that the elites are unlikely to maintain that monopoly. The commitment of the governments to the process, the fundamental bargain, is expressed by the end of the single-nation veto system, which changed the logic of Community decision making. Europe's states have thrown themselves into the drive for a unified market, unleashing business processes that in themselves are recasting the terms of competition within Europe. The terms of the final bargains are open.

The effort to reshape the European Communities has so far been guided by three groups: Community institutions, industrial elites, and governments. The Commission proposes and persuades. Important business coalitions exercise indispensable influence on governments. Governments are receptive because of changes in the world economy and shifts in the domestic political context. The domestic context has changed in two key ways:

1 with the failure of traditional models of growth and purely national strategies for economic management; and
2 with the defeat of the left in some countries, and with its transformation because of the weakening of communist parties in others.

These changes opened the way for an unlikely set of elite alliances. In this context,

EC initiatives began to demonstrate that there were joint European alternatives to failed national strategies.

Delors built on the budding sense of optimism and gave energy and leadership to the notion of a genuine single market. Whether a broader range of political groups will become involved is an open issue, one that may determine both whether the process continues and what form it takes.

The outcomes are quite unknowable, dependent on the timing and dynamics of a long series of contingent decisions. But the story, and consequently the analysis, concerns political leadership in creating a common European interest and then constructing a set of bargains that embody that understanding.

Document 44: H. Kastendiek, 'Convergence or a persistent diversity of national interests?', in C. Crouch and D. Marquand (eds), *The Politics of 1992: Beyond the Single European Market* (Oxford, 1990), pp. 68, 76–80, 82–4

In many discussions of 1992 it has been taken for granted that the introduction of the single market as a major step towards economic integration will also have a significant impact on national politics in Western Europe. The shift of author-itative decision-making from national arenas to transnational institutions and mechanisms will establish a new power centre to which the member states of the Community have to adjust, however reluctantly in some cases . . .

. . . In reaction to the economic competition tightened up by the introduction of the single market, this process will often take the form of a cross-national imitation of those policy-styles and political structures which have proved or promise to be most effective. The combined effects of these multiple pressures for mutual adaptation, it is assumed, have initiated a general trend towards a political convergence.

In this paper, I want to argue that this assumption is precipitate because it neglects an analysis of previous patterns of political change in and across individual Western European countries and misinterprets recent changes in the politics of the Community. Consequently, it does not consider the fact that formerly proclaimed theses of convergence have regularly failed and thus have rather confirmed the alternative view of a persistent diversity of national patterns of politics and society . . .

Europe 1992: economic integration and political convergence?

What is so significant about the debate on the single market and its political implications is the shift in the perception of the Community. Seen as a 'lame duck' only a few years ago, it is now reputed to be a main asset of the European economy and of European politics. The introduction of the single market, defined as an absolute economic necessity, has been regarded as a starting point of a new dynamic of political integration. This new dynamic has been concluded from recent changes in the institutions and policy-making mechanisms at the level of the EC, but also from the momentum coming from below as the member states have to respond to the quest for an integrated Europe demanded by business and industry as well as to the social and cultural changes resulting from a multitude of integrationist trends in Western Europe. It is this combination of economic and political consequences expected from the introduction of the single market which has created the present 'Euro-fever' and fuelled the notion of a political convergence.

In my attempt to counterbalance the present debate I want to pose the question whether this notion once more interprets a cross-national constellation of change as a constellation of identical national changes. The introduction of the single market and the new dynamic of political integration seem to indicate an adaptation to new imperatives for change, in particular to the requirements of a techno–economic restructuring imposed by international competition. The problem is, however, whether these changes necessarily point to a process of mutual adaptation of national politics, supported and reinforced through the mechanisms of the EC . . .

. . . Thus, the present situation may again prove to be a constellation of parallel rather than convergent developments, i.e. a constellation of simultaneous changes which may, in the geometric sense of a 'parallelism', not dissolve but reproduce the patterns of political diversity. However, for a discussion of these points, it would be precarious simply to extrapolate my former argument. The question at stake is whether, in recent years, (a) a substantially new constellation of change has emerged which (b) demands or at least supports rather uniform changes of national politics.

The prospects of present and future political change in general and within the EC in particular have been concluded from a variety of problem constellations, ranging from the secular trend towards an accelerating internationalization of economic, social, political and cultural relations or the future obsolescence of national politics resulting from impending worldwide environmental catastrophes on the one hand to the more traditional themes of the political implications and consequences of techno–economic change or of the trend towards regional integration on the other. Clearly the third point has been at the forefront of the present discussion. It may have been forgotten that the present 'Euro-fever' did not start immediately after the decision to introduce the single market had been taken in 1985. It did so only when the debate on '1992' became articulated with the public campaigns for a techno–economic and, subsequently, socio-political restructuring as a solution to the economic crisis –campaigns which had gathered momentum in the second half of the eighties . . .

. . . By the middle of the eighties, as a result of these experiences, academic analyses had often departed from previous interpretations of integration. Former analytic models had relied on a rather unilinear advance of European politics. By 'sticking closely to the terms of the Treaties establishing the European

Communities', they had postulated 'integration as a stage-by-stage process, in which the ultimate target of economic union would be preceded by the pooling of significant national instruments for the management of economic policy', and some of them had woven 'an ingenious political schema around this step-by-step formulation of economic integration, emphasizing the transfer of political loyalties which would accompany a shift in the focus of economic policy-making towards a new centre in Brussels'.[1] Obviously, at that time, neither this functionalist view of European integration nor a federalist interpretation assuming the emergence of a new institutional and constitutional order in the spirit of a European Union fitted to the process and outcome of actual Community affairs. Thus, a more realistic analysis was suggested which had to focus on the uneven and disjointed character of the EC's decision-making, to grasp the intergovernmental rather than supranational or even federal patterns of EC politics, and even to question the very notion of integration and to possibly replace it by more 'modest' concepts like 'policy coordination', 'intergovernmental cooperation', or 'politics of interdependence'. Not surprisingly, this view – based on a series of detailed policy-making studies presented in the same volume[2] – was very much inclined to stress the impact of national politics and thus of political diversity on the performance and the prospects of the Community.

The problem of diversity even became the central theme of a further study by the author cited, published two years later.[3] The entire argument now revolves on the thesis that, from the very onset, diversity has been the inherent characteristic of the European Communities and has become even more so as a result of the enlargements of the membership in 1973, 1981 and 1986. Therefore, the solution to the shortcomings and difficulties of the EC cannot be seen in attempts to overcome the heterogeneity but only in attempts to cater for the requirements of adapting to this diversity! Consequently, the various proposals for a revitalization of the Community, discussed by other authors as initiatives for a new dynamic of European integration, appear as 'strategies for managing diversity'.

Strategies for further market integration are explicitly – and bluntly – included in this argument: 'Attachment to the pursuit of market liberalization implies giving priority to decentralized and efficient competition which preserves diversity.'[4] Seen from the perspective of the present debate on '1992' this is clearly a provocative statement.

The 'natural focus of Community policies', it is maintained, has already 'shifted towards cooperation or collaboration rather than full integration'.[5] The 'very language of policy coordination as distinct from harmonization, let alone integration . . . also suggests implementation of agreement by parallel national action rather than by common instruments'.[6] . . .

'1992' or what has changed?

Pronounced as it was, the reported interpretation of the 'pre-1992' Community may have overstated the case. But obviously it reflected (in the double sense of the term) salient features of the EC until the mid-eighties. Thus, the question necessarily follows whether the present debate has neglected a 'realistic' view of the Community or whether the EC has changed substantially and dramatically.

For a discussion of this question I want to comment further on the two major strands in the debate already mentioned in this paper. The first derives the new dynamic of the Community from the observation that the economic rationale of West European integration has gained a new persuasive power, and argues that this has paved the way for a political redefinition of the EC; the second deduces the new drive of the integration process from a genuine political response to the former shortcomings and deficiencies of Community affairs. As the first strand is based on a functionalist interpretation and as the second more or less assumes a trend towards a federalist organization of Western Europe, the two main approaches rejected by the 'realists' have become prominent again. Both share a Euro-optimist view (if not attitude) and therefore do not conflict with each other. On the contrary, in their respective concentration on the economic and political aspects of 1992 they are rather complementary, and thus contribute jointly to the notion that there has been a process of accelerating integration in which the economic and political objectives are directly interrelated, if not coordinated.

The picture becomes more complicated, however, when we look at the initiatives for a revitalization of the Community launched from the early eighties onwards. Again, there was much evidence that Community affairs had developed in a rather uneven and disjointed way. In the course of events the main emphasis of successive proposals for reform shifted from the political to the economic side and vice versa; individual initiatives became watered down in bargaining processes; some initiatives were taken to counterbalance others; and generally there was a propensity or custom to present the final results in the well established mode of Eurorhetoric. We should also be well aware of the fact that the proclamation of the 1992 exercise in 1985 fits this pattern of ('normal') politics. It should be fair to say that the plan for the 'single European market' (or 'internal market' as it was called in the first instance) hardly presented a new vision of Western Europe. Basically, it was a reaffirmation of the main goals already agreed in the Treaty of Rome in 1957, and accordingly the newly introduced terms actually offered new designations for a long existing model, i.e. the Common market. This reaffirmation was important enough when we recall the state of Community affairs of the seventies and early eighties. Although the 1992 plan was linked with changes in EC decision-making procedures . . . its main emphasis was on the revitalization of economic integration . . .

. . . The new drive of the Community has not resulted, I think, from a process set in motion by revitalized EC institutions or from a new commitment of national governments to promote the European Union. Rather it resulted from a notion that the EC offers favourable conditions for a far reaching techno–economic restructuring generally seen as an imperative for the future development of all national economies. Only when the case of European integration became broadly discussed in terms of a solution to the crises of the seventies and early eighties, when it no longer appeared to be a zero sum affair, and when it could be seen as a logical trans-national extension of basically similar policies pursued in all the member states, only then the new EC process gathered its present momentum . . .

. . . What has changed in the Community, then, is not so much its basic institutional design or the definition of its main goals but the expectations from further integration. To some extent the present situation resembles that of the sixties when the creation of the EEC had triggered an increase in intra-Community trade and thus promoted a climate of Euro-optimism which in turn had contributed to a relatively smooth process of interest intermediation between the member states. What is celebrated at present as a new stage of European integration could well prove to be just another conjuncture of Community affairs, supported by relatively favourable economic conditions (if compared to the seventies and early eighties) and by a widespread trust in the positive effects of 1992. The political progress of the Community in recent years (extended policy scope and procedural changes) is obvious, but it has not yet been transformed into a structural change towards a new type of supranational organization, already assumed or anticipated by many commentators. Thus 1992 and even more so a political reshaping of the Community have still to be achieved.

Concluding remark

The introduction of the single market and the additional drive for economic and social integration which may follow from it demand policies which are not as technical as they often appear to be. This may explain why they are not left to the Eurocrats but often are dealt with as matters of high politics in top-level bodies of the Council of Ministers. Thus, the decision to introduce the single market has not at all discontinued the bargaining processes within the Community and especially between governments which try to preserve or to promote what is regarded to be in the national interest. The present Euro-fever has not resulted in a consensual type of decision-making, and it is only the general acceptance of the ultimate goal which conceals the fact that the procedural changes within the institutional setting of the Community have not really led to a shift of authoritative decision-making from the Council of Ministers to the Commission and the Parliament. Therefore we should be sceptical about the general argument that 1992 will be a matter of centralized decision-making kept away from national actors. The often-mentioned 50 to 80 per cent of legislation enacted in the member states which will have its origin in EC institutions is not imposed by an external body but is decided in a way in which each member state is participating, especially via its national government.

As a result, there is good reason to assume that the diversity of national politics within the Community will not be overcome in the foreseeable future but will be expressed in a continuing policy of differentiation which will allow a 'diversity of practice' . . .

Notes

1 H. Wallace *et al.* (eds), *Policy-Making in the European Community* (London, 1983 edn) pp. 7–8.
2 H. Wallace *et al.* (eds), ibid. (1983 edn).
3 H. Wallace and A. Ridley, 'New wine in old bottles', in *Europe: The challenge of diversity* (London, 1985).
4 ibid., pp. 10–11.
5 ibid., p. 10.
6 ibid., p. 53.

Document 45: A. Bressand, 'Futures for economic integration. Beyond interdependence: 1992 as a global challenge', *International Affairs* Vol. 66: 1990, pp. 53–5, 58–61

An economic perestroika in search of its political glasnost

The least visible yet the most fundamental part of the challenge of 1992 is that neither economists or politicians have fully grasped yet the new political economy of regional integration from which 1992 derives its unexpected momentum as well as its international impact. Hence the paradoxical situation in which European political leaders find themselves . . .

. . . In my view, the most enlightening perspective on the 1992 process is to be gained by focusing on this discrepancy between the visions of European integration that led European politicians to give their blessing to the Single Act and the process that they have actually unleashed.

Three political versions of European integration are at the centre of the debate to which 1992 is gradually giving birth – the federalist one, the policy coordination one and the deregulatory 'roll-back' one. The two extreme views are obviously the 'roll-back' one – today's re-expression of the 'free trade zone' approach, in which all that is at stake is to eliminate trade barriers and to deregulate within each country – and the federalist one – to which Jacques Delors alluded in the summer of 1988 when he mentioned the prospect of 80 per cent of the key decisions being taken in Brussels against 20 per cent in the national capital. While these two extreme views polarize the political debate, both seem quite at odds with observable trends.

While 'deregulation' is a fundamental source of economic dynamism, it is also a far more complex – and regulation-intensive – process than commonly realized . . .

1992 as a post-interdependence dynamic

. . . Coming back to the economic forces behind the present rebirth and momentum of European integration, two aspects of the 1992 process stand out and provide insights into the actual dynamic at work. The first one relates to corporate strategies, or cross-border networking. The second seminal change revolves around mutual recognition and its implications for national sovereignty and for global economic openness.

The new dynamic of corporate interconnection

Rather than simply seeking exports and economies of scale, European-based companies are now focusing on developing Europe-wide delivery systems, corporate alliances, production networks and electronic marketplaces. Rather than just shipping goods across borders, they are seeking customized, in-depth interactions with clients, suppliers and partners, through an expanding gamut of networking strategies, many of which have a strong information and advanced communication content. In this sense the physical elimination of custom houses is an almost narrow symbol of the deeper and more complex ways in which corporate strategies are reshaping the new phase of economic integration . . .

. . . To achieve the economies of scale in customized products that we label mass customization, corporations need a depth and quality of interactions that goes beyond the arm's length relationship associated with markets, even when market forces are actually shaping such relationships. A concrete example is the move of US and European car manufacturers from piecemeal subcontracting aimed at short-term cost optimization to the development of long-term strategic relationships with suppliers. Such depth and quality of relations is made possible by two types of factors, namely access to infrastructures through which inter-actions can be conducted, and definition of – and adherence to – common sets of rules to which we might refer as infostructures. Without going into details here, this combination of infrastructures and infostructures might be called 'net-works', thereby giving to this term a broader sense than is usually implied.

While this parenthesis on corporate strategies and the new wealth-creation process may sound out of place here, a lot of the restructuring at work in Europe falls within this type of interaction rather than under the traditional trade specialization and economies-of-scale paradigm. While high technology and services (finance, transport, communications, advertising, etc.) are presently the key fields of applications, such strategies and the policies explicitly or implicitly supporting them are at the heart of the 1992 dynamic, and go a long way in accounting for the discrepancy between traditional political visions of Europe and the unexpected renaissance of regional integration.

Seen at the level of individual actors, this new type of interaction appears to rest on four types of 'network'. Two of them are data networks . . .

. . . Two other types of networks are of a strategic nature: intercorporate networks include alliances of all types, while metacorporate networks are intended to influence the corporate environment through lobbying, standard setting, etc. These four types of networks are presently at the forefront of European integration.

Obviously, many obstacles may develop in the way of this unprecedented development of cross-border networking in Europe. But a number of policies in place within the 1992 White Paper framework, as well as outside it, can be seen as facilitating or fostering these various types of corporate networking strategies . . .

. . . Present EC and national policies have however tended to develop piece-meal, do not cover the whole gamut of the cross-border dynamic, and still lack a unified strategic concept. Indeed, the discrepancy between the visions held at the political level and the actual process of cross-border integration has prevented Europeans from seeking higher coherence and effectiveness in what is already a ground-breaking exploration of the post-interdependence world economy.

The new citizenship of mutual recognition

The second critical dimension of the 1992 dynamic has, in my view, to do with the watershed decision by the twelve European Community countries to break away from previous and increasingly futile efforts to harmonize regulations and technical norms in favour of an amazingly speedier process based on a limited number of core principles and on mutual recognition. In many ways, mutual recognition reinforces the relevance and the impact of the corporate cross-border networking strategies just described.

The implications of mutual recognition are quite fundamental, as national authorities will now accept that other governments grant establishment rights to their own national firms as well as to third-country firms, taking into account their own regulatory criteria rather than those of the host country. To the extent that some core principles are adhered to, banks, financial service providers and many other corporations will be able to carry a number of activities on a European scale under their home country regulations. By the same token, in the light of the European Court's landmark 'cassis de Dijon' decision, standards and norms considered acceptable in one of the EC countries will have to be accepted in all others.

As remarked by Michel Albert, chairman and chief executive of the AGF insurance group, mutual recognition as will be practised in Europe has no equivalent in the world, and goes beyond the federalist vision borrowed from the US experience. As he likes to stress, Europeans have accepted direct interaction and competition between national regulations and tax structures without creating the political institutions with which a transfer of sovereignty of that order had always been associated.

Towards an OECD-wide 1992?

Such an analysis of the European integration process would obviously call for much more detailed analysis. Yet it seems clear already that the 1992 process must be seen as a watershed not just for Europe but for the overall global economy. As suggested above, this has little to do with exceptional foresight on the part of European leaders, and much more to do with unanticipated synergies between the broad policy framework available in the European context and a new global economic dynamic that can no longer be understood and managed in the traditional narrow trade framework.

Document 46: A. Smith, 'National identities and the idea of European unity', *International Affairs* Vol. 68: 1992, pp. 57–60, 62, 64–5, 67, 70, 72–3, 74–6

First considerations: method

Though there have been many studies of the economic organizations and political institutions of the European Community, relatively little attention has been devoted to the cultural and psychological issues associated with European unification – to questions of meaning, value and symbolism. What research there has been in this area has suffered from a lack of theoretical sophistication and tends to be somewhat impressionistic and superficial. This is especially true of attitude studies, in which generalizations over time are derived from surveys of particular groups or strata at particular moments. In few areas is the attitude questionnaire of such doubtful utility as in the domain of cultural values and meanings.

Clearly, what is needed in this field is a series of case-studies over time of changes in collective perceptions and values, as recorded in literature and the arts, in political traditions and symbolism, in national mythologies and historical memories, and as relayed in educational texts and the mass media. Such studies rarely focus on the European dimension as such. Rather, they address changes in the content of national symbolism and mythology, ethno-history and collective values and traditions, which may or may not include an opening towards a wider, European dimension, but whose central focus is the continuing process of reconstructing or re-imagining the nation.

Such studies form a useful point of departure for investigations into the complex relationships between national identities and the processes of European unification in the sphere of culture and values. Here I shall concentrate specifically on the cultural domain and its links with politics, leaving on one side the processes of economic and political integration that form the main concern of European studies. I shall focus on five interrelated areas.

- The impact and uses of the pre-modern 'past' or 'pasts' of ethnic communities and nations in the continent of Europe, and the ways in which pre-modern structures and images continue to condition modern processes and outlooks.
- The origins and nature of collective, cultural identities, and more specifically of national identities, and their consequences for social and political action.
- The growth of globalizing tendencies in communications, education, the media and the arts, which transcend national and even continental boundaries, bringing a truly cosmopolitan character to society that surpasses internationalism.
- Allied to these tendencies, fundamental geopolitical and ecological changes in the world at large – often of an unpredictable nature, like the dangers of a

shrinking Soviet Union or a Middle Eastern vortex, or of pollution and epi-demic disease – which affect changing values.

- The processes of regional or continental unification, of which Europeanization is only the most explicit and advanced example. Here the question is not just the history of an idea or process, but the changing contents and boundaries of 'Europe' in the context of a rapidly evolving world.

Multiple identities

A comparative method using case-studies of national identity and culture needs some kind of theoretical framework; and given the nature of our problem, a logical starting-point is the concept of collective cultural identity. This would refer not to some fixed pattern or uniformity of elements over time, but rather to a sense of shared continuity on the part of successive generations of a given unit of population, and to shared memories of earlier periods, events and person-ages in the history of the unit. From these two components we can derive a third: the collective belief in a common destiny of that unit and its culture. From a subjective standpoint, there can be no collective cultural identity without shared memories or a sense of continuity on the part of those who feel they belong to that collectivity. So the subjective perception and understanding of the communal past by each generation of a given cultural unit of population – the 'ethno-history' of that collectivity, as opposed to a historian's judgement of that past – is a defining element in the concept of cultural identity, and hence of more specific national and European identities.

From this starting-point we might go on to characterize the cultural history of humanity as a successive differentiation (but also enlargement) of processes of identification . . .

. . . Collective identities, however, tend to be pervasive and persistent. They are less subject to rapid changes and tend to be more intense and durable, even when quite large numbers of individuals no longer feel their power. This is especially true of religious and ethnic identities, which even in pre-modern eras often became politicized. It is particularly true of national identities today, when the power of mass political fervour reinforces the technological instruments of mass political organization, so that national identities can outlast the defection or apathy of quite large numbers of individual members. So we need to bear this distinction between the collective and the individual levels of identity in mind and to exercise caution in making inferences about collective sentiments and communal identifications on the basis of individual attitudes and behaviour.

National identity: some bases and legacies

This preliminary survey of the types and levels of cultural identity provides a general framework for analysing specifically national identities. Here it may be useful to take together the first two areas of analysis – the impact of the pre-

Documents

modern past and the nature and consequences of national identity – since in Europe at any rate it is mainly through such identities that these 'pasts' have been retained and mediated.

The concept of national identity is both complex and highly abstract. Indeed the multiplicity of cultural identities, both now and in the past, is mirrored in the multiple dimensions of our conceptions of nationhood. To grasp this, we need only enumerate of few of these dimensions. They include:

- the territorial boundedness of separate cultural populations in their own 'home-lands';
- the shared nature of myths of origin and historical memories of the community;
- the common bond of a mass, standardized culture;
- a common territorial division of labour, with mobility for all members and ownership of resources by all members in the homeland;
- the possession by all members of a unified system of common legal rights and duties under common laws and institutions . . .

. . . This reiterated reference to a community of common public culture reveals the continuing influence of ethnicity and its common myths, symbols and memories in the life of modern European nations. On the one hand, these nations seek to transcend their ethnic origins, which are usually the myths and memories of the dominant ethnic community (the English, the northern French, the Castilians); on the other hand, in a world of growing interdependence, they very often feel the need to revert to them to sustain community as well as to justify their differences. The link with the distinctive pre-modern past serves to dignify the nation as well as to explain its mores and character. More important, it serves to 'remake the collective personality' of the nation in each generation . . .

. . . In this respect, national identifications possess distinct advantages over the idea of a unified European identity. They are vivid, accessible, well established, long popularized, and still widely believed, in broad outline at least. In each of these respects, 'Europe' is deficient both as idea and as process. Above all, it lacks a pre-modern past – a 'prehistory' which can provide it with emotional sustenance and historical depth . . .

A globalizing culture?

Against these predictions must be set the 'major trends' of world history that so many have discerned and welcomed. These include:

- the rapid growth of vast transnational companies, with budgets, technologies, communications networks and skill levels far outstripping those of all but the largest and most powerful of contemporary national states;
- the rise and fall of large power blocs based on one or other military 'super-power', and forming a military–political network of client-states in an increasingly interdependent international system of states; and

- the vast increase in the scale, efficiency, density and power of the means of communication, from transport to the mass media, from telecommunications to computerized information and transmission.

What this means, in the most general terms, is an accelerating process of globalization: of trends and processes that transcend the boundaries of national states and ethnic communities, and that serve to bind together into common economic, political and cultural patterns the various populations into which the globe is at present divided.

That such trends and processes can be observed is not in question. It is not difficult to point to processes that transcend national boundaries, and appear to unite different populations in those respects. This is as true of patterns of world trade, nuclear proliferation and diplomatic language as it is of styles in modern art, fashion and television serials. The question is whether there is anything new in such boundary-transcending activities and processes, and whether they serve to unite distinctive populations in more than superficial respects. Do they, in other words, portend that global cosmopolitanism of which Marx and Engels, as well as so many liberals, dreamed? . . .

. . . It is undeniable that we are witnessing an immense and rapid growth of communications and information technology, spanning the globe; and with it a slower but definite, albeit uneven increase in literacy and mass education in many countries. There is also considerable convergence in parts of each state's education system: an emphasis on technology, a concern with mathematics and science, and interest in at least one other lingua franca, and so on. In other parts of each education system, however, there is a conscious retention of national difference: in literature, in history, in the arts. In so far as the state can control and use the instruments of mass education effectively, this policy of national self-maintenance is not to be underestimated . . .

. . . Herein lies the paradox of any project for a global culture: it must work with materials destined for the very projects which it seeks to supersede – the national identities which are ultimately to be eradicated.

The European 'family of cultures'

This, then, is where the European project must be located: between national revival and global cultural aspirations. Thus expressed, it makes the old debate between pan-Europeans and anti-Europeans seem faintly antiquated.

That debate centred on the possibility and desirability of creating a unified Europe 'from above', through economic and political institutions, perhaps on the model of German unification in the nineteenth century. Pan-Europeans conceded that there would be local delays and problems, but believed that European unity was imperative to prevent a recurrence of any European 'civil war', to create a third power between East and West and to secure a prosperous future for Europe's peoples. They also argued that the route of 'state-making' from above through bureaucratic incorporation and the building of institutions was the only way forward. Just as in the past dynastic states had moulded the first nations in the West, so today the framework of a United States of Europe and swift political union, based firmly in the Western heartlands, would forge a European consciousness in place of the obsolete national identities.

Anti-Europeans countered by pointing to the 'unevenness' of Europe's peoples and states, to the difficulties of deciding the boundaries of 'Europe', to the continuing strength of several European national states and to the linguistic and ethnic pluralism of Europe's mixed areas. But at the root of their opposition to pan-Europeanism, whether unitary or federal in character, was their belief in the overriding importance of existing national identities and the ethnic histories and cultures they enshrined. Behind the economic facade and the agonizing over subsidies and monetary union, the embattled camps of Brussels and Bruges agreed on the mutual incompatibility of 'Europe' and 'national' identity.

But is there any warrant for this dichotomic view of cultural identities and for the battle cries on either side? We have already seen that, sociologically, human beings have multiple identities, that they can move between them according to context and situation, and that such identities may be concentric rather than conflictual. None of this is to deny the cultural reality and vivid meanings of these identities, which, transmitted through successive generations, are not exhausted by the often fickle volitions and changing perceptions of individuals. At the same time, there is plenty of historical evidence for the coexistence of concentric circles of allegiance . . .

. . . So what is common to all Europeans? What can they be said to share and in what respects can they be said to differ from non-Europeans? To these kinds of questions there can never be satisfactory answers. Europeans differ among themselves as much as from non-Europeans in respect of language (Basques, Finns, Hungarians), territory (Russians, Greeks, Armenians), law (Roman, Germanic), religion (Catholic, Orthodox, Protestant) and economic and political system (democracy, communism, unitary state, federalism, etc.) – as well as in terms of ethnicity and culture.

On the other hand, there are shared traditions, legal and political, and shared heritages, religious and cultural. Not all Europeans share in all of them; some share in particular traditions and heritages only minimally. But at one time or another all Europe's communities have participated in at least some of these traditions and heritages, in some degree . . .

. . . Some changes are occurring in these areas, and given the political will of the elites, more rapid changes may soon take place. But the question still remains: how will the new 'European message' be received? Will it be reinterpreted by audiences and pupils in ethnic and national terms, as with so many cultural products? For until the great majority of Europeans, the great mass of the middle and lower classes, are ready to imbibe these European messages in a similar manner and to feel inspired by them to common action and community, the edifice of 'Europe' at the political level will remain shaky. This is all too clear today in respect of foreign policy and defence, where we are witnessing the need for European governments to respond to their national public opinion and the failure of Europeans to agree on a common policy. Once again, the usual divisions of public opinion between European states have been exposed, and with them the tortuous and divided actions of Europe's governments . . .

. . . The 'European failure' only underlines the distance between the European ideal and its rootedness in the popular consciousness of Europe's national populations – and hence the distance between European unification at the political and cultural levels and the realities of divergent national identities, perceptions and interests within Europe . . .

. . . Here lies the new Europe's true dilemma: a choice between unacceptable historical myths and memories on the one hand, and on the other a patchwork, memoryless scientific 'culture' held together solely by the political will and economic interest that are so often subject to change. In between, there lies the hope of discovering that 'family of cultures' briefly outlined above, through which over several generations some loose, over-arching political identity and community might gradually be forged.

Europe in a wider world

At present the tide is running for the idea of European unification as it has never done before. This is probably the result of dramatic geopolitical and geocultural changes, which remind us that the future of 'Europe', as indeed of every national state today, will be largely determined by wider regions, or global, currents and trends . . .

. . . There is another and equally important issue raised by the project of European unification and its relationship with nations and nationalism. Identities are forged out of shared experiences, memories and myths, in relation to those other collective identities. They are in fact often forged through opposition to the identities of significant others. . . . Who or what then, are Europe's significant others? Until now, the obvious answers were the protagonists of the ideological Cold War. In this context Europe was often seen as a third force between the respective super power blocs, though there was always something unreal about such a posture. Now, however, the problem of relationship to other identities has become more perplexing. To whom shall Europe be likened, against whom shall it measure itself? . . .

. . . Facing and understanding these problems is a precondition for forging a pan-European identity that will eschew these undesirable and self-defeating images and features. Shaping a cultural identity that will be both distinctive and inclusive, differentiating yet assimilative, may yet constitute the supreme challenge for a Europe that seeks to create itself out of its ancient family of ethnic cultures.

Notes to Chapters 1–6

1 THE QUEST FOR EUROPEAN INTEGRATION

1 F. Melian Stawell, *The Growth of International Thought* (London, 1929), pp. 97–120.
2 Denis de Rougemont, *The Meaning of Europe* (London, 1965), reviews these early proposals for European unity.
3 Kant's essay is included as an appendix in C. Friedrich, *The Philosophy of Kant* (1954 edn), p. 444.
4 R. Aron and A. Marc, *Principles du federalisme* (Paris, 1948), p. 108.
5 A. Cobban, *The Nation State and National Self Determination in Europe* (London, 1969 edn).
6 See E.J. Hobsbawm, *The Age of Empire, 1875–1914* (London, 1987), especially Chapters 4, 6, and 7.
7 Richard Coudenhove-Kalergi's, *Pan Europa*, was first published in 1924; see also his *An Idea Conquers the World* (New York, 1954 edn).
8 Ibid., (2nd edn) p. ix of the Preface.
9 A. Milward, *The Reconstruction of Western Europe 1945–51* (Methuen, 1984); and the sequel to this seminal work, ibid., *The European Rescue of the Nation-State* (London, 1992).
10 W. Lipgens, *A History of European Integration: Vol. One 1945–1947* (Oxford, 1982), especially pp. 44–58.
11 A. Spinelli, *European Union in the Resistance, Government and Opposition* Vol. 2: 1967, pp. 321–9.
12 See the account in D.E. Ellwood, *Rebuilding Europe: Western Europe, America and Postwar Reconstruction* (Harlow, 1992).
13 S. Andersen and K. Eliassen, 'Policy-making in the new Europe', in Anderson and Eliassen (eds), *Making policy in Europe: The Europeification of National Policy-making* (London, 1993), p. 256.
14 J.A. Caporaso, 'Theory and method in the study of international integration', *International Organization* Vol. 25: 1971, p. 228.
15 B. Hughes and J. Schwartz, 'Dimensions of political integration and the experience of the European Community', *International Studies Quarterly* 1970–1, pp. 263–94.
16 A.J.R. Groom and A. Heraclides, 'Integration and disintegration', in M. Light and A.J.R. Groom (eds), *International Relations: A Handbook of Current Thought* (London, 1985), p. 174.
17 D. Puchala, 'Of blind men, elephants and international integration', *Journal of Common Market Studies* Vol. 10: 1972, pp. 267–84.
18 J.N. Rosenau, 'A pre-theory revisited: world politics in an era of cascading interdependence', *International Studies Quarterly* Vol. 28: 1984, especially pp. 298–300.

19 K. Kaiser, 'L'Europe des savants: European integration and the social sciences', *Journal of Common Market Studies*, Vol. 4: 1965–66, pp. 36–46.
20 C. Pentland, *International Theory and European Integration* (London, 1973), p. 16.
21 Ibid. (1973), pp. 20–1.
22 W. Wallace, *The Transformation of Western Europe* (London, 1990), p. 54.
23 R. Pryce and W. Wessels, 'The search for an ever closer Union: a framework for analysis', in R. Pryce (ed.) *The Dynamics of European Union* (London, 1987), p. 3.

2 THE SUPRANATIONAL PARADIGM (1): THE FEDERALIST APPROACH

1 See H. Bull and A. Watson (eds), *The Expansion of International Society* (Oxford, 1984), especially Chapters 26, 27 and the Conclusion.
2 L.N. Lindberg and S.A. Scheingold, *Europe's Would-be Polity: Patterns of Change in the European Community* (Englewood Cliffs, NJ, 1970), p. 6.
3 See R. Mayne, J. Pinder and J.C. de V. Roberts, *Federal Union: The Pioneers* (London, 1990).
4 A group of federalist thinkers did eventually update the federalist doctrine to take proper account of the social roots of political change. See, for instance, H. Brugmans', *L'idée européene* (Bruges, 1965) and A. Marc, *L'Europe dans le Monde* (Paris, 1965).
5 L. Lindberg, *The Political Dynamics of European Integration* (Stanford, Cal. 1965), p. 6.
6 P. King, *Federalism and Federation* (London, 1982).
7 H. Brugmans, *La Pensée Politique Federalism* (London, 1969), especially Chapter 5.
8 L. Levi, 'Recent developments in federalist theory', *The Federalist* Part Two, 1987, p. 106.
9 For a critical review of the federalist legacy see C.J. Friedrich, 'Trends of federalism', in *Theory and Practice* (New York, 1968) and M. Vile, 'Federal theory and the "New Federalism"', in D. Jaensch (ed.), *The Politics of New Federalism* (Adelaide, 1977).
10 A. Lijphart, 'Consociation and federation: conceptual and empirical links', *Canadian Journal of Political Science* Vol. 12: 1979.
11 K.C. Wheare, 'What federal government is', in P. Ransome (ed.), *Studies in Federal Planning* (London, 1990), pp. 23–4.
12 A. Bosca, *The Federal Idea: The History of Federalism from Enlightenment to 1945*, published in two volumes by the Lothian Foundation (London, 1991), for a contemporary account see Edouard Herriot, *The United States of Europe* (London, 1931).
13 W. Lipgens, 'European federation in the political thought of resistance movements during World War II', *Central European History* Vol. 1: 1968, pp. 5–19.
14 A. Spinelli and E. Rossi, *The Ventotene Manifesto* (Pavia, 1989 edition).
15 Among some of the most influential contributions here were, H.P. Kerr, in J. Pinker and A. Bosca (eds), *Pacifism is not Enough: Collected Speeches of Lord Lothian/Philip Kerr*, (London, 1990); L. Robbins, *The Economic Causes of War Conflicts* (London, 1939); L. Curtis, *Civitas Dei, The Commonwealth of God* (London, 1939); W. Beveridge, *Peace by Federation?* (London, 1940); I. Jennings, *A Federation for Western Europe* (Cambridge, 1940); and R.G. Mackay, *Federal Europe* (London, 1940).
16 A. Spinelli and E. Rossi, op. cit. (1989 edn), pp. 40–1 and 45–9.
17 W. Lipgens, *Documents on the History of European Integration, Vol. 1, Continental Plans for European Union 1939–1945* (Berlin, 1985), pp. 666–8.
18 A. Bosca, op. cit. (1991) Vol. 1, p. 3.
19 See the discussion in S. George, *Britain and European Integration Since 1945* (Oxford, 1991), Chapter 1.
20 Steffan Zetterholm, 'Why is cultural diversity a political problem? A discussion of cultural barriers to political integration', in S. Zetterholm (ed.), *National Cultures and*

European Integration (Oxford, 1994), pp. 65–82; see also Bruno de Witte, 'Cultural Linkages', Part III of W. Wallace (ed.), *The Dynamics of European Integration* (London, 1990), pp. 171–91.

21 D.J. Elazar, 'The role of federalism in political integration', in D. Elazar (ed.), *Federalism and Political Integration* (Jerusalem, 1979), pp. 42–4.

22 For an account of Monnet's realism, see F. Duchêne, *Jean Monnet* (London, 1995).

23 J. Monnet, press conference, May 1962, cited in J. Pinder, 'European Community and nation-state: a case for a neo-federalism?', *International Affairs* Vol. 62: 1986, p. 45.

24 Jean Monnet, *Memoirs* (London, 1978), pp. 346 and 367.

25 Monnet's inaugural speech as president of the ECSC referred to what he regarded as that organization's federalist nature. J. Monnet, *Les Etats-Unis d'Europe ont commencé* (Paris, 1955), pp. 56–7.

26 R. Mayne *et al.*, op. cit. (1990), p. 55.

27 See A.W. MacMahon (ed.) *Federalism: Mature and Emergent* (New York, 1955), Introduction to Part IV, pp. 411–12 for a brief account of these factions.

28 L. Levi, *Altiero Spinelli and Federalism in Europe and the World* (Turin, 1990).

29 See A. Spinelli, 'The growth of the European movement since World War II', in C. Grove Haines (ed.) *European Integration* (Baltimore, 1957).

30 Daniela Preda, 'From defence community to a political community: the role of De Gasperi and Spinelli', in A. Bosca, op. cit (1992) Vol. 2, pp. 186–206.

31 On the split in European federalism, see H. Brugmans and P. Duclos, *Le Fédéralisme Contemporain*, (Leyden, 1963), pp. 143–9; and M. Forsyth, 'The Political Objectives of European Integration', *International Affairs*, Vol. 43: 1967, pp. 489–91.

32 M. Burgess, 'Federalism and federation in western Europe', in M. Burgess (ed.) *Federalism and Federation in Western Europe* (Beckenham, 1986), p. 26.

33 J. Lodge, 'European Union and the first elected European Parliament: the Spinelli initiative', *Journal of Common Market Studies* Vol. 22: 1984, especially pp. 395–8; this is consistent with her earlier expression of cautious optimism concerning the EC's federalist potential. See J. Lodge, 'Direct elections to the European Parliament: towards a federal future?', *Cooperation and Conflict* Vol. 13: 1978, pp. 215–30, and especially p. 30; see, in similar vein, J.L. Homan, 'Which Europe?', *Journal of Common Market Studies* 1970–71, pp. 67–92.

34 See F. Rosenthiel, 'Reflections on the Notion of Supranationality', *Journal of Common Market Studies* Vol. 2: 1963.

35 Andrew Marshall, 'Federalism that will never lie down', *The Independent* 11 December 1991.

3 THE SUPRANATIONAL PARADIGM (2): FUNCTIONALIST MODELS

1 The historical roots of functionalism are discussed in F. Parkinson, 'The philosophy of international relations: a study in the history of thought', *Sage Library of Social Research* Vol. 52, (Beverly Hills, Cal. 1977), Chapter 6.

2 Inis Claude, 'Swords into plowshares', *The Problems and Progress of International Organization* (London, 1965), p. 31.

3 J. Martin Rochester, 'The rise and fall of international organization as a field of study', *International Organization* Vol. 40: 1986, pp. 777–813.

4 The Mitranian vision lives on in the idealist tradition of international theory. See J. Galtung, 'The European Community: a superpower in the making' (London, 1973); and T. Kamo, 'International integration and the dynamics of peace: behavioural trends in the European Community', *British Journal of International Studies* Vol. 5: 1979, pp. 150–70.

5 D. Mitrany, *A Working Peace System: An Argument for the Functional Development of International Organization* (London, 1993), p. 28 (reprinted).

6 D. Mitrany, ibid. (1966 edn).

7 D. Mitrany, *The Progress of International Government* (London, 1933), p. 118. His other major works on this theme include: *The Problem of International Sanctions* (Oxford, 1925); 'The functional approach to world organization', *International Affairs* Vol. 24: 1948, pp. 350–61; 'The functional approach in historical perspective', ibid. Vol. 47: 1971, pp. 533–43; *International Security* (National Peace Council, 1944).

8 D. Mitrany, *The Progress of International Government*, (1933) p. 88.

9 D. Mitrany, in *International Affairs* (1948), p. 356.

10 D. Mitrany, op. cit. (1933), p. 101.

11 D. Mitrany, *A Working Peace System* (1943 edn), p. 31.

12 Technocratic determinism has been a persistent theme in the functionalist account of the social process. As such, it has attracted some articulate critiques. See, for instance, J.K. Galbraith, *The New Industrial State* (New York, 1967), especially p. 405; and B. Crick, *In Defence of Politics* (Harmondsworth, 1964), pp. 92–3 and 110.

13 For a review of this critique see R. Tooze, 'The progress of international functionalism', *British Journal of International Studies* Vol. 3: 1977; M. Imber, 'Re-reading Mitrany: a pragmatic assessment of sovereignty', *Review of International Studies*, Vol. 10: 1984; and R. McLaren, 'Mitranian functionalism: possible or impossible?', *Review of International Studies* Vol. 11: 1985.

14 See the critique in R.J. Harrison, 'Testing functionalism', in A.J.R. Groom and P. Taylor (eds), *Functionalism: Theory and Practice in International Relations* (London, 1975), pp. 112–37.

15 J.P. Duroselle, 'General de Gaulle's Europe and Jean Monnet's Europe', in C. Cosgrove and K. Twitchett (eds) *The New International Actors: The UN and the EEC* (London, 1970), pp. 187–200.

16 See W. Diebold, 'The relevance of federalism to western European economic integration', in A.W. Mackintosh (ed.), *Federalism: Mature and Emergent* (New York, 1955).

17 R. Schuman speaking in the Consultative Assembly of the Council of Europe, Records of the Fourth Sitting, 10 August 1950, pp. 174 and 180.

18 D. Urwin, *The Community of Europe: A History of European Integration Since 1945* (Harlow, 1991), pp. 43–57.

19 W. Yondorf, 'Monnet and the action committee: the formative years of the European Communities', *International Organization* Vol. 19: 1965.

20 Quoted in S. Patijn (ed.), *Landmarks in European Unity* (Leyden, 1970), p. 101.

21 J. Pinder, 'Positive integration and negative integration: some problems of economic union in the EEC', *The World Today* January 1968.

22 R.J. Harrison, 'Neofunctionalism', in A.J.R. Groom and P. Taylor (eds), *Frameworks for International Cooperation* (London, 1990), pp. 139–40.

23 H.J. Kusters, 'The Treaties of Rome, (1955–57)', in R. Pryce (ed.), *The Dynamics of European Union* (London, 1987).

24 J. Monnet, *Memoirs* (1978), pp. 431–2.

25 For an early insight into this incipient neofunctionalist approach, see E.B. Haas, 'Regionalism, functionalism, and universal international organization', *World Politics* 1956, pp. 238–63, especially pp. 260–3.

26 E.B. Haas, 'The study of regional integration: reflections on the joy and anguish of pre-theorising', *International Organization* Vol. 24: 1970, p. 610.

27 See A.J.R. Groom, 'The functionalist approach and East/West cooperation in Europe', *Journal of Common Market Studies* Vol. 13: especially pp. 21–8.

28 And, for that matter, subsequent attempts to explain the impulse to transnational integration couched in normative rather than empirical terms. See, for instance,

J.W. Sloan and H.R. Targ, 'Beyond the European nation-state: a normative critique', *Polity* Vol. 3: 1973, pp. 501–20.
29 E.B. Haas, *The Uniting of Europe: Political, Social and Economic Forces, 1950–1957* (Stanford, Cal., 1958), p. 16.
30 E.B. Haas, 'Technocracy, pluralism and the new Europe', in J.S. Nye (ed.), *International Regionalism* (Boston, 1968), p. 159.
31 E.B. Haas, ibid. (1968), p. 155.
32 See, for instance, his account of change in E.B. Haas, 'International integration: the European and the universal process', in *International Political Communities: An Anthology* (New York, 1966).
33 The efforts of Haas's colleagues to define the elemental nature of international change were no less confused in these terms. See for instance, E.B. Haas and P.C. Schmitter, 'Economics and differential patterns of political integration', in *International Political Communities: An Anthology* (New York, 1966), pp. 259–99.
34 Haas explores this critical technocratic theme in E.B. Haas, *Beyond the Nation State* (Stanford, Cal., 1964); see also E.B. Haas, 'Technocracy, pluralism and the new Europe', in J.S. Nye, op. cit, (1988).
35 Another neofunctionalist theorist, P.C. Schmitter, in 'A revised theory of regional integration', *International Organization* Vol. 24: 1970, pp. 232–64, discussed the critical interaction between national and transnational elites in determining the shape and outcomes of international policy making.
36 E.B. Haas, 'International integration: the European and the universal process', in *International Political Communities: An Anthology* (New York, 1966).
37 For an account of the neofunctionalist perspective on the determinitive role of elites, see E.B. Haas, 'The study of regional integration: reflections on the joy and anguish of pre-theorizing', *International Organization* Vol. 24: 1970, p. 616; E.B. Haas, 'International integration: the European and the universal process', op. cit. 1966, pp. 7–12; and L.N. Lindberg, 'Political integration as a multi-dimensional phenomenon requiring multivariate measurement', *International Organization* Vol. 24: 1970, pp. 682–702.
38 E.B. Haas, *Beyond the Nation State* (Stanford, Cal., 1964), p. 35.
39 M. Brenner, quoted in J. Caporaso, 'Functionalism and regional integration', *Sage Professional Papers* 1972, p. 26.
40 Some contributors to the neofunctionalist paradigm placed undue emphasis on cultural spillover. See, for instance, R. Inglehart, 'An end to European integration', *American Political Science Review* Vol. 61: 1967, pp. 91–103, where he somewhat glibly opines that 'the response by a majority [of young people] is overwhelmingly favourable to European integration; it swamps all differences of social class and region'; see also R. Inglehart, 'Public opinion and regional integration', *International Organization* Vol. 24: 1970, pp. 165–8. For an altogether more perceptive assessment of the cultural context of integration, see J. Lodge, 'Loyalty and the EEC: the limits of the functionalist approach', *Political Studies* Vol. 26: 1978, pp. 232–48.
41 Puchala addresses precisely this critical issue; see D. Puchala, 'The Common Market and political federation in western European public opinion', *International Studies Quarterly* Vol. 14: 1970, pp. 32–59, especially p. 58.
42 L.N. Lindberg, *The Politics of European Economic Integration* (Stanford, Cal., 1963), p. 5.
43 Carole Webb, 'Introduction: variations on a theoretical theme', in H. Wallace, W. Wallace and C. Webb (eds), *Policy Making in the European Communities* (2nd edn, London 1983), especially pp. 9–17.
44 E.B. Haas, in *International Regionalism* (1968), pp. 151 and 159; L. Lindberg, 'Political integration as a multi-dimensional phenomenon requiring multivariate measurement', in L. Lindberg and S. Scheingold (eds), *Regional Integration, Theory and Research* (Cambridge, Mass., 1971), pp. 45–127.

45 L.J. Cantori and S.L. Spiegel, 'The analysis of regional international politics: the integration versus the empirical systems approach', *International Organization* Vol. 22: 1973.

46 E.B. Haas, *The Uniting of Europe* (1958), p. 311; Lindberg, however, was noticeably more cautious about the implied logic of spillover. See L.N. Lindberg, op. cit. (1971) at p. 293.

47 E.B. Haas, *The Uniting of Europe* (2nd edn, 1968), p. 297.

48 See J.S. Nye, 'Comparing Common Markets: a revised neofunctionalist model', *International Organization* Vol. 4: 1970.

49 P.C. Schmitter, 'A revised theory of regional integration', in L. Lindberg and S. Scheingold, *Regional Integration, Theory and Research*, (1971), pp. 232–3.

50 As did other leading regional theorists. See particularly, the attempt to quantify and measure the relevant variables in J.S. Nye, 'Comparative regional integration: concept and measurement', *International Organization* Vol. 22: 1968, pp. 855–80.

51 R.D. Hansen, 'European integration: forward march, parade rest, or dismissed?', *International Organization* Vol. 27: 1973, pp. 225–54.

52 B.M. Russett, 'Transactions, community, and international political integration', *Journal of Common Market Studies* Vol. 9: 1971, pp. 224–45, especially p. 230; see also B.M. Russett, *International Regions and the International System* (Chicago, 1967); B.M. Russett, '"Regional" Trading Patterns, 1938–1963', *International Studies Quarterly* 12: 1968, pp. 360–79.

53 R.D. Hansen, 'Regional integration: reflections on a decade of theoretical efforts', *World Politics* Vol. 21: 1969, pp. 242–71.

54 E.B. Haas, 'The "uniting of Europe" and the "uniting of Latin America"', *Journal of Common Market Studies* Vol. 5: 1967, pp. 315–43.

55 See, for instance, the disclaimers in J.S. Nye, 'Comparing Common Markets: a revised neofunctionalist model', *International Organization* Vol. 24: 1970, pp. 796–835.

56 E.B. Haas, 'The study of regional integration: reflections on the joy and anguish of pre-theorising', *International Organization* Vol. 24: 1970; reprinted in L. Lindberg and S. Scheingold, op. cit. (1971), p. 27.

57 E.B. Haas, 'The obsolescence of regional integration theory', (University of California Institute of International Studies (1976), p. 3.

58 Ibid. p. 6.

59 Ibid. pp. 86–93.

60 Ibid. pp. 87–89.

61 D. Puchala, 'Patterns in west European integration', *Journal of Common Market Studies* Vol. 9: 1970, pp. 117–42.

62 See the account of this reprise in Chapter 6 of this book.

63 M. Holland, *European Integration: From Commonality to Union* (London, 1994), pp. 56–7.

4 THE STATECENTRIC PARADIGM

1 See R. Aron, 'Old nations, new Europe', *Daedelus* Winter 1964, pp. 43–66, especially his conclusions, pp. 65–6.

2 A. Milward, *The Reconstruction of Western Europe, 1945–51* (London, 1983); and A. Milward, *The European Rescue of the Nation State* (London, 1992).

3 A. Milward, ibid. (1992), p. x.

4 As this debate became ever more frenetic in Britain during the 1990s, Lord Howe was moved in a radio comment, on 19 February 1995, to draw a clear distinction between mere 'Europscepticism' and outright 'Europhobia'. This distinction is less clear cut in the writings of those of a sceptical disposition who have contributed to this debate. See the medley of views from prominent members of the Bruges Group (K. Minogue,

P. Minford, N. Stone, A. Walters, A. Sked, *et al.*), in P. Minford (ed.) *The Cost of Europe* (Manchester, 1992).

5 R. Dahrendorf, 'A new goal for Europe' (excerpt from 'Wieland Europa', *Die Zeit* 9 July 1971 and 16 July 1971) and reprinted in M. Hodges (ed.), *European Integration* (Harmondsworth, 1972), pp. 74–87.

6 H. Wallace, 'The impact of the European Communities on national policy making', *Government and Opposition* Autumn 1971; and H. Wallace, *National Governments and the European Communities* (Chatham House/PEP, 1973).

7 W. Wallace, 'Walking backwards towards unity' in W. Wallace, H. Wallace and C. Webb (eds), *Policy Making in the European Communities*, (2nd edn, London, 1983), p. 302.

8 Thucydides, *History of the Peloponnesian War* (Harmondsworth, 1982), p. 15.

9 N. Machiavelli, *The Prince*, Chapter 25.

10 W. Nicholl, 'The Luxembourg compromise', *Journal of Common Market Studies* Vol. 23: 1984, pp. 35–43; for a more recent account, see A. Teasdale, 'The life and death of the Luxembourg compromise', *Journal of Common Market Studies* Vol. 31: 1993, pp. 567–9.

11 For a summary of de Gaulle's philosophy of the state and his international outlook, see S. Hoffmann, 'De Gaulle, Europe and the Atlantic Alliance', *International Organization* Winter, 1964, pp. 1–28.

12 F. de la Serre, 'The EEC and the 1965 crisis', in R. Willis (ed.), *European Integration* (New York, 1975).

13 C. Johnson, 'De Gaulle's Europe', *Journal of Common Market Studies* Vol. 1: 1962.

14 C. de Gaulle, *Memoirs of Hope: Renewal and Endeavour* (London, 1971), p. 148.

15 M. Camps, *European Unification in the Sixties: From the Veto to the Crisis* (New York, 1966); J. Lambert, 'The constitutional crisis: 1965–66', *Journal of Common Market Studies* Vol. 4: 1966.

16 E. Kolodziej, *French International Policy Under de Gaulle and Pompidou: The Politics of Grandeur* (Ithaca, 1974), pp. 336–8.

17 S. Hoffmann, 'Reflections on the nation state in western Europe today', *Journal of Common Market Studies* Vol. 21: 1982, p. 35.

18 S. Hoffmann, 'Obstinate or obsolete? The fate of the nation-state and the case of western Europe', *Daedelus* Vol. 95: 1966, pp. 863–6.

19 S. Hoffmann, 'Fragments floating in the here and now', *Daedelus* Winter, 1979, pp. 13 and 14.

20 E. Burke, 'Reflections on the revolution in France', *Works* (1790), Vol. II, p. 359.

21 S. Hoffmann, 'The European process at Atlantic cross purposes', *Journal of Common Market Studies* Vol. 3: 1964, pp. 87–91.

22 S. Hoffmann, 'Obstinate or obsolete?', (1966), pp. 881–9.

23 S. Hoffmann, 'The European process at Atlantic cross purposes', (1964), pp. 89–91 and 93.

24 S. Hoffmann, 'Europe's identity crisis: between the past and America', *Daedelus* Vol. 93: 1964, p. 1276.

25 Ibid. p. 1274.

26 Ibid. p. 1269.

27 S. Hoffmann, 'Obstinate or obsolete?', (1966), p. 909.

28 Ibid. p. 910.

29 'Europe's identity crisis' (1964), p. 1272.

30 S. Hoffmann, 'Obstinate or Obsolete?', (1966), p. 865.

31 Ibid. (1966), pp. 866–7.

32 Ibid. (1966), p. 901.

33 S. Hoffmann, 'Reflections on the nation-state in western Europe today', *Journal of Common Market Studies* Vol. 21: 1982, p. 21.

34 See H. Simonian, 'France, Germany and Europe', *Journal of Common Market Studies* Vol. 19: 1981, pp. 203–19 for an account of the Community's principal internal axis.

35 S. Hoffmann, 'Fragments floating in the here and now', *Daedelus* Winter, 1979, p. 26.

36 Ibid. p. 26.

37 Murray Forsyth, *Unions of States: The Theory and Practice of Confederation* (Leicester, 1981).

38 John Pinder, 'The Single Market: a step towards union', in J. Lodge (ed.), *The European Community and the Challenge to the Future* (2nd edn, London, 1993), pp. 61–7.

39 G. Edwards and H. Wallace, 'The Council of Ministers of the European Community and the President in Office', (Federal Trust for Education and Research, London, 1977); W. Wallace and D. Allen, 'Political cooperation: procedure as a substitute for policy', in H. Wallace, W. Wallace and C. Webb (eds), op. cit. 1977 edn, pp. 227–46; and J. Lodge, 'Towards the European Political Community: EEC summits and European integration', *Orbis* December 1974, for a contemporary account of these institutional developments.

40 Ralf Dahrendorf drew conclusions on the basis of his experience as one of West Germany's commissioners, which confirmed the confederal rather than the supra-national prognosis. See his 'Possibilities and limits of a European Communities foreign policy', *World Today* April 1971, and his 'A new goal for Europe', in M. Hodges (ed.), *European Integration* (Harmondsworth, 1972).

41 W. Wallace, *Europe as a Confederation* (1982), p. 66.

42 M. Forsyth, op. cit. (1981), p. 184.

43 Not least, the development – albeit tentative – of monetary cooperation. See V. Barattieri and A. Thomas, 'EEC monetary and economic cooperation', *International Affairs* October 1975, pp. 499–517.

44 Taylor's main contribution to this debate and his most cogent account of European confederalism was contained in his book, *The Limits of European Integration*, published in 1983.

45 P. Taylor, 'The functionalist approach to the problem of international order: a defence', *Political Studies* Vol. 16: 1968, pp. 393–410.

46 See his balanced account of the conflicting tendencies and variable options available within the European project in P. Taylor, 'Britain, the Common Market and the forces of history', *Orbis* Vol. 16, Fall, 1972, pp. 743–59.

47 P. Taylor, 'The limits of gradualist integration', Chapter 2 of *The Limits of European Integration* (London, 1983), p. 53.

48 P. Taylor, 'Intergovernmentalism in the European Communities in the 1970s: patterns and perspectives', *International Organization* Vol. 36: 1982, p. 764.

49 P. Taylor, 'The politics of the European Communities: the confederal phase', *World Politics* Vol. 27: 1975, p. 346.

50 P. Taylor, ibid. (1975), pp. 340–7.

51 See W. Connor, 'Nation-building or nation-destroying?', *World Politics* April, 1972.

52 W. Wessels, 'The dynamics of administrative interactions: towards a European system of cooperative states', in W. Wallace (ed.), *The Dynamics of European Integration* (London, 1990); W. M. Blumenthal, 'The world economy and technological change', *Foreign Affairs* Vol. 66: 1988; M. Sharp and C. Shearman, 'European technological collaboration', *Chatham House Papers* (London, 1987); and E. Thiel, 'Patterns of monetary interdependence', in W. Wallace (ed.), op. cit. (1990).

53 For a flavour of this debate, see A. Bressand and K. Nicolaidis, 'Regional integration in a networked world economy' in W. Wallace (ed.), *The Dynamics of European Integration* (London, 1990), pp. 27–49; and De Anne Julius, *Global Companies and Public Policy: The Challenge of the New Economic Linkages* (London 1990).

54 Roy Pryce had observed this ultimately creative dialectic between politics and theory as early as 1962. See R. Pryce, *The Political Future of the European Community* (London, 1962), pp. 22–4 and 56–9.

55 R. Pryce, 'Relaunching the European Community', *Government and Opposition* 1984, pp. 486–500.
56 M. Richonnier, 'Europe's Decline is not Irreversible', *Journal of Common Market Studies* Vol. 22: 1984, pp. 227–43.
57 For a flavour of the gathering revisionist mood in the academic community, see L. Tsoukalis (ed.), 'The European Community past, present and future', a special issue of the *Journal of Common Market Studies* Vol. 21: 1982. The papers contained here were the proceedings of a conference held in Oxford in 1982 which coincided with the 25th anniversary of the signing of the Rome Treaty.
58 See the discussion reflecting the changing state of play in the mid 1980s as the Single Market project gathered momentum, in B. Langeheine and U. Weinstock, 'Graduated integration: a modest path towards progress', *Journal of Common Market Studies* Vol. 23: 1984, pp. 185–97; H. Wallace, 'Negotiations and coalition formation in the European Community', *Government and Opposition* 1985, pp. 453–72; and W. Nicholl, 'Paths to European unity', *Journal of Common Market Studies* Vol. 23: 1985, pp. 199–206.

5 THE SYNCRETIC PARADIGM: THE AMBIGUITIES OF EUROPEAN INTEGRATION

1 B. Laffan, *Integration and Cooperation in Europe* (London, 1992), pp. 13–15.
2 U. Everling, 'Possibilities and limits of European integration', *Journal of Common Market Studies* Vol. 18: 1980, p. 228.
3 F.W. Scharpf, 'The joint decision trap: lessons from German federalism and European integration', *Public Administration* Vol. 68: Autumn, 1988, p. 239.
4 A. Giddens, *The Nation State and Violence* (Cambridge, 1985).
5 L. Hurwitz, *The European Community and the Management of International Cooperation* (New York, 1987).
6 P. Katzenstein (ed.), *Between Power and Plenty: Foreign Economic Policies of Advanced Industrial States* (Madison, Wisconsin, 1985).
7 R. Keohane and J.S. Nye Jr, *Power and Interdependence: World Politics in Transition* (Boston, 1977), pp. 11–19.
8 R. Keohane and J.S. Nye Jr, 'Transgovernmental Relations and International Organizations', *World Politics* Vol. 27: 1974, pp. 41–2.
9 S.J. Michaelek Jr, 'Theoretical perspectives for understanding international interdependence', *World Politics* Vol. 31: 1979, pp. 136–50.
10 H. Wallace, 'National governments and the European Communities', (Chatham House/PEP, 1973), Chapter 2; see also H. Wallace, 'The impact of the Communities on national policy making', *Government and Opposition* Vol. 6: 1971.
11 Simon Bulmer, 'Domestic politics and European Community policy-making', *Journal of Common Market Studies*, Vol. 21: 1983; S. Bulmer, 'The European Council's first decade: between interdependence and domestic politics', *Journal of Common Market Studies* Vol. 24: 1985; for a case study approach see S. Bulmer, *The Domestic Structure of EC Policy Making in West Germany* (New York, 1986).
12 S. George, *Politics and Policy in the European Community* (Oxford, 1st edition, 1985; 2nd edition, 1991), especially Chapter 14.
13 See the discussion of this issue in P.B. Potter, 'Universalism versus regionalism in international organization', *American Political Science Review* Vol. 37: 1985, pp. 850–62.
14 See R.O. Keohane and J.S. Nye Jr, *Power and Interdependence* (1977); R.O. Keohane and J.S. Nye (eds), *Transnational Relations and World Politics* (1971); R.O. Keohane and J.S. Nye, 'International interdependence and integration', Chapter 5 of F. Greenstein and N. Polsby (eds), *Handbook of Political Science* Vol. 8 (Reading, Mass., 1975), pp. 363–414; and

R.O. Keohane, *After Hegemony: Cooperation and Discord in the World Political Economy* (Princeton, 1984).

15 R.L. Gilpin, *The Political Economy of International Relations* (Princeton, 1987); and P. Robson, *The Economics of International Integration* (London, 3rd edn, 1987).

16 R.O. Keohane and J.S. Nye Jr, 'International interdependence and integration', Chapter 5 of F. Greenstein and N. Polsby, op. cit. (1975), p. 365.

17 W. Wallace in H. Wallace, C. Wallace and C. Webb (eds), *Policy Making in the European Community* (London, 1977 edn), p. 315.

18 C. Webb, 'Theoretical perspectives and problems', in H. Wallace *et al.*, *Policy Making in the European Community* (London, 1983 edn), p. 33.

19 See the discussion in M. Zacher, 'The decaying pillars of the Westphalian temple: implications for international order and governance', in J. Rosenau and E.J. Czempiel (eds), *Governance without government: order and change in world politics* (Cambridge, 1992), pp. 58–101.

20 R. Putnam, 'Diplomacy and domestic politics: the logic of two-level games', *International Organization* Vol. 12: 1988, p. 433.

21 M. Edberg, 'The fourth level of government: on the standardisation of public policy within international regions', *Scandinavian Political Studies* Vol. 3: 1980, pp. 239–40.

22 P. Gourevitch, 'The second image reversed: the international sources of domestic politics', *International Organization* Vol. 32: 1978, pp. 881–911.

23 R. Putnam, op. cit. (1988) p. 434.

24 W. Wessels, 'The EC Council: The Community's decision making center', in R. Keohane and S. Hoffmann (eds), *The New European Community* (Boulder, Col., 1991), p. 135.

25 S. Hoffmann, 'Restraints and choices in American foreign policy', *Daedelus*, Fall, 1962.

26 C. Webb, 'Theoretical perspectives and problems', in H. Wallace *et al.*, (eds), *Policy Making in the European Community* 2nd edn, (London, 1983), p. 32.

27 S. Williams, 'Sovereignty and accountability in the EC', *Political Quarterly* July–September, 1990, pp. 299–302.

28 A.M. Burley and W. Mattli, 'Europe before the court: a political theory of legal integration', *International Organization* Vol. 47: 1993.

29 W Wallace, 'Walking backwards towards unity', Chapter 12 of H. Wallace *et al.*, *Policy Making in the European Communities* (London, 1977 edn), pp 301–23 for a clear exposition of the hybrid qualities of the EC at this stage in its evolution.

30 R.O. Keohane and J.S. Nye Jr, op. cit. (1977), p. 19.

31 R.O. Keohane and J.S. Nye, 'Transgovernmental relations and international organizations', *World Politics* Vol. 27: 1974, p. 61.

32 For a survey of some of the key issues raised in the current debate on the regime concept, see F. Kratochwill and J. Ruggie, 'International organisations: the state of the art', in P.F. Diehl (ed.), *The Politics of International Organizations: Patterns and Insights* (Chicago, 1989), pp. 17–29; S. Haggard and B.A. Simmons, 'Theories of international regimes', *International Organization* Vol. 41: 1987; J. Ruggie, 'International regimes, transactions and change: embedded liberalism in the postwar economic order', in S. Krasner (ed.) *International Regimes* (Ithaca, 1975), pp. 195–232.

33 For a useful attempt to define some testable hypotheses about the relative prospects for regime formation in different sets of circumstances, see O.R. Young, 'The politics of international regime formation: managing natural resources and the environment', in *International Organization* Vol. 43: 1989, especially pp. 366–75.

34 P.F. Diehl, op. cit. (1989), p. 15.

35 For a notable critique, see S. Strange, 'Cave! Hic dragones: a critique of regimes analysis', in S. Krasner (ed.) op. cit. (1975), pp. 337–54.

36 O.R. Young, 'International regimes: towards a new theory of institutions', *World Politics* Vol. 39, 1986, at pp. 104–21.

37 O.R. Young, 'International regimes: problems of concept formation', *World Politics* Vol. 32: 1980, pp. 331–56.
38 E.B. Haas, 'Why collaborate? Issue linkage and international regimes', *World Politics* Vol. 32: 1980, p. 405.
39 D. Puchala and R. Hopkins, 'International regimes: lessons from inductive analysis', *International Organization* Vol. 36: 1982, pp. 245–75.
40 F. Kratochwill and J. Ruggie, op. cit. (1989), p. 29.
41 S. Haggard and B. Simmons, op. cit. p. 511.
42 Ibid. p. 496.
43 D. Puchala, op. cit. (1972), p. 277.
44 Cited in Ian Davidson, 'Agenda for a change', *Financial Times* 20 September 1995.
45 S. Hoffmann, 'Reflections on the nation-state in western Europe today', *Journal of Common Market Studies* Vol. 21: 1982, p. 33.
46 S. Hoffmann, ibid. p. 33.
47 S. Hoffmann, ibid. p. 35.
48 C. Pentland, *International Theory and European Integration* (London, 1973), p. 154.
49 C. Pentland, ibid. p. 240.
50 For an overview of the balance of intergovernmental and supranational competences see M. Holland, *European Integration: From Community to Union* (London, 1994), Chapter 8.
51 J. Lodge, 'EC policymaking: institutional dynamics', in J. Lodge (ed.), *The European Community and the Challenge of the Future* (1993), pp. 1–36.
52 Fritz Scharpf, 'The joint decision trap: lessons from German federalism and European integration', *Public Administration* Vol. 66: 1988.
53 For a summary of the different federalist experiences, see A. Sbragia, 'Federalism in comparative context', in A. Sbragia (ed.), *Euro-Politics. Institutions and Policymaking in the 'New' European Community* (Washington DC, 1992), pp. 259–68.
54 For a thorough review of the Maastricht Treaty proposals, see A. Duff, J. Pinder and R. Pryce (eds), *Maastricht and Beyond* (The Federal Trust, London, 1994).
55 M. Richonnier, 'Europe's decline is not irreversible', *Journal of Common Market Studies* Vol. 22: 1984, pp. 227–43.
56 *Financial Times* 18 June 1991.
57 See D. Edward, 'The impact of the Single Act on the institutions', *Common Market Law Review* Vol. 24: 1987, pp. 19–30.
58 *Official Journal of the European Communities*, 256, 3 October 1980, pp. 2–3.
59 J. Pinder, *European Community: The Building of a Union* (Oxford, 1991), pp. 71–6.
60 D. Allen, D. Llewellyn and D. Swann, 'A forward view', in D. Swann (ed.), *The Single European Market and Beyond: A Study of the Wider Implications of the Single European Act* (London, 1992), p. 267.
61 C.O'Nuallain (ed.) with J.M. Hoscheit, *The Presidency of the European Council of Ministers. Impacts and Implications for National Governments* (London, 1985); H. Wallace and G. Edwards, 'European Community: the evolving role of the Presidency of the Council', *International Affairs* October 1976, pp. 535–50.
62 H. Wallace is more optimistic about the Community's cooperative potential. See H. Wallace, 'Making multilateral negotiations work', Chapter 12 of W. Wallace (ed.) *The Dynamics of European Integration* (London, 1990), especially pp. 214–16.
63 J. Fitzmaurice, 'An analysis of the European Community's cooperation procedure', *Journal of Common Market Studies* Vol. 26: 1988, pp. 389–400; J. Lodge, 'The Single European Act and the new legislative cooperation procedure: a critical analysis', *Journal of European Integration* Vol. 9: pp. 5–28.
64 W. Wessels, 'Administrative interaction', in W. Wallace, op. cit. (1990), p. 238.
65 S. Hoffmann, 'The European Community and 1992', *Foreign Affairs* Vol. 68: 1989, p. 32.
66 R. Keohane and S. Hoffmann, 'Institutional change in Europe in the 1980s', in R.

Keohane and S. Hoffmann (eds), *The New European Community: Decision Making and Institutional Change* (Boulder, Col., 1991), especially pp. 8–18.

67 J. Lodge, 'Towards a political union?', in J. Lodge (ed.) *The European Community and the Challenge of the Future* (2nd edn, London, 1977), p. 377.

68 L. Cornett and J. Caporaso, '"And still it moves!" State interests and social forces in the European Community', in J. Rosenau and E.O. Czempiel (eds), op. cit. (1992), p. 248.

6 THEORETICAL *DÉJÀ VU*?

1 H.C. Brenn, 'The European Community: a union of states without unity of government', *Journal of Common Market Studies* Vol. 26: 1987, pp. 1–23.

2 See A.W. Cafruny and G.G. Rosenthal, 'The State of the European Community: theory and research in the post-Maastricht era', in A.W. Cafruny and G.G. Rosenthal (eds), *The State of the European Community (Vol. 2): The Maastricht Debates and Beyond* (London, 1993), pp. 1–3.

3 M. Burgess, *Federalism and European Union, 1972–1987* (London, 1989), pp. 4–6.

4 For an account of this initiative, see J. Lodge, 'European Union and the first elected parliament: the Spinelli initiative', *Journal of Common Market Studies* 1984, pp. 377–402.

5 M. Burgess, Chapter 2 in M. Burgess (ed.), *Federalism and Federation in Western Europe* (Beckenham, 1986), pp. 23–4.

6 M. Burgess, op. cit. (1989), at pp. 7 and 218.

7 W. Stewart, 'Metaphors, models and the fevelopment of federal theory', *Publius* Vol. 12: 1982, pp. 5–24.

8 See the discussion of this functionalism in J. Roemheld, *Integral Federalism: Model for Europe – A Way Towards a Personal Group Society, Historical Development, Philosophy, State, Economy and Society*, trans. H. Bongert (Frankfurt am Main, 1990), pp. 147–71.

9 L. Levi, 'Recent developments in federalist theory', *The Federalist* No.2, 1987, p. 102.

10 M. Burgess, op. cit. (1989), p. 1.

11 Ibid. p. 5.

12 Ibid. p. 2.

13 E. Wistrich, *The United States of Europe* (London, 1994), pp. 164 and 170.

14 R. Keohane, 'International institutions: two approaches', *International Studies Quarterly* Vol. 32: 1988, pp. 379–96.

15 J. Pinder, 'Economic integration vs national sovereignty: differences between eastern and western Europe', *Government and Opposition* Vol. 24: 1989, pp. 320–1.

16 J. Pinder, 'European Community and nation state: a case for a neo-federalism?', *International Affairs* Vol. 62: 1986, pp. 41–54.

17 J. Pinder, ibid.; see also J. Pinder, 'The Single Market: a step towards union', in J. Lodge (ed.), op. cit. (1993) especially pp. 512–52, 561–3 and 565–7.

18 R. Nathan, 'Implications for federalism of European integration', Chapter 1 of J. Ornstein and M. Perlman (eds), *Political Power And Social Change: The United States Faces A United Europe* (London, 1991), especially pp. 16–21.

19 I.D. Duchacek, *Comparative Federalism: The Territorial Dimension of Politics* (1970), p. 20.

20 D.J. Elazar, *Exploring Federalism* (University of Alabama, 1987), pp. 11–12.

21 D. Muttimer, '1992 and the political integration of Europe: neofunctionalism reconsidered', *Journal of European Integration* Vol. 13:1, 1989, p. 78; see the more conditional account of the prospects for neofunctionalism in T. Pedersen, 'Problems of enlargement: political integration in a pan-European EC', *Cooperation and Conflict* Vol. 25 1990, pp. 83–99.

22 D. Muttimer, ibid. (1989), p. 101.

23 J. Tranholm-Mikkelsen, 'Neofunctionalism: obstinate or obsolete? A reappraisal in the

light of the new organism of the EC', *Millennium: Journal of International Studies* Vol. 20: 1991, p. 18.

24 J. Tranholm-Mikkelsen, ibid. (1991), p. 18.

25 Ibid. p. 18.

26 E. Kirchner, *Decision Making in the European Community: The Council Presidency and European Integration* (Manchester, 1991), p. 123.

27 See the discussion in D. Puchala, 'The Common Market and political federation in western European public opinion', *International Studies Quarterly* Vol. 14: 1970, pp. 35–59.

28 See R. Keohane, *Neorealism and Its Critics* (New York, 1986).

29 J. Snyder, 'Averting anarchy in the new Europe', *International Security* Vol. 14: 1990, p. 15.

30 R. Axelrod and R. Keohane, 'Achieving cooperation under anarchy: strategies and institutions', *World Politics* 1985, pp. 226–54.

31 P. Taylor, 'The European Community and the state: assumptions, theories and propositions', *Review of International Studies* Vol. 17: 1991, pp. 109–25.

32 P. Taylor, 'Regionalism and functionalism reconsidered', in A.J.R. Groom and P. Taylor (eds), *Frameworks for International Cooperation* (London, 1990), pp. 234–54.

33 J. Storey, 'Europe's future: western union or common home?', in C. Crouch and D. Marquand (eds), *The Politics of 1992* (Oxford, 1990), especially pp. 44–67.

34 K.M. Waltz, *Theory of International Politics* (Reading, Mass., 1979).

35 J.M. Grieco, 'Anarchy and the limits of cooperation: a realist critique of the newest liberal institutionalism', *International Organization* Vol. 42: 1988, pp. 485–507.

36 R. Gilpin, 'The richness of the tradition of political realism', *International Organization* Vol. 38: 1984, p. 304.

37 L. Cornett and J.A. Caporasa, "And still it moves! State interests and social forces in the European Community', in J.N. Rosenau and E.O. Czempiel, *Governance Without Government: Order and Change in World Politics* (Cambridge, 1992), p. 232.

38 R. Keohane, 'International institutions: two approacches', *International Studies Quarterly* Vol. 32: 1988, pp. 379–96.

39 J.N. Rosenau, 'Governance, order and change in world politics', in J.N. Rosenau and E.O.Czempiel (1992), op. cit. Chapter 1.

40 E. Haas, *The Uniting of Europe* (Stanford, Cal., 1968), Preface, p. xix.

41 S. Hoffmann, 'The European Community and 1992', *Foreign Affairs* Vol. 68: 1989, pp. 34–5.

42 R. Keohane and S. Hoffmann, (eds) *The New European Community* (Boulder, Col., 1991), p. 15.

43 A. Moravcsik, 'Negotiating the Single European Act: national interests and conventional statecraft in the European Community', *International Organization* Vol. 45: 1991.

44 A. Moravcsik, 'Preferences and power in the European Community: a liberal inter-governmentalist approach', *Journal of Common Market Studies* Vol. 31: 1993, p. 474.

45 Ibid. p. 474.

46 Moravcsik has, more recently still, applied his intergovernmental model to the post-Maastricht dissensus. See A. Moravcsik, 'Idealism and interest in the European Community: the case of the French referendum', *French Politics and Society* Vol. 11: 1993, pp. 45–56; for a rejoinder, see S. Meunier-Aitsahalia and G. Ross, 'Democratic deficit or democratic surplus? A reply to Andrew Moravcsik's comments on the French Referendum', *French Politics and Society* Vol. 11: 1993, pp. 57–69.

47 P. Taylor, 'The new dynamics of EC integration in the 1980s', in J. Lodge (ed.), *The European Community and the Challenge of the Future* (London, 1st edn, 1989), pp. 3–25.

48 J. Pelkmans and A. Winters, 'Europe's domestic market', (Chatham House/PEP 43, London, 1988).

49 J. Rosenau, 'A pre-theory revisited: world politics in an era of cascading inter-dependence', *International Studies Quarterly* Vol. 28: 1984, pp. 245–305.

50 C. Brewin, 'The European Community: A union of states without unity of government', *Journal of Common Market Studies* Vol. 26: 1987, pp. 1–23.
51 C. Webb, 'Introduction: variations on a theoretical theme', in H. Wallace, W. Wallace and C. Webb (eds), *Policy Making in the European Communities* (London, 1983 edn), especially pp. 32–6.
52 H. Wallace, ibid. (1977 edn), p. 65.
53 J. Peterson, 'The European Community and policy networks', pp. 151–69 of P. Dunleavy and J. Stanyer, *Contemporary Political Studies 1994*, (Proceedings of the Annual PSA Conference, 1994).
54 W. Sandholtz and J. Zysman, 'Recasting the EC bargain', *World Politics* Vol. 42, 1989, p. 127.
55 H. Wallace, 'Making multilateral negotiations work', Chapter 12 of W. Wallace (ed.), *The Dynamics of European Integration* (London, 1990), pp. 225–6.
56 R. Jordan and W. Feld, *Europe in the Balance. The Changing Context of European International Politics* (London, 1986).
57 H. Kastendiek. 'Convergence or a persistent diversity of national politics', in C. Crouch and D. Marquand, *The Politics of 1992* (Oxford, 1990), pp. 68–84.
58 A. Bressand, 'Beyond interdependence: 1992 as a global challenge', *International Affairs* Vol. 66: 1990, pp. 47–65.
59 D. Allen, D. Llewellyn and D. Swann, 'A forward view', in D. Swann (ed.), *The Single European Market and Beyond: A Study of the Wider Implications of the Single European Act* (London, 1992), p. 267.
60 For a flavour of this by now super abundant literature, see H. Wallace, 'The Europe that came in from the cold', *International Affairs* Vol. 67: 1991, pp. 647–63; A. Smith and H. Wallace, 'The European Union: towards a policy for Europe', ibid. Vol. 70: 1994, pp. 429–44; W. Wessels, 'Rationalizing Maastricht: the search for an optimal strategy of the new Europe', ibid., Vol. 709: 1994, pp. 445–58; A. Williams, *The European Community: The Contradictions of Integration* (Oxford, 1991); W. Reinicke, *Building a New Europe: The Challenge of System Transformation and Systemic Reform* (The Brookings Institution, Washington DC, 1992).
61 T. Pedersen, 'Problems of enlargement: political integration in a pan-european EC', *Journal of Cooperation and Conflict* Vol. 25, 1990, pp. 85–6.
62 R. Keohane, 'International institutions: two approaches', *International Studies Quarterly* Vol. 32: 1988, pp. 379–96.
63 H. Wallace and A. Ridley. 'New wine in old bottles', in *Europe: The Challenge of Diversity* (Chatham House Papers, 29, London, 1985), pp. 14–28 and 'Strategies for managing diversity', ibid. pp. 29–49.
64 B. Langeheine and U. Weinstock, 'Graduated integration: a modest path towards progress', *Journal of Common Market Studies* Vol. 23: 1984, pp. 185–7.
65 M. Wilke and H. Wallace, 'Subsidiarity: approaches to power-sharing in the European Community', *RIIA Discussion Paper* No. 27.
66 H. Wallace, 'Widening and deepening: The European Community and the new European agenda', *RIIA Discussion Paper* No.23; and A. Michalski and H. Wallace, 'The European Community: the challenge of enlargement', (London, 1992).
67 P. Bongers and J. Chatfield, 'Regions and local authorities in the governance of Europe', in A. Duff (ed.), *Subsidiarity and the European Community* (Federal Trust, London, 1993), pp. 77–85.
68 C. Harvie, *The Rise of Regional Europe* (London, 1993).
69 E. Zimmermann, 'Political unrest in western Europe: trends and prospects', *West European Politics* Vol. 12: 1989; K. Lawson and P.M. Merkl (eds), *When Parties Fail: Emerging Alternative Organizations* (Princeton, 1988).
70 Paul Taylor argued a convincing case for this particular theoretical approach when the academic study of European integration was in its infancy. See P. Taylor, 'The concept

of Community and the European integration process', *Journal of Common Market Studies* Vol. 6: 1968, especially pp. 99–100.

71 See on this theme, H. Rattinger, 'Public attitudes to European integration in Germany after Maastricht: inventory and typology', *Journal of Common Market Studies* Vol. 32: 1994, pp. 525–40.

72 R.C. Eichenberg and R. Dalton, 'Europeans and the European Community: the dynamics of public support for European integration', *International Organization* Vol. 47: 1993; and R. Inglehart and K. Reif, 'Analysing trends in West European opinion: the role of the Eurobarometer surveys', in K. Reif and R. Inglehart (eds), *The Eurobarometer* (Basingstoke, 1991), pp. 1–26.

73 J. Janssen, 'Postmaterialism, cognitive mobilization and public support for European integration', *British Journal of Political Science*, Vol. 21: 1991, pp. 443–68; M. Hewstone, *Understanding Attitudes to the European Community* (Cambridge, 1986).

74 A. Rijksbaron *et al.* (eds), *Europe from a Cultural Perspective: Historiography and Perceptions* (The Hague, 1987).

75 S. Serfaty, *Understanding Europe. The Politics of Unity* (London, 1992), pp. 170–2.

76 W. Reinicke, *Building a New Europe: The Challenge of System Transformation and Systemic Reform* (The Brookings Institution, Washington DC, 1992), pp. 141–6.

77 See A.M. Sbragia in the Introduction to *Euro-Politics: Institutions and Policy Making in the 'New' European Community* (The Brookings Institution, Washington DC, 1992), pp. 1–22.

78 Suzanne Boddenheimer, 'The "Political Union" debate in Europe: a case study in international diplomacy', *International Organization* Winter, 1967, pp. 53–4.

Index